# Crafting Scholarship in the Behavioral and Social Sciences

D0165772

*Crafting Scholarship* helps readers improve their writing and publishing success in academia. Framed within the context of the editorial and peer-review process, the book explores writing, editing, and reviewing in academic publishing. As such it provides unique coverage of how successful writers work, how they manage criticism, and more. Examples from successful scholars provide helpful tips in writing articles, grants, books, book chapters, and reviews. Each chapter features tools that facilitate learning, including *Best Practices* and *Writer's Resource* boxes to maximize success, discussion questions and case studies to stimulate critical thinking, and recommended readings to encourage self-exploration. A Facebook page provides an opportunity for readers to post writing updates and for instructors to share materials.

   *Highlights:*

- Provides insight on working with journal boards, reviewers, and contributors drawn from the author's 30 years of experience in editing journal articles and writing books.
- Describes writing quantitative and qualitative reports, theory and literature reviews, books and chapters, grants, and book reviews.
- Identifies common problems academics face in writing and publishing along with practical solutions.
- Explores best practices in writing peer reviews, responding to reviewers and editors, and how to calculate and interpret acceptance rates and impact factors.
- Addresses how to write each section of a journal article and select keywords that facilitate digital search engines to help potential readers find an article.
- Includes examples of published work and tips on writing research syntheses using meta-analytic techniques or narrative analyses.
- Examines the practices of successful writers, the pros and cons of collaborations, what publishers look for, and managing criticism.

- Reviews pertinent empirical literature on the core topics of writing, reviewing, and editing.

Intended for graduate or advanced undergraduate courses in professional development, writing in an academic field, or research methods taught in psychology, education, human development and family studies, sociology, communication, and other social sciences, this practical guide also appeals to those interested in pursuing an academic career and new and seasoned researchers.

**Robert M. Milardo** is Professor of Family Relations at the University of Maine.

# Crafting Scholarship in the Behavioral and Social Sciences

## Writing, Reviewing, and Editing

Robert M. Milardo

Routledge
Taylor & Francis Group

NEW YORK AND LONDON

First published 2015
by Routledge
711 Third Avenue, New York, NY 10017

and by Routledge
27 Church Road, Hove, East Sussex BN3 2FA

*Routledge is an imprint of the Taylor & Francis Group, an informa business*

*Library of Congress Cataloging-in-Publication Data*
Milardo, Robert M.
   Crafting scholarship in the behavioral and social sciences : writing, reviewing, and editing / Robert M. Milardo.
       pages cm
   Includes bibliographical references and index.
   1. Social sciences—Authorship.   2. Social science literature—
Editing.   3. Social sciences—Research.   I. Title.
   H61.8.M56 2015
   808.06'63—dc23
   2014012839

ISBN: 978-1-138-78783-4 (hbk)
ISBN: 978-1-138-78784-1 (pbk)
ISBN: 978-1-315-76608-9 (ebk)

Typeset in Sabon
by Apex CoVantage, LLC

Printed and bound in the United States of America by Publishers Graphics, LLC on sustainably sourced paper.

# Contents

# About the Author

**Robert M. Milardo** is Professor of Family Relations at the University of Maine, his academic home for over three decades. He has published extensively in leading journals and books and served as the founding editor of the *Journal of Family Theory & Review* owned by the National Council on Family Relations. He was elected fellow of NCFR in 2005. Bob is active in the developing science of personal relationships and was elected the first president of the International Association for Relationship Research. He served as a visiting Hofstede Research Fellow at the Netherlands Interdisciplinary Demographic Institute in The Hague and as visiting research professor in the School of Psychology at Victoria University in Wellington, New Zealand. He is the author of *The Forgotten Kin: Aunts and Uncles*, published by Cambridge University Press in 2010. Commentaries on family issues have appeared in *Psychology Today*, *The Guardian*, the *Wall Street Journal*, the *Washington Post*, *USA Today*, and various local and regional media. Bob lives in rural Maine with his partner Renate Klein, two cats, Bea and Smoke, and a very large stack of wood.

# Preface

## Overview of the Book

*Crafting Scholarship in the Behavioral and Social Sciences* aims to improve your writing and success in academic publishing. The book consists of three units on the particulars of writing articles and books, the ordinary experiences and practices of successful writers, and the best practices in reviewing, responding to reviews, and working with editors. Throughout, the book draws on a measure of my experience in more than three decades of writing, reviewing, and editing; the experiences of other successful authors and editors; and a variety of empirical literatures in the behavioral and social sciences, including compositional studies. From these sources we can learn a good deal about writing well, the most effective practices in establishing a writing life, positioning our work for publication, and the importance of writing with an audience in mind that includes both critics and supporters.

The first unit consists of four chapters on writing articles and grants, book reviews, books, and chapters in edited books. Chapter 2 focuses on writing effective empirical articles, which, for many of us, is the bread and butter of our academic work. The chapter addresses how editors and successful writers view the importance of the overall quality of writing and adherence to technical issues regarding style and formatting. The chapter details the core sections of typical journal articles, how to write each section, the issues editors and experienced writers consider critical, and the special requirements of writing qualitative research reports. The chapter addresses the importance of crafting descriptive titles, writing abstracts, and selecting keywords that facilitate digital search engines that guide readers to your work. Although writing grants can be highly specialized, many of the issues in this chapter and the following chapters apply to the core requirements of successful grant writing.

Chapter 3 offers instructive methods for writing successful theoretical articles and gives examples of published work that illustrates the essential ways theoretical work is presented and purposed. The chapter details writing research syntheses using meta-analytic techniques or narrative analyses, and the chapter includes a primer on searching bibliographic databases and other sources.

Book reviews represent one of the most underdeveloped forms of scholarship. Chapter 4 is unabashed in attempting to elevate the stature, sophistication, and contribution of book reviews. The chapter details results of surveys across a wide variety of disciplines that demonstrate how faculty use book reviews, how often they read them, and how often they write reviews. The chapter defines the forms book reviews can take, ranging from reports announcing a book's publication to more advanced reviews that critique a book's merit or engage in a broader discourse about the development of a field of inquiry. The chapter uses examples of recently published reviews to illustrate the potential growth of this form of scholarship—for instance, new developments in cross-disciplinary reviews, comparative critical reviews of multiple volumes, and the complementary use of Web 2.0 platforms. No current book details the capacity of this brand of scholarship for growth or details the varied forms contemporary book reviews take.

Chapter 5 examines why scholars write books and the advantages and disadvantages in writing them. The chapter details the requirements of publishers and the necessary components of successful book proposals. In addition, we explore writing chapters for edited or collaborative volumes and the many advantages in doing so.

The second unit is comprised of three chapters on the experience of writing. Chapter 6 explores managing risk and criticism. This chapter is about how the experience of writing is similar across disciplines, how writing is a risky business, and how successful writers manage that risk. Managing risk is a critical aspect of successful publishing and largely overlooked in books on writing for the behavioral and social sciences.

Chapter 7 follows with an exposé on the routine practices of successful writers. I draw on interviews with new writers, those in mid-career, and senior faculty. The chapter explores the essentials of successful practices, including scheduled writing times, intensive writing and binge writing, the advantages or shortcomings of collaboration, the role or irrelevance of "the muse," prewriting, logging progress, working to deadlines, and managing criticism. All are key issues in successful writing and publishing, and no book covers these issues in such depth, comprehensiveness, or minty freshness.

The exposé continues in Chapter 8, which explores the curious ways in which writers work. We address where they work and how they manage space and time to suit the requirements of their writing, writing in groups, writing in public venues, and how writers balance writing time with the sometimes unpredictable requirements of children and family caregiving, yet another issue overlooked in books on writing, but often center-stage for writers and especially women.

The final two chapters of the book illuminate best practices in reviewing and editing. Chapter 9 concerns the peer-review process, reviewing grant proposals, and writing effective reviews of articles submitted to scholarly journals as well as responding effectively to reviews of one's own submissions. The chapter draws on the pertinent empirical literature on reviewing in addition to interviews with successful authors regarding their experience of being reviewed and completing reviews as members of journal editorial boards or invited reviewers (often referred to as ad hoc reviewers). The chapter includes the findings of a content analysis of more than 100 anonymous reviews from which I developed a set of best practices, and some practices to be avoided in completing reviews.

Chapter 10 details the essential practices of editors and editorial offices. Of course, I draw on my own experience as an editor, but I am fully aware that editors vary in their beliefs, which translates into distinctly different practices. Then, too, journals vary in their purpose, culture, preferred style of work they publish, and workload. To broaden the scope of the chapter, and to better represent common practices, I interviewed editors in general psychology, social psychology, family studies, and sociology and supplemented this with a review of empirical reports on editorial practices. All these diverse sources inform an understanding of the work of editors and editorial offices. In addition, the chapter details critical issues for authors such as the calculation and interpretation of acceptance rates and the importance and meaning of journal impact factors. The chapter details the key concerns reported by authors regarding issues of the reliability, validity, and fairness of the peer-review process and follows this with a discussion of how editors construct decision letters and how authors can best respond to them. The chapter closes with a discussion of ethical concerns in editorial practices.

Each chapter includes features that facilitate learning and quickly establishing successful practices. These features include:

- Highlights of recommended **Best Practices** boxed for emphasis. Included are essential habits of successful academic writers, managing risk and criticism, and responding to reviewers and editors.
- **Writer's Resources** that highlight useful materials that supplement the primary text, including recommended apps for writers and tips for establishing writing groups.
- Direct quotes from interviews with experts, faculty in mid-career, and new professionals as they comment on their experiences and the issues discussed in each chapter.
- Discussion questions, activities, and case studies that encourage readers to engage topics discussed in each chapter.
- Recommended readings that supplement the material covered in each chapter and a comprehensive reference list.

## Unique Features

*Crafting Scholarship in the Behavioral and Social Sciences* has a number of unique features that distinguish it from other books on academic writing and publishing.

- The book is informed by my years of writing articles and books in the behavioral and social sciences and my experience in editing three journals: Associate Editor, *Journal of Social and Personal Relationships*; Editor, *Journal of Marriage and Family*; and Founding Editor of the *Journal of Family Theory & Review*, which, taken together, represent over 30 years of experience in editing and working with journal boards, reviewers, and authors representing an array of interests and disciplines. I also currently edit the *Textbooks in Family Studies* series for Routledge.

- The book includes chapters on topics often omitted in similar books, including chapters on writing qualitative reports, theory, and comprehensive literature reviews. Additional chapters detail how academic writers work and experience writing as well as best practices in reviewing, editing, and responding to critics.

- The chapters are informed by a wide array of materials, including interviews with editors, senior scholars, scholars at mid-career, and junior scholars. Each of the chapters draws on the pertinent applied empirical literatures on the core topics of writing, reviewing, and editing. For the chapter on reviewing, I examined more than 100 anonymous reviews to uncover the best and not-so-helpful practices of reviewers.

- The book emphasizes similarities in the experience of behavioral and social scientists and fiction writers and, in doing so, visits books on writing fiction penned by novelists (e.g., Anne Lamott, Alice Munro, and Stephen King) and other writing masters (e.g., Natalie Goldberg, Ralph Keyes, and Betsy Lerner).

- This is a book about identifying the common problems academics face in writing and publishing, and the chapters provide practical solutions.

- A Facebook page, Crafting Scholarship (https://www.facebook.com/CraftingScholarship), supports the book and writing community. Writers are encouraged to post updates on their writing, photos of their writing paraphernalia and writing spaces, and otherwise share their practices, challenges, and successes. Writing instructors can share pedagogical materials, writing exercises, and syllabi.

## Audiences

The primary audience for this book is graduate students, new professionals (e.g., lecturers and assistant professors), and mid-career and more senior faculty in the behavioral and social sciences in North America and abroad. I draw many of my examples from family and relational studies, and I expect readers in fields such as family studies, family psychology, family communication, sociology, child and human development, and social psychology will soon feel at home. My intention and the book's oeuvre is broader in scope. I am hoping the issues of writing well, the practices of successful writers, and the analyses of reviewing and editorial practices will resonate with authors across many disciplines, including those working in the sciences and largely concerned with writing empirical reports, both quantitative and qualitative, and those working in more applied venues such as policy analysis, education, and a variety of clinical settings. The interviews, for example, were conducted with a diverse representation of scholars in multiple disciplines with different interests and specializations. The book applies to graduate students and faculty working throughout the behavioral and social sciences, and every effort is made to provide examples from multiple disciplines.

Graduate programs typically include classes on writing or professional practices where the book would be appropriate and of practical value. I imagine the book could be used in undergraduate classes on professional practices, but it is not specifically written as an undergraduate text. The book assumes readers have mastered the rudiments of English composition; if not, there are legions of appropriate books and some masterful books on style (see Recommended Readings for Chapter 2).

## Acknowledgements

To the many authors, reviewers, and editors with whom I have had the pleasure of working over the years, my sincere thanks for teaching me about the basics: writing, reviewing, and editing. A passel of talented reviewers provided some exceptionally useful suggestions, and the book has benefited as a result. To the reviewers Deborah Biggerstaff, University of Warwick, UK; David H. Demo, University of North Carolina at Greensboro; Peggy S. Meszaros, Virginia Tech; Jennifer Rose, Wesleyan University; and Claudia J. Stanney, University of West Florida: Many thanks for your thoughtful suggestions. I recorded hours of interviews for the book, and to the dramatis personae I am wondrous and grateful. Many thanks to: Anisa Zvonkovic, Paul Amato, Libby Balter Blume, Rachelle Brunn-Bevel, David Brunsma, Julie Fitness, Heather Helms, Michael Johnson, William Marsiglio, Harry Reis, R. Kelly Raley, Ron Sabatelli, Sarah Schoppe-Sullivan, and Elizabeth Sharp. Some entirely unplanned and unexpected conversations occurred along the road, and thanks are due to Renate Klein, Karin Lindstrom Bremer, Helen Marrow, Jennifer Rose, Paul Silvia, and the many scholars with whom I spoke at conferences, workshops, and via e-mail. Debra Riegert, senior editor at Routledge/Taylor & Francis, and her exceptionally capable assistant, Angela Halliday, offered great suggestions for the book's organization and design for which I am thankful. Thanks to the Committee on Publication Ethics (www.publicationethics.org) for permission to reprint a Code of Conduct for editors. To the many students and workshop participants I infected with an obsession for writing well, either congratulations or apologies are in order.

# 1 Crafting Scholarship
## An Introduction

Great writing underscores influential contributions in the sciences and in all of their applied iterations. The social psychologist Ellen Berscheid (2003) clearly values great writing as she reflects on the nature of influential contributions in psychology.

> The ability to express a new vision of the world simply, regardless of the underlying complexity of the idea and regardless of how much it defies conventional belief, [is] essential to those who wish their work to have an impact. Disciples are unlikely to be attracted if the vision is poorly articulated or expressed in a way that seems discouragingly complex, even though great complexity often underlies ideas that seem simple on the surface.
>
> (p. 121)

I am always amazed how significant contributions can appear so obvious, often rudimentary, regardless of the complexity of the phenomena being described. Ted Huston's (2000) model of close relationships is one example. The model is inclusive of the full array of attributes that describe relationship development from properties of individuals like personality attributes, emergent conditions like love and trust, relationship features like interaction sequences, and contextual influences like a couple's contact with friends and relatives, or their experience of work and coworkers. Virtually all scholarship on marriage and intimate partnerships can be organized with the close relationships model and the complex interactions of personal, relational, and contextual factors depicted. The model's simplicity belies the complexity it portrays. Great writing is deceptive, neither simple to execute nor elementary in meaning or implication.

Great writing permits us to read efficiently. When an article or book is well organized and clearly articulated, we understand an author's intention, we anticipate the line of argument, and there is little ambiguity. The effect is true for readers and just as importantly for the publishing gatekeepers—reviewers and editors.

Great writing is technically astute and conforms to accepted standards of style and usage, standards that buttress clarity of expression. Well-crafted articles and books are built on essential writing skills like an understanding of effective sentence structure, but they are also strategic. Great writing is consciously directed at an audience that includes general readers as well as critics, reviewers, and editors. At its core, this book is about writing strategically for an explicit and critical audience and, in doing so, crafting scholarship that is effective and influential.

## Purpose and Organization of Crafting Scholarship

*Crafting Scholarship* intends to improve your writing, success in publishing, and success in being read and cited—all of which are the building materials of influence and growth in the sciences and their applications. The book is organized in three parts. Part I includes four chapters on **writing journal articles, grants, books, book chapters,** and **book reviews,** all with an intended audience in mind. I assume we all have at least reasonably mastered the fundamentals of English composition, although I am the first to admit I am always learning more about style and grammar. And I assume we are familiar with the basic forms that journal articles take in our respective disciplines. You may not have written many journal articles, for instance, but I'm sure you are familiar with the typical forms they take. This first unit lifts off from a basic foundation and proceeds to think about crafting articles and other scholarly works strategically.

A second unit focuses on the **experience of writing,** how successful writers in the behavioral and social sciences approach their writing, their common practices, quirky rituals, and the issues that typically interfere with writing. I am immensely intrigued by how writers write and where and when they do so. A curiosity about writing habits initially led me to write this book.

I am interested in how the experience of writing for the behavioral and social sciences is similar to writing in other venues and genres. For instance, do novelists experience writing in ways similar to social scientists? Stephen King (2000), in his musing on the craft, says: "Writing is a lonely job. Having someone who believes in you makes a lot of difference. They don't have to make speeches. Just believing is usually enough" (p. 74). And: "When you write a story, you're telling yourself the story. When you rewrite, your main job is taking out all the things that are *not* the story" (p. 57). Both observations apply whether crafting fiction or a rigidly organized journal article. There are differences. King aims to write 2,000 words per day. I'm happy with 250, and that's a good day, but still there is similarity in our experience. The three chapters in this unit explore the phenomenology of writing as well as the issues of risk and criticism, and the practices successful writers fold into their routine writing habits.

The final unit includes two chapters, one on **reviewing journal articles** and one on the **common practices of editorial offices** and **responsibilities of editors**. These chapters aim to improve success in writing effective reviews, encourage an understanding of how editors work, and ultimately improve your success in publishing. I based much of the material for these chapters on a content analysis of peer reviews of journal articles taken from the archives of the *Journal of Family Theory & Review* and from the pertinent empirical literatures. I liberally supplemented this material by drawing on interviews with experienced editors to further interrogate core issues. I paired this mixture of source material with my own experience as a writer, reviewer, and editor.

## The Wherewithal: Why Write This Book?

Writing, reviewing, and editing have been constants in my academic life. I like writing and the challenges it represents: the challenge of discovery represented by mastering a new literature, honing an insightful review or new conceptualization, or following the intrigue of an empirical inquiry. In all these ordinary activities that consume so much of my time, and I imagine yours as well, I like thinking about writing strategically and executing that writing as well as possible. Doing science well and writing well are co-conspirators.

Reading about writing and writers is another part of the conspiratorial process; it helps me to become a better writer, but, truth be told, I find writers a curious lot. I find writers and writing practices endlessly fascinating, and most certainly patterned. My colleague Elizabeth prefers writing in cafes—not just any café, but a café of a certain size, with a large corner table where she can spread out her writing accouterments and command a view of the entire room. In some ways Elizabeth's writing practices are unique, but they are also deliberate and responsive to her own needs as a writer. Successful writers are aware of their requirements and constantly adjust circumstance with their writing needs. Uncovering some of the practices of successful writers is entertaining, instructive, and a major purpose of this book.

There is another conspirator. In 1983, Jetse Sprey, then the editor of the *Journal of Marriage and Family* published an editorial in which he suggested scholars interested in serving on the journal's board write and so indicate their interest. I did so and, after completing several reviews, was appointed to the board a year later. Reviewing was interesting, yet another way to venture into the intrigue of producing great science and a way to hone my skills as a writer and a reviewer. Although I had not anticipated a career as an editor, my interest in writing crossed paths with several unexpected, and entirely fortunate, opportunities. I served six years as associate editor of the *Journal of Social and Personal Relationships*, which was founded by Steve Duck a few years earlier. Another six-year term as editor of the *Journal of Marriage and Family* followed. These experiences led to an opportunity to develop a journal specializing in theory and review. I believed then and now that the broad field of family studies needed a home for encouraging the publication of integrative literature reviews and theoretical developments. I became the founding editor of the *Journal of Family Theory & Review* in 2008 and served as editor for seven years. I've read a heap of manuscripts and their incumbent reviews. And I've written scores of decision letters to authors. I don't know the exact number but over a thousand would be a conservative estimate. This book is the outcome of my unexpected, provocative, and rewarding career as an editor.

Although many books exist on technical writing and issues of style, *Crafting Scholarship* frames writing for academic and applied audiences within the larger context of the peer-review process. You might think of developing skills in reviewing, in the companion process of responding to reviews and editors, as additional elements in the foundation of great writing. Reviewers and editors are additional co-conspirators.

The literature on the writing for the behavioral and social sciences is well developed, with several instructional articles (Ambert, Adler, Adler, & Detzner, 1995; Belgrave, Zablotsky, & Guacagno, 2002; Bem, 1995; Matthews, 2005; Sabatelli, 2010; White, 2005), book chapters (Bem, 2004; Sternberg, 2000), and books devoted to the craft (Becker, 2007; Silvia, 2007). Authors typically address issues of grammar and style, and most address the specific requirement of technical writing. Most refer to the now classic books by Strunk and White, *The Elements of Style* (1999), Williams and Colomb's *Lessons in Clarity and Grace* (2010), or Gower's *The Complete Plain Words* (1973), and none substantially improve on these classics. However, few systematically explore the experience of writing, and none base their work on a well-designed empirical study of what authors say about their experience. Previous work is well intentioned, and sometimes useful, but often largely editorial. Previous work is neither broadly based on the experience of multiple authors, nor systematic in how the topic is interrogated, nor firmly positioned within an empirical literature on writing, reviewing, and editing. This book adds to what we know about the experience of writing across disciplines and venues. I am hopeful you will find *Crafting Scholarship* a useful and comprehensive treatment of the three pillars of academic publishing: writing, editing, and reviewing.

## Dramatis Personae

I spoke with many people about writing, some rather informally, although not always briefly. Others I interviewed in depth with a specific set of questions in mind. I asked about their writing practices, when and where they wrote, their views on reviewing work for journals, and their experience in being reviewed and responding to reviews. I interviewed new professionals, those in mid-career, parents with young children, and some well-established and successful senior scholars. I interviewed editors with considerable experience about their views on writing and publishing. The interviews are liberally cited throughout the book, and I think they form an important empirical foundation for the best practices identified. Brief biographical statements for each of our players are included below.

**Anisa Zvonkovic** is department head and professor of human development at Virginia Tech. She presided as president of the Groves Conference on Families and is a recipient of several awards for her teaching, mentoring, and research. Her research interests concern the effects of work and other contextual demands on individual and interpersonal lives and feminist and postmodern perspectives on close relationships. She is principle investigator for a National Institutes of Health–funded project on work travel and families and the health and family relationships of people experiencing high work demands.

**Paul Amato** is the Arnold and Bette Hoffman Professor of Sociology and Demography at the Pennsylvania State University. Paul is best known for his research on marital quality and the consequences of divorce on children. His many research awards include the Ernest Burgess Award for outstanding scholarly and career achievement in the study of families, four Reuben Hill Awards for excellence in research, and a Distinguished Career Award from the American Sociological Association.

**Libby Balter Blume** is professor and director of the programs in developmental psychology and family life education at the University of Detroit Mercy. Libby is the coauthor of textbooks on middle childhood and adolescence, series editor of *Groves Monographs on Marriage & Family*, and past book review editor for the *Journal of Family Theory & Review*, for which she is now editor-in-chief. Her research interests center on feminist and queer theories.

**Rachelle Brunn-Bevel** is assistant professor of sociology and anthropology at Fairfield University. Rachelle's research examines how students' race, ethnicity, class, gender, and immigrant status intersect to influence their educational experiences and outcomes. She has additional interests in racial-ethnic disparities in standardized test scores among K–12 students, and the unique experiences of female faculty.

**David Brunsma** is professor of sociology at Virginia Tech. With research interests in race, racism, human rights, and critical sociologies, he is co-editor with his colleagues Keri Smith and Brian Gran of the *Handbook of Sociology and Human Rights* (2013). David is active in the leadership of the American Sociological Association and is the founding co-editor of *Sociology of Race and Ethnicity*.

**Julie Fitness** is department head and professor of psychology at Macquarie University in Australia. Julie's research concerns rejection and forgiveness in relationships. She is a former deputy editor of *Psychological Science* and editor of *Personal Relationships,* published by the International Association for Relationship Research.

**Heather Helms** is associate professor of human development and family studies at the University of North Carolina, Greensboro. She is the recipient of several awards for excellence in research and teaching. Her research interests center on marital and family process, work and family relationships, and the social context of marriage. Her current projects focus on marital quality for new parents of Mexican origin and the link between sociocultural stressors and marital well-being during the early years of parenthood.

**Michael P. Johnson** is emeritus professor of sociology, women's studies, and African and African American studies at the Pennsylvania State University. His most recent book is the highly influential *A Typology of Domestic Violence* (2008). Michael continues to lead workshops on domestic violence throughout North America and Europe.

**William Marsiglio** is professor of sociology at the University of Florida. Bill's research focuses on the social psychology of men's sexuality and reproduction, fathering, and paid or volunteer work with children outside the home. Among his many books on fathers is the most recent *Nurturing Dads: Social Initiatives for Contemporary Fatherhood,* cowritten with Kevin Roy (2012).

**Harry Reis** is professor of psychology at the University of Rochester. Harry is former editor of the *Journal of Personality and Social Psychology* (Interpersonal Relations and Group Processes) and *Current Directions in Psychological Science*. Harry studies the factors that influence the quantity and closeness of social interaction and the consequences of different patterns of socializing for health and psychological well-being.

**R. Kelly Raley** is professor of sociology and training director at the Population Research Center, University of Texas at Austin. Kelly is the current editor of the *Journal of Marriage and Family*, the oldest and most influential family science journal. Her research investigates family trends, the social determinants of family formation, and the impact of family change on social stratification. As part of a larger agenda examining the economic, social, and cultural contributors to marriage disparities in the United States, she recently completed a project that investigated the influence of social contextual factors on adolescent relationship formation.

**Ron Sabatelli** is professor and head of the Department of Human Development and Family Studies at the University of Connecticut. Ron served as editor of *Family Relations* and is well known for his theoretical work on exchange theory. His research interests include processes mediating the formation, maintenance, and disruption of intimate relationships.

**Sarah Schoppe-Sullivan** is associate professor of human development and family sciences, and psychology at Ohio State University and a recent recipient of an award for distinguished teaching as well as a National Science Foundation CAREER Award for her work on maternal gatekeeping.

**Elizabeth Sharp** is associate professor of human development and family studies at Texas Tech University. Her research interests include gender and family ideologies, qualitative methodology, and the intersection of dance and theater with the social sciences.

# References

Ambert, A. M., Adler, P. A., Adler, P., & Detzner, D. (1995). Understanding qualitative research. *Journal of Marriage and Family, 57,* 879–893.

Becker, H. (2007). *Writing for the social sciences.* Chicago, IL: University of Chicago Press.

Belgrave, L. L., Zablotsky, D., & Guacagno, M. A. (2002). How do we talk to each other? Writing qualitative research for quantitative readers. *Qualitative Health Research, 12,* 1427–1439.

Bem, D. (1995). Writing a review article for *Psychological Bulletin. Psychological Bulletin, 118,* 172–177.

Bem, D. (2004). Writing the empirical journal article. In J. M. Darley, M. P. Zanna, & H. L. Roediger (Eds.), *The compleat academic* (2nd ed.). Washington, DC: American Psychological Association.

Berscheid, E. (2003). Lessons in "greatness" from Kurt Lewin's life and works. In R. J. Sternberg (Ed.), *The anatomy of impact* (pp. 109–124). Washington, DC: American Psychological Association.

Brunsma, D., Smith, K.E.I., & Gran, B. (Eds.). (2013). *Handbook of sociology and human rights.* Boulder, CO: Paradigm Publishers.

Gowers, E. (1973). *The complete plain words.* Boston, MA: D. R. Godine.

Huston, T. (2000). The social ecology of marriage and other intimate unions. *Journal of Marriage and the Family, 62,* 298–321.

Johnson, M. P. (2008). *A typology of domestic violence: Intimate terrorism, violent resistance, and situational couple violence.* Lebanon, NH: Northeastern University Press.

King, S. (2000). *On writing: A memoir of the craft.* New York, NY: Simon & Schuster.

Marsiglio, W., & Roy, K. (2012). *Nurturing dads: Social initiatives for contemporary fatherhood.* New York, NY: Russell Sage Foundation.

Matthews, S. H. (2005). Crafting qualitative research articles on marriage and families. *Journal of Marriage and Family, 67,* 799–808.

Sabatelli, R. (2010). Writing for a scholarly journal. *Report, 55,* F2–F5. Minneapolis, MN: National Council on Family Relations.

Silvia, P. J. (2007). *How to write a lot.* Washington, DC: American Psychological Association.

Sternberg, R. J. (Ed.). (2000). *Guide to publishing in psychology journals*. New York, NY: Cambridge University Press.

Strunk, W. Jr., & White, E. B. (1999). *The elements of style* (4th ed.). New York, NY: Simon & Schuster.

White, L. (2005). Writes of passage: Writing an empirical journal article. *Journal of Marriage and Family, 67*, 791–798.

Williams, J. M., & Colomb, G. G. (2010). *Style: Lessons in clarity and grace*. Boston, MA: Longman.

# Part I
# Writing for Journals, Grants, and Books

# 2 Writing Journal Articles

Some of the most significant writing we do as academics consists of crafting journal articles. Tenure and promotion decisions in no small way depend on success in publishing, especially in journals with the greatest influence, which are sponsored by leading professional organizations. And just to keep things in perspective, gaining tenure and promotions is important, but equally important is crafting great work in articles that are likely to be influential and contribute to the growth of our respective fields.

The style in which empirical articles are written is straightforward, with an introduction and literature review, a methods section, results and discussion, and conclusion. The formula differs modestly for theory, research syntheses, case studies, and applied work but is standard for empirical work. This chapter details writing effective articles with the implicit goal of seeing them published in influential journals. In focusing on empirical reports, including quantitative and qualitative work in all their variations, I don't wish to exclude case studies, analysis of social policies, or other forms of journal articles. Many, and perhaps most of the issues we discuss are generic and apply to nearly all form of articles. The writing and review of theory and review articles is dear to my heart, because I edited such a specialized journal for seven years, and so this topic has its own chapter. Many of the signatures defining great writing or best practices in composing the body of articles also apply to writing other forms of scholarship, including grant proposals.

This chapter begins with some general comments about the preparation and presentation of journal submissions, and then details preparing articles reporting on empirical work. I assume you have previously read heaps of journal articles, are familiar with the form, and have written literature reviews for previous assignments, and perhaps completed a thesis or written a journal article. If you are entirely new to the process or simply wish to improve your skills, do continue with the chapter, but in addition, consider visiting any of the suggested resources at the end of the chapter. Like any skill, improvement, and in this instance writing well and gaining success in publishing, comes from continuing education and practice. Some readers may be more interested in writing case studies, applied or policy essays, grants, or work directed toward lay audiences. For this, I hope you will find the chapter helpful and encourage you to visit more specialized textbooks (e.g., Green & Simon, 2012; New & Quick, 2003).

## Quality of Writing

The overall quality of writing—including issues of style, grammar, and appropriate use of the English language—are important in some regards, but they aren't necessarily deal breakers. Reviewers and editors are not expecting Woolf or Hemingway; they are expecting a reasonable level of competence. Otherwise reviewers and editors vary in the importance they attach to the quality of writing. Personally I enjoy writing and vastly favor a well-written article. I admire authors who write well. I suspect they are more successful in publishing, their work more assessable and influential, and from the perspective of an editor, they are much easier to work with. Some view the issue of writing well as relatively unimportant, assuming an author has achieved a minimal level of competence; the quality of the science or contribution to the discipline is privileged. When I asked Mike Johnson about how important are matters of style or grammar in the evaluation of manuscripts under review, he responded:

> Not at all. In terms of my decision whether to recommend accepting or rejecting a paper, not at all. It would come up in a recommendation for revision and I would include a note to the editor [about the writing] if needed. To me the overall quality of writing is not that important. Although I should say, it very rarely comes up. Most of the things that I review are well written. It is possible that editors are screening out things that are horribly written.

Harry Reis shared a similar view: "I consider it important in that I think we ought to write well. I would *never* use that to accept or reject a paper."

The disposition of a manuscript is largely dependent on the quality of the science or application and the importance of the contribution. Great writing is not a prerequisite for either, but then neither is it entirely inconsequential. Harry Reis shared a position that appeared often in my interviews. "Writing well helps to get your ideas across . . . and it's kind of a delight to read. I think that certainly promotes [an author's] work." Heather Helms amplified the issue and added some thoughts:

> Good writing is pretty important to me. . . . If I review an article and think this is really well written, then I have almost an emotional reaction. It's a positive feeling. You enjoy reading it. It's not a struggle

to get from paragraph to paragraph. You do not have to constantly reread a sentence over and over again to understand the author's intention. It makes the process more enjoyable. I like reading good writing. So if a paper is written well, then you can concentrate on [substantive issues]. If it's not well written, you spend all your time struggling through the paper asking what did this sentence or paragraph mean. I can actually get a little bit grouchy if the writing is so poor I can't understand the writer's intention.

Paul Amato is a professor of sociology and has won the prestigious Reuben Hill Award more than any other author (see Appendix 1).[1] Like Michael and Heather, he is very productive and among the most skilled authors I know in crafting journal articles. Paul takes a similar perspective to both Michael and Heather regarding the importance of the quality of writing in evaluating a manuscript.

I think there are situations where a manuscript is not particularly well written but the research still seems useful or valuable. There are a lot of social scientists who are not very good writers . . . it is something I weigh heavily because I do believe clear writing reflects clear thinking. If a manuscript is very poorly written, it makes me wonder if the whole theory and analysis are questionable. Good writing in our field needs to be as clear as possible. Here is my theory, this is what I did, here are my results, and here is what I think it means.

RM: *Are matters of house style or grammar important?*

It's not a deal breaker but poor grammar does irritate me. Mixing up verb tenses, run-on sentences, and so on are bothersome, but not necessarily a deal breaker.

Later in the interview, Paul commented on the importance of learning to write well in his career.

I realized in graduate school that I needed to learn how to write. So I spent an entire summer immersing myself in learning grammar and reading books on style and I learned an awful lot. So I tell my students you've got to learn how to write. I don't think we stress that enough in our curriculum.

Ron Sabatelli, editor of *Family Relations*, considers the issue of style important but prefers to rely on professional copy editors to correct such issues and reserve his editorial commentary to more substantive issues. And not to belabor the point, I asked Kelly Raley, the editor of the *Journal of Marriage and Family,* her thoughts on the issue of writing and its importance in evaluating a manuscript.

I think there is a strong relationship between the quality of writing and the quality of thinking. It's not a correlation of one; they are not the same thing, but oftentimes people who struggle with writing also don't have the tools to organize their thoughts as strongly as people who have strong writing skills.

Matters of style are probably less important to me than to other editors, but as I'm in this position longer I understand why it is important to people, because when people don't adopt the expected style of presenting things it just takes readers a lot more effort to understand what the authors are trying to do. But having said that, it is really not the thing I'm paying attention to when reading an article. I'm really paying much more attention to the nature of the contribution and whether the method is appropriate for making that contribution.

In summarizing the commentary of our judges—Michael, Heather, Harry, Kelly, and Ron—good science, intelligent and knowledgeable practices are necessary, and good writing services all.

When the quality of writing detracts from a reader's understanding or ease of understanding, it becomes an important issue. We write technical work that requires considerable background knowledge on the part of readers and concentration in trying to understand complex arguments. A well-organized work, clearly written with few distracting errors in style or grammar, can only help in generating a more positive evaluation. Typographical errors or lapses in house style (e.g., APA style) are things I can control as a writer, and in the end I want to give evaluators as few reasons to be critical as possible. Other elements of good writing are more difficult to achieve but nonetheless are important to consider. For instance, the precise and consistent use of concepts throughout a manuscript is a simple prescription but sometimes difficult to obtain. The clarity and logic of an argument are also important but decidedly difficult to judge. Heather Helms shared her thoughts on these issues.

To be honest, journal writing is kind of boring. Creative writing, like fiction, is much more expressive. I actually think some of us like creative writing; I have to battle through that side of myself when I'm writing an empirical article. I remember being edited by Susan McHale [a mentor]. "Synonyms are not good," she would say. In creative writing you don't necessarily want to use the same word all the time for describing something, and in empirical writing you do. There is the need for this conceptual clarity that is kind of boring but it is actually really important.

I am writing this paper now that comes from the economic hardship literature, and people throw terms around like economic pressure, economic hardship, economic strain, stress; there is zero conceptual clarity. The problem is that these concepts all mean different things, and are operationalized differently. I've become attuned to the importance of conceptual clarity throughout a paper, being clear how concepts fit with the literature, and operationalizing constructs in ways that make sense and fit with the theoretical base. So I think that empirical writing is different. I think there is a method to doing it well that new writers need to understand.

Heather identifies a common problem I see in editing submissions: an inconsistent use of language and incomplete definition of core concepts. In her example, she draws on the economic hardship literature and the many concepts directed at similar themes. Often authors can make important contributions by carefully distinguishing between related but distinct concepts, a contribution built upon exacting definitions.

---

**BOX 2.1 WRITER'S RESOURCE: USEFUL WRITING APPLICATIONS**

### The Writer's Diet
*http://writersdiet.com/WT.php*
This app was developed by Helen Sword and provides a supplement to her books *Stylish Academic Writing* (2012) and *The Writer's Diet* (2007). The app is a diagnostic tool that evaluates writing samples (maximum 1,000 words per run) over five grammatical categories such as the use of verbs and adverbs. The app is well designed, simple to use, and informative. I enjoy using it and find it helpful in evaluating writing samples and pinpointing areas needing shoring up.

### Edit Minion
*http://editminion.com*
This is another great app that evaluates writing samples for common grammatical hot points. The app highlights passive verb constructions, sentences ending in a preposition, weak words, clichés, tricky homonyms (e.g., your and you're), frequently used words, adverb usage, and common misspellings. Once you've used this app a bit you'll begin to recognize weaknesses in your writing and correct them. Running an evaluation of an entire manuscript is modestly time-consuming and worth the effort. I ran this chapter in three batches of text, and it took about three hours to read through the analysis and make changes in the text. The approach adds some features I like, handles large selections of text, and improves my writing.

**Word Web**
*http://wordweb.info*
Word Web is an English thesaurus and dictionary. The application duplicates existing features of Windows but adds some additional functionality. I've been using the Pro version for years and find it very helpful.

There are a variety of additional writing applications, but these are the three I find most useful. You may wish to explore the possibilities a bit more. For instance, *Write or Die 2* is an application that makes procrastination consequential. A writer sets a goal, for instance 250 words in 60 minutes, and things happen if the goal is not met. It's like video gaming meets scientist. (No worries—it's nonviolent and nonshocking.) The whole business is kind of fun, but that's what I mean by distracting. If you find additional apps useful, please let me know on the *Crafting Scholarship* Facebook page.

## Clarity and Precision in Writing

The heart of great journal writing is clarity. Using an exacting language can be quite difficult and commonly appears as an issue in manuscripts under review. For instance, it is quite common for authors to use **family** to mean members of a household such as parents and children, and in the same manuscript use family to refer to the wider tracings of kin including children, parents, uncles, aunts, and grandparents. In this instance, how would we understand the following prediction? "Families are important determinants of positive well-being." I can think of at least a half-dozen possible meanings to this sentence. Without knowing the author's definition of *family*, readers are left to create their own image, which may be fine when writing a novel, but science requires precision.

Imprecision in the use of language and the definitions given to core concepts, or lack of explicit definitions, often leads to divergent recommendations among reviewers, because each interprets core issues differently and consequently reaches different conclusions. In my conversations with Rachelle Brunn-Bevel, a talented new professional at Fairfield University, she regarded the issue of divergent reviews as disturbing, even when the decision letters of editors were clear and instructive. "It leaves me a little bit unsettled knowing that different people come up with different recommendations about the same paper." Authors can't control how reviewers will evaluate and understand their work, but they can avoid unnecessary confusion by writing clearly, using consistent language and well-defined concepts.

Sometimes this goal of conceptual clarity leads to some dull, but precise writing. For example, consider the following sentence about **family myths**:

> Family myth refers to "a number of well-systematized beliefs, shared by all family members, about their mutual roles in the family and the nature of their relationship."
>
> (Ferreira, cited in Bennett, Wolin, & McAvity, 1988, p. 213)

By this definition we understand a family myth to be a belief shared by family members about themselves and their relationships. Like all good social scientists, we might question the particulars of the definition (e.g., must a family myth be held by *all* family members?), or we might question the connection to related concepts (e.g., family rituals). As a conceptual definition, it serves the purpose of providing the author and reader with some common ground, an initial definition on which to build an understanding of this one aspect of family life. Intellectually, the definition provokes additional questions all directed at achieving a clearer understanding of the inner workings of people and their relationships. The definition functions as it should.

Consider the following example, one with a different purpose but still on the topic of family myths.

> A family myth is an enriched pattern, a two-faced proposition, allowing its operator to say one thing and mean another, to lead a double life.

To my ear, this is a wonderfully evocative sentence taken from Anne Carson's essay on *The Beauty of the Husband* (2001). Carson's **fictional tangos** play with my sense of curiosity, introducing an element of ambiguity, of mystery. I am intrigued. In reading her work, I am not at all clear how to describe it to you; it is short story, poem, and essay. I settled for calling it a fictional tango, as the author does, a dance of thought. This is all very nice, but as you've guessed, great fiction is terrible science, although it may inform science or be informed by it (Blume, 2011).

Of course there is more to preparing a manuscript than simply providing clear definitions of key concepts and using those concepts consistently, although this is a great start. Sword (2012) asked more than 70 academics about what they considered stylish academic writing and paired this with an analysis of how a sample of 1,000 journal articles in various disciplines (including psychology, higher education, and medicine) were actually written. Taken together, Sword's analysis identifies the core qualities that identify great writing, all of which should sound familiar and most of which are emphasized throughout this book.

The defining qualities of great writing include: writing with precision and clarity, penning well-crafted sentences, communicating a sense of energy and intellectual commitment, engaging readers in a compelling story, avoiding unnecessary jargon, and writing with imagination. Some qualities are not terribly transparent, such as "providing readers with aesthetic and intellectual pleasure" or "writing with imagination and creative flair." I guess what all this really means is writing with conviction and a good deal of curiosity. Then, too, there are some prerequisites to great writing: competence in the subject matter and rewriting heaps.

Other elements of great writing emerged from Sword's analyses of exemplary books and articles. Some qualities of great writing apply to books, but I would not recommend them as useful techniques in writing for journals. For example, using eye-catching titles, humor, or extended examples that draw on literary or historical sources, or nonessential figures or photographs. There are exceptions, of course. In a study of how fatherhood is depicted in the media, consulting historical documents and quoting them would be perfectly appropriate (LaRossa & Reitzes, 1995). When such material is but remotely germane, it would not be entirely appropriate for a journal article.

---

**BOX 2.2  BEST PRACTICE: THE BASICS OF WRITING WELL (AND GETTING PUBLISHED)**

- Aim for clear, precise language.
- Keep your subjects and verbs close by. They are good friends to clear writing.
- Engage readers in the story line of an argument with examples and illustrations.
- Avoid jargon when a simple expression will do.
- Mind the cadence, and vary the length of sentences. Longer sentences can be split up and still be friends.
- Favor active verbs.
- Write with conviction and ownership.
- Never say "the ways in which" when "how" will do.
- Never say "studies find" when actually people do.
- Read Howie Becker's book (recommended below), Strunk and White again, Williams and Colomb, or Gowers if you favor the UK brand of English.

## Crafting Effective and Successful Manuscripts

Many great instructional resources are available on how to construct a journal article, and especially an article reporting on empirical research; to a lesser extent there are useful resources for constructing theoretical articles or literature reviews (see Chapter 3). Some of the resources my students, workshop participants, and I have found most helpful are detailed at the end of the chapter. Here I assume you can write reasonably well and you understand the essentials of conducting research. You have read a number of empirical reports and have a good idea of how they are constructed. You have identified work that you consider exceptional and well written and are planning to model this work; and you've already read some of the instructional resources available.[2] I also assume you are not an expert. The skill sets necessary for writing research reports, case studies, grant applications, and other technical documents are substantial. Nonetheless, having a good foundation in basic writing skills in addition to understanding the fundamental construction of a journal article are great places to begin. Like any craft or sport, exceptional competence builds upon basic skills and emerges from effort and experience. It's also nice to have a responsive mentor and this book, or so I hope. There are no shortcuts to producing publishable work, but it does help to understand the issues editors and reviewers find to be important and how they approach those issues.

Incidentally, much of what we have discussed thus far and will discuss in the following sections applies to different types of written work. For instance, although grant applications can be written for a variety of purposes, including the support of new empirical work, they commonly address applied interests such as program development or community-based projects. In nearly all instances, grant applications will include core elements similar to writing empirical reports, including statements of purpose and literature reviews.

## Introductions and Problem Statements

Reviewers and editors are quick to point out the importance of a clear and concise **statement of purpose**. Ideally this should occur in the first few paragraphs. Editors clearly emphasize this, as do experienced authors. Kelly Raley, editor of the *Journal of Marriage and Family*, and Ron Sabatelli, editor of *Family Relations,* share similar views on the importance of the first few pages of a manuscript. Ron says, "among the most important issues for me is that the contribution to the research literature is clear in the first couple of pages." Heather Helms stated this quite directly: "If I don't know by the end of the third paragraph what the study is about I am not optimistic about the paper."

I have received manuscripts with long, belabored introductions as authors take the reader through the many conceptual pathways they traversed in coming to a particular question. Often this sort of long, detailed introduction is unnecessary and detracts from communicating a clear focus. In such cases, I often suggest authors condense their introductory comments to no more than a page or two. Editor Julie Fitness comments on the issue similarly:

> I would expect to see the purpose stated within the first couple of paragraphs. The first paragraph is sort of a stage setter and describes how or why a particular topic is important. A statement of the research question follows. By the end of the introduction, the reader should be curious about what you're going to find. Here's the area of interest, here's the question and by the time we get to the methods section it is going to be so inevitable that you can see what our question was and why it was necessary to answer (in this way).

An introduction establishes the context for the study, succinctly states the essential purpose or question, and, in achieving these ends, engages the reader's curiosity by describing why the topic is of interest and what the unique contribution of this particular work will be. We don't need a memoir or a tome; a few well-constructed paragraphs will do. A common error is to include detail in the introduction that is more appropriate to the literature review, and in this way the two sections become fused. Keep these sections separate. They have very different purposes. As a rule, the number of references included in an introduction is minimal.

You may draft an introduction early in the process of writing a paper, but it is often helpful to return to this section when the paper is mostly complete and you've got a better idea of what you actually wrote, which may be different from what you initially thought you were going to write. Once you have completed a draft, let it sit for a week or more before returning to it with a fresh perspective. Paul Amato revises many times but does so within a fairly short period of time. Other authors I spoke with take longer, but often less than a few months.

My colleague Anisa Zvonkovic goes a few steps further. When ready to revise a paper, she prints a hard copy of the manuscript to physically view it differently, and she does her final revising in a different space. Rather than her typical writing space, a kitchen table at home, to revise she visits a public space, usually a local café or a library. She says, "A different place helps to put on a different perspective." In this way she manipulates form and place to encourage a fresh perspective on her developing work. Anisa prefers a bit of activity around her when she's revising and shies away from working in seclusion.

Revisiting an early draft of the introduction and statement of the research question once you have completed the remainder of the paper is important. Experienced scholars know this and revise accordingly. In the course of completing a paper, subtle shifts may occur in the direction of the analyses or their interpretation that require complementary refinements in the original introduction and problem statement. Most certainly writers want to make the best possible impression in the first page or two and for a halo effect to ensue once the remainder of the paper is reviewed. However, it's best to keep in mind: "a carefully woven opening paragraph will catch no readers if, on the very next page, you slacken the net and let all the fish go" (Sword, 2012, p. 87).

## Literature Reviews

Much is written on the construction of literature reviews as preludes to grant proposals or empirical work, theory, policy briefs, case studies, or similar kinds of journal-length articles. The purpose is to establish a context for the work that is to follow. This includes a critical review of the pertinent literature, including work that establishes what is currently known about a topic and how the present study will build upon earlier work and contribute to a body of knowledge. In the case of empirical work, some is largely descriptive (e.g., an estimate of population demographics or a study that intends to enumerate the number of friends spouses share in common); some are exploratory with the stated purpose of developing theory inductively (e.g., qualitative interviews); but frequently among the best and most influential empirical work, and the grant applications that support such work, are studies based in a theoretical perspective that needs to be explicitly stated. Theory directs the assembly of empirical work by suggesting testable hypotheses, measurement and design, and the later conduct of analyses. Recent developments in adult attachment theory perfectly illustrate each of these outcomes. The articulation of adult attachment styles prompted the development of new measures, and an extraordinary array of research followed that led to advancements in theory (for a review, see Mikulincer & Shaver, 2012).

A literature review needs to establish the context for a study, at times providing a detailed critical review of work that is especially relevant, but all in the service of deriving specific research questions and, when appropriate, explicit hypotheses. In empirical work, as well as other forms of journal articles, we are not writing a detailed history, and citing all the relevant work is not the best use of limited space. A great introduction and accompanying literature review identifies a research question and establishes the importance of the topic. Relevant theory and empirical work are synthesized and critiqued. Research questions and hypotheses are clearly based upon the accumulated evidence, both theoretical and empirical. In the end the reader is left with an appreciation for the importance of the study and how it is designed to contribute to the literature.

At least that is the goal. Crafting all of this in about five to eight pages is challenging. As with any craft, mastery derives from understanding the goals, emulating the work of successful authors, practice, and heaps of rewriting. It also helps to trust in the force, but we'll talk more about that later.

Some years ago I worked with Steve Duck, the founding editor of the *Journal of Social and Personal Relationships*, as an associate editor responsible for the Family Studies and Sociology section of the journal. Publishers limit the number of pages available for each volume of a journal, and Steve was determined to use that allocation well and in this way publish as much as possible in each issue and thereby serve the field of personal relationships and establish the journal. Steve encouraged authors to eliminate nonessential text, including nonessential citations, and referencing only that work which was most recent and relevant; he encouraged his editorial team to be just as stern. Eliminating nonessential references is tedious, sometimes unwelcome by authors, and seemingly a bit compulsive on the part of an editor, but it had the effect of permitting us to publish a few more articles in each volume. Publishing an additional article or two meant the journal grew along with its impact, authors and the field were better served, and the fledgling journal became a major influence in the emerging science of personal relationships.[3] In any case, an effective literature review need not denote the entire historical record, but rather establish the raison d'être for the current study and in doing so cite that literature distinctly pertinent for theoretical, methodological, or empirical reasons.

## Writing for Editors and Reviewers

Editors and reviewers look for introductions and literature reviews that build a strong rationale for a study and demonstrate an understanding of the relevant literature. Heather Helms comments on how she approaches reviewing manuscripts and evaluating the front end:

> I'm looking for a certain level of complexity in thought, depth of understanding, critical analysis, and the ability to pull all that together into testable research questions that make sense, and the ability to adequately and appropriately test those questions with the appropriate methods and analyses.

Reviewers are often quick to point out citations missing from a review, although most editors with whom I spoke do not consider this a deal breaker. Like Heather Helms, we look for a reasonable level of understanding and complexity of thought. A missing citation can be rectified in a revision.

More difficult are manuscripts written from the perspective of one discipline that fail to cite literature from neighboring disciplines. For instance, a study of siblings might benefit from literatures developed by psychologists, communications scholars, and sociologists. In my own work on uncles and aunts, it was quite a pleasant surprise to discover interesting and relevant work done on siblings in evolutionary biology, an area far removed from the journals I typically graze.

Some journals are directed at scholars in a number of related disciplines, and the work published in these journals reflects that multidisciplinary focus (e.g., education, family studies, human development). For example, research on domestic violence appears in many neighboring disciplines. Michael Johnson comments on the issue:

> I want to say [failing to cite work in a neighboring discipline] is not very important, but I work in the area of domestic violence where there is work done in so many disciplines that you do want people to cross over. What I think I do is tell the authors they need to look at something in a neighboring discipline. I won't reject it because they haven't cited something and I'll give them citations and encourage them to incorporate pertinent work in the literature review and conclusion.

Introductions and their companion reviews end with a set of questions or predictions that are derivative of the theory and research reviewed. For the reader, there should be no surprises; the review should clearly forecast the questions, hypotheses, and the variables upon which they are built. If a review centers largely on gender differences in spouses' friendships, the reader can reasonably expect the research questions will center on those variables. We would not expect a hypothesis regarding a previously unmentioned variable. Readers would be surprised if a question appeared about age differences in friendship formation if these variables and their pertinent literatures had not appeared earlier. More often there are subtle shifts in the focus of the review and research questions. For instance, it would be disconcerting if the review focused on spouses and their friendships, and the concluding research questions shifted from spouses to courtship among young adults and accompanying changes in friendship networks.

In the end, we aim for a clear, compelling, and focused introduction that ends with a statement of purpose, and a well-designed review of pertinent literature that sets the context for the work that will follow. This is all straightforward, but paradoxically it can be difficult to execute. From my experience as an author, a well-executed introduction and literature review is devilishly difficult to articulate and assemble, and often takes many drafts before I begin to get it right. From the perspective of an editor or reviewer, the quality, logic, and precision of this front matter, presages all that is to follow. If the front matter is well executed, I expect great things from the body of the article.

## Reporting Methods

The description of a research design, the methods employed to collect data, and measures used need to be entirely in keeping with the requirements of the research questions. There should be a clear symmetry in the variables about which the study has questions or hypotheses and the variables that are measured.

The core elements of the study should be described clearly but succinctly. This includes the design, which may be quite straightforward in the case of an Internet-based survey, or quite complex in the case of a longitudinal panel involving multiple times of measurement and multiple methods (e.g., questionnaires and personal interviews). The sample is described, including how participants were solicited and any pertinent descriptors that help in locating the study (e.g., age, gender, income, sexual orientation, relational status). Measures should be fully described, and such descriptions often include sample items, details about response choices, and informative statistics such as means, standard deviations, and estimates of measurement qualities (e.g., coefficient alpha). Complex analytical tactics are explained in the methods section if they are apt to be new to readers or represent unfamiliar applications. If you are unsure what to report, model similar studies published in the journals of interest.

Harry Reis likens a well-written methods section to:

> describing a new car in terms of the mechanical design of the engine. Engine specifications are what make the car work, but rarely does one leave the showroom excited about engine mechanics. Nevertheless, with a flawed design, the car will sputter and die, but a vehicle with a well-structured engine will keep its passengers sailing smoothly in pursuit of their goals.
>
> (Reis, 2000, p. 81)

Methods sections are important because they give readers the necessary information to evaluate the research and understand the outcomes of that research. For editors and reviewers, a well-designed, comprehensive, and articulate methods section is essential material in evaluating a manuscript and later interpreting findings.

I asked Sarah Schoppe-Sullivan what she considered important in reviewing a manuscript.

> I think there are a couple of things. I focus a lot on the study design. Measurement is important I think because of my background in

psychology. I tend to focus a lot on measurement and whether the measures are appropriate and their psychometric properties [robust].

Effective method sections are comprehensive in providing a reader with the details necessary to understand the execution of a study. They are intended to be functional, clearly written and well organized. I consider this the easiest section of a manuscript to write, but still it typically takes me several drafts to get all the ducks in a row.

## Reporting Results

A well-constructed methods section foretells the organization of the results that follow. Great results sections represent great storytelling. You can make reporting results duller than doornails, but you need not do so. The best results sections are compelling narratives that continue the story begun in the introduction. Mark Edwards, in his book *Writing in Sociology* (2012), likens an effective results section to a great museum tour. A knowledgeable tour guide can dramatically increase the pleasure and appreciation of a museum visit or art walk by signaling how a particular art form might be interpreted and given meaning. The walk, in its design, planning, and articulation, illustrates the core of presenting results in a way that is informative, pertinent, and interesting.

In an art walk and a results section, avoid the banal. Tell the story, but avoid all the portraits and analyses you considered but later abandoned. Keep your eyes on the prize(s), which means the original questions with which you began the inquiry. Use parallel structures so that the order of the presentation of findings is consistent with the order in which the initial questions and hypotheses were presented, and ideally the same order in which the measures were described.

Some findings are essential but not exactly gripping news, and much of this material can be presented in the methods section. Descriptions of the sample and measures—for instance, incomes, average ages, or mean scores on dependent measures—can be included in tables or text in the methods section. Descriptive details on the participants or measures are important in locating the study, but as a rule avoid beginning the reporting of results with your dullest detail. Result sections begin with a reporting on the core questions, which makes for a better story and more interesting read.

In nearly all empirical work, I end up conducting far more analyses than I actually report; usually it is a matter of wanting to design the most elegant analyses that clearly address the questions I have. There are other instances where I simply wish to rule out alternate interpretations. A reader doesn't need to know about all the background work. Although some auxiliary analyses can be important to share, the first priority is to explore a research question or test a hypothesis and report on the conduct and outcome of that inquiry in a way that is precise and informative.

I prefer results written in ways that favor narrative descriptions of findings that review the question being addressed and offer interpretations of those findings. Consider two examples.

- The main effects of gender, $F(1, 198) = 6.74$, and marital status, $F(4, 195) = 4.65$, were highly significant at $p < .01$ (see Table 1).
- Women reported more close friendships than men for all groups as predicted, with means of 5.2 and 1.4, respectively. This pattern of gender differences is repeated for all marital statuses, although recently divorced individuals report the fewest friendships, and married individuals report fewer close friends than unmarried individuals. The means and standard variations are presented in Table 1 along with the relevant test statistics.

In the first instance, the results of an analysis of variance are reported succinctly and the reader is referred to Table 1, presumably for additional details. We know the value of the $F$ statistic and the $p$ value but not the actual number of friends reported on average or the direction of the main effects. The interpretation of the findings is deferred to the discussion section. For most readers, the precise value of a statistic, in this case an $F$ ratio, is not terribly interesting in of itself, although it is necessary to report somewhere.

In the second example, the findings are stated in straightforward prose. We know how the number of friendships differs across gender and marital status, and those differences were as predicted. In this instance, the actual finding becomes the subject rather than the value of a statistic. Social scientists are a bit geeky, but even for the geekhood of social scientists, narrative accounts are more interesting to read and they can more quickly communicate information. Statistical details are sequestered in tabular format in most cases.

Where sophisticated or unusual statistical procedures are employed, some additional interpretation may be required. This includes providing readers with explicit explanations of the material presented in tables or figures—for instance, the literal interpretation of a coefficient.

The coefficients presented in Table 2 can be interpreted as partial correlations. For example, controlling for income and parental status, the number of close friendships is predictive of marital satisfaction for men with a coefficient of .34 in column 1 ($p < .01$), but not women, a coefficient of .09 in column 2 (*ns*). The number of close friendships predicts marital satisfaction for men but not women.

It can be helpful to have a clear and explicit narrative interpretation of the statistics presented in a table and, conversely, somewhat tiresome without such readers' aids. In the example above, the actual values of the partial correlations may not be terribly crucial, but they are included to quickly illustrate for the reader the interpretation of the statistics presented in the table. As a reader, I prefer clear and instructive narratives. They allow a reader to quickly understand complex statistical procedures and what they mean. We are all busy people with many demands on our time. Clear and instructive writing permits a more effective use of our time.

## Discussion and Conclusions

The concluding section of the paper reviews the purpose and major findings, discusses why the findings are important, and explains how they add to the literature. The section provides some speculation about unexpected findings or underlying causal mechanisms or otherwise adds some discussion of the theoretical contributions. In the example above, the concluding section of the paper might discuss why the number of close friendships varies across gender and marital status and why these findings are important, for instance, by influencing marital processes. Customarily there is some discussion of the major limitations of the study and some suggestions for further research. Reviewers and editors alike are impressed with a thoughtful and well-written conclusion, as are readers.

## Titles and Keywords

Titles generally fall into two camps: those that include a literary element designed to attract a reader's attention and those that are entirely descriptive and inform a reader of the purpose, variables, or findings. Titles can suggest themselves at any time in the process, and I often keep a running list of possibilities at the front end of the manuscript. A great title should be interesting and informative. Great titles give the reader a concise explanation of the subject of an article. Consider these examples. Which do you prefer?

- *The Gender-Equality Paradox: Class and Incongruity Between Work-Family Attitudes and Behaviors* (Usdansky, 2011)
- *Financial Strain and Stressful Events Predict Newlyweds' Negative Communication Independent of Relationship Satisfaction* (Williamson, Karney, & Bradbury, 2013)
- *Mothers' Attitudes About and Goals for Early Adolescents' Cross-ethnic Peer Relationships: A Qualitative Analysis* (Mount, Karre, & Kim, 2013)
- *Early Family Ties and Marital Stability Over 16 Years: The Context of Race and Gender* (Orbuch, Bauermeister, Brown, & McKinley, 2013)

- *Pulling the Strings: Effects of Friend and Parent Opinions on Dating Choices* (Wright & Sinclair, 2012)
- *Connecting Here and There: A Model of Long-Distance Relationship Maintenance* (Merolla, 2012)
- *A Little Help From Our Friends: Informal Third Parties and Interpersonal Conflict* (Eaton & Saunders, 2012)
- *Between Family and Friendship: The Right to Care for Anna* (Nelson, 2011)
- *Locating Multiethnic Families in a Globalizing World* (Trask, 2013)

All these titles are effective, some more than others, and share a similar purpose. They briefly summarize the essential focus of the article to which they refer. In scanning a title, a reader should have a fairly good idea of the main topic, including the major variables, the theoretical approach, and possibly the method. References to a qualitative method, an analysis of census data, or a reference to a meta-analysis further alerts the reader to the author's purpose and means to achieving that purpose, and can be appended to the main title (e.g., Mount et al., 2013, in the list above).

Titles may include a semblance of humor or literary style, but in referencing pop music or metaphor, a search of the literature for that particular phrase might suggest something more original is in order. Phrases like "with a little help from my friends," a reference to a Beatles tune, or "an embarrassment of riches," an idiom used in the titles of articles, a novel, a history of Dutch culture, film, and several dramatic works, are frequently used and consequently tired. Phrases such as "a study of" or the equivalent are not useful, and copy editors will often strike them. Titles in the range of 12 to 15 or fewer words are just about right. The examples noted above range from 7 to 15 words, with the longer titles being more descriptive and therefore more effective (mean = 12 in case you're wondering).

The titles noted above vary in subtle ways. For instance, the first two are quite specific, with the key variables of the work included in the title. This is especially true of the second example, where the core finding of the study becomes the title (Williamson et al., 2013). There is little ambiguity about the subject of this work. Another example includes the qualifying phrase "a qualitative analysis" (Mount et al., 2013), and another implies a longitudinal design (Orbuch et al., 2013). This is useful information for readers who are particularly interested in such work.

The next three titles begin with implied metaphors: "pulling the strings," "connecting here and there," and "a little help from our friends." They pique interest, and in each case, once we read the second half of the title, we begin to understand the subject matter of the article. In this way, they are fine titles, but perhaps they are not the most useful.

Authors often rely on search engines to locate articles of interest, searches that are based on keywords linked to the article or included in titles or abstracts. When readers rely on keyword searches, literal titles based upon a variable language are most effective in facilitating a literature search, while titles that include metaphors, like "pulling the strings," are unhelpful in facilitating a search. Where a metaphor is used in a title, authors need to be especially particular in selecting an appropriate set of keywords to accompany the article. When submitting an article to a journal, authors are asked to suggest keywords either on the title page or when prompted in a digital submission process. Submission portals like *Scholar 1,* which a number of journals use, or similar systems, permit an author to review a list of potential keywords and make selections accordingly. Because potential readers find work of interest through search engines that rely on keywords, it is in an author's best interest to select applicable keywords carefully and comprehensively, and to include such keywords in the title.

The final two titles in our list are among the briefest: "Between Family and Friendship: The Right to Care for Anna" and "Locating Multiethnic Families in a Globalizing World." They are suggestive of the subject matter but not terribly so. We cannot know from these titles whether the content represents critical literature review, theory, case study, or empirical work. The number of keywords represented in the first instance is two (family and friendship), and in the second instance one or possibly two (multiethnic families and possibly globalizing world). Incidentally, they are both quite interesting works; they would be better served, and more easily found by database searches, with more informative titles that emphasize keywords that are representative of the subject matter.

## Abstracts

Abstracts appear following the title page and are often among the last elements of a manuscript to be written. An abstract is a succinct summary of subject and purpose, and often a reader's first exposure to an article. Consequently, abstracts are among the most important parts of an article. They permit a reader to quickly assess the subject matter, method, and essential findings. Along with titles and keywords, they fuel algorithms for searching databases that index journal articles.

Abstracts typically include a sentence describing the subject and purpose of the work being reported on and a brief description of the research method, participants, central measures, and major findings for empirical work. Abstracts close with a statement about the work's conclusions, implications, and applications as appropriate. Journals vary on the recommended length for abstracts. In the range of 75 to 150 words is about average for many journals. It is wise to consult the instructions for authors published by each journal and construct an abstract accordingly.

## Qualitative Research Reports

Crafting articles based on qualitative methods shares some similarities and some important differences with their quantitative cousins. Many pedagogical resources offer guidelines for writing and evaluating, research based upon direct interviews, observations, ethnographies, memoir, and the array of methods available for conducting qualitative research that are listed in the recommended readings at the conclusion of this chapter.

The family sociologist Ralph LaRossa (2012) provides a useful metaphor for positioning the varied types of qualitative work along three dimensions or coordinates: **latitude, longitude,** and **altitude.** The model allows a reader or reviewer to gage the intent of a study and to understand or evaluate the work accordingly. For instance, it makes little sense to criticize a work for having a small sample without first knowing the study's purpose and where it resides on the three coordinates. The dimension of latitude defines where a work resides in relation to the humanities versus sciences. Susan Orlean's wonderful book *Saturday Night* (1990), on how ordinary citizens, young and old, spend their Saturday nights, is great journalism but not intended to be a systematic inquiry. She writes in the introduction to the work's thesis:

> Saturday night is different from any other night. On Saturday night, people get together, go dancing, go bowling, go drinking, go out to get dinner, get drunk, get killed, kill other people, go out on dates, visit friends, go to parties, listen to music, sleep, gamble, watch television, go cruising, and sometimes fall in love—just as they do every other night of the week, but they do all these things more often and with more passion and intent on Saturday night. Even having nothing to do on a Saturday night is different than having nothing to do on, say, Thursday afternoon, and being alone on a Saturday night is different from being alone on any other night of the week. For most people Saturday is the one night that neither follows nor precedes work, when they expect to have a nice time, when they want to be with their friends and lovers and not with their parent, bosses, employees, teachers, landlords, or relatives—unless those categories happen to include friends or lovers. (pp. xii–xiii)

If we were to treat the book as a qualitative study of leisure, time, and the meaning of these ideas, it falls somewhere between journalism and ethnography. (Orlean often accompanied people on their Saturday-night pursuits much like an ethnographer.) It is curious work; I am not sure it is science, but it certainly is suggestive of some intriguing issues, and the book happens to be a great read on a Saturday night.

Longitude captures the idea of an inquiry's length and the degree to which it is built on direct data excerpts such as the use of direct quotes from interviews to establish and illustrate core themes. Susan Orlean's book falls somewhere in the middle of this spectrum as she relies on her own observations but includes the voices of the people she observed to anchor those observations.

The final coordinate refers to altitude or the level of theorizing in a particular work. Some qualitative work is deeply immersed in representing the voice of participants and generalizing about the underlying themes represented by those voices. In my own work on aunts and uncles and their relationships with nieces, nephews, and parents, I relied on what participants shared in their interviews to develop an understanding of the importance of such relationships for the individuals involved (Milardo, 2010). The work falls in a corner of space defined by a reliance on data and the subsequent derivation of theory. From the voice of the aunts, uncles, nieces, and nephews I interviewed, I came to better understand how generativity, or a concern for other generations, is expressed. Aunts and uncles throughout their interviews routinely express generative concerns as they recounted instances of mentoring their nieces and nephews, and just as commonly nieces and nephews mentored their aunts and uncles.

Although Orlean writes from the perspective of a journalist and I from that of a social scientist, our respective works can be located on the three coordinates in ways that emphasize both similarities and differences. Similarly, the interviews with experts I used throughout this book to illustrate themes in writing, reviewing, and editing are located at different positions along all three coordinates, and especially altitude, or the level of theorizing. LaRossa's three-dimensional perspective helps us to locate the wide variety of work that falls under the mantle of qualitative research and, in doing so, adapt the criteria we employ to evaluate work relative to its coordinates, which is to say intended purpose.

Good qualitative work can be assembled and evaluated in several ways. Some believe qualitative work is entirely distinct from its quantitative brethren; others take a different position and view qualitative work in ways similar to quantitative work and judge each by similar standards. Writers would do well to understand how their work falls along the three coordinates and submit their work to publications that favor that blend.

Journals in family studies favor work that is science based, often highly reliant on direct ties to data excerpts, and aimed at theory building. The *Journal of Marriage and Family*, for instance, instructs reviewers to evaluate all submissions based upon eight criteria:

- Relevance of the work to family scholars
- Importance of the research question(s)
- Novelty of the idea or methods
- Explicit reliance on the development or testing of theory
- Integration with the existing literature

- Quality of the data
- Quality of the data analysis
- Clarity and soundness of writing and underlying reasoning

Some of these criteria are rather standard fare for journals that publish empirical work. We might add, and some journals do add, concerns about the ambiguity of findings and their interpretation, the application or practical significance of the findings, or the broad applications of the theoretical or empirical contribution (Sternberg & Sternberg, 2010). In most instances, there is little distinction made for qualitative and quantitative studies, and the same criteria apply.

I asked Kelly Raley, editor of the *Journal of Marriage and Family*, if she evaluated qualitative work differently. She replied, "No, I don't think so," but then detailed some of the difficulties editors and reviewers report in evaluating qualitative work.

> An area of concern for me is that the standards for evaluating qualitative research are unclear. For example, what must be included in the methods section and how early in the analysis does an author need to be presenting a theoretical framework? Key issues are just not standardized.
>
>   RM: *Does that seem problematic to you?*
>
>   Well, yes, I think it is problematic. I think it is important to have some standards of evaluation. At the same time I think it is completely reasonable for authors to challenge those standards and say that this limits us in this way, or whatever, but I think it is important to have the standards out there.

Other outlets are more explicit about the distinguishing criteria for evaluating the methods used in qualitative work. Journals such as the *Journal of Marital and Family Therapy*, *Family Relations*, and *Qualitative Health Research* commonly publish award-winning qualitative work (see Appendix 2: Anselm Strauss Awards).

I asked Michael Johnson if he evaluated qualitative work differently from quantitative work when reviewing for family science journals.

> You do have to look at [the two general forms of conducting research] differently. The same issues are there, but those issues are harder to evaluate for qualitative work because qualitative work doesn't have the obvious markers. You really have to trust the authors. They tell you what they did and then give you examples. For example, in qualitative work [part of an evaluation] depends on whether the case was well made for what the authors are arguing about what the data say. You have to trust that the authors didn't just cherry-pick the quotes that supported an argument and ignore the ones that didn't.

I just had a conversation with someone the other day who asked: "Well, where does the trust come from?" I think it comes from how well the authors explain what they did in the method section; how they made decisions about what the themes were. Sometimes people will say they are doing grounded theory, but then they don't exactly lay out the process they use in the grounded theory framework to analyze their data. And that leaves you wondering if they really just came in with their own ideas, and then just picked out what supported that in their data, and ignored things that weren't supportive.

Michael's concern for the conduct and quality of data, and the representation and interpretation of data are common concerns that appeared in my interviews with reviewers and editors. Knowing how reviewers and editors evaluate qualitative work helps in assembling and writing our own work and matching a submission to an appropriate journal. Within the manuscript, authors can aid reviewers by being clear about where their work falls along the dimensions of latitude, longitude, and altitude, and in doing so possibly anticipate potential criticisms and avoid them before they occur. Reviewers and editors have responsibilities as well to evaluate qualitative research in ways appropriate for the method being employed and the subsequent analysis of data. It makes no sense, for instance, to criticize a qualitative study for failing to generalize or be representative of a particular population, unless, of course, an author makes such an unsubstantiated claim. Then, too, qualitative methods are diverse in their design, execution, and purpose in the same way that quantitative methods include a wide array of particular research designs ranging from direct observations of participants to automated mass surveys. Fundamentally we evaluate research submissions on the broad criteria noted above, such as clarity of the research question, quality of the data, and contribution to the field, and we apply these criteria in ways consistent with the purpose, method, and choice of analysis.

## Impression Management

Occasionally, editors receive a manuscript assembled in a style particular to a specific behavioral or social science journal, although not the style requested. For instance, perhaps the sections of the paper are numbered consecutively. The journal *Social Science Research* prefers this style, but it is not otherwise common in the behavioral and social sciences and is not used in the journals published by the leading organizations representing education, communication sciences, family studies, psychology, social work, and sociology. In these cases, the editor and the reviewers may wonder if an article formatted in this way was recently submitted to and rejected by another journal. If so, upon resubmission, was the manuscript revised with the comments of the first round of reviewers in mind? If the authors did not make the effort to correct simple matters of style and formatting, what is the likelihood they attended to the substantive comments of the first round of reviewers? In this way, before we even begin to review the content, questions regarding the sophistication of the manuscript are raised. This is not the best way to make a positive first impression or begin a review cycle.

Authors make the best impressions with reviewers and editors when they are clearly aware of the journal's mission, recent publication record, and particular style guidelines, all of which should be on the journal's website. If you wish to draw the attention of reviewers and convince them of your naiveté, label your abstract "Executive Summary" and include direct citations in the body of an abstract arranged as three separate paragraphs. Add citations to a variety of journals but entirely omit citations to the journal to which you are submitting your work, which then begs the question, "Why this journal?" Of course, there may be good reasons that an author does not cite articles published in the journal to which a manuscript is being submitted. Perhaps the journal has not recently published anything especially germane. That is possible but not very likely with regard to broad-based journals with long publication histories. In any case, be sure you are entirely familiar with a journal's recent publication record before submitting. I recently received a manuscript on involving parents in schools, a noble activity and I'm happy folks are working on this, but it is hardly relevant to a family theory journal. Had the authors simply reviewed the journal's mission statement and a recent issue, they could have avoided the expense of a submission fee and delay in appropriately seeking publication. Errors in manuscript preparation and journal selection can appear as lazy scholarship or simply incomprehensible, but sometimes they are more a matter of inexperience and a lack of training. After all, the review and publication process can appear formidable and the array of specialized journals considerable, at least at first glance. Writing successful articles or grant applications requires familiarity with what editors and reviewers look for in evaluating manuscripts and, just as importantly, knowing a journal's mission, publication record, and submission requirements, and, similarly, the requirements of funding agencies.

---

## BOX 2.3  BEST PRACTICE: WRITING JOURNAL ARTICLES

- Write clearly and unambiguously. This only happens after multiple drafts.
- First drafts are not clearly written. Rewrite.
- Write and then read each sentence like it matters, because it does. "A poorly crafted or uncrafted sentence . . . functions more like a shapeless log tossed into a river: it might or might

not help you get to the other side, depending on how strong the current is and how hard you are willing to kick" (Sword, 2012, p. 48).

- The most successful introductions are brief (about one or two pages), include few references, and end with a question or statement of purpose.
- Literature reviews establish the context of the work and the writer's expertise. End with a set of questions or hypotheses that are clearly derivative of the review.
- Begin a sentence with the critical subject matter, which is typically not the name of the author(s) whose work you are citing.
- Methods sections fully explain the necessary detail. There are no mysteries regarding what was done, with whom, or how measures were constructed.
- Results are systematically presented for each question or hypothesis. Complex analyses are explained and clearly interpreted. Tables are self-explanatory, and sample interpretations are included in the text.
- Never end with "further research is needed." Write a thoughtful discussion of your work's meaning and implications and tell the reader about the kind of research needed in some detail.
- Stellar titles and abstracts are rich in keywords.
- The story line throughout the article is clear, consistent, and ever present.
- Write for the intended audience, and your likely reviewers.
- Know the journal or granting agency to which you're submitting your work.

## Summary

The psychologist Daryl Bem (2004) likens the structure of a research report to an hourglass. We begin rather broadly and become increasing more specific as we move through the precise questions, methods, and analyses and conclude with a broader statement about the implications of the study. The analogy reminds us of the simple structure of a typical journal article. Executing the structure successfully is hardly simple and takes great care in all phases of the research process and reporting on that process. Here we have detailed the importance of writing clearly and unambiguously, more important in writing for journals and grant applications than for any other form. We also described what editors and reviewers consider important in evaluating manuscripts as well as grant applications, and especially in regard to the quality of the writing. We have detailed the purpose of the essential parts of a manuscript and how to approach writing each section, and we have described the important consideration of fueling keyword searches in crafting titles and abstracts. Finally, we described the importance of appropriately selecting journals for submissions based upon a journal's mission and the execution of that mission. Developing an understanding of these fundamental practices will hopefully add to your skill and success in crafting articles.

## Activities

1.  Select one issue of a favored journal and review the titles of the articles appearing in that issue. How would you evaluate them? Are there some you would rewrite? Can you identify the keywords in each title? Which titles are likely to be most effective in facilitating literature searches?
2.  Try writing a title of your own work that is rich in keywords.
3.  Try writing a title without a colon.
4.  Abstracts are important parts of an article because they fuel digital searches based on keywords, and just as importantly, they function to inform potential users of the article's content, hopefully encouraging them to continue reading. Select two or more abstracts and evaluate them in terms of the two functions noted above. Can you identify the keywords in each abstract? How well will each serve a digital search engine? How would you rate each abstract in terms of the *blue note*, or how well each captures your interest? Does each abstract represent its respective article fully and fairly, or in ways that are useful to readers?
5.  In your experience, how important is good writing in crafting scholarship? Is great writing important for qualitative work? More or less so compared to quantitative work?
6.  Identify a qualitative work you admire or in which you have a particular interest. This may be a manuscript you are currently writing or the work of another, perhaps an article from the list of the winners of the Anselm Strauss Award (see Appendix 2). Map your selection using the dimensions of altitude, latitude, and longitude.

## Recommended Readings

The recommended readings that appear at the end of each chapter are listed in order of utility or importance if not alphabetically.

### Core Writing Skills

The foundations of successful publishing and great writing are rooted in understanding some basic principles. Reviewing these resources improved my writing immensely, and the fun in doing so. They are all highly recommended.

Becker, H. (2007). Chapter 1: Freshman English for graduate students (pp. 1–25) and Chapter 4: Editing by ear (pp. 68–89), in *Writing for the social sciences*. Chicago, IL: University of Chicago Press.

The entire volume of Howard Becker's book is excellent, but if you're pressed for time, I highly recommend these two chapters. They provide general advice on writing and editing your own work. Regardless of how complex our work, there is no excuse for an overabundance of jargon or for language that distances the reader. This book will improve your writing and success in publishing. I list it first because it is such a quick read and a good place to begin.

Strunk, W. Jr., & White, E. B. (1999). *The elements of style* (4th ed.). New York, NY: Simon & Schuster.

Get this book. It is the classic statement on great writing style in 105 pages. First published in 1959, it quickly became a favorite and remains so. It's a no-nonsense explanation of the rules of composition and great advice on matters of style. There are several newer editions. Take your pick.

Sword, H. (2012). *Stylish academic writing*. Cambridge, MA: Harvard University Press.

Once you've read the first two selections, this book includes chapters on the core elements of great writing. The book is brilliant; the chapters are brief and littered with examples.

Williams, J. M., & Colomb, G. G. (2010). *Style: Lessons in clarity and grace*. Boston, MA: Longman. (Revised by G. G. Colomb, the 10th edition is superb.)
Gowers, E. (1973). *The complete plain words*. Boston, MA: D. R. Godine.

Williams/Colomb and Gowers are excellent style guides, and the latter is a classic British style guide. They will change your life and style.

Billig, M. (2013). *Learn to write badly*. Cambridge, UK: Cambridge University Press.

Michael Billig's book is an interesting critique on how academics are trained and how they write. The sensibility of a sociological imagination meets the rigor of compositional studies or rhetorical analysis. Billig is none too impressed with academic writing in the behavioral and social sciences: "Modern academia is increasingly competitive yet the writing style of social scientists is routinely poor and continues to deteriorate." The position is similar to Sword (2012), who writes: "There is a massive gap between what most readers consider to be good writing and what academics typically produce and publish" (p. 3). I am not sure I completely agree with either author, but they have got my attention. Billig's rhetorical analysis is certain to make you question how you write. The final chapters of the book provide a compositional critique of work in social psychology and sociology. The book ends with several recommendations worth attending to.

### Writing and Publishing Journal Articles

Bem, D. (2004). Writing the empirical journal article. In J. M. Darley, M. P. Zanna, & H. L. Roediger (Eds.), *The compleat academic* (2nd ed.). Washington, DC: American Psychological Association.

If you read anything on crafting a research article, this should be first on the list. Although written by a psychologist for psychologists, this is by far the finest article on constructing the research report. It is filled with clear advice and helpful examples. New professionals and old hats will find valuable advice here.

Sabatelli, R. (2010). Writing for a scholarly journal. *NCFR Report, 55*, F2–F5.

The editor of *Family Relations* draws on his many years of experience in the world of publishing and offers his observations.

White, L. (2005). Writes of passage: Writing an empirical journal article. *Journal of Marriage and Family, 67*, 791–798.

A helpful guide written by an experienced author and former associate editor of the *Journal of Marriage and Family*.

Edwards, M. (2012). *Writing in sociology*. Los Angeles, CA: Sage.

A useful book with thoughtful advice on writing quantitative and qualitative articles. Chapters are brief and typically under 10 pages, which makes for a quick read.

Sternberg, R. J. (Ed.). (2000). *Guide to publishing in psychology journals*. New York, NY: Cambridge University Press.

This edited book on writing journal articles includes 14 chapters written by senior psychologists and former editors. The chapters are generally quite thoughtful treatments of the basic components of a journal article and include chapters on strategy, such as writing with reviewers in mind, responding to reviews, and advocating for your work. Overall, highly recommended.

Sternberg, R. J., & Sternberg, K. (2010). *The psychologist's companion: A guide to writing scientific papers for students and researchers* (5th ed.). New York, NY: Cambridge University Press.

This book is a comprehensive guide to organizing and writing an empirical article, with additional chapters on writing grants and finding a book publisher. The chapter on selecting a journal includes useful details (e.g., impact factors) on over 50 psychology journals, although most family and personal relationship journals are absent, as are journals in allied fields (such as communication, education, sociology, and social work).

## A Style of Our Own

American Psychological Association. (2010). *Publication manual of the American Psychological Association* (6th ed., 2nd printing). Washington, DC: Author.

This is an important reference work for all, and the one most behavioral and social science students should learn first. Many journals use APA style or something similar. The sixth edition provides all the details on essentials such as creating headings, citing references in text, preparing tables, reference lists, matters of style, and much more. This manual has spawned its own cottage industry of textbooks and websites. Some are useful, especially one hosted by Purdue University. First buy or borrow the full manual. (The second printing has fewer internal errors but an inaccurate page index, making it difficult to use. Watch for later printings. Even the master occasionally sneezes.)

American Sociological Association. (2010). *American Sociological Association style guide* (4th ed.). Washington, DC: Author.

The 128-page *Style Guide* provides complete information on style, format, and other specifications for manuscript submissions. Chapters are included on Matters and Mechanics of Style, Preparing Your Manuscript for Submission, Copyeditor's Notations, Reference Sources, and Reference Formats. Even if you never plan on submitting to an ASA journal, the suggestions regarding matters of style will definitely improve your writing. The *Style Guide* is inexpensive for members and recommended.

Acock, A., van Dulmen, M., Kurdek, L., Buehler, C., & Goldsheider, F. (n.d.). Constructing tables for the *Journal of Marriage and Family*. Retrieved from http://oregonstate.edu/~acock/tables/

This is a great site with sample tables that can be downloaded and serve as templates for presenting most forms of analyses. The tables are done in a variation of APA style required by the *Journal of Marriage and Family*, but they can be used in many venues and are highly recommended.

## Qualitative Research

LaRossa, R. (2012). Writing and reviewing manuscripts in the multidimensional world of qualitative research. *Journal of Marriage and Family, 74*, 643–659. doi:10.1111/j.1741-3737.2012.00978.x

This is a masterful article on the construction and evaluation of qualitative work. The lead article is followed by several commentaries, each written by an accomplished qualitative researcher. All highly recommended.

Ambert, A. M., Adler, P. A., Adler, P., & Detzner, D. (1995). Understanding qualitative research. *Journal of Marriage and Family, 57*, 879–893.

This article and the next were recommended to me by Alexis Walker, a former editor of the *Journal of Marriage and Family*. Ambert and her colleagues give useful advice on writing up qualitative research and reviewing it. Highly recommended.

Belgrave, L. L., Zablotsky, D., & Guacagno, M. A. (2002). How do we talk to each other? Writing qualitative research for quantitative readers. *Qualitative Health Research, 12*, 1427–1439.

It's as the title says and a nicely written article with useful tactical suggestions for communicating qualitative research. I wish all reviewers would read it.

Matthews, S. H. (2005). Crafting qualitative research articles on marriage and families. *Journal of Marriage and Family, 67*, 799–808.

The intended audience for this article are authors new to publishing qualitative work, and its stated purpose is to "reduce the number of 'revise and resubmits' if not outright rejections." Most certainly this article will help you improve the presentation of your work, lower the potential for rejections, but expect revisions of anything you submit. Outright acceptances are rare.

### Grant Writing

Browning, B. A. (2011). *Grant writing for dummies*. Hoboken, NJ: John Wiley.

From the now ubiquitous series, this is a useful and general guide to locating funding sources and writing proposals.

New, C. C., & Quick, J. A. (2003). *How to write grant proposals*. Hoboken, NJ: John Wiley.

This book provides a comprehensive guide to writing proposals with thoughtful, illustrative examples of complete proposals along with case studies.

### Of the Spoken Word

Issever, C., & Peach, K. (2010). *Presenting science: A practical guide to giving a good talk*. Oxford, UK: Oxford University Press.

This is a short and to-the-point guide to oral presentations. Personally I appreciate a well-organized talk with useful slides. When a talk is well honed, I am more inclined to expect an important publication and look for such work. The book is written for physical scientists, and it's curiously geeky in spots (check out the cover, for instance), but it is surprisingly thoughtful.

## Notes

1. The award is given annually to the best empirical article published in the previous year.
2. For examples of award-winning work, see Appendices 1 and 2.
3. The number of articles published in an annual volume is positively correlated with the impact factor. By increasing the number of articles published, we have the potential to increase the rate of citations. All the boats rise when there are more ships in the harbor.

## References

Bem, D. (2004). Writing the empirical journal article. In J. M. Darley, M. P. Zanna, & H. L. Roediger (Eds.), *The compleat academic* (2nd ed.). Washington, DC: American Psychological Association.

Bennett, L. A., Wolin, S. J., & McAvity, K. J. (1988). Family identity, ritual, and myth: A cultural perspective on life cycle transitions. In C. J. Falicov (Ed.), *Family transitions: Continuity and change over the life cycle* (pp. 211–234). New York, NY: Guilford Press.

Blume, L. B. (2011). Freedom roundtable: Families in fiction—fact or fantasy? *Journal of Family Theory & Review, 3*, 303–304. doi:10.1111/j.1756-2589.2011.00105.x

Carson, A. (2001). *The beauty of the husband*. New York, NY: Alfred A. Knopf.

Eaton, J., & Saunders, C. B. (2012). A little help from our friends: Informal third parties and interpersonal conflict. *Personal Relationships, 19*, 623–643.

Edwards, M. (2012). *Writing in sociology*. Los Angeles, CA: Sage.

Green, W., & Simon, B. L. (Eds.). (2012). *Columbia guide to social work writing*. New York, NY: Columbia University Press.

LaRossa, R. (2012). Writing and reviewing manuscripts in the multidimensional world of qualitative research. *Journal of Marriage and Family, 74*, 643–659. doi:10.1111/j.1741-3737.2012.00978.x

LaRossa, R., & Reitzes, D. C. (1995). Gendered perceptions of father involvement in early 20th century America. *Journal of Marriage and Family, 57*, 223–229.

Merolla, A. J. (2012). Connecting here and there: A model of long-distance relationship maintenance. *Personal Relationships, 19*, 775–795.

Mikulincer, M., & Shaver, P. R. (2012). Adult attachment orientations and relationship processes. *Journal of Family Theory & Review, 4*, 259–274. doi:10.1111/j.1756-2589.2012.00142.x

Milardo, R. M. (2010). *The forgotten kin: Aunts and uncles*. New York, NY: Cambridge University Press.

Mount, N. S., Karre, J., & Kim, H. (2013). Mothers' attitudes about and goals for early adolescents' cross-ethnic peer relationships: A qualitative analysis. *Family Relations, 62*, 312–325.

Nelson, M. K. (2011). Between family and friendship: The right to care for Anna. *Journal of Family Theory & Review, 3*, 241–255.

New, C. C., & Quick, J. A. (2003). *How to write grant proposals.* Hoboken, NJ: John Wiley.

Orbuch, T. L., Bauermeister, J. A., Brown, E., & McKinley, B. (2013). Early family ties and marital stability over 16 years: The context of race and gender. *Family Relations, 62*, 255–268.

Orlean, S. (1990). *Saturday night.* New York, NY: Alfred A. Knopf.

Reis, H. T. (2000). Writing effectively about design. In R. J. Sternberg (Ed.), *Guide to publishing in psychology journals* (pp. 81–97). Cambridge, UK: Cambridge University Press.

Sternberg, R. J., & Sternberg, K. (2010). *The psychologist's companion: A guide to writing scientific papers for students and researchers* (5th ed.). Cambridge, UK: Cambridge University Press.

Sword, H. (2007). *The writer's diet.* Auckland, NZ: Pearson Education.

Sword, H. (2012). *Stylish academic writing.* Cambridge, MA: Harvard University Press.

Trask, B. S. (2013). Locating multiethnic families in a globalizing world. *Family Relations, 62*, 17–29.

Usdansky, M. L. (2011). The gender-equality paradox: Class and incongruity between work-family attitudes and behaviors. *Journal of Family Theory & Review, 3*, 163–178.

Williamson, H. C., Karney, B. R., & Bradbury, T. N. (2013). Financial strain and stressful events predict newlyweds' negative communication independent of relationship satisfaction. *Journal of Family Psychology, 27*, 65–75.

Wright, B. L., & Sinclair, H. C. (2012). Pulling the strings: Effects of friend and parent opinions on dating choices. *Personal Relationships, 19*, 743–758.

# 3  Writing Theory and Review

*I find it hard enough to tackle facts, Holmes, without flying away after theories and fancies.*

Arthur Conan Doyle (1892)

Theory papers and literature reviews vary in form, but they all begin with an introduction that states the topic or problem of interest in much the same way as an empirical paper. Thereafter, the substance of theory papers often takes one of two forms. A **theory review** summarizes and critically reviews existing theory or empirical work, and often both, for the purpose of adding new theoretical contributions as well as evaluating existing theory. A **research synthesis** summarizes and evaluates the current knowledge on a selected issue, without any particular intent to make a theoretical contribution. For instance, summarizing and critically reviewing the literature on the impact of divorce on children could be useful quite apart from any interest in furthering an explicit theoretical perspective. The distinction between the two types of contributions is somewhat arbitrary, because some influential literature reviews are driven by theory and suggest theoretical advances, and, conversely, papers largely directed at developing theory are often rooted in empirical work and inform the interpretation and future direction of continuing research.

This chapter explains the basic types of theory and review papers and distinguishes between the various forms these contributions can take. Three approaches to writing a paper based in theory are illustrated in some recent work on attachment. We then address the core issues in conducting comprehensive digital literature searches, which is an essential skill in producing scholarship.

## Theory Development

Theory papers can be purposed and written in several ways. This includes work directed at developing new theory or conceptual models and work directed at metatheoretical issues that apply to multiple theoretical approaches. The majority of theoretical work is more modest in scope. The intention is not to develop new theory per se, but rather to evaluate and, to a certain extent, refine existing theory, critically assess the research generated, or make comparative assessments of different theoretical approaches sometimes paired with an integrative function. These various purposes are illustrated by recent contributions to **attachment theory.**

Mikulincer and Shaver (2012) provide an overview of recent advances in adult attachment theory and follow this with a substantive review of attachment research on core issues likely to be of interest to researchers in many areas. They provide some initial background on attachment in the early development of infants and more recent developments in the application of attachment theory to adults and their relationships. They follow this overview of theory with a review of research on the links between early experience and the later development of adult attachment styles or orientations, and then examine how attachment orientations influence patterns of communication in couples, the management of couple conflict, the expression of caregiving and support to relationship partners and family members, as well as the experience of parenting and emergence of attachment patterns within families.

---

### BOX 3.1 WRITER'S RESOURCE: THE THEORY CONSTRUCTION AND RESEARCH METHODOLOGY WORKSHOP

The Theory Construction and Methodology Workshop was founded in 1970 and represents a loosely organized group of scholars interested in improving family theory, research, and methodology. The group sponsors a preconference workshop that occurs annually prior to and in part overlapping with the annual meeting of the National Council on Family Relations (usually in November). If you have a theory or method paper in development, it is well worth submitting a working paper to the workshop.

Each session of the workshop focuses on one or two papers and lasts about 90 minutes. Papers are circulated to workshop participants early so they can be read prior to the conference. At each session, discussants assigned to a paper provide a formal evaluation of the paper's strengths and shortcomings, authors are given time for a brief response, and the lion's share of each session is given over to a dialogue between the audience, discussants, and the author(s). Graduate students and new professionals are quite welcome. Details about the workshop are available at ncfr.org, where you can also find the full text of all articles presented in the workshop since its inception.

Pittman and his colleagues (2011) pen a different sort of theoretical paper, one in which the purpose is less to review pertinent research than to integrate divergent theoretical perspectives: Bowlby and Ainsworth's attachment theory, and Erikson's **psychosocial theory of development**. The authors draw parallels in the central concepts of each theory and apply them to the issue of identity formation in adolescence and early adulthood, including the formation of relationship identities. They articulate how individual development and identify formation occur in a relational context and how individual development is influenced by that context. They offer predictions regarding the implications of attachment styles on the expression of intimacy and commitment in close relationships. In reviewing two well-established theoretical models, Pittman and his coworkers offer a synthesis and new theoretical propositions with implications for some inventive avenues for future research.

Bell (2009) visits Bowlby and Ainsworth's attachment theory as well but from a different perspective, the rapidly developing field of **neurobiology**. Bell demonstrates how research in neurobiology confirms many of the original hypotheses of Bowlby and Ainsworth, but, in addition, Bell takes a deeper look at the neurobiological research. In doing so Bell extends the reach of attachment theory by detailing attachment processes not considered in the original theory. Bell incorporates elements of trust, caregiving, and empathy and offers new theoretical insights with implications for future research.

The three works by Mikulincer and Shaver, Pittman and his colleagues, and Bell share a fundamental interest in a common theoretical model, but their purposes are quite different. Mikulincer and Shaver organize an integrated review of a realm of research all of which is fueled by attachment theory. Their review is not so much a critical assessment of the theory but an accounting of what is known about adult attachment as it applies to issues of concern to relationship scholars. Pittman's team advances theory development by integrating psychosocial developmental theory and attachment theory for the purpose of theorizing about identity formation. Bell visits current research in neurobiology and uses this empirical work to advance the development of attachment theory. While theory can inform or direct empirical inquiry, seemingly unrelated avenues of empirical inquiry can inform theoretical advances. The process of theoretical development is reflective.

Theory papers can take additional forms. In my own work with Heather Helms, Eric Widmer, and Stephen Marks (2014), we developed a model of **social capital** that is based upon an individual's or family's investments in personal relationships with kin, friends, coworkers, and other personal associates, and the organization of those ties in networks. The purpose of the work is to advance a new understanding of social capital, suggest new approaches to measurement, and use selected research to illustrate the application of the model.

Other examples of theory development include the work of Jetse Sprey and of David Bell and his colleagues. Sprey (2013) approaches questions about how knowledge is created and argues that a focus on social relationships, rather than individuals, creates opportunities for higher levels of abstraction. Sprey draws on the concepts of **nonlinearity** and **chaos,** more commonly used in the natural sciences, and then suggests ways of building understandings of communities and the relationships that comprise them.

Bell, Atkinson-Schnell, and DiBacco (2012) approach theory development in a similar fashion. They question how stable, peaceful societies emerge from individual motivations, and they apply recent advances in the **neurosciences** to advance their theoretical toolbox. We can view each of these papers as metatheoretical works because their goal is to inform new directions in the development of theory, which can be used to inform the design of new research.

Theory can additionally emerge from immersive empirical inquiry, including some grounded theoretical approaches. Ingrid Connidis (2012) compares two common narrative sources, **personal interview** and **memoir,** because each contributes in unique ways to understanding the ties of gay men with their parents and siblings.[1] Her work explores the boundaries of social science and humanity, narrative theory and qualitative method, personal biography and community. Qualitative researchers engage in various ways of inventing theory, including peering into the core of what we mean by theory (LaRossa, 2012).

The design and purpose of theoretical papers varies in the ways we have described. Authors would do well to understand precisely the purpose of their work, communicate this with readers, and organize their arguments and critical reviews of the relevant literature accordingly.

## Research Synthesis

Literature reviews commonly focus on synthesizing areas of inquiry, and in doing so make important contributions. The cornerstone of an exceptional review is a comprehensive literature search, and therein resides the first challenge for authors.

Research on families and other forms of personal relationships appears in a wide variety of journals that represent multiple disciplines. In a recent review of the kinship literature, I found much of the pertinent literature in a few generalist family journals (e.g., *Journal of Marriage and Family*), but well over 50 journals published important contributions, and many are not commonly regarded as "family" or "relationship" journals (Milardo, 2010). Significant research on kinship appeared in major journals that represent a broad array of psychological or sociological issues (e.g., *American Journal of Sociology*), highly specialized journals (e.g., *Fathering, Child Abuse and Neglect, Journal of Divorce and Remarriage,*

*Journal of Gerontology*), journals published outside of North America (e.g., *British Journal of Sociology, Journal of Psychology in Africa*), and journals from neighboring disciplines that I don't read regularly (e.g., *American Anthropologist, Child Clinical Psychology and Psychiatry, Ethology and Sociobiology, Human Nature, Journal of Applied Communication*). In addition to the journals were books and handbook chapters that presented important empirical work, reviews, and theoretical contributions. In some areas, conference proceeding can be valuable sources (e.g., De Reus & Blumb, 2011; Widmer & Jallinoja, 2008). The diversity of sources and the volume of research are impressive given that kinship studies is an understudied area of research. More popular topics in the behavioral and social sciences (e.g., early child development, poverty, and divorce) receive even greater attention, and work in these areas appears in even more journals and books. Similar challenges exist for scholars working in any field that is inherently multidisciplinary, including for instance education, communication, and social work.

---

### BOX 3.2 WRITER'S RESOURCE: THEORY AND REVIEW JOURNALS

Some journals specialize in publishing theory and critical reviews. In the field of family studies, there are several key journals and many more throughout the behavioral and social sciences. Journals like the *Journal of Marriage and Family* and *Family Relations* routinely publish such work as well as the more typical empirical fare. In addition, many disciplines are represented by journals that specialize in publishing theory or reviews. Examples include:

- *Annual Review of Psychology*
- *Annual Review of Sociology*
- *Clinical Child and Family Psychology Review*
- *Clinical Psychology Review*
- *Developmental Review*
- *Journal for the Theory of Social Behavior*
- *Journal of Theoretical and Philosophical Psychology*
- *Merrill-Palmer Quarterly*
- *Review of Educational Research*
- *The Sociological Review*
- *Trauma, Violence & Abuse: A Review Journal*

A few journals specialize in publishing theory and research syntheses of work having to do with families and other forms of close relationships. Four are described below.

*Journal of Family Theory & Review*
An innovative quarterly journal sponsored by the National Council on Family Relations and specializing in publishing theory and review.

*Psychological Bulletin*
A venerable journal in psychology long known for publishing influential reviews. The journal is published bimonthly and sponsored by the American Psychological Association.

*Psychological Review*
A quarterly journal sponsored by the American Psychological Association and specializing in publishing theory.

*Sociological Theory*
A quarterly journal sponsored by the American Sociological Association that occasionally publishes theory directly relevant to family and relationship scholars.

The volume of research and diversity of outlets in nearly every area of the behavior and social sciences require a skillful approach to designing and executing literature searches. Manual searches of tables of contents of journals or books are typically inadequate because of the number of journals that publish work on any particular topic. In many areas of research, well-planned and executed literature reviews are essential for understanding core theory, findings, and methods. Reviews are needed that synthesize research findings over multiple studies, conducted in multiple disciplines, and published in an array of journals and books. "Many areas of social science research are in less need of further research than they are in need of organization of the existing research" (Card, 2011, p. 4).

A research synthesis may focus on summarizing research on broad topical areas, such as changes in marital or relational quality over time (Bradbury & Karney, 2004) or the predictors of divorce (Amato, 2010). Others focus on narrower topics, such as mothers' part-time employment and its effects on family and child outcomes (Buehler, O'Brien, & Walls, 2011), parenting athlete children (Bremer, 2012), or the interface of gender and class in work and family life (Usdansky, 2011). Regardless of whether a review examines a broad or more refined area of concern, a research synthesis takes essentially one of two forms: **narrative review** or **meta-analysis**.

## Narrative Reviews

Narrative reviews evaluate and summarize research on a particular topic. Authors are charged with clearly defining the topic of interest and the methods used in identifying the pertinent literature (Card, 2011; Cooper, 2010; Cooper, Hedges, & Valentine, 2009; Eisenburg, 2000). Authors of narrative reviews are encouraged to include a methods section much like an empirical report. Authors report on the keywords used to conduct a search, the databases searched, and the period of time over which the search was conducted (e.g., all work published between 2010 and 2014). There are often additional details, such as the rules used to include pertinent literature and those used to exclude literature that is not entirely germane to the questions being addressed. This is often followed by a description of how results were coded and summarized. Methods sections are important because they define the parameters of a review, but they are not intended to be great reads. A relatively concise statement is all that is needed.

Blair Glennon (2012) addressed the literature on heterosexual parents of gay or lesbian children. The question concerned how parents viewed their interactions with others, including other family members, following a disclosure of a child's sexual orientation as gay or lesbian. The narrative review is theory based, using Erving Goffman's **theory of stigma**, and systematically reviews data from published research, case studies, and autobiographical accounts. In describing the conduct of her literature review, Glennon details the keywords used (e.g., "gay" or "lesbian" and "family relation") as well as the databases searched (e.g., *PsycINFO, ERIC, Academic Search Premier, Sociological Abstracts*, and *ProQuest Dissertations and Theses*). She then details the kind of research included in the review, and just as importantly the criteria used to exclude research. She refrained from including work on the reactions of parents from the point of view of their children, for example, preferring to base the review on an understanding of parents from their own perspective. She then details how the findings of each study are coded, and she draws on a theoretical rubric to further define a coding scheme. The end result is a detailed accounting of how the pertinent literature was identified and subsequently analyzed. The reader has a clear road map of the method and can easily judge the parameters of the literature search, its scope and thoroughness, as well as the manner and quality of the analysis. Although the findings of the work reviewed are not analyzed in any empirical way (such as would be the case with a quantitative meta-analysis), the design and conduct of the review is nonetheless systematic and derivative of an explicit theoretical perspective.

The entire accounting of Glennon's method is approximately 750 words and appears as an appendix to the journal article. This is not always the case. The methods governing a review are just as often included in the text following the introduction (e.g., Arditti, 2012; Bremer, 2012) or at a point appropriate to the presentation and typically following a description of the underlying theory guiding the review (e.g., Niehuis et al., 2011). As an editor and reader, I prefer having the details available in an appendix unless the details are essential to understanding the body of the review. Journals vary in their requirements, and authors need to attend to the pertinent instructions for the preparation of manuscripts, usually available on a journal's website. In some instances, a full description of the method for identifying the literature being reviewed is not described in detail, especially when the purpose is theory or conceptual development, although greater detail benefits readers (e.g., Anderson & Branstetter, 2012; Usdansky, 2011).

## Meta-analyses

Quantitative meta-analyses are another form of research synthesis based upon a host of statistical techniques for combining the results of several studies on a specific issue (Card, 2011; Cooper, 2010). Meta-analyses focus on examining the specific findings of multiple studies, rather than the conclusions reached by authors, and provide an empirical measure of effect sizes.

Chris Proulx, Heather Helms, and Cheryl Beuhler (2007) examine a long-standing question in family studies, the association of **marital quality** and **personal well-being**, using a meta-analysis of 93 empirical reports. The question has intrigued researchers and practitioners for many years and undoubtedly has important implications for public policy. We know individuals experiencing marital strain or dissatisfaction generally report higher levels of depressive symptomatology compared to those who are relatively satisfied with their marriages, but the causal sequence is not always clear. Can we be sure that the effects on well-being are due to relationship processes rather than any number of situational variables such as conditions at work or issues regarding personal health? We also might expect the effects to vary by gender. Fortunately, there is a substantial empirical literature on the topic, including research based on cross-sectional and longitudinal designs.

Among the first tasks in engaging a meta-analytic review is to comprehensively search for relevant work. As in the case of narrative reviews, Proulx and her colleagues detail the methods used to identify pertinent literature, including the databases visited and keywords used to search them, supplementary manual searches of key journals, and the specific rules for including as well as excluding work. The real labor of meta-analyses comes in the detailed coding of results for each study and in this case included calculating **primary effects** based on **product-moment correlations** of marital quality and well-being. Given that individual researchers use different measures and different ways of conducting analyses, coding for effects is challenging. In addition, Proulx and her team accounted for factors that are likely to act as moderators in the association of marital quality and individual well-being, including gender and marital duration. We are left with a powerful, systematic, and detailed analysis of marital quality, which varies positively with well-being. Spouses who report higher levels of marital quality also report higher levels of personal well-being, and, contrary to expectations, these effects appear consistent for husbands and wives. In regard to the causal sequence, in case you are as intrigued as I am, marital quality has stronger effects on well-being than the converse.

Meta-analyses are important ways to synthesize research findings and assess effect sizes. They require a sufficient body of research to realize their potential and, like all empirical analyses, require careful attention to assembling the relevant data and designing appropriate coding schemes for comparing findings across studies.

Here I have emphasized meta-analyses based on quantitative techniques; some exceptionally inventive analyses are rooted in conceptual models that govern the conduct of analyses (e.g., Singh, Allen, Scheckler, & Darlington, 2007). Other methods, such as **scoping reviews**, seek to eliminate bias in narrative reviews or meta-analyses by distinguishing between the design and implementation of a literature search and the personal qualities, and potential biases, of those involved (e.g., unique methodological expertise or interests) (Landa et al., 2011).

## Searching the Literature

Whether the purpose is to write an introduction to an empirical report, write a research synthesis, or conduct a meta-analysis, a search of the pertinent literature is fundamental. Just as the conduct of an experiment, survey, or qualitative inquiry requires a certain degree of methodological sophistication, conducting a literature search requires an understanding of standard search techniques and tools, such as library holding catalogues, periodical references, and databases. The basics of library and database searches are covered in a number of useful sources, such as *Library Use: Handbook for Psychology* (Reed & Baxter, 2003, with a partial update in Reed & Baxter, 2009). It also helps to have access to a knowledgeable librarian skilled in the art of bibliographic searching in the behavioral and social sciences.

---

### BOX 3.3 WRITER'S RESOURCE: ACADEMIC ABSTRACTING SERVICES

For social scientists and practitioners, databases can be helpful in uncovering literature of interest, and often it is necessary to search several specialized sources. Among the many useful resources are the following indexing services.

### Academic Search Premier
A broad-based resource that indexes more than 13,000 journals across the sciences, including biology, chemistry, engineering, physics, psychology, and religion.

### Child Development & Adolescent Studies
*Child Development & Adolescent Studies*™ searches literature related to the growth and development of children, adolescents, and young adults (to age 21). This database includes all of the issues of *Child Development Abstracts & Bibliography* from 1927 to 2001 previously published by the Society for Research in Child Development and searches over 200 journals as well as additional sources, including books, book chapters, theses and dissertations, and technical reports.

### Dissertation Abstracts or Dissertation Abstracts International
This database is a bibliography of American and international dissertations published by University Microfilms International/ProQuest since 1938. The database covers doctoral dissertations accepted at an accredited American institution since 1861, and selected theses since 1962. In 1988 the database began including citations for dissertations from 50 British universities that are available at The British Document Supply Centre. A limited number of dissertations from the rest of the world are included.

### ERIC (Education Resource Information Center)
ERIC provides bibliographic records of journal articles and other education-related materials, including books, conference papers, and technical reports.

### Family and Society Studies Worldwide
This database covers research, policy, and practice literature in the fields of family science, human ecology, human development, and social welfare. Over 800 journals are searched with about 200 relevant to family issues.

### Family Studies Abstracts
This database searches more than 200 journals publishing work relevant to family scholars.

## JSTOR

JSTOR (rhymes with "way more" and short for *journal storage*) is a digital library that includes digitalized back issues of journals not typically included in other sources. For instance, the entire backlog of the *Journal of Marriage and Family* (founded in 1939) and *Family Relations* (founded in 1951) are included. The database provides full-text searches of more than 2,000 journals and also includes some books and other primary sources.

## PsycINFO™

This popular database abstracts scholarly journal articles, book chapters, and books and dissertations and is owned and operated by the American Psychological Association. The database currently abstracts over 2,500 peer-reviewed journals in behavioral science and mental health.

## Social Science Citation Index (SSCI)

The SSCI citation database searches more than 2,000 social science journals over more than 50 disciplines. It is entered through the *Web of Science* and permits descendant searches in which articles that have cited earlier work are identified. For instance, a search of Arlie Hochschild's *The Second Shift* published in 1989 would reveal all the journal articles that subsequently cited this influential book on the distribution—or lack thereof—of household labor.

## Sociological Abstracts

This resource abstracts and indexes the international literature in sociology and related disciplines in the social and behavioral sciences. The database provides abstracts of journal articles and citations to book reviews drawn from over 1,800 serial publications and includes abstracts of books, book chapters, dissertations, and conference papers. [Excerpt from http://www.asanet.org/journals/st/st.cfm]

In a typical literature search, the universe of potential sources consists of all the material—journal articles, books and chapters in books, theses and dissertations, and conference proceedings—published on a given topic. Other useful materials include technical reports published by individuals, private agencies, public agencies at the state or federal level, or by other governments. Often I concern my own work with materials available in journals and books, but on occasion other documents can be important. For instance, a technical report on a gathering of scholars discussing the execution of qualitative research sponsored by the National Science Foundation proved to be interesting and useful in my own work (Ragin, Nagel, & White, 2004). A report on military families published by the Rand Corporation provided a summary of research that complemented other empirical work and reviews (Karney & Crown, 2007). Several mass surveys of Internet use and the use of computer-mediated communications conducted by the Pew Internet & American Life Project have proved to be exceptionally interesting and important in my own research and teaching (Boase, Horrigan, Wellman, & Rainie, 2006). A master's thesis on aunts and uncles and their relationships with nieces and nephews proved to be one of the first empirical studies and a useful resource (Chebra, 1991).

In my work, technical reports published by public or private agencies, theses, and dissertations are useful. I search for such documents when I need to be comprehensive, but they are typically not the first places I look, or the kinds of materials in which I am initially interested. I begin with the assumption that most of the important work—including the more important theses, dissertations, and technical reports—will be published in peer-reviewed journals and books. Consequently, the search begins with identifying journal articles and books or chapters, and this becomes the kind of material I read first.

Whether browsing the Internet or the holdings of an academic library, it quickly becomes apparent that not all the available work is equivalent or worth retrieving or reading. Peer-reviewed journals and journals sponsored by professional organizations are preferred over all other sources. Similarly, books published by major university presses and international publishers are preferred over locally produced work, vanity presses, or other forms of individual platforms whether in print or digital form (e.g., iBooks). Materials produced by professional organizations or interest groups and available in print or on websites can be informative, but in most cases are secondary and do not replace professional journals and books. There are exceptions, but early in the search of a literature it pays to keep an eye on the prize and that largely means peer-reviewed materials.

## Searching Bibliographic Databases

How do we go about identifying the population, all the available material published on a given topic, or at least the core materials defining that population? Several strategies exist for conducting a comprehensive search. They all begin with a solid foundation: a clearly defined subject of interest. For instance, if we began a search with the term *parenting* without any refinements that would confine the search, we would quickly discover an overwhelming volume of literature. To illustrate these issues, I conducted a search using the Family and Society Studies Worldwide database, which is useful for searching most family topics. A search of database on the keyword *parenting* yielded over 22,000 citations. This search included all sources covered by the database, which includes journals and books but also magazine articles and materials from the popular press. If we limit the search to peer-reviewed journals, about 13,000 items are identified, still far too many to examine. We need to limit the search further and how we do so depends on our precise interest. Let's say we are interested in fathers. A refined search for *parenting* and *fathers*, excluding *mothers* refines the search and yields a manageable 553 citations, and if we further limit the search to peer-reviewed journal articles published in the last year, the search become still more manageable with 37 citations identified. At this point we might begin to read through the titles of each citation and decide which to pursue further, but one more step can be useful to narrow the citations to be perused more carefully.

In the search on parenting and fathers, several journals are represented. Some are quite specialized: the *Journal of Substance Abuse Treatment*, *Journal of Autism and Developmental Disorders*, and *Community, Work & Family*. Unless we have a specific interest in the general topic of the journal, we might well forgo examining these entries.

The list of citations narrows at each step and now includes articles that appear in more generalist family journals. There are two varieties of such journals: those that are sponsored by professional groups and those that are privately owned. Journals sponsored by major professional organizations typically publish the most sophisticated and influential research. The *Journal of Marriage and Family* and *Family Relations* are distinguished journals with a long history and published by the National Council on Family Relations. The *Journal of Family Psychology* is published by the American Psychological Association and publishes exceptional research. The search of the fathering literature yields citations to these journals; consider perusing their abstracts first and judging their pertinence. In addition, there are citations to works published in peer-reviewed journals not sponsored by professional groups. These include citations to work on fathering in the *Journal of Family Issues* and a journal aptly entitled *Fathering: A Journal of Theory, Research, and Practice About Men as Fathers*. For these journals, read the abstracts and judge their pertinence accordingly.

Strategic decisions about what to examine further by reading abstracts and perhaps the full text are made on the basis of prioritizing peer-reviewed journals over all other sources and further refining the selection by considering the source journals and their scope and sponsorship. In all cases, the initial goal is to read material likely to be of the highest quality and directly relevant to the question of interest.

---

**BOX 3.4  WRITER'S RESOURCE: BOOLEAN BASICS**

This group of logical terms is named after George Boole a 19th century mathematician and dance partner (not widely known) who invented a form of logic that underscores all of digital thinking and devices.

There are 3 Boolean operators used in searching a database. Knowing how each performs in selecting a citation is useful and allows a more efficient search, and use of time.

*Search term A AND search term B* selects all citations including both terms. Excluded are all citations with neither keyword and all citations with only one of the two keywords. For example searching on aunts and uncles selects all articles with both of these keywords, but none of the citations that include only one of the keywords. The operator AND can be omitted which means a space separating two keywords is interpreted as AND.

*Search term A OR search term B* selects all citations including one term or the other. For example, searching on aunts OR uncles selects all citations with one keyword or the other, or both. Which set is larger, a search of two keywords linked by AND or a search of two keywords linked by OR?

*Search term A AND NOT search term B* selects all citations including A but not B. For instance a search of aunts AND NOT uncles would yield all articles that include the keyword aunts but none of the articles that include aunts and uncles, or just uncles.

AND NOT is equivalent to NOT or a minus sign.

---

There are other issues to consider in conducting manageable searches. The *Family and Society Studies Worldwide* database, mentioned above, searches several hundred family journals. Other databases are available and detailed in Box 3.3 that may be more appropriate given a particular interest. Again, thinking tactically, we begin a search with the resources most likely to produce pertinent material using a database most suited to a particular interest, and we later continue with resources that may buttress our first attempts, including searching other databases.

There is also the issue of the appropriate selection of **keywords**. Even fairly simple variations can make a difference in the scope or relevance of the literature cited. For instance, if I add *fathering* to the search so that now I am searching peer-reviewed journal articles published in the last year with the search terms *parenting* and *fathers* or *fathering, not* *mothers,* the number of hits increases from 37 to 171. The simple addition of one keyword increased the number of citations uncovered significantly.

To keep a search manageable, limit the first iteration to the previous year of publication. Once a few pertinent references are identified, it will be possible to identify some of the important earlier work simply by checking the references in each article. Later, additional searches of previous years can be launched.

## Searching Books

In addition to searching for journal articles, books and chapters in edited books can be useful. *Attachment in Adulthood* by Mario Mikulincer and Phil Shaver (2007) would be an excellent resource giving a comprehensive review of the field of attachment theory and research as it applies to adults. Edited books that are composed of chapters written by experts in particular topical areas are also useful. *The Cambridge Handbook of Personal Relationships* edited by Anita Vangelisti and Daniel Perlman (2006) is a fine example of an edited volume that includes the work of many authors, all of whom specialize in their assigned topic.

Both books mentioned above were published several years ago, and work on them likely began a year or more earlier. One of the problems with books is that they quickly become outdated, at least to a degree. In areas with heaps of research being conducted and published each year this is a more significant issue relative to areas that see less activity. Nonetheless, even ancient work—say, something published in the darkness of the disco era or even earlier[2]—could be quite relevant with important conceptual or theoretical insights and should not be overlooked (e.g., Bott, 1971; Levinger, 1979).

## Searching Authors and Citations

Whether working from journal articles or books, another useful strategy is to search citations and particular authors. I know that Eric Widmer does exceptional and quite sophisticated work on kinship networks. Any search of the keywords **kinship** and **social networks** will likely uncover Eric's most recent research, or I could search directly for his name. Searching the names of authors whose work is especially important is more efficient and ensures that the work of a particular author will not be missed.

Once we have identified work that is especially relevant we can then evaluate the references cited by that work. Eric is Swiss and a senior faculty member in the Department of Sociology at the University of Geneva. He often learns of important work published by Europeans more quickly than I do and so provides an entry to work I might not otherwise locate as easily. It is another instance of a well-established principle in social network theory: There is strength to weak ties.[3]

Another play on the theme of searching particular authors is to search classic books or articles that have been particularly influential. Elizabeth Bott's *Family and Social Network* was originally published in 1957 and among the first to establish a link between the configuration of a social network of kin and marital outcomes. A search of Bott's book on the *Social Science Citation Index* entered through the *Web of Science* finds that more than 800 articles have cited this work. This indexing service uses a descendant approach to identify groups of work that have cited an earlier work. The search could be delimited in a variety of ways. For instance, we could limit the search to those journal articles published in the last five years that cited Bott and in this way identify current work on social networks and families, the primary subject of Bott's book. Incidentally, the August 2000 issue of *Journal of Marriage and Family* published reviews of the most influential books published in the family field over the past century and thereby provided a partial accounting of books worth an ancestral search.

### Searching the Invisible College

A profitable addition to searching databases and library catalogues is directly accessing the **invisible college** (Cooper, 2009). This includes posting queries to professional interest groups and typically through a listserv or similar computer assisted communication medium. Professional organizations such as the National Council on Family Relations and the American Sociological Association maintain several electronic mailing lists for members. They typically serve particular interest groups. The family section of the American Sociological Association, for instance, maintains an electronic mailing list for members. The National Council on Family Relations offers electronic mailing lists for each of the organizations sections (i.e., interest groups), including the feminist and family section, ethnic minorities, and research and theory. These groups can easily link researchers with common interests who can then share resources. However, a word of caution is in order; you might think of it as a matter of electronic mailing list etiquette. Do your homework before broadcasting a query to a group or individual. I recently received an e-mail from a doctoral student asking whether I knew anything about the literature on generativity. I do and in fact have published recently on the topic. In the heap of e-mail I get daily, this one query sank quickly. I felt the student should have gone to the library and completed a simple search on the topic before contacting me. The bottom line is not to ask other people to do your work for you but rather ask them to contribute to the work you have already done.

On another occasion, a doctoral student from another university wrote saying she was planning research on aunts. She had clearly read the current literature and wanted to know whether I knew of any more recent work. I wrote back, shared a few as-yet-unpublished resources, and encouraged her. Her research was eventually published (Davis-Sowers, 2011).

Accessing the invisible college can be an important way to add to your knowledge of an area and otherwise learn of materials that might not appear in a formalized literature search. A trusted colleague may be able to help you quickly sift through the literature by suggesting work that is especially relevant or especially well done. Personal contacts are helpful in many ways, but they do not replace doing your homework.

---

**BOX 3.5 BEST PRACTICE: WRITING THEORY AND REVIEW**

- Select keywords thoughtfully and revise as needed to make the outcomes of a search manageable.
- Learn the 3 Boolean operators.
- Limit the initial search to the last few years of publication to make things more manageable.
- With any literature review include a description of how the literature search was conducted, the keywords used and databases searched. Keep detailed notes and treat the topic formally as you would any method section in an empirical report.
- Reviewers and editors are impressed with well-articulated and carefully designed literature searches.
- For academic work, use established bibliographic databases. For shoe shopping and related activity use Google.

---

## Summary

This chapter has described several forms of theory papers, narrative research reviews, and meta-analyses. All theory and research synthesis begins with searches of the relevant literature, and we identified several strategies for conducting searches. Often the first and most important tactic involves searching an academic bibliographic database that abstracts a broad array of literature and journals likely to be relevant to our interest. In addition, the chapter detailed other secondary tactics for locating materials of interest, such as queries posted to web-based electronic mailing lists and personal contacts with experts. Searching for literature, especially in an unfamiliar area, is time-consuming and tedious; it pays to be tactical in the design of the search and in the selection of databases and search terms and discerning what material is subsequently read.

## Activities

1.  Identify a topic of interest and conduct a literature search using some of the more readily available databases such as *Family and Society Studies Worldwide, PsycINFO, ERIC, Academic Search Premier*, or *Sociological Abstracts*. Broad topics such as *parenting* will produce vastly more hits than more refined topics such as *parenting adolescents*, and you may wish to adjust the scope of your search accordingly. Write a description of the methods you used in conducting your search, including the databases and keywords used, the years searched, and the criteria for including or excluding literature. For example, will you include dissertations and theses or material published in non–peer-review sources? Material published in English only? Include details on the conduct of the search and your evaluation of the method and outcomes.
2.  Identify a classic work in an area of interest. This may be a journal article or a book that was especially influential. Once you have identified an article or book, search the *Social Science Citation Index* for all the work that subsequently cited that book or article. How useful is this tactic for identifying research of interest?
3.  Identify a topic of interest and compare the result of a search of any two or three databases. How do they differ from or complement each other?

## Recommended Readings

Bem, D. (1995). Writing a review article for *Psychological Bulletin. Psychological Bulletin, 118*, 172–177.

  This is sound advice for crafting a review article. The article was written for psychologists publishing in a specific journal, but nonetheless it is great advice. There are more recent articles, but I still think this is about the best.

Cooper, H. M. (2010). *Research synthesis and meta-analysis: A step-by-step approach* (4th ed.). Thousand Oaks, CA: Sage.

  The book presents a thorough discussion of quantitative meta-analysis and how to conduct and evaluate one. Chapter 3: Searching the Literature (pp. 46–83) provides a detailed and very useful discussion of conducting a literature search and the variety of sources available.

Eisenburg, N. (2000). Writing a literature review. In R. J. Sternberg (Ed.), *Guide to publishing in psychology journals* (pp. 17–34). New York, NY: Cambridge University Press.

  A brief but useful chapter on writing reviews from a former editor of *Psychological Bulletin*.

Reed, J. G., & Baxter, P.M. (2003). *Library use: Handbook for psychology* (3rd ed.). Washington, DC: American Psychological Association.

Reed, J. G., & Baxter, P. M. (2009). Using reference databases. In H. Cooper, L. V. Hedges, & J. C. Valentine (Eds.), *The handbook of research synthesis and meta-analysis* (pp. 73–101). New York, NY: Russell Sage Foundation.

The 2003 book is intended for undergraduates and graduate students early in their careers. The book provides an accounting of the basics of conducting library searches. Although the third edition (2003) is slightly dated, much of the material remains current and very useful. The 2009 book chapter is a crash course in conducting a literature search.

## Notes

1. For her comparative work on interview and memoir in theory building, Ingrid was awarded the Alexis Walker Research Prize, among the most distinguished awards given to recognize excellence in research on families.
2. This is a reference to a period similar to the late Beatles era, but with less imagination.
3. The phase is from Granovetter (1979) and refers to the idea that acquaintances provide access to resources not otherwise easily available. Whereas my good friends know many of the same people I know, my intermediate friends and mere acquaintances know many people I do not know and so provide access to information and resources that would not otherwise be available to me.

## References

Amato, P. R. (2010). Research on divorce: Continuing trends and new developments. *Journal of Marriage and Family,* 650–666. doi:10.1111/j.1741-3737.2010.00723.x

Anderson, R. J., & Branstetter, S. A. (2012). Adolescents, parents, and monitoring: A review of constructs with attention to process and theory. *Journal of Family Theory & Review, 4,* 1–19. doi:10.1111/j.1756-2589.2011.00112.x

Arditti, J. A. (2012). *Parental incarceration and the family.* New York, NY: New York University Press.

Bell, D. C. (2009). Attachment without fear. *Journal of Family Theory & Review, 1,* 177–197.

Bell, D. C., Atkinson-Schnell, J. L., & DiBacco, A. E. (2012). Explaining society: An expanded toolbox for social scientists. *Journal of Family Theory & Review, 4,* 48–66. doi:10.1111/j.1756-2589.2011.00113.x

Boase, J., Horrigan, J. B., Wellman, B., & Rainie, L. (2006). *The strength of Internet ties.* Washington, DC: Pew Internet & American Life Project.

Bott, E. (1971). *Family and social network* (2nd ed.). New York, NY: The Free Press.

Bradbury, T. N., & Karney, B. R. (2004). Understanding and altering the longitudinal course of marriage. *Journal of Marriage and Family, 66,* 862–879. doi:10.1111/j.0022-2445.2004.00059.x

Bremer, K. L. (2012). Parental involvement, pressure, and support in youth sport: A narrative literature review. *Journal of Family Theory & Review, 4*, 235–248. doi:10.1111/j.1756-2589.2012.00129.x

Buehler, C., O'Brien, M., & Walls, J. K. (2011). Mothers' part-time employment: Child, parent, and family outcomes. *Journal of Family Theory & Review, 3*, 256–272. doi:10.1111/j.1756-2589.2011.00110.x

Card, N. A. (2011). *Applied meta-analysis for social science research*. New York, NY: Guilford Press.

Chebra, J. M. (1991). *Aunts' and uncles' relationship with their nieces and nephews: An exploratory study* (Unpublished master's thesis). Kent State University, Kent, OH.

Connidis, I. A. (2012). Interview and memoir: Complementary narratives on the family ties of gay adults. *Journal of Family Theory & Review, 4*, 105–121.

Cooper, H. M. (2010). *Research synthesis and meta-analysis: A step-by-step approach* (4th ed.). Thousand Oaks, CA: Sage.

Cooper, H., Hedges, L. V., & Valentine, J. C. (Eds.). (2009). *The handbook of research synthesis and meta-analysis* (2nd ed.). New York, NY: Russell Sage Foundation.

Cooper, M. L. (2009). Problems, pitfalls and promise in the peer-review process: Commentary on Trafimow & Rice (2009). *Perspectives on Psychological Science, 4*, 84–92.

Davis-Sowers, R. (2011). "It just kind of like falls in your hands": Factors that influence black aunts' decisions to parent their nieces and nephews. *Journal of Black Studies, 42*, 1–20.

De Reus, L. A., & Blumb, L. B. (Eds.). (2011). *Social, economic, and environmental justice for all families*. Groves Monographs on Marriage and Family. Ann Arbor, MI: University of Michigan Library.

Doyle, A. C. (1892). *The adventures of Sherlock Holmes*. London, UK: George Newnes. (Available at Project Gutenberg.)

Eisenburg, N. (2000). Writing a literature review. In R. J. Sternberg (Ed.), *Guide to publishing in psychology journals* (pp. 17–34). New York, NY: Cambridge University Press.

Glennon, B. (2012). Heterosexual parents of gay and lesbian individuals: Social interaction issues. *Journal of Family Theory & Review, 4*, 332–353. doi:10.1111/j.1756-2589.2012.00138.x

Granovetter, M. (1979). The strength of weak ties. *American Journal of Sociology, 78*, 1360–1380.

Karney, B., & Crown, J. S. (2007). *Families under stress: An assessment of data, theory, and research on marriage and divorce in the military*. Santa Monica, CA: Rand Corporation.

Landa, A. H., Szabo, I., Le Brun, L., Owen, I., Fletcher, G., & Hill, M. (2011). An evidence-based approach to scoping reviews. *Electronic Journal Information Systems Evaluation, 14*, 46–52.

LaRossa, R. (2012). Writing and reviewing manuscripts in the multidimensional world of qualitative research. *Journal of Marriage and Family, 74*, 643–659. doi:10.1111/j.1741-3737.2012.00978.x

Levinger, G. (1979). A social exchange view of the dissolution of pair relationships. In R. Burgess & T. Huston (Eds.), *Social exchange in developing relationships* (pp. 169–193). New York, NY: Academic Press.

Mikulincer, M., & Shaver, P. R. (2007). *Attachment in adulthood.* New York, NY: Guilford Press.

Mikulincer, M., & Shaver, P. R. (2012). Adult attachment orientations and relationship processes. *Journal of Family Theory & Review, 4,* 259–274. doi:10.1111/j.1756-2589.2012.00142.x

Milardo, R. M. (2010). *The forgotten kin: Aunts and uncles.* New York, NY: Cambridge University Press.

Milardo, R. M., Helms, H. M., Widmer, E. D., & Marks, S. R. (2014). Social capitalization in personal relationships. In Christopher R. Agnew (Ed.), *Social influences on close relationships* (pp. 33–57). New York, NY: Cambridge University Press.

Niehuis, S., Lee, K-H., Riefman, A., Swenson, A., & Hunsaker, S. (2011). Idealization and disillusionment in intimate relationships: A review of theory, method, and research. *Journal of Family Theory & Review, 3,* 273–302. doi:10.1111/j.1756–2589.2011.00100.x

Pitman, J. F., Keiley, M. K., Kerpelman, J. L., & Vaughn, B. E. (2011). Attachment, identity, and intimacy: Parallels between Bowby's and Erikson's paradigms. *Journal of Family Theory & Review, 3,* 32–46.

Proulx, C. M., Helms, H. M., & Beuhler, C. (2007). Marital quality and personal well-being: A meta-analysis. *Journal of Marriage and Family, 69,* 576–593.

Ragin, C. C., Nagel, J., & White, P. (2004). *Workshop on scientific foundations of qualitative research.* Arlington, VA: National Science Foundation.

Reed, J. G., & Baxter, P. M. (2003). *Library use: Handbook for psychology* (3rd ed.). Washington, DC: American Psychological Association.

Reed, J. G., & Baxter, P. M. (2009). Using reference databases. In H. Cooper, L. V. Hedges, & J. C. Valentine (Eds.), *The handbook of research synthesis and meta-analysis* (pp. 73–101). New York, NY: Russell Sage Foundation.

Singh, K., Allen, K. R., Scheckler, R., & Darlington, L. (2007). Women in computer related majors: A critical synthesis of research and theory from 1994–2005. *Review of Educational Research, 77,* 500–533. doi:10.3012/0034607309919

Sprey, J. (2013). Extending the range of questioning in family studies through ideas from the exact sciences. *Journal of Family Theory & Review, 5,* 51–61. doi:10.1111/jftr.12002

Usdansky, M. L. (2011). The gender-equality paradox: Class and incongruity between work-family attitudes and behaviors. *Journal of Family Theory & Review, 3,* 163–178.

Vangelisti, A. L., & Perlman, D. (Eds.). (2006). *The Cambridge handbook of personal relationships.* New York, NY: Cambridge University Press.

Widmer, E. D., & R. Jallinoja, R. (Eds.). (2008). *Families as configurations.* Geneva, Switzerland: Peter Lang.

# 4 Writing Book Reviews

Book reviews in all their variations are among the most underdeveloped and underappreciated forms of scholarship. In this chapter we review the traditional forms of reviews and how they are written as well as some of the more innovative forms of reviews, including longer comparative essays and the use of author interviews and other types of web-based supplemental material. We detail the importance of books in the behavioral and social sciences, the qualities of great reviews, why reviewers write them, and why readers read them.

## Types of Reviews

Just as empirical reports can take many forms, ranging from brief reports of essential findings to complex theory-driven articles reporting on multiple studies, so, too, book reviews can vary in their complexity, scope, and purpose. We can usefully speak of four types of reviews.

### The Watson

Basic reviews are relatively brief and describe the purpose and content of a book. They typically include some form of evaluation, although in their most elementary form, critical commentary is minimal or entirely absent.

**Elementary reviews** list the details of a publication and follow with a description of the book's stated purpose and a brief summary of the content. They are typically around 500 words. Restating the table of contents is unnecessary; a thoughtful and fair-minded summary will do. In writing the review, keep the journal's audience in mind, which often means explaining technical jargon. In a psychology or sociology journal, you can assume a reader understands terms such as **cognitive dissonance** or **role**, but don't assume a reader will necessarily understand **role balance**. Use your discretion. The goal is to write a review that readers can read and understand quickly and efficiently. Watsons function to inform a community of readers about the new addition to the field.

**BOX 4.1 WRITER'S RESOURCE: ESSENTIAL INFORMATION COMMON TO BOOK REVIEWS**

All reviews begin with locating the book or books being reviewed in the publishing world. A reader should be able to easily find a library copy or make a purchase, and librarians understandably rely on accurate details to locate books. Formatting such detail is tedious and varies across journals. Fortunately major journals employ copy editors who can whip into shape the appropriate pesky details and punctuation. It does help if review authors provide accurate details. The *Journal of Family Theory & Review* uses the following format:

- Title of the book
- The authors' or editors' names and initials
- Edition
- Place of publication and publisher
- Date of publication
- Number of pages
- ISBN number
- Price
- Format (hardback, paperback, soft cover, or e-book)
- Web page (if available)

Journals vary, but a standard style is as demonstrated in the following example.

> *Is Marriage for White People? How the African American Marriage Decline Affects Everyone.* Ralph Richard Banks. New York: Dutton, Penguin Group USA. 2011. 304 pp. ISBN 9780525952015. $25.95 (hardcover).

## Comprehensive Reviews

**Comprehensive reviews** include all of the details common to their briefer cousins but add a more systematic appraisal of the work and in doing so locate that work in its academic ancestry. Reviews of this sort "help fellow social science students and colleagues understand if and how the book accomplishes something useful and how that accomplishment was achieved" (Edwards, 2012, p.121). Comprehensive reviews can be quite thoughtful and interesting to read when the critique has the outcome of guiding a reader through an intellectual enterprise. Reviewers have the option of first summarizing the content, describing the central thesis or purpose of the book, and denoting the intended audience. This largely descriptive material is followed with an appraisal of the book's strengths and shortcomings. The goal is a thoughtful and engaging text, so assemble the writing accordingly.

Sometimes reviewers can seem a bit overzealous or perhaps occasionally self-serving. I recall an instance where a colleague had recently published a book on friendships in children. The purpose and scope of the book were clear and were represented in the title of the book and subsequent preface. The reviewer criticized the book for not including a review of research on adult friendships. It's a nutty comment. My guess is the reviewer wanted to read a book about adult friendship—and, in of itself, this is an interesting topic—but it was not the focus of this particular book. A more interesting comment might have been a discussion of how the study of friendships in children could inform the understanding of friendships in adulthood, or vice versa. In this way, rather than offering a vacuous criticism, the reviewer might take the opportunity to engage in theory building and encourage advancements in the understanding and study of friendship across the life span. The review might have also addressed issues of race, class, and gender and how friendships in children are influenced by social locations. The point is to write a review that addresses the overall quality of the work relative to the stated purpose and intended audience, to offer criticism where appropriate, and to use the content of the book to launch a discussion of curious issues. The comprehensive review is a public enactment of the peer-review process where all the actors are known, and many of the elements of useful reviews of journal articles discussed in Chapter 9 apply.

As in the case of reviewing journal articles, reviewers should recuse themselves when there is a conflict of interest or the appearance of a conflict. Examples include cases where a significant relationship exists between a book's author and the reviewer (e.g., close friendship, mentoring relationship, adversarial relationship), or a case in which the reviewer might realize a professional gain from a positive or negative review (e.g., where a book is largely based upon a reviewer's work, offers a contrary position, or is dismissive of a reviewer's work). Similarly, it would be inappropriate for an author to suggest a reviewer to an editor or approach a colleague and request a review when there is a conflict of interest or the appearance of same. Senior faculty should avoid requesting reviews of their work by junior faculty when the elder may later influence a tenure or promotion decision, for instance. Academic advisors should avoid requesting reviews by current or former students. If there is any question of whether you should write a review, you might share the dilemma with a few trusted colleagues or share the issue with your editor and ask for an opinion.

Book reviews sometimes are plagued by minutiae. Reviewers lament the absence of a particular reference or two. Use endless direct quotes from the book. State the content of the book in excruciating detail. List in military fashion the title of each and every chapter. Go bonkers or completely Pollyanna. None of these minutiae serve the purpose of engaging a thoughtful discourse and consequently are to be avoided.

Book reviews are not literature reviews, but a few pertinent citations can be appropriate, particularly when they illuminate an argument or ground an argument in a relevant theoretical, applied, or empirical literature. Citing your own work can seem self-serving, so keep this in mind and concentrate on presenting issues and cite material judiciously (including your own work if relevant). A particularly well-chosen quote from the book can be appropriate, but again the key is to do so sparingly. As a rule, if you have more than one direct quote per three pages of text, you have too many. A compliment on the author's writing or on the execution of a thoughtful argument is appropriate, but remember perfection is not of this world. It is quite possible to write a complimentary review acknowledging a book well done but still provide a critical analysis of issues, and, in fact, doing so is the heart of an interesting review.

Comprehensive reviews vary in length; a review in the range of 2,000 to 5,000 words is typical. Reviews of this sort announce a book's birth, establish the purpose and content, evaluate the book's merits and contributions to the existing literature, and serve as a platform for encouraging a discourse. Having accomplished all that, readers can decide whether to pursue the book. It is customary to end a review with some sort of recommendation.

## Cross-disciplinary Reviews

In this form of review the intent is to review a book from different perspectives. The emphasis is less on evaluating a particular book than on assessing how the book informs inquiry across disciplines. The *Journal of Family Theory & Review* publishes this form of review. In one instance, Libby Balter Blume commissioned reviews of Jonathan Franzen's novel *Freedom*, winner of a National Book Award, a *New York Times* best-seller, and selection of *Oprah's Book Club*, among other notable achievements. In an interview with *PBS Newshour*, which Libby cites in her preface to the reviews (Blume, 2011), Franzen reflects on how his experience of family, of siblings, of parents who were at times clashing contemporaries, and of being in a long-term marriage all contribute to a fictional account of a family ensemble. The evolving story tells of Patty and Walter Berglund's courtship, marriage, deteriorating relationship, and postdivorce adjustment, or lack thereof; the book dwells on their families of origin and their parenting of their own children, and we witness the coming of age of their children and the changes that emerge in parents and their relationships with adult offspring. The novel is a compelling story but still leaves us with the question of whether literature informs science. Libby viewed the book as an opportunity for family scholars to "comment on the characters' fictional family lives by addressing questions as: Are Franzen's

characters normative? Are their stories consistent with the research literature on families? Do family theories influence popular culture?" (Blume,
2011, p. 303). Libby solicited reviews from family scholars representing
different disciplines and expertise: Ingrid Connidis on the issues of intergenerational relations and ambivalence, Jeffery Jensen Arnett on emerging
adulthood, Dana Berkowitz on gender and sexuality, and Michael Bam-
berg on narrative identity. In the staid culture of behavioral and social
science journals, and the rarified air of theory journals, this is a bit of twist
in the more usual discourse. Personally I welcomed the exchange; I hope
readers did as well. At the least the exchange illustrated how interpretative communities who rarely meet can promote a new realm of discourse.

Although the comprehensive review style aims to offer some evaluation
of a book's quality, the cross-disciplinary review may not. In the case of
Franzen's novel, there was no intention of evaluating the novel, nor any
pretense that behavioral and social sciences researchers have any expertise in evaluating literature.

In yet another example of a cross-disciplinary review, Tessa le Roux
(2011) reviewed *The Immortal Life of Henrietta Lacks*. Written by Rebecca
Skloot, a journalist, the book is a medical and social history of the Lacks
family and the intersection of the worlds of family, medicine, and science.
Henrietta Lacks died of cervical cancer in 1951; she left behind five children and a Petri dish of cancerous cells taken without her knowledge. The
cell strain became known as **HeLa** and continues to be used in the laboratory studies of several illnesses. Le Roux examines the book as a platform
to inquire about issues of social justice and ethics, race, poverty, and class.
The HeLa strain of cells is used in research facilities worldwide, and that
use unquestionably led to many medical advances and a corresponding
multimillion dollar industry. Yet the Lacks family realized no direct benefit, and ironically was without health insurance. Le Roux complemented
the review published in the March 2011 issue of the *Journal of Family
Theory & Review* with a supplemental interview with Sharon Terry, chief
executive officer and president of the Genetic Alliance, an advocacy organization committed to transforming health through genetics and promoting an open dialogue with all concerned parties (see http://ncfr.org/jftr/
book-bits). Although the book was written for a broad audience, le Roux
explores issues of particular relevance to family scholars. The appeal of
the book is undeniable to both a general audience as well as the readers
of the journal in which the review was published. The review remains one
of the most popular articles published by the journal, with over 1,000
downloads at this writing, which means readers' interest in this particular
book review exceeds readers' interest in nearly all other work published
by the *Journal of Family Theory & Review* or its sister journals, *Family
Relations* and the *Journal of Marriage and Family,* in 2011.

Cross-disciplinary reviews that showcase books not typically viewed in
the realm of one discipline—such as family studies, where the focus is less

on evaluation than promoting a discourse—can have an influence on the field at least equal to the more typical fare of theoretical articles, literature reviews, and empirical reports. Whereas brief book reviews represent a service to the field, cross-disciplinary and longer review essays are creative and scholarly contributions and should be considered as such. Comprehensive and critical reviews are influential; people read them, although they are not frequently cited as a rule (East, 2011; Harley et al., 2010).

### Comparative Reviews

Comparative reviews are an iteration of a comprehensive review in which one writer, or a team of writers, reviews several related books. For example, Brandy Renee McCann (2012) wrote an essay evaluating three books reporting on studies of kinship. This form of review serves many of the same purposes as single source reviews but emphasizes the multiple and comparative contributions of several related books to a particular area of inquiry. McCann's review explores how relationships with extended kin advance an understanding of how families operate across multiple households, a network of individuals and relationships that figure in how families understand and define themselves. The books she reviewed take different approaches to kinship both conceptually and methodologically, but taken together they allow the reviewer to develop a more comprehensive discussion of the meaning of family and kinship to participants: how kin define family membership and who is included in or excluded from that group; how family members practice doing family through their routine interaction and ritual; and how the broader landscape of family influences individuals and the personal relationships that comprise family networks. The comparative review of multiple volumes and its various iterations advances a discourse about common themes and thus represents another instance of creative scholarship.

---

**BOX 4.2  WRITER'S RESOURCE: AN INTERVIEW
WITH LIBBY BALTER BLUME**

Libby Balter Blume is professor and director of the Developmental Psychology and the Family Life programs at the University of Detroit Mercy. Libby served as the book review editor of the *Journal of Family Theory & Review* from 2009 to 2011, and later was appointed senior editor. I asked her about her experience as a book review editor, her views about the purpose and contributions of reviews, and how the experience of being a book review editor influenced her career.

RM: *What are the qualities of a great book review?*

A book review should provide an overview of the content, but more importantly it should provide a critical review of the topics or issues, especially how that book might influence family theorizing or be relevant for theory, research, and pedagogy in the field. In other words, it shouldn't just be descriptive; it needs to also contribute to the mission of the journal that it is being written for. So in the case of the *Journal of Family Theory & Review*, a great review needs to advance family theorizing, or to explain how it fits into a field of research.

It goes without saying that it's got to be quality writing, clearly written, and not necessarily written to promote the author or the book.

RM: *Let's say you receive a really scathing review. How much can or should a book review editor influence the content or tone of a review without interfering with a free exchange of ideas?*

I expect a reviewer to take a balanced view and contribute her own perspective, but I wouldn't want a review to trash a book simply because the [reviewer] disagreed with it.

My goal would be to tone down any judgmental qualities but not interfere with the content of the review. I would also look carefully to make sure the reviewer is including adequate references, source material, and justifications for his own position. I have often made suggestions to authors of reviews [when reading their initial submissions]. Generally I don't accept reviews that are just an author's opinion of a book; the review has to also contribute to the discourse, and contribute to the field.

In the comparative reviews of multiple books, the reviews became less about the content of the books and more about how each book contributed to the field, in which case the review became an original piece of scholarship itself and an important contribution.

RM: *So the purpose of the longer book review essays was to expand the scholarly contribution of the review?*

Exactly. That was also true of the reviewer roundtables with people completing a review of [a common book] from several different perspectives. The point was that it would advance the field in some way. It would not necessarily advance **the book**. For example, I selected Jonathan Franzen's novel *Freedom* for review because it was widely read and it had something to say to us about how we understand families and do research [see Blume, 2011].

RM: *Why do authors write book reviews?*

Usually because they're asked, or because I present them with a book that really [is apt to] interest them, that is a good match with their area of research, and it is really something they would probably get around to reading anyway. So it's because the editor has done a good job of matchmaking. Essentially, I think most authors are doing it because they want to make a contribution to the field in general, because they think their perspective is important, and I am speaking of associate and full professors. I mostly contacted more senior people whenever I could.

RM: *Why select senior scholars?*

Because they don't have to worry about tenure and promotion. The book reviews are not juried so they don't count [in tenure and promotion reviews]. Occasionally, I would get a request from an assistant professor to review a book, and if the title was relevant to us I would say yes. I'm not sure what their motivations were, but some were at institutions [where reviews might be more highly regarded], or, for the same reason as the senior people, they just wanted to share their perspectives on a book they thought was interesting or relevant. They don't get credit. It's more important to be writing articles.

RM: *Did you find editing rewarding?*

Yes, I did, because I really liked having access to authors and their critical reviews of these titles. Probably I wouldn't have read all these reviews otherwise because they weren't necessarily in my field, but I also enjoyed giving feedback to reviewers and sending them suggestions for revision.

RM: *Do you think the experience helped you to become a better journal editor?*

I feel most of my hands-on experience was editing the book reviews. At the time, I was constantly communicating with authors on editorial issues. [Libby often requested minor revisions and occasionally more involved revisions of the reviews submitted.]

RM: *Was being book review editor rewarded by your home institution?*

No, not at all. It was just regarded as a service to a professional association.

It's terrible. I mean editing in general is not recognized [to the same extent] as original research.

Book reviews appear in some additional styles. One style is having multiple reviewers representing different areas of expertise or academic disciplines write comprehensive and critical reviews of one particular book (e.g., Fortner, 2012). In another variation, the *Journal of Marriage and Family,* as part of its *Decade in Review*[1] series, commissioned reviews of 14 books published in the 20th century and deemed to be classics, books that had and continue to have a significant impact on the field. The reviewers were charged to "assess each classic book anew with the purpose of reflecting on its importance, the nature of the influence, and its current place in the development of family science and allied disciplines" (Baranowski, 2000, p. 847).

All of these forms of book reviews, with the exception of the Watsons, are instances of creative scholarship with the purpose of enhancing the field and promoting discourse. In each form, a progressive review requires considerable knowledge and understanding of the field, and perhaps allied disciplines. Successful reviews negotiate a delicate balance of appropriate praise, denoting what is novel or well executed, and appropriate criticism, denoting what is lacking in a constructive way that informs continuing theory, empiricism, and practice.

## Are Book Reviews Relevant?

Books communicate theory, research, and professional practices in the behavioral and social sciences and more so than in neighboring biological and physical sciences, which consistently rely on brief empirical reports (Hyland, 2004). In the field of family studies, for instance, we rely on books to advance theory and present findings from empirical work in greater depth than is possible in an empirical article. Monographs based on empirical work, both quantitative and qualitative, are common. As a consequence, book reviews in the behavioral and social sciences (and humanities) tend to be longer and more reflective than those appearing in the other sciences. Comparisons of reviews appearing in multiple disciplines and journals find distinct differences (East, 2011; Hyland, 2004). In sociology, for instance, greater attention is placed on the quality of exposition, and book reviews in this field are longer, more discursive, and more critical of both content and style of argument relative to reviews of books in the physical sciences.

Faculty in the behavioral and social sciences and humanities routinely write and read book reviews (Hartley, 2006; Lindholm-Romantschuk, 1998), although many journals that previously published reviews no longer do so (e.g., *Family Relations, Journal of Marriage and Family, Journal of Social and Personal Relationships*). This presages an eventual decline in the number of participants. Nonetheless, book reviews remain popular among writers and readers alike. Across the humanities, behavioral and social sciences, academics by in large browse book reviews and find them useful or very useful (Hartley, 2006). They remain a popular means to monitor the development of the field and are an important way in which scholars filter new scholarship (East, 2011; Harley et al., 2010). They offer authors recognition and, to a certain extent, feedback on their books as well as generating a discourse (Lindholm-Romantschuk, 1998). Cross-disciplinary reviews offer unique ways to promote exchanges between the behavioral and social sciences, physical sciences, and humanities—interpretative communities that may not otherwise enjoy routine contact.

Books reviews are an easy way for new professionals to gain experience in working with editors and academic publishing, hone their writing and critical skills, and establish a publication profile. On the other hand, some journals favor reviews written by well-established scholars because of the experience and sophistication they bring to bear, and presumably such reviews carry more weight and are more influential. There are exceptions. Recently I read a review of a textbook written by two doctoral students. The review was carefully written and applied a critical lens to the text from the point of view of a student user. The review was engaging and informative and provided a perspective unavailable to anyone other than a new professional (Aducci & Johnson, 2011).

Why do authors pen book reviews? Hartley (2006) found the most common responses from scholars in the behavioral and social sciences were:

- I am asked to by the editor (67%).
- I wish to inform my colleagues about the value (or otherwise) of a new book that may be of interest to them (62%).
- I wish to clarify my own ideas about a set of issues in my field (50%).
- I will get a free copy of the book (38%).
- I think the title sounds interesting (33%).
- I initially think a book will be an important contribution (29%).

The reasons for writing reviews have little to do with career advancement, although a significant minority indicate writing a book review would be "useful for my c.v." (36%). This is not particularly surprising. Book reviews are unlikely to become citation classics, and they are not widely regarded by promotion and tenure committees (East, 2011; Harley et al., 2010). I can't imagine a wildly successful academic career based upon writing reviews. On the other hand, reviews vary substantially, as we have seen, in their purpose and complexity. Some are complex, grounded in a literature and offer advances in theory building and critical discourse. Over the course of my career I've written a half dozen and found them a pleasant diversion from writing more typical empirical reports. Like many reviewers, I chose books I had reason to read for my own research or teaching as well as books that were poised to make an important contribution or advance a particularly interesting dialogue.

## Elevating a Brand of Scholarship

Superlative contributions are derivative of creative innovation, innovations that are often contrary to accepted practice. The various forms of comprehensive, comparative, and critical book reviews are an instance of emerging innovation. Given the importance of books and monographs to the field, and the importance of peer review, it is disingenuous to minimize the place of well-crafted book reviews in the realm of scholarship. Faculty across disciplines are, as a rule, surprisingly tepid with regard to innovative practices in the dissemination of knowledge (Harley et al., 2010). We rely on a rather narrow band of practices for publishing our work. Journal articles, and to a lesser extent monographs, are the core venues for presenting scholarship, but they need not be the sine qua non of publishing. Book reviews represent opportunities to advance scholarship through critical discourse and to make the essentials of the peer-review process an instance of public discourse and engage a broad array of writers and readers in that process. The privatized peer-review process that consists of communications between an editor, a select group of reviewers, and authors serves us well. Nonetheless, there are advantages to a more public peer-review process that consists of a reviewer and audience, and yields a communication stream that adds to the advancement of scholarship by engaging unbounded interpretive communities.

Although faculty across disciplines express fairly traditional preferences for disseminating scholarship, including new professionals with formative exposure to Web 2.0 platforms and the varied communication mediums these platforms provide (Harley et al., 2010), curious instances of innovation do exist. For instance, in her work with choreographer Genevieve Durham-DeCesaro, Elizabeth Sharp (2013) explores performance social science, where transcripts of interviews with women are set to dance. Other scholars are recognizing the need for models of publication that can accommodate arguments of varied length; rich media; embedded links to diverse sources of data such as still photos, voice, and video; and interviews with authors. At the same time, journals and their publishers are designing platforms to accommodate such developments as all parties begin to recognize the extraordinary advantages of web-based publishing. Book reviews limited to a singular iteration of content are useful, in much the same way a univariate comparison of group means is a useful descriptive statistic in an empirical report. Without diminishing the contributions of Watsons in the world of book reviews or empirical reports, there are contributions with a more expansive purpose: empirical reports framed in multivariate analyses, theory-rich qualitative inquiries, and critical book reviews. Book reviews can make significant contributions that can be enhanced with the integration of rich media—especially reviews that are grounded in critical thinking, including comprehensive or cross-disciplinary reviews.

BOX 4.3  BEST PRACTICE: ELEMENTS
OF PREFERRED REVIEWS

Hartley (2006) surveyed faculty in the behavioral and social sciences, biological sciences, and humanities and asked them about their experiences writing and reading book reviews. Their characterization of likes and dislikes is instructive.

**We dislike reviews that:**
- Are poorly written.
- Do not appropriately match the skill or background of the reviewer with the content.
- Contain incorrect and/or unsubstantiated claims.
- Are written to show the superiority of the reviewer.
- Fail to discuss the book's argument and worth.
- Are "too short, long, terse, shallow, pedestrian, self-serving, bitchy, negative, sarcastic, etc." (p. 1200).

**We like reviews that:**
- Clearly note the book's strengths and weaknesses.
- Are comprehensive and succinct.
- Provide a useful critique of theory in the field and a book's position within that field.
- Go beyond criticism to draw conclusions of broader importance.
- Indicate how the reviewer's views changed as a result of reading the book.

## Summary

This chapter has detailed the common, and not so common, forms of book reviews that vary in their intended purpose and complexity. Watsons, or elementary reviews, announce a book's arrival and describe the content without an evaluation. Comprehensive reviews add a critical component by considering a book's strengths and weaknesses. Longer forms of comprehensive reviews place a book within a disciplinary context, adding critical commentary regarding that context. In these instances, comprehensive reviews treat the book under review as a platform to engage readers in a critical analysis of pertinent theory, research, or applications. Cross-disciplinary reviews pair one or more reviewers representing perspectives or disciplines distinct from that of the book's author. In still another style of review, an author compares the contributions of multiple volumes written on similar topics. To describe this type of review, we used the example of a review of three books published on kinship. In comprehensive reviews, sometimes referred to as review essays, in cross-disciplinary reviews, and in comparative reviews, authors provide evaluations of the books being reviewed, but the more important and probably more interesting purpose is to engage readers in a broader discourse about the interpretation and creation of knowledge. For this reason, book reviews represent a form of scholarship that, like the common empirical report, varies in purpose, complexity, and merit. We detailed why authors pen reviews, and why readers read them, and the chapter closed with a nod to embracing innovations in the production of scholarship and the forms in which it is presented.

## Activities

1.  You are asked to review a book that is very critical of your work and also appears to misrepresent that work. You don't want to disappoint the editor, whom you admire. How do you respond?
2.  You are asked to review a book that happens to be written in an area you are clearly knowledgeable about. The book was written by your former dissertation chair, with whom you have had little contact in the last few years. How do you respond?
3.  Are there gender differences in the way reviews are written? (If you're interested in pursuing the topic, there is an empirical literature on gender and the construction of academic identities in book reviews, see Hartley, 2005; Tse & Hyland, 2009).
4.  What journals in your particular field publish book reviews? Are they written by established scholars, new professionals, or a mix of both?
5.  Locate a journal in your field that publishes book reviews. What types of reviews are published in the journal? How long are they? Are references typically included?
6.  Identify a review you particularly admire as well as one you believe falls short. What are the elements of an especially interesting review? Or the elements of one that is not particularly useful?

## Recommended Readings

Hartley, J. (2006). Reading and writing book reviews across disciplines. *Journal of the American Society for Information Science and Technology, 57,* 1194–1207.

An interesting empirical study of scholars in the social sciences, humanities, and sciences addressing questions about how often scholars read and write book reviews, how useful they find them, and the features they regard as important.

Peh, W. C. G., & Ng, K. H. (2010). Writing a book review. *Singapore Medical Journal, 51,* 685–688.

Although written for readers of a medical journal, the article is largely based on Hartley (2006) and provides a succinct set of instructions for writing a basic book review.

Edwards, M. (2012). Chapter 15: Writing a book review. In *Writing in sociology* (pp. 121–124). Los Angeles, CA: Sage.

This brief chapter is also based on Hartley (2006) and reiterates how to write a basic literature review. Read Hartley first, then lots of reviews in the journals you frequent, and then either Edwards or Peh and Ng. Writing more complex reviews requires an understanding of the essential details presented in these readings in addition to some skill in writing literature reviews, so you might consult that chapter as well.

## Note

1. At 10-year intervals, the *Journal of Marriage and Family* devotes one or more issues to publishing comprehensive reviews of the work done in core areas over the previous decade.

## References

Aducci, C. J., & Johnson, M. D. (2011). A review of "Theory construction and model-building skills: A practical guide for social scientists." *Journal of Family Theory & Review, 3,* 58–61.

Baranowki, M. (2000). Classic book reviews: The past revived. *Journal of Marriage and Family, 62,* 847.

Blume, L. B. (2011). Freedom roundtable: Families in fiction—fact or fantasy? *Journal of Family Theory & Review, 3,* 303–304. doi:10.1111/j.1756-2589.2011.00105.x

East, J. W. (2011). The scholarly book review in the Humanities: An academic Cinderella? *Journal of Scholarly Publishing, 43,* 52–67.

Edwards, M. (2012). *Writing in sociology.* Los Angeles, CA: Sage.

Fortner, M. (2012). Widening the lens on the discussion of race and marriage: Introduction to reviews of *Is Marriage for White People? Journal of Family Theory & Review, 4,* 354–355.

Harley, D., Acord, S. K., Earl-Novell, S., Lawrence, S., & King, C. J. (2010). *Assessing the future landscape of scholarly communication: An exploration of faculty values and needs in seven disciplines.* Berkeley, CA: University of California, Berkeley, Center for Studies in Higher Education.

Hartley, J. (2005). Is academic writing masculine? *Higher Education Review, 37,* 53–62.

Hartley, J. (2006). Reading and writing book reviews across disciplines. *Journal of the American Society for Information Science and Technology, 57,* 1194–1207.

Hyland, K. (2004). *Disciplinary discourses: Social interactions in academic writing.* Ann Arbor, MI: University of Michigan Press.

Le Roux, T. (2011). Review of *The Immortal Life of Henrietta Lacks* by Rebecca Skloot. *Journal of Family Theory & Review, 3,* 54–65.

Lindholm-Romantschuk, Y. (1998). *Scholarly book reviewing in the social sciences and humanities: The flow of ideas within and among disciplines.* Westport, CT: Greenwood.

McCann, B. R. (2012). The persistence of gendered kin work in maintaining family ties: A review essay. *Journal of Family Theory & Review, 4,* 249–254.

Sharp, E., & Durham-DeCesaro, G. (2013, November). *Making space for innovative methodologies: Publicizing "ordinary" women's lives through transdisciplinary dance and social science collaborative project.* Paper presented at the Theory Construction and Methodology Workshop at the annual meeting of the National Council on Family Relations, San Antonio, TX.

Tse, P., & Hyland, K. (2009). Discipline and gender: Constructing rhetorical identity in book reviews. In K. Hyland, & G. Diani (Eds.), *Academic evaluation: review genres in university settings* (pp. 105–121). Hampshire, England: Palgrave Macmillan.

# 5 Writing Book Proposals, Books, and Chapters in Edited Books

This chapter examines why authors write books in the behavioral and social sciences and some of the distinct advantages, and disadvantages, of doing so. We address the types of books written, including edited books with multiple contributors, and how to initiate contact with potential publishers. All publishers, or nearly so, require a book proposal, and the form this takes is relatively standard. We detail the critical elements of fetching proposals and the habits of successful writers. In the end, "writing a book is like writing anything else: you sit down and type" (Silvia, 2007, p. 109).

Writing a book involves a significant investment of time and energy and is only accomplished with a well-organized and consistent effort over a considerable period of time. Developing a strategy for getting the work done, developing a routine writing schedule, and managing the ever-present doubts are keys to success.

Much of this chapter applies to the broad class of books referred to as theory or research monographs, clinical or applied professional books, and textbooks like this one. Writing texts for undergraduate classes, particularly introductory classes, is beyond the scope of this chapter. Although much of the discussion applies to all forms of books, introductory textbooks often include a wide array of sophisticated pedagogical and auxiliary materials.

## Why Write Books?

We write books for a variety of reasons not the least of which is the intellectual and personal challenge. Books allow us to fully explore a topic without the structure or page limitations of journal articles. Books tell a story, albeit one based on the development of new theory, conduct of empirical inquiry, comprehensive review, policy analysis, or clinical application, but a story nonetheless. Successful research monographs, whether based upon the structure of quantitative analyses or some form of personal interview or fieldwork, call upon authors to engage a reader in a line of argument, a story however complex or abstract (e.g., Hansen, 2005). Some stories are best told in book form.

Laura Ellingson and Patricia Sotirin (2006) first reported on their study of *aunting* in a brief journal article; the complete report of their empirical work appears in the form of a far more detailed and interesting monograph (Ellingson & Sotirin, 2010). Karen Hansen's (2005) book on parenting challenges the view of self-contained **nuclear families** raising children independently and without connection to a wider community of kin, friends, and other personal associates. Her work reconstructs the way we view families by contextualizing the ordinary business of parents and children. Parents, for instance, regularly call on their siblings for help in child care, and their siblings respond. Families live in what Hansen describes as *not-so-nuclear families*. It is intriguing work with significant implications for how families are understood and studied. Books can, and often do, tell larger stories than is possible in a brief article.

Bill Marsiglio began his career writing empirically based journal articles and more recently has turned to qualitative research on **fathers** and reporting his work in monographs (e.g., Marsiglio & Roy, 2012). Bill comments on his joy in writing books:

> I am a lot more excited now that I started writing qualitative pieces, and particularly writing books. One of my more exciting moments is when I feel I'm in the process of creating a meta story of other people's stories and figuring out a way to introduce a reader to individual people and their stories, providing a reader with a sense of how these stories matter, and then writing conceptually about critical ideas. And so there is a creative side to doing that and the kinds of writing that I do.

We write books to report on a long-term program of research or other professional activity. Terri Orbuch and her colleagues reported on their longitudinal study of **early marriage** (Holmberg, Orbuch, & Veroff, 2004). Joyce Arditti (2012) wrote about families with an incarcerated member and the effects on children, an area in which she has long conducted research. Paul Amato and his colleagues examined the changing enactment of marriage, family, and community in America (Amato, Booth, Johnson, & Rogers, 2009). Research and applied monographs contribute to developing new theory, research, or applied programs throughout the behavioral and social sciences.

Writing books can be personally and professionally rewarding. Many scholars are known for their books, not their journal articles: Hal Kelley, Arlie Hochschild, Urie Bronfenbrenner, and Lillian Rubin come to mind. Nonetheless, there are issues to consider before taking the leap. Books take time, sometimes quite a lot. For new professionals, multiyear commitments to writing books may not be the most strategic choice when applications for tenure and promotion are on the horizon.

Yet another motivation for writing books in the behavioral and social sciences may be the prospect of amassing great wealth, a desire that overwhelms the joys of teaching and academic service, in which case some form of reality therapy might be in order.

## Types of Books

Books vary in their purpose and intended audience. Monographs report on research, method, and theory for a rather sophisticated audience of advanced graduate students and new and established professionals. Textbooks are crafted with some specific audience in mind, and this may include undergraduate or graduate students or professionals working in applied settings. Occasionally, we write books that are intended to cross over into trade and be of interest to a wider audience. Authors need to be abundantly clear about their intended audience and write for that group.

Books can be cowritten with colleagues with the obvious advantage of spreading out the workload into more manageable units. When collaborating successfully, writing 6 chapters of a 12 chapter book is significantly easier and carries the added advantage that the book may appear in print more quickly. Coauthors can help make hard decisions about the structure, organization, and coherence of a book. Ideally, they add expertise and can edit one another's drafts. They can also be terribly unhelpful; selecting someone you are going to mind-merge with for a significant time is an important decision. In his little book of great wisdoms, Paul Silvia (2007) suggests selecting coauthors who write a lot.

At the extreme, the contributors can be multiple, with nearly every chapter written by a different author. My colleague Jim Ponzetti is currently working on such an edited book, with the working title *Evidence-Based Parent Education Programs*, for which he is writing some of the introductory chapters; the remaining chapters and lion's share of the book are being written by well-known experts. Jim's goal is to provide a textbook on the best practices in designing and implementing parent education programs and to engage experts with firsthand knowledge to pen the contributing chapters. More commonly, edited books are assembled to cover a particular area of research. In the field of communications sciences, Anita Vangelisti edited the comprehensive *Handbook of Family Communication* (2013). Cindy Hazan and Mary Campa edited *Human Bonding: the Science of Affectional Ties* (2013), a book that provides a comprehensive treatment of attachment from infancy to adulthood. Sally Lloyd, April Few, and Katherine Allen's *Handbook of Feminist Family Studies* (2009) offers a critical treatment of feminist theory and methodology.

Edited books can be rewarding to design and see through the publication process. They provide a useful service to their intended audience and an efficient way to review a topic of interest. For editors, they provide opportunity to work with colleagues in other disciplines or at other institutions, often quite distant, with whom one might not otherwise have the opportunity to collaborate, and of course they provide the opportunity to hone editing skills.

Writing individual chapters for an edited book can be rewarding. Such opportunities permit one to develop, establish, and share an expertise. Writing an invited chapter for an edited book can offer the opportunity to engage in theory building in a way that might not be possible in a journal article, or to summarize a body of work, including one's own and that of others. Invited chapters do not generally have the same authority as an article placed in a major journal, and consequently they are not as valued by tenure and promotion committees. Chapters have a relatively short shelf life and are less broadly distributed than articles in major journals. In my own experience, invited chapters I wrote in the past are rarely cited, while aged journal articles continue to be acknowledged.

## Selecting a Publisher

Books require investors, someone willing to take a chance on your work and invest in its production and subsequent marketing and sale. For most academic books, this means identifying potential publishers and contacting them. There are several issues to consider:

- Who is the likely audience for the book, and which publishers market to this audience? Publishers vary in their target audiences, with some marketing to academic or professional groups and libraries and some specializing in crossover books that are intended to appeal to professionals and the lay public. Deciding on the primary audience is among the first decisions to be made because it determines the structure, organization, and writing style of the book as well as the domain of potential publishers.
- Which publishers produce books in your field? Publishers may specialize in marketing books to distinct professional groups (e.g., clinical psychologists, social workers) or disciplines (e.g., developmental psychology, communication sciences, sociology).
- Publishers vary in the types of books they consider, with some producing textbooks exclusively and others producing clinical or research monographs. For the most part, it is a simple matter to identify likely publishers by virtue of the titles and types of books currently in their list.
- Some publishers have well-deserved reputations for carefully producing books. Independent reviews of early drafts are solicited for the purpose of helping authors to improve their work. Some publishers place more resources in copyediting books prior to publication, and this can improve the overall quality of the work. Some publishers

market more effectively. Some package with well-designed jackets and covers, and perhaps endorsements by Pulitzer Prize winners on the back, or at least authors well known to the intended audience. All these services are costly; they add to the quality of the book and the cost to consumers.

- Consider the cost of a book to its intended audience. Publishers vary in how they price books. Ideally I want great service, high-quality production, global marketing, and an affordable paperback edition and e-book.
- Talking with authors about their experiences with publishers can be helpful; otherwise, it would be difficult to know which publishers engage in more effort and expertise in soliciting reviews, copy editing, book and cover designs, and marketing. An author may also be able to introduce you to an editor.
- Talk with editors. Many attend conferences, and they are there to show their books and, just as importantly, speak with potential authors. Otherwise, contact information for editors is often included on publishers' websites. Incidentally, an editor's attendance at a conference that represents a book's audience is an important bit of information.
- Once a few potential publishers are identified, review their list. Are there books on similar topics to your work? How are the books priced? Are affordable paperback and e-book editions typical? How well are the books packaged?

Once the preliminaries are completed, the primary audience identified, and a few potential publishers selected, the next steps involve writing a book proposal. In some cases, an author may first write a query letter to an editor describing in a few paragraphs the book and the author's credentials. In most cases, even if I have spoken with an editor about a book to assess his or her interest, I will follow up with a query letter. The letter is brief if I happen to know or have a working relationship with an editor and longer if I have little relationship with an editor. A letter of about a page transmitted by e-mail is fine. If the editor responds favorably, then follow up with a well-crafted book proposal that follows the publisher's guidelines. Typically, editors respond within a week or so of receiving a query. There are exceptions, but in my experience publishers are prompt and often helpful. They may encourage or express an interest in the book, and occasionally they do not. Perhaps the book is not in keeping with their current publishing interests. Nonetheless, in most fields, there are a number of potential publishers seeking new titles. The well-publicized experience of trade authors and fiction writers who submit proposals to a legion of publishers before finding a home for their books is not typical of academic book authors, at least not in my experience (Keyes, 2003).

Among the most prestigious publishers are university presses. They differ from commercial presses in a number of ways (Lindholm-Romantschuk, 1998). University presses are sponsored by their parent institutions and, to a certain extent, are less dependent on commercial success. Publishing books and monographs is part of a university's commitments to producing scholarship and a public service mission. University presses keep books in print longer, and this accounts in part for their impact, although recently developed methods of producing books on demand makes the issue less relevant than it was in the past. University presses often employ rigorous manuscript selection processes involving multiple levels of editorial and peer-based reviews. The result is a higher quality book in most instances.

Then there is the issue of "unselecting" a publisher. Options abound for self-publishing, and certainly a slew of trade books select this option. Amazon, iBooks, and others offer platforms for designing books with a unique professional look. The wave of popularity in self-publishing has yet to significantly influence academic books but perhaps will do so in the future. There are some advantages and not a few disadvantages to selecting this route. Although some self-published books are profitable, most are not (Keyes, 2003). Marketing an academic book to university libraries, instructors, and professionals is a formidable task, and not one to be taken lightly. Then again, there is a long history of self-publication by some noteworthy authors, including Thoreau, Whitman, Dickens, and, more recently, Dave Eggers, who self-published his novel *A Heartbreaking Work of Staggering Genius*, which is some pretty good company to keep.

## Writing a Book Proposal

Most academic publishers require book proposals. Although publishers vary in the content, order, and degree of detail they prefer, proposals include a short list of key sections or components. In addition to the proposal, including one and preferably two sample chapters is a good idea and may be required by some publishers before they will review your work.

Publishers will also want to know about you, the author, and particularly your experience in publishing, so include a CV. If you have previously published books, highlight this; if not, highlight your other publications and related scholarly work. This is not the place to append a complete record of your academic work; rather an abbreviated CV will suffice. Omit material that is not pertinent, and include documentation of your academic ancestry, current position, publishing successes, grants, and awards. In short, anything that will convince a publisher of your expertise and establish why you are the perfect person to write this particular book.

Before you write a proposal, complete your homework: Visit the publisher's website, read the guidelines for proposals, be sure you understand them, and write the proposal accordingly. I've reviewed more than a few book proposals over the years, and they vary widely. Some are carefully crafted, well written and researched; each section addresses the relevant issues succinctly; the purpose, content, and audience is clear. Great proposals are in the range of 8 to 10 pages. In other circumstances, I have read proposals that were sparse. There was no indication the author had read the guidelines for preparing a proposal. To be honest, great proposals are sometimes declined by publishers because the book does not fit with current interests of the publisher, because the market is soft, or other reasons. I have also seen contracts offered to sparse proposals consisting of a scant few pages. The book happened to match a publisher's interests. As an author, I can't control market factors or completely predict a publisher's current interests, but I can control the quality of the presentation.

It is possible to submit a proposal to several publishers simultaneously. Most authors I know avoid this. If a publisher is tardy in completing a review (i.e., taking more than two months), then I would interpret this as an indication of minimal interest or simply as an indication of editorial disarray, and I would submit the proposal elsewhere. Otherwise, I'm content to submit to one publisher at a time; it's less confusing and more respectful of the time publishers invest in reviewing book proposals. Whichever your preference, a great proposal includes a few key components.

## Overview

In a few paragraphs, describe the essentials: the overall purpose, intended audience, and rationale or need for the book. This is your opportunity to get an editor's or reviewer's attention, so write clearly and succinctly, no more than a page (double-spaced, always, no exceptions).

## Outstanding Features

Briefly list the outstanding or unique features of the book. Perhaps it is the first substantial study of a topic, an in-depth treatment of an emerging topic, a comprehensive advanced textbook, or an upper-level textbook taking a novel pedagogical approach. What makes your book unique and different from other books on similar topics? Craft this section carefully, and then include a sentence or two about why you are the person to write this book. Incidentally, my hunch is that when you began working on this book, there were moments when it was an exciting prospect. When you talked about the project with a colleague, the words just poured out. That is the energy to capture when you write this section.

*Assessing the Competition*

Identify the existing books in the field that are similar, even if only in part, to your book. What are the strengths and weakness of the competition? Avoid any semblance of hyperbole, and provide a frank assessment of the competing books. For instance, in writing the initial proposal for this book, I identified about a dozen books on writing. I noted the primary focus of each; their strengths, particularly if I thought something was especially notable or well done, as well as weaknesses or areas that I thought didn't work well; and how my book differed. Although there are other books on writing for the behavioral and social sciences, *Crafting Scholarship* includes topics rarely addressed elsewhere, such as editorial practices, writing and responding to reviews, and special features like interviews with editors and authors.

Add a bit of feminist sensibility to your assessment: A competing book need not be a disaster for your book to be a triumph. Finally, if you believe your teaching, research, clinical practice, or other professional experience led you to write a book very different from the competition, say so. In my case, I believed my several decades of experience as an editor and author was relevant and led to a unique book, so I said so. In the end, a publisher or a reviewer should know how your book differs from the competition in style, content, and depth.

*Pedagogy and Apparatus*

The style in which a book is written, the overall purpose, and intended audience all contribute to the kind of features an editor or reviewer might expect. For a quantitative research monograph, I would expect a number of tables, figures, and other features that serve the overall purpose of the book. For a textbook, editors and reviewers expect a structure and content that enables learning. This could mean identifying learning goals in the introduction to each chapter, summary paragraphs that guide a student's review, and closing with a review, discussion questions, and suggested exercises. Describe features like case studies, interviews with leading professionals, or boxed text in which special topics are presented. Describe any additional features such as glossaries, recommended readings, references, or appendices. Detail whether the book includes supporting or supplemental materials such as social media sites, websites, study guides, laboratory manuals, and the like.

*Audience and Market Considerations*

Among the first tasks in designing a book is deciding on the intended audience. This might include a selection of undergraduates, graduates, new professionals, applied audiences, researchers, or libraries, but it is unlikely to be all of the above. Authors often exaggerate their markets;

aim for a realistic description of the audience for whom you are writing and who is most likely to purchase your book. In the case of textbooks, include details on of the types of classes that would use your book, including disciplines and typical class titles and enrollments. If the book could be used in a variety of classes, disciplines, or departments, prioritize the list and state where the book is mostly likely to be adopted; if appropriate, denote other classes where it might also generate interest.

For monographs, handbooks, and more general books directed at professional audiences, who is likely to buy the book? What makes this book unique and different from other books on the market? How would you estimate the total market for the book? If the primary market is professionals in child development programs, how many such programs are there? If there are professional organizations, newsletters, blogs or mailing lists that would be useful in promoting the book, mention them. Later in the process, once you have been offered a contract and submit the final copy, you will be asked to complete an author questionnaire in which additional details on potential ways to promote the book are requested.

### Status of the Book

Here publishers look for details on the length of the book in double-spaced pages and word counts, the estimated number of chapters, how much you have already written, and the time line for completing the book. If there are display materials such as photos, drawings, figures, and tables, estimate the number. Estimate the time available to write, how long it takes to complete a chapter, and provide a realistic timetable.

Authors may approach publishers early in the process or later, when the book is nearly complete. Some complete a draft of a table of contents and one or two sample chapters and pair this with book a proposal. I prefer writing the lion's share of a book before contacting publishers, but only when I am fairly confident a publisher will find the project attractive. If I were writing a more typical textbook, particularly for an undergraduate audience, I would secure a publisher much earlier in the process. I want to be sure of a contract before fully committing to writing the entire book and benefit from any suggestions an editor and reviewers might offer in assembling the book.

### Suggested Reviewers

Publishers will select their own preferred reviewers, but they may also appreciate suggestions. If the book has several distinct markets or potential audiences, consider recommending people representing the breadth of the market. I suggest reviewers who are apt to find the book useful and respond to it favorably. If I am unsure of a potential reviewer's response, I don't suggest that person. Avoid recommending reviewers who are major figures in the field but people with whom you have had little or no contact or professional exposure. Reviewers are typically not identified to authors, but there is no reason to nominate reviewers whose response to your book is uncertain.

### *Annotated Table of Contents*

An editor and reviewer need to know as much as possible about the book's content. Include a list of chapter titles and a paragraph about the probable content and purpose of each chapter. This is an important section of the proposal, so it should be well written, but reviewers understand the book is a work in progress and the order of chapters as well as the precise content might change.

## Getting to the Page

Writing books is like writing articles or writing for any other venue. Books are more formidable, but the process still involves outlining sections, crafting each paragraph, and rewriting heaps. Like writing articles, establishing a consistent and routine writing schedule is necessary. For some, this means writing daily, even for brief periods (e.g., an hour per day); for others (like myself), it means writing for longer blocks of scheduled time each week plus stolen moments (unscheduled writing times). The precise schedule may vary from semester to semester, but there is always a plan in place. My classes are assigned meeting times; my writing blocks are also assigned. A typical writing schedule is about three scheduled blocks of time per week: two 2-hour blocks and one 4-hour session. (I don't write profitably for more than four hours per day. There are occasionally exceptions, but generally this is my experience.) I treat scheduled writing times much like a class. There are exceptions, and times when I miss a session, but they are exceptions. I miss writing sessions because of the occasional meeting that I simply must attend, or I miss a session because I am attending a conference. There are times I skip a writing session because I sense a need to take some time off. In these circumstances, I may need relief from the fray of academic life, or the material I am about to work on needs additional thought. Often the material at hand is being processed, and the time away from my desk and laptop is well spent. I recently scheduled some time to write the proposal for this book. I struggled with starting the proposal and ended up just blowing off the day and taking a hike. In the next writing session, the proposal just sort of poured out and over three or four sessions was completed. A day or portion of a day off may seem like idle time but in fact is often a productive strategy. Take the time off when needed, and then write.

Bill Marsiglio recounts his common experience in writing and recognizing the need for time off. I expect the experience is common to all writers.

> If I get stuck in a manuscript, if time permits, I'll go for a bike ride. Usually cycling is a place where I will process ideas. I go cycling with the anticipation that something will come to me. I don't know how it's going to come to me, but it will come to me while I'm cycling.

Like many experienced writers, Bill is well aware of his typical writing process and has learned to recognize how to respond to the cues: when it's time to take a break and when it's necessary to keep "butt in chair."

Stolen moments are also important writing times, moments when I have completed class preparations or other tasks assigned to the day and can manage to pour a bit more time into writing. I don't mean to say that all the many tasks I must attend to are completed; this is rarely, if ever, the case, but rather I prioritize writing above most all other work except teaching. I make room for stolen moments. If all the tasks assigned to a particular day are completed, I turn to writing for an hour or two. I don't turn to the many other tasks I must complete; they will get done in their assigned times.

One of my colleagues gets much of her writing done in stolen moments. Recently she described completing the conclusion of a journal article in her car while her tween and teen children were shopping for clothes and otherwise cavorting at the local shopping district. She manages to complete most of her writing in stolen moments. For writers who are primary caregivers of children, elderly parents, or other family members, scheduling and then executing writing time is not always possible. For the rest of us, if you are unable to write routinely because there are too many papers to grade, too many committee meetings to attend, or a host of other important stuff that occupies our professional lives, this is normal. Write anyway, just write.

If you haven't already figured it out, to pen books, or articles for that matter, we need to prioritize writing. If you would rarely miss teaching an assigned class, you might consider rarely missing an assigned writing session. For this active writing model to work, we need to support each other. If I happen to be chairing a committee, I don't expect my colleagues to attend a committee meeting when they are teaching, and I don't expect them to attend when they are scheduled to write. Committee and department chairs, deans, and other administrators can support scholarship when they privilege writing time much as we privilege classroom teaching and, in this way, directly and actively support faculty scholarship.

Sabbaticals have always been important in my writing, and time when I can focus on writing and little else. About five chapters of this book were completed in draft form during a sabbatical. Nonetheless, as useful as they are, I still accomplish the vast majority of writing during semesters in which I teach two or three classes.

Consider establishing a writing plan with an initial table of contents, working chapter titles, expected length, and projected completion dates. Chapters often take longer than expected, although with experience I can better estimate just how long in a typical semester it will take to write a chapter.

Prewriting takes time. These tasks include preparing data, designing and implementing analyses, thinking through interpretations and potential theoretical models, reading literatures in a variety of disciplines and areas of inquiry, and following leads. Plan on this sort of activity and include it in a writing plan as much as possible.

Keeping a log of progress can be helpful in several ways. It can act as a reminder of accomplishments and help to estimate the time required to write chapters. A log serves as a place to record notes on each chapter on material that you want to go back to and notes on other material to be consulted or analyses to be completed before considering the chapter done.

Often I move on to another chapter before the previous one is entirely completed. I'll return to the earlier chapter after a few weeks, and often with a fresh perspective. My notes will remind me of what I wanted to review, or add, at a later date.

## Managing Risk

The hardest part of writing a book may be managing the internal doubts successfully. Books are an enormous undertaking. I rarely start with the conviction that I have enough material and all will go quickly and smoothly. Mostly I just trust in the force and enjoy the moments when a sentence or argument goes especially well. I fully expect that some days won't go well and I won't feel particularly clever. I also know the doubts are much like white noise, ever present but never terribly important or requiring much attention.

Given the enormity of the task, start with what seems the easiest chapter to write. This could mean a chapter that feels most compelling or one on a familiar topic and for which you have completed most of the background reading or core analysis. Write regularly regardless of how difficult it is or how doubtful you feel. Just keep working.

Rarely do I ever feel a chapter, or article, is completely done. There is nearly always more material to be considered: articles or books to read, data to be reanalyzed, cases to be reviewed. Certainly address the most critical work, but be mindful that there will always be more material pertinent in some small way, or material that is not entirely relevant but just plain interesting.

Start-ups of any writing task are uncomfortable, and especially for books. I always feel intimidated. I expect this sort of reaction and write anyway. I also expect that the initial reservations and doubts will dissipate once the piece I'm working on starts to take shape. Helen Marrow, an assistant professor of sociology at Tufts University and author of *New Destination Dreaming: Immigration, Race, and Legal Status in the Rural American South* (2011), recently shared a similar experience. Although in this instance she was speaking of writing an article, the experience generalizes to writing books.

> I am feeling good! After two weeks or so of trying to "trust the process" and begin writing this first draft paper, I think I am finally beginning to see the light and hit the top of its curve. I always find my writing process to be really slow and painful until it reaches a peak point where the paper finally feels like it is coming together, but also where I usually realize I've written too much and will have to cut the word count back down eventually. So my plan for the next two weeks is to keep my excitement and forward movement and to prioritize writing whenever I can.

Starting a new project can be difficult, at least initially. With books, I always feel unconvinced I have enough material or enough original thought to make a book of any length. This was also true of the current work. I expected the book to be much shorter with fewer chapters. As I read material from the behavioral and social sciences, from neighboring disciplines like compositional studies, or from the humanities, ideas matured and developed and the chapters expanded in scope and depth in ways that I had not anticipated. It is one of the joys of writing, the discovery of new ideas. I think it is a mistake to think writers come to the page with a bunch of ideas fully worked out. My suspicion is that contributions in theory or clever interpretations of data come from engaging the act of writing. The creative contributions are inseparable from the writing.

## Contracts and Production Issues

Contracts for academic books are fairly standard. Publishers offer a royalty that is often graded, increasing as the number of books sold reaches a threshold (usually above 1,000 or 1,500 copies). The royalty rate is negotiable and ranges from 2% to 10%, sometimes higher for digital versions of the book. Royalties are built into the pricing, so be aware that a higher royalty will translate to a high sticker price for buyers. Advances on royalties are not typical in my experience, but they are possible. For most academic books, it is not much of an issue. You draw income and tax liabilities now or later.

The contract will specify how the book will be produced. Hardcover editions, in part directed at libraries, and digital versions are typical;

paperback editions less typical but desirable because they are more affordable. The issue is important and one you might raise with a publisher before signing a contract. More than one author has been disappointed that his or her book was issued in an expensive hardcover but not in paperback, which limited sales. In the near future, the issue may become moot as digital copies become the norm, but it is an issue to discuss with an editor early in the process. Many prefer digital copies for their light weight and portability.

Production issues of consequence appear once a final copy of the manuscript is submitted to a publisher. If material from other work under copyright is used, authors are responsible for seeking permissions, although publishers will provide instructions for doing so (e.g., reprinting a figure or substantial quote of text). Authors also may be responsible for constructing an index—yet another issue to discuss prior to signing, but expect little more than instructions for completing the task. Indexes serve to guide readers in locating topics of interest and are based upon identifying authors, keywords, phrases, or topics and their locations in a text. Microsoft Word has an indexing function that is flexible and efficient.

I have yet to meet an author thrilled with the marketing for his or her book. It is perhaps the most common complaint among both academics and those who write for trade (Keyes, 2003). Publishers frequently request pertinent information on marketing in the form of an author questionnaire. The typical form requests information on the potential readers and the organizations that represent them, journals and newsletters that might review the book, potential awards for which the book might be eligible, brief (one paragraph) and even briefer (two sentences) descriptions of the book for use by salespersons, and a host of other issues. The detail provided by authors will position the marketing folks; whether they use all the information provided is a mystery.

In the end, authors are left with a choice of diving into the marketing fray or not. Some writers (like me) would rather spend their time working on the next writing project than marketing a recently published work, but my colleague Sandy Caron enjoys marketing her books, and surely there are other academics who enjoy the challenge. Of course, one can always hire a marketing firm to do the deed. Other than that, it is typical for authors, at least authors of trade books, to construct websites, invoke social media, Twitter feeds, and the like.

Then there is the issue of book covers and art. My partner, Renate Klein, designs her own covers, which her publisher seems to welcome (Klein, 2013). Consider designing your own cover or have a friend do so. Alternatively, public sites like *Shutterstock* contain legions of photos for every occasion. It may be debatable whether cover art matters for academic books, but surely many readers value a well-designed, artful cover.

---

**BOX 5.1  BEST PRACTICE: WRITING BOOKS**

- Plan a writing schedule.
- Write routinely, which means daily or multiple times per week.
- Recognize the need for process time or time off.
- Build a time table of writing objectives with time for prewriting (outlining, reading, and analysis).
- Log progress for each session.
- Learn to manage risk and self-doubt.
- Start-ups are bumpy. Keep working.
- You will never read or analyze everything. Keep writing.
- Never judge the merit of your work as you do it. Keep writing.
- Creative thought is derivative of active writing. Keep the order straight and write.

---

## Summary

Writing books can be complex, difficult, sometimes downright ornery, time-consuming, and personally rewarding. Despite the many challenges, the essentials of writing books and articles remain the same. Scholarship in any form is difficult and requires amassing considerable expertise, organizing that expertise, and establishing a routine writing schedule that involves weekly, if not daily, writing sessions. Writing also requires managing the ever-present risks and the complex array of emotions that accompany the pen and screen. In this chapter, I have described the experience of writing and all its incumbent personal challenges. Writers have their idiosyncrasies for sure, but the basics of the experience are common among all writers, whether writing from the perspective of the behavioral and social sciences, where most of the readers of this book reside, or the perspective of fiction writers and the many others who ply the trade in one form or another. We are most successful when acknowledging the many semblances of personal risk, and perhaps comforted when recognizing writing is a wee bit maddening for all the masses.

## Activities

1. Identify a book you admire. What about this book was well done? How was the book organized? What would you change or do differently? How well did the author introduce each chapter? Did the stated goals match what actually transpired?
2. Construct an outline with chapter titles of the book you would like to write.

3.  Books are longer, but the process of writing them is identical to writing much shorter journal articles. In what ways is the process of writing identical across virtually any medium in your experience?

## Recommended Readings

Keyes, R. (2003). *The writer's book of hope*. New York, NY: Scribner.

The book was written mostly for those who pen fiction, but the experiences described transcend disciplines and apply to all writers. The stories of other writers, some well known, are curious and well worth reading. Erskine Caldwell, for instance, is among my favorites. He found it easier to write if he stayed in motion and managed to ride buses all day; during the evening, he sailed on ferries running between Boston and New York and wrote in transit. Then there is the advice of Australian writer Janette Turner Hospital for dealing with rejections: "Have one stiff drink, say five Hail Mary's, and then five [expletive], and get back to work" (p. 140). It is comforting to know that I am not the only writer to feel addled at times.

Rabiner, S., & Fortunato, A. (2002). *Thinking like your editor: How to write great serious nonfiction—and get it published*. New York, NY: W. W. Norton.

Written by two experienced editors, the book includes great advice on writing proposals and presenting them to publishers. The book is directed at authors of nonfiction written for trade but applies well to academic books.

Silvia, P. (2007). *How to write a lot*. Washington, DC: American Psychological Association.

This masterful and inspiring text includes a brief chapter on writing books.

Golash-Boza, T. M. (2011, March 22). How to write a book proposal for an academic press (Web log post). Retrieved from http://getalifephd.blogspot.com/2011/03/

This commentary on writing a book proposal is brief, insightful, and nicely written.

VandenBos, G. R., Frank-McNeil, J., & Amsel, J. (2008). Reviewing book proposals. In R. J. Sternberg (Ed.), *Reviewing scientific works in psychology* (pp. 79–88). Washington, DC: American Psychological Association.

This chapter provides an overview of reviewing book proposals and the kinds of issues in which publishers are most interested, such as market, tone, appropriateness, and organization of the content.

# References

Amato, P. R., Booth, A., Johnson, D. R., & Rogers, S. J. (2009). *Alone together: How marriage in America is changing.* Cambridge, MA: Harvard University Press.

Arditti, J. A. (2012). Child trauma within the context of parental incarceration: A family process perspective. *Journal of Family Theory & Review, 4,* 181–219. doi:10.1111/j.1756-2589.2012.00128.x

Ellingson, L. L., & Sotirin, P. J. (2006). Exploring young adults' perspectives on communication with aunts. *Journal of Social & Personal Relationships, 23,* 483–501.

Ellingson, L. L., & Sotirin, P. J. (2010). *Aunting.* Waco, TX: Baylor University Press.

Hansen, K. V. (2005). *Not-so-nuclear families: Class, gender, and networks of care.* New Brunswick, NJ: Rutgers University Press.

Hazan, C., & Campa, M. I. (Eds.). (2013). *Human bonding: The science of affectional ties.* New York, NY: Guilford Press.

Holmberg, D., Orbuch, T. L., & Veroff, J. (2004). *Thrice told tales: Married couples tell their stories.* Mahwah, NJ: Erlbaum.

Keyes, R. (2003). *The writer's book of hope.* New York, NY: Scribner.

Klein, R. C. A. (Ed.). (2013). *Framing sexual and domestic violence through language.* Hampshire, UK: Palgrave Macmillan.

Lindholm-Romantschuk, Y. (1998). *Scholarly book reviewing in the social sciences and humanities: The flow of ideas within and among disciplines.* Westport, CT: Greenwood.

Lloyd, S. A., Few, A. L., & Allen, K. R. (Eds.). (2009). *Handbook of feminist family studies.* Los Angeles, CA: Sage.

Marrow, H. (2011). *New destination dreaming: Immigration, race, and legal status in the rural American South.* Stanford, CA: Stanford University Press.

Marsiglio, W., & Roy, K. (2012). *Nurturing dads: Social initiatives for contemporary fatherhood.* New York, NY: Russell Sage Foundation.

Silvia, P. J. (2007). *How to write a lot.* Washington, DC: American Psychological Association.

Vangelisti, A. (Ed.). (2013). *Handbook of family communication* (2nd ed.). New York, NY: Routledge.

# Part II
# The Experience of Writing

# 6 Managing Risk, Criticism, and the Drunken Monkeys

For many academics, writing is central, a core part of the profession. We write varied forms: letters, brief and not so brief; responses to the daily queries through e-mail and messaging; letters of recommendation; lectures and all the materials that support our teaching; committee reports and white papers; blogs, editorials, and newsletter entries; grant proposals; journal articles; book reviews; invited chapters in edited books and, more recently, handbook chapters and encyclopedia entries; and the occasional monograph and book. We write for a variety of routine professional needs, not the least of which is publishing. We are as academics professional writers but oddly enough rarely describe ourselves this way (Goodson, 2013). Our success in the academe depends on an ability to write well and efficiently, perhaps like no other occupation.

Writers infrequently talk about their experiences of writing, or so it seems from the many writers in the behavioral and social sciences with whom I've spoken. As students we learn the basic mechanics of writing and the composition of empirical reports, and little else. When we write, we do so in isolation. Much of my own work has been in collaboration with other scholars, yet my coauthors and I rarely—in fact I can't think of a single instance—talk about the process of writing or our experience of it. We do share thoughts about conceptualization, designs, and analyses, but we speak little about how we write and experience that writing.

I recently collaborated with Eric Widmer, Heather Helms, and Stephen Marks on an invited chapter (2014). The chapter presents a new model of social capital. In preparing to write the chapter, we talked about our understanding of the core concepts, what we did and didn't like about the available literature, research that illustrated basic elements of our conceptual model, and other issues. We agreed on who would write each section and established deadlines. Yet I know little about the processes my coauthors use in writing, about where they write, whether they schedule writing time as a routine part of each week, the length of a writing session, or how much they write in a session. We have never spoken about such issues or our experience of writing, and yet I'm often friends as well as professional colleagues with the people with whom I collaborate. We are silent about the practice and experience of writing. In my conversations with scholars, comments acknowledging the silence were common. Paul Amato is an extraordinarily prolific family sociologist. After speaking with him about his experience of writing, he offered: "You know I've never really talked to people about this before." It is a common sentiment. Bill Marsiglio, a leading scholar in the field of fatherhood, shared: "I haven't talked a whole lot about writing."

Because we work in silence, we are unable to make critical social comparisons that can help us to understand our experiences and emotional reactions to writing as well as develop writing skills. Quite apart from the practical value of talking about writing, writers are nearly universally quirky, often intensely curious, and fun to speak with about their practices. Before I began speaking with the lot, I had no idea just how quirky; I wasn't alone in my personal experiences.

This chapter is about the experience of writing and the commonality of experience across professions. We detail the inherent risk of writing, the common personal experience of writers, and how they manage risk and criticism. Whether we are speaking with new or experienced professionals, risk is ever present.


## Common Experience Across Professions

For some, writing is torturous and, if not, then simply maddening. Even Stephen King, a popular and prolific novelist who has authored 50 novels and sold more than 350 million books, finds writing challenging.

> Stopping a piece of work just because it's hard, either emotionally or imaginatively, is a bad idea. Sometimes you have to go on when you don't feel like it, and sometimes you're doing good work when it feels like all you're managing is to shovel s*** from a sitting position.
>
> (King, 2000, pp. 77–78)

I am glad to hear that. Not that I wish unpleasantness on a fellow writer and Mainer (Stephen lives in central Maine, as do I), but it's nice to know I'm not the only one who sometimes struggles with the written word. There are days when writing is an enormous effort, nothing feels quite right, and an articulate sentence a distinct impossibility. It is only later that I begin to experience pleasure—the day after, when the solution to a conceptual issue, or even just a particularly handsome sentence written the previous day, seems well crafted and I can take some pride in my work. Then, the voices of doom and judgment, anxiety and ambiguity, are silenced. Anne Lamott, in her wonderful memoir on writing, *Bird by Bird* (1994), calls such voices the "drunken monkeys" (pp. 6–7).

Heather Helms speaks about her experience, implying elements of drunken monkeys and the converse, something we might call the happy camper:

> Writing and being published is really, really hard. Sometimes it's all day for a paragraph, but then sometimes I'll come back from a run and, bam, I'll write four or five pages.
>
> Then sometimes I'll go back and read what I've written and feel "Wow, I really wrote that." So that is a nice experience. That's the fun part. I have to write for my job, but I'm really doing it because it's stimulating.

Some writers find the work difficult but in most regards rewarding. Bill Marsiglio and I spoke for well over an hour about his experience of writing:

> Someone once wrote "I hate writing but I love having written."[1] Well, I never found that to be the case. I actually enjoy most of the process of writing especially the process of writing books. And I definitely like seeing that final product.
>
> I can work or sit for longer periods of time if I'm writing a book than if I'm writing an article because I feel I have less opportunity, it's more formulaic and not as much fun. But if I'm writing a book I feel more at ease and there is a creative aspect to it.
>
> There are lots of people who talk about writing blocks and so forth. Fortunately I never really experience that. There are times when I struggle here and there but usually I don't get so anxious or annoyed with the process. I don't think of myself as having struggles.

For many writers, some form of despair, anxiety, or fear goes with the craft, and although it does not appear to be characteristic of all writers, it is a surprisingly commonly reported set of experiences. Like many of the behavioral and social scientists with whom I've spoken, some successful novelists—such as Stephen King, Sue Grafton, Margaret Atwood, and John Grisham, to name a few—experience trepidation at the page and, for that matter, at virtually every phase of the publishing process. In 1924, F. Scott Fitzgerald wrote his publisher on the day of *Gatsby*'s publication: "I am overcome with fears and forebodings. . . . In fact all my confidence is gone" (Keyes, 2003, pp. 16–17). The foreboding Fitzgerald experienced is not one of my drunken monkeys, but then this is not 1924. Times and sensibilities have changed, but the sense of fear and shaking confidence, that's familiar turf. Paired with the difficulty of writing and all its attendant drunken monkeys is a cast of critics. In publishing fiction as well as behavioral and social science, our work is open to criticism, and the gatekeepers are sometimes fierce.

## A Risky Business

At the core, writing is about risk and criticism. Writers are quick to point out examples of great work that was less than warmly received by publishers when first presented. J. K. Rowling, in response to her own difficulties and sense of depression in writing, created the *dementors*, a brand of ghoulish denizens who prey on good citizens and vacuum out all happy memories, leaving only despair (Keyes, 2003). Rowling submitted the first book in the Harry Potter series to 12 publishing houses, all of which declined the opportunity to publish this previously unknown author. Rowling has at this writing sold more than 450 million books translated into 73 languages. Not too shabby.

Similar stories abound among novelists and social scientists, including Nobel and Pulitzer Prize winners (Gans & Shepherd, 1994; Keyes, 2003). John Kennedy Toole ended his own life after one too many publishers rejected his first novel. His mother, Thelma Toole, took up the cause, and eventually the Louisiana State University Press published the book. Twelve years after his death, Toole's book, *The Confederacy of Dunces*, won a Pulitzer Prize for fiction and has sold over 1 million copies. Rejection, like confusion, has its costs.

Behavioral and social scientists routinely experience rejection. In a survey of 3,597 of authors across the sciences, 78% reported their last journal submission was rejected. Authors in the humanities and social sciences fare no better, reporting rejection rates of 76% (*Peer Review Survey*, 2010). Nearly all resubmit their previously rejected work to another journal and are eventually published. Prior to publication, nearly all completed at least one revision, and the vast majority (91%) believed that the review process improved the quality of their paper.

Rejection is a common experience and, in some regards, to be expected, but it is not experienced uniformly. Authors of textbooks on writing journal articles for the social sciences, of which there are many, assume rejection is the norm (Edwards, 2012; Thyer, 2008).

> Rejection is a fact of life in the world of scholarly publishing. It is painful and it is unpleasant, but it is the price you pay for entering the field and playing the game. In order to score touchdowns, you must take a lot of hits. Or to put it another way: in order to find your prince, you have to kiss a lot of toads.
>
> (Edwards, 2012, p. 72)

In my conversations with authors who are prolific, rejections happen, but they are not necessarily the dominant experience. Authors vary in their experiences but estimate that most of their work is accepted following revision to their journal of first choice, and some rarely, if ever, experience rejections. Heather Helms is among the latter group. "I don't submit something if I don't think it can be published," she said. "It's a waste of my time and everybody else's time." Among the authors I interviewed, an acceptance rate in journals of first choice of about 75% or more is standard. The point is rejections happen; they need not be commonplace when authors attend to the issues detailed here and in the accompanying chapters.

I asked Paul Amato about his experience of being reviewed, about how he typically responds when receiving a decision letter from an editor and the accompanying reviews.

> Every time you send an article out to a journal you know it is going to be criticized. Even if you think it is a pretty good article and eventually gets published and cited a lot, it's going to be torn down. In some ways, it's kind of a harsh system.
>
> The emotional stuff is really important. Intellectually you think about the reviews that we get and we try and assess in a fairly objective way the validity of the criticism; how we might deal with it; how we are going to respond. Emotionally there is all this churning going on. We're thinking: "How did this person not like my work? How come they didn't love it? I am deeply offended by this." Or "I'm never going to write anything ever again, ever. That's it. I'm finished." So you have to deal with all this emotion that goes on, and you have to get through it if you're ever going to have your work published.
>
> RM: *How long does it take to get through the process? A week?*
>
> Hopefully not that long.
>
> RM: *Is it any different now than when you were an assistant professor?*
>
> I tell my graduate student to get ready to have your work rejected because that is how you get published. You get published by having your work rejected. I tell them that I've been doing this for three decades now; I've published a lot. I get my work rejected all the time. I just had an article rejected last month. The more that you get published, the more that you have to have your work rejected. Get ready for criticism. Get ready for outright rejection and just tell yourself, "Okay, it was rejected; I'm going to dust it off, I'm going to revise it, and I'm going to send it out again." And if you believe in that piece you're working on, eventually you can get it published. It might be the second or third journal you send it to, but that is the way the system works. You pick yourself up, you dust yourself off, and you keep moving forward.
>
> At the same time it is not always easy to live up to that advice. It's hard to get your work rejected. It surprises my students when I tell them I get my work rejected a lot even now because they just think: well, how can that be? But realizing that even people who are fairly experienced, and have been doing it for a long time and have been

reasonably successful at having their work published and cited, even they have trouble with this process. [It] makes them realize that is just the way the system works and we need to anticipate this or we're going to be really unhappy.

Paul has several decades of experience and has published more than 100 articles, and yet there is nothing all that easy about the process. The major difference is that with experience we can become more aware of our reactions to writing and to being reviewed. Successful writers are conscious of their mood states and act accordingly. They are mindful of momentary experiences that can impede productive writing; they learn to expect turbulence and yet stay engaged.

Critical reviews are to be expected, some of which will be helpful, perhaps challenging, and encourage new ideas. Hopefully none will cause one to reach for the hemlock. From the perspective of an author, there will be times when a critical review appears reasonable and times when a review will appear unreasonable, and there may be elements of both themes in a review cycle. Perseverance most certainly is characteristic of successful authors. Again, Heather comments:

> Good writing is about perseverance. You've got to have the skills and ability to do critical analysis, but it's also about perseverance. My mentors would publish in *Child Development*, *Developmental Psychology*, and the *Journal of Marriage and Family*, and they would get these scathing reviews, but they would just bounce back from it. They also taught me not to shoot too low. Don't assume you won't get into [prestigious journals]. So that was good advice.

If there is one quality that characterizes successful authors, perseverance is surely in the running. All the authors I spoke with had this quality, and it commonly appears as a central theme in advice to fiction writers. Author and writing instructor Natalie Goldberg adds: "One must be persistent under all circumstances and it's not always exciting. . . . It is a long quiet highway" (Goldberg, 1993, p. xii).

Behavioral and social science writers sometimes find reviews helpful, sometimes disagreeable, but they universally put the pen to paper and revise; often within weeks of receiving critical reviews, papers were revised and resubmitted. At times revisions can take longer. Rachelle Brunn-Bevel comments on her response to calls for revision and resubmission:

> If [the reviews] are more about packaging, that is something I can do quickly depending on the time in the semester. But if it is something more substantive like, you know, including another wave of data or something like that, it is going to take more time. I might end up taking two months.

## Managing the Drunken Monkeys

Successful writers are superb at risk management. Writing is simply a risky business. The risk of being found out that I'm not that talented a scholar, that I have nothing much to say that hasn't already been said better, that what I've written is all gibberish, that others who once thought so highly of me will now regard my written work and my entire person as questionable, that when you come right down to it, I'm just a fraud with nothing much to say. And, to boot, there are the criticisms of journal submissions in pdf files, indisputable and unchangeable. In the miasma of the drunken monkeys there is always someone to confirm all fears. Stephen King observes: "If you write someone will try to make you feel lousy about it." Later he adds: "Writing is a lonely job. Having someone who believes in you makes a lot of difference. They don't have to make speeches. Just believing is usually enough" (p. 50).

Regardless of how successful a writer is, there are drunken monkeys and a continuous internal chatter of self-doubt as well as a few critics who will question your work. In my experience as an editor, whether I'm working with a new professional or a well-established scholar, writers experience doubts about the quality of their work. The entries in my writing log speak of what is my own typical experience, and I suspect of many others as well, including Stephen King.

> May 6: The chapter is rolling. Wrote about half or more of the section on risk today.
> May 7: About two pages written today. Progress but I'm not at all happy with it. Still stuttering along.

My experience of writing is much the same regardless of whether I'm writing a brief article or a longer monograph. There are good and bad days, and it doesn't have much to do with what is written but more about the momentary ambiguities of direction and worth. It is not always a simple matter to decide how to organize an argument, chapter, or section on risk. At times—and to be honest, this is more often true than not—it is not at all clear how to organize a chapter, or how to theorize a set of findings, or how to correct an ill-defined concept. Sometimes—in my experience, nearly always—writing is difficult emotionally and intellectually. I surely enjoy the latter, but I can't say that about the drunken monkeys. I have simply learned to expect their appearance—they are quite predictable—and control their influence. Once accomplished, writing is a welcome challenge, but it is not exactly fun like hanging out with my buddies in the Martini Club. I'm guessing that most writers are more like me than not.

This is my typical experience, and perhaps yours is similar. Then again, it is nearly always worthwhile to confront the difficulties, because doing so is more likely to lead to a contribution and a better quality manuscript. If writing a new piece begins with trial and tribulation, it ends with the triumph.

At the moment a section is written, I am not always sure of the quality or worth, and in part I think that has to do with the residuals of ambiguity. It is only later, and usually the next writing session, when I can judge the quality of the previous session's work. This experience has remained unchanged over the course of my career, and the only difference is that it is predictable; I know the drill. I know exactly how the writing will go and how I'll feel about it. When beginning an article or chapter, the ambiguity and doubt is ever present and heightened. I know this and can plan accordingly. I limit writing sessions to two to four hours, decide on a specific stop time, plan something more immediately enjoyable following the session, and set my goals or number of words per session fairly low (about 250 words). Harry Reis calls this phase of writing: "butt to chair." I know, too, that once a piece begins to take shape, I'll find the writing easier and more rewarding. As a consequence, sessions will be longer when time permits, and the writing may go faster. The drunken monkeys are still present, but less active.

Boice (2000) compared two groups of writers: a group of "blockers" and a group of "non-blockers" who experienced some occasions of fluent writing. Blockers experienced more negative thoughts, but for both groups the most common negative thoughts were about the hard work of writing (about 65% of the blockers and 43% of the non-blockers). Concerns about perfection were present and more likely among the blockers, but they were not the primary issue. In the end, both groups reported surprisingly high levels of negative thoughts. The non-blockers directed more self-talk at quitting the negative intrusions (e.g., "This will be pleasant enough once I get going.").

At all phases of writing, success comes from perseverance, and this means expecting doubts about quality and worth and designing writing sessions that take these feelings into account. Plan for the drunken monkeys and trust in the force.

## Mindful Writing Practices

Many practices accompany successful writing, and they all require a certain degree of self-observation—what Robert Boice (2000) refers to as a *mindful* approach to writing, as well as teaching for that matter. In his observations of new faculty spanning many years, productive writers evidence a persistent consistency in their approach to writing. They write regularly with moderate expectations. They eschew expectations of experiencing great insights, preferring to simply work steadily at their craft. They have occasional bouts of peaceful "not-doing" or periods when they are planning a project, or thinking through an argument or conceptual model. All this activity is part of the writing process, largely welcome, and integrated into writing sessions. Great work derives from consistency of effort—butt in chair. Productive writers avoid negative emotions, the drunken monkeys, or at least set them aside as much as possible and seek out moderation in their emotional responses to writing. It takes suspending doubt, self-criticism, and disbelief, placing one's trust in the efficacy of constant effort. Then, too, a mindful practice means knowing that a first draft is apt to be less than stellar, but still a necessary part of the process. They transform criticism into a welcome process that has the potential to improve the quality of their work. They are not angelic, nor necessarily immediately embracive of criticism, but simply persistent.

---

**BOX 6.1 BEST PRACTICE: WRITING MINDFULLY AND MANAGING RISK**

- Compare your writing practices with a colleague.
- Know thyself, which is to say your writing self; the other selves can wait.
- Cage the drunken monkeys.
- Expect criticism, and seek out kudos.
- Never let bits of foul weather disturb your vision.
- Practice mindful writing strategies.
- Remember: Writing produces insight, not the converse.
- Keep writing.

---

## Summary

Although writing is a routine part of university life, faculty in the behavioral and social sciences rarely see themselves as writers, and they rarely talk about their experience of writing. The inherent risks of writing are fueled by elements of self-doubt and ample opportunities for criticism and rejection. Successful writers learn to anticipate the drunken monkeys and the external critics, and they persist in improving their writing and welcoming their successes. Success derives from mindful writing, a constant awareness of personal process.

## Activities

1. Do you typically describe yourself as a writer? In what ways does the label apply or not?
2. Create a list of all the reasons you are unable to write. Compare your list to similar lists assembled by your colleagues.

3.  Describe how you go about beginning to write an article or chapter. What are the feelings that accompany this initial writing?
4.  Why is writing difficult? What reasons quickly come to mind? Jot them down in a few minutes without self-editing.

## Recommended Readings

Richards, P. (2007). Risk. In H. Becker (ed.), *Writing for the social sciences* (pp. 108–120). Chicago, IL: University of Chicago Press.

Pamela Richards wrote this chapter about her personal experience in writing and the risk involved. It is well worth reading.

King, S. (2000). *On writing: A memoir of the craft.* New York, NY: Simon & Schuster.

Stephen King muses about writing fiction, but the book is filled with wit and wisdom. Some of writing is universal. Highly recommended.

Day, N. E. (2011). The silent majority: Manuscript rejection and its impact on scholars. *Academy of Management Learning and Education, 10,* 704–718.

It is remarkable that so little is written about the emotional experience of writing and the inherent risks. Nancy Day engages the issue directly, reviews the available and meager empirical literature, and offers some strategies for dealing with the drunken monkeys.

## Note

1.  The quip is attributed to Dorothy Parker, a writer, poet, satirist, and funny woman who once wrote in a theatrical review this comment on a player: "Runs the gamut of emotions from A to B." Her epitaph, which she penned, reads: "Excuse my dust."

## References

Boice, R. (2000). *Advice for new faculty members: Nihil Nimus.* New York, NY: Pearson.

Edwards, M. (2012). *Writing in sociology.* Los Angeles, CA: Sage.

Gans, J. S., & Shepherd, G. S. (1994). How are the mighty fallen: Rejected classic articles by leading economists. *Journal of Economic Perspectives, 8,* 165–180.

Goldberg, N. (1993). *Long quiet highway: Waking up in America.* New York, NY: Bantam Books.

Goodson, P. (2013). *Becoming an academic writer: 50 exercises for paced, productive, and powerful writing.* Los Angeles, CA: Sage.

Keyes, R. (2003). *The writer's book of hope.* New York, NY: Scribner.

King, S. (2000). *On writing: A memoir of the craft.* New York, NY: Simon & Schuster.

Lamott, A. (1994). *Bird by bird: Some instructions on writing and life*. New York, NY: Anchor Books.

Milardo, R. M., Helms, H. M., Widmer, E. D., & Marks, S. R. (2014). Social capitalization in personal relationships. In C. R. Agnew (Ed.), *Social influences on close relationships* (pp. 33–57). New York, NY: Cambridge University Press.

*Peer Review Survey 2009: Full Report*. (2010). London: Sense about Science.

Thyer, B. A. (2008). *Preparing research articles*. New York, NY: Oxford University Press.

# 7 Establishing Successful Writing Practices

In the first few years, over two-thirds of new assistant professors produce nothing in the way of journal articles, the kind of work that is most prominent in tenure and promotion reviews (Boice, 2000). It is a startling finding and one that commands attention. Here we detail the reoccurring themes that define productive writing practices across disciplines as well as document practices that interfere with productivity. We can learn much from the empirical literature on writing for the behavioral and social sciences and the collective wisdom of other writers.

We explore the routine and ritual practices of new professionals, those in mid-career, and some accomplished senior scholars. Success in writing derives from some very different approaches grounded in a few key principles. Contrary to the common wisdom of popular writing texts, productive authors are diverse in their writing habits. They are consistent in regard to their persistence and interest in scholarship, but they organize their writing in ways that are responsive to their personal preferences and social conditions. Regardless of personal preferences, writing occurs in a social context: an overstimulating academe requiring several competing commitments that are often unsupportive of writing time as well as a gendered relational context comprised of family relations with partners, children, and elderly parents in which caregiving responsibilities largely fall on women. I may plan a writing session on Friday, but if my dean calls a meeting, my partner's car breaks down, a child is ill, or my mother falls and injures her hip, all bets are off. The array of unanticipated interruptions is a constant challenge, especially for those who write as part of a complex of professional obligations like teaching and service. Having a quiver of effective responses that help to normalize writing time improves one's chances of success.

## Scheduling Writing Time

Productive writers share one common attribute: They write regularly. Scheduling writing sessions is among the most consistent recommendations for writers, and for good reason. Productive faculty report that scheduling regular writing sessions is among the most important strategies (Boice, 2000; Keyes, 2003; Mayrath, 2008; Silvia, 2007). The question is, just how often is *regular*. In her book on *Becoming an Academic Writer*, Patricia Goodson (2013) recommends scheduling daily writing sessions, if only for brief periods, for instance, 30 minutes per day. Paul Silvia, in *How to Write a Lot* (2007), recommends allotting time for writing each week starting with about four hours at minimum allocated over one or more days. Before becoming a parent, Paul wrote for two hours each morning, Monday through Friday. Now with two toddlers, some change in Paul's writing schedule has occurred, but the commitment to daily writing has not. He says:

> I have two children now, so the writing schedule I described in the book—write every weekday from 8 am to 10 am—seems like a feverish delusion. As parents of young children know, 8 am is almost lunchtime. Now I write from 5 am to 6:30 am each weekday, which is something my pre-parenthood self would have found startling and irrational. The writing room depicted in the book, with its spacious desk and toddler-unfriendly furnishings, has become a child's bedroom. I no longer have a room in my house to write, just a lounge chair at the end of a hallway with a lamp, a printer, and a shelf for a coffee cup and a few cherished books about writing.

Paul's commitment to writing regularly continues unabated and is a consistent message throughout his book (Silvia, 2007). In interviews with productive faculty in the field of educational psychology, authors consistently emphasized the need to schedule writing time as a regular entry in a weekly calendar, and many wrote daily (Mayrath, 2008).[1]

In Boice's studies (2000), new faculty failed to learn to write with regularity and efficiently in graduate school, often writing in binge sessions to meet a particular deadline. The average time to write dissertations is a stunning four years post data collection. This doesn't suggest routine weekly writing sessions were part of the mix, and it doesn't bode well for success in the academe. It also suggests some inefficient mentoring and a lack of institutional support.

New faculty shared the belief that writing is best done in large blocks of time, which may never come or come irregularly. This is an issue I, and many others, struggle with most. Boice, Goodson, and Silvia all emphasize writing daily in whatever times are available, even 30-minute sessions. I've never done this and always thought it near impossible. I write regularly, but not daily. Mostly I write in scheduled writing sessions consisting of a single four- to six-hour session and a few shorter two-hour slots per week, and I grab a stolen moment here and there. As I write this chapter, I am averaging a whopping 12 to 16 hours per week. Incidentally, I teach three classes most semesters, often chair a major committee for my college, and have spent the better part of my career as a journal editor. I like writing and I'm determined to write regularly, if not quickly, so I schedule time for writing each week. The exceptions to this schedule are conferences when I am away from campus, and advising week each semester, which I enjoy thoroughly. There are some other exceptions, but they are not common or predictable. And to be honest, as I mentioned earlier, I occasionally take some time off when I'm fatigued or just need some free time to wander. I think my colleagues do as well, but we don't talk about it.

Boice (2000) described a group of new faculty who were productive early in their careers. They learned to work in brief sessions daily. These quick starters worked efficiently and were mindful of their writing habits. They are rare birds; thriving new faculty comprise about 3% to 5% of the total Boice interviewed. Their work habits are unique among their peers, but not especially unusual or unfamiliar.

In my interviews, productive writers are rarely as consistent in their writing habits. They fall into several camps. Some write regularly when time permits during the week. They may not keep to a precise schedule because of unpredictable events (e.g., child care), but they still manage to complete some writing each week. Others prefer to write in intensive bursts or multiday sessions. A minority write in prescheduled sessions of a few hours duration each week, which is my typical schedule. Although most find brief sessions inadequate, they follow this practice out of necessity, because their schedules don't permit longer sessions. Preferences aside, they write when they can, and do so with regularity.

I asked Heather Helms about her writing and whether she schedules time each week.

> I know that is such good advice. Well, I try and then children get ear infections. People get sick, and the dean calls you for a meeting, and you get put on a committee. . . , I try, but it becomes harder and harder to protect my time. I do try to have a set number of hours in a week, four hours, that I can dedicate to writing. I need chunks of time. An hour just doesn't work for me. When I write I get really lost in it; if I'm at home I forget to shower or eat and then I look at the clock and think, oh my gosh, I have to pick my child up from school or an activity and I haven't taken a shower or eaten anything.
>
> It is just the way I write. It is just who I am, and I've learned to embrace it. It also means I don't publish at the same rate as people [who write more regularly and during prescheduled times]. The people who gave me that advice are just machines. They are also men, and they also tend not to have children. [laughs] They also tend to have power that I don't have. So I just accept who I am. The bigger chunks of time I can give myself, the better, but I know that hurts me because if that's the only way I can write, it's hard to find big chucks of time.

Heather prefers to schedule blocks of time for writing, but, like many of her colleagues (and my own), she finds that children get unexpected illnesses, deans call meetings, and we might add that elderly parents have mishaps. These relational commitments and the unexpected attentions they require are paired with an overstimulating academic environment. I can't remember a time when I had nothing to do, for instance.

There is competition for our time and attention, and then there are family obligations that largely fall on women. As in all matters of work and home, gender rules, although there are exceptions. When I asked Bill Marsiglio if he scheduled time for writing, he replied: "I have a five-year old." Bill specializes in qualitative research on fathering, has published books on the topic, and fathering his young son is clearly important.

> I write in spurts, and it's not always predictable when they happen. If my son is here, I typically don't work while he is at home. I choose to spend time with him rather than writing. So right now by life revolves around working around his schedule. Sometime I'll have a block of time [for writing], but it is a day-to-day thing.
>
> Early in my career I could do whatever I wanted. In the last five years, having a young son has really altered the way I organize my life and particularly my writing life. . . . I wake up early and mornings have always been a very productive time for me academically. I would go to my computer and write from a half-hour to an hour and then eat [breakfast] and then go right back to my computer and work for a huge chunk of time, and this was for days I wasn't teaching. On any days I wasn't teaching and on weekends in particular, [I'd write]. And depending on my life circumstances, I might work in the afternoons and evening as well.

Bill may not write as often or for such long sessions as he once did, but he does manage to continue writing with some regularity—in spurts, as he says—and if not daily, then for several sessions each week. This may not be Bill's preference, but he finds stolen moments and writes when he can. His recent book on fathering with Kevin Roy (2012) attests to his continuing productivity. On the day we spoke, he was preparing to interview a father participating in his current research project and subject of his next book.

The comments of Paul (Silvia), Heather, and Bill also demonstrate how writing lives vary over time. Although prior to becoming parents they were able to regularly schedule ample time for writing, parenting a young child altered the available time for and the predictability of executing schedules. In a similar fashion, over time as faculty move into senior positions, they become involved in faculty governance, chairing committees, departments, and graduate programs; supervising graduate students;

and an array of leadership positions in professional organizations, all of which compete with writing time.

Nonetheless we still manage to meet with our classes. We don't *find* the time to teach; we meet our classes regularly, and all other activities, other than a family emergency or sick child, become secondary. In over three decades of teaching, I don't recall missing more than a class or two. I can't say that about writing sessions. I suppose if I were a parent, my teaching record would not be as unblemished, but I'm sure you get the point. So why is writing secondary activity and one that only occurs when time permits? Regularity seems fleeting for most academic writers. Typical responses to my queries about scheduling writing time were consistent. It is viewed as impossible, or simply unworkable.

> "It doesn't work for me." Harry Reis
> "No, I have tried to work that way. It has not worked thus far for me." Sarah Schoppe-Sullivan
> "No, I don't. I write anytime. I often write throughout the day with lots of breaks." Michael Johnson
> "These days I write whenever I find the time. A lot of scholars reach a point in their careers where they suddenly discover that all of their time is eaten up; it's a gradual thing: committees, students, [leadership positions in the] ASA [American Sociological Association] and NCFR. If I get a free Saturday, I'll just go for it." Paul Amato

Scheduling routine writing time is unlikely for many, including those with very productive careers, those who are parents of young children, and those who are not so encumbered, as well as those in early, middle, and later stages of their careers. There were exceptions. Rachelle Brunn-Bevel remarked:

> Yes, well, I didn't always work this way. I would fall into scheduling everything else first, like teaching and meetings and then fit writing in between those things, which was a problem because everything else had more pressing deadline [and] writing would get pushed off. I definitely realized I needed to schedule a time for writing way in advance and have it on my calendar like a regular appointment so that I don't schedule other things at that time or writing continually gets pushed back for what I perceive as more pressing deadlines.
>
> RM: *How long is a session?*
>
> It depends on the semester, but this semester I have scheduled three two-hour blocks for myself on nonteaching days. So two hours on Monday morning, two on Friday morning, and then two hours on Wednesday afternoon.
>
> I've tried to use four-hour blocks, and it can work sometimes, but I feel for a weekly schedule four hours is a lot to block out without

interruption. The only time I've been able to write for four hours is when I'm with several people who are writing at the same time. But it doesn't seem to work for me on a weekly basis.

RM: *Is the issue that it is hard to find a four-hour block of time or that four-hour blocks are just too long for you?*

I think that four hours is just too long for me, but finding four hours free is really hard to do. I don't check e-mail during [writing] time, because I find that e-mail almost always takes me in another direction. . . . To stay away from e-mail for a four-hour block in the day, I find that when I do that, I'm really behind, or I've missed some pertinent thing that came, so that is why I don't feel I can schedule four-hour blocks weekly.

Rachelle quickly developed some productive habits that frequently appear in the recommendations of writing mentors (e.g., Boice, 2000; Goodson, 2013; Keyes, 2003; Silvia, 2007). She makes writing a priority, establishes bounded writing times, manages distractions like e-mail, and sets clear goals. Like many of the writers with whom I spoke, Rachelle is reflective about her own process. She knows what works for her and why, and she arranges her writing sessions accordingly. All the writers I spoke with were clear about their own preferences for writing and the conditions that were conducive to productivity. Some, like Rachelle and Elizabeth, preferred sessions of a few hours, and others, like Heather, Paul, and Michael, preferred longer sessions of four hours or more. They are clear about their preferences, although they cannot always arrange for them and often had to accept less than ideal conditions.

Among the many faculty whose careers Boice (2000) followed, writing was left to what new faculty did when they had time, when everything else was done. It's a simple matter to put off writing, and not very likely to put off teaching. At times, I, too, confuse what's important with what is merely urgent.

## Intensive Writing Sessions

Writing authorities discourage **binge writing** because it is less effective as a long-term strategy for **productive writing** (Boice, 2000; Goodson, 2013; Silvia, 2007). To a large extent this advice has validity as far as it goes, and a consistent pace in writing is preferred. Interviews with outstanding scientists, athletes, artists, and writers find that they work regularly; those who write, do so daily; those who run, run daily. Effective writers, regardless of whether they are writing fiction or science, rely less on binges than consistency and write in brief daily sessions (Boice, 2000). Then, again, there are exceptions. Some writers I've met are clearly effective; they publish consistently, and do so in influential journals, and yet they prefer writing in long, focused sessions. Paul Amato is one example.

My ideal is that I like to completely immerse myself in one thing, like a journal article. So I will set aside an entire week, and I'll pull all the [readings] together, I'll do the analysis, and I will get the first draft of an article finished in a week. That is working every day, 10 hours a day on it through the weekend, and after seven or eight days I'll have an article. Then, of course, I'll polish it up for the next few days. I like to work in this sort of feverish, intense mode, where I'm just obsessed by this topic and I'm living and breathing it for a chunk of time, and then I'm done with it. I like this really intensive focus on something.

I can't do that anymore these days. I can't get a free week. So I'm working a few hours each day whenever I can. It is really hard for me to write like that. I forget what I'm doing. I lose the thread.

I hesitate to refer to Paul's preferred style as binge writing, and I think it more accurate to refer to this style as **intensive writing**. In fact, several of the authors I spoke with preferred writing in longer sessions. For professional writers, whose primary occupation is writing, the issue doesn't emerge because writing for a long block of time each day may be a simpler matter, although some distractions persist in the form of book promotions, meetings, e-mail, and family obligations. For an academic with a teaching, student supervision, and service load, dedicating writing time is a major issue. Finding large blocks of time is difficult to pull off with any regularity, especially if you have young children or other family members to care for. What struck me about Paul's comments, and really those of other writers who shared a preference for long blocks of time, is the adaptability. Paul is clear that finding a full week to devote to writing is nearly impossible at this stage of his career, and so he says: "I'm working a few hours each day whenever I can." It is characteristic of the writers I interviewed that they are clear about their preferences, but they adapt to circumstances and find ways to write under virtually any condition. Persistence furthers.

Incidentally, Paul is planning a yearlong sabbatical in which he can write full time. It is a strategy I use as well. At my home university, tenured faculty are eligible to apply for sabbaticals every four years. It is an exceptional opportunity for writing daily and, in fact, is how I wrote much of this book. I wrote for about four or five hours a day, sometimes a bit longer, for four days each week. One additional day is set aside for other responsibilities such as supervising graduate students and journal editing. It's a pleasant way to work. I would not refer to it as binge writing, although it has some intensity at times. Of course, sabbaticals are only available intermittently; they don't replace routine weekly writing sessions. About half of this book was written in those daily sessions. Paul, Heather, Bill, and, to a certain extent, myself, may prefer long periods of time that can be devoted to writing, but when they are not possible, we find the time to write anyway. Persistence furthers.

## Collaboration

Faculty learn to work in isolation, and, as noted earlier, this habit of working alone is characteristic for tenured faculty. We rarely talk about writing, myself included (at least prior to writing this book).

Collaborations in research and writing remain a significant issue. Productive faculty often report collaborations with peers, with more experienced senior scientists, and with new professionals, including students, as one explanation for their productivity (Kiewra & Creswell, 2000; Mayrath, 2008).

Collaboration has many benefits. Working with Eric Widmer in a recent project, I benefited from his knowledge of the current research on the configuration of kin networks and their impact on family outcomes. In the same project, Heather Helms contributed her expertise on disadvantaged families. Collaborations can add a measure of efficiency in the completion of a project as well as levels of expertise that improve the overall quality, sophistication, and success in eventual publication.

There is another side to collaborations. When I commit to having something written to a friend and colleague, I don't want to disappoint them. The writing gets done. Social deadlines shared with collaborators are a consistent attribute of productive authors (Mayrath, 2008).

## Chasing the Muse: Inspiration

New faculty embraced beliefs about writing that are not terribly helpful, such as the belief that writing successfully requires inspiration, a magical moment in which the muse visits with reams of great sentences pouring forth with abundance (Boice, 2000). Astonishing theories are born of pure inspiration. The expectation of inspiration saving the day is common among fiction writers as well.

Somerset Maugham was once asked whether sudden and unexpected inspiration suggested a play or character. He replied that he never got ideas in that way. "I just write for several hours a day at the same time every day. Sometimes I just write my name until an idea occurs" (Keyes, 2003, p. 49).

The importance of inspiration from parts unknown is vastly overrated. Sometimes it does seem like the muse visits; I do gain some new insights unexpectedly and a sentence arrives with surprising lucidity, but I don't wait for these moments, I just keep on truckin'. Butt to chair. Although truth be told, I have had some great insights simply appear while driving around in my truck. The inspiration to study uncles and their relationships with nephews came in this way, but it was more like a skeleton of an idea. The book got written after years of sloshing around collecting data, transcribing interviews, and otherwise engaging in some rewarding but difficult work. For sure, the interviews were wonderfully interesting and fun; transcribing hours of interviews was not so fun, rather tedious actually. Once the data were collected, transcribed, and coded, writing the book took another three years, and that was with weekly writing sessions and a sabbatical. During much of that writing, I didn't feel all that inspired; I just felt determined, intensely curious, and willing to corral the ever-present drunken monkeys. Butt to chair. Great work comes not from inspiration but from long hours engaged in the craft. The act of writing produces the inspiration and enacts its articulation. You must write to produce good ideas, and not the other way around. On the issue of inspiration, Stephen King writes: "Amateurs sit and wait for inspiration, the rest of us just get up and go to work. . . . Your job is to make sure the muse knows where you're going to be every day from nine 'til noon. . . . " (2000, p. 157).

## Prewriting

Like Boice's thriving new faculty, success in writing comes from consistent practice, and typically this means writing weekly at the least. As always, there are exceptions. There are times when I am simply not writing. Because my time for research and writing is so limited, I prefer to take the time needed to let new ideas percolate before fully engaging in a new line of research and the incumbent writing. I think of this as a prewriting stage, and time to mindfully and deliberately plan new work and set a foundation in place. In the academe there are many opportunities to pursue; it is wise to consider each carefully and select projects that will have long-term benefits consistent with your research goals.

Boice's productive new faculty work patiently but consistently as they calmly prepare materials, and they begin by accumulating ideas and completing background work that then propels their writing. Setting goals is part of the process of writing and a legitimate focus of a writing session. "Planning is part of writing, so people who write a lot also plan a lot" (Silvia, 2007, p. 30).

In my own work, writing often begins in a "notes" file. I take notes on the pertinent background readings, and often these notes morph into extensive commentary, material that later becomes part of the substance of the work I'm about to write. Taking notes on background readings is a form of prewriting and properly belongs in the time allocated for a writing session. At some point in the note taking, I begin to draft outlines of the work. This can take the form of a topical outline or a preliminary drawing of a conceptual model that will later organize the writing. Although I have not found it helpful to use larger-format drawing, like posters or white or black boards, some writers do (Silvia, 2007). Whether large or small, conceptual images are a useful way to flesh out ideas and order the presentation.

Among the writers I interviewed, drawing conceptual models as a form of prewriting was common and highly recommended, and far more common than creating formal outlines. With a reasonable amount of practice, writing empirical articles is fairly straightforward, and perhaps a formal outline is unnecessary—particularly for a methods section, where the order of essentials is rather formulaic (i.e., a description of the method, sample, measures, and so on), or a results and discussion, where the order of presentation is governed largely the earlier literature review. In my own experience as an editor, a well-defined conceptual model provides structure to a manuscript and underscores an invitation to revise and resubmit an article and eventually see its publication. A well-defined conceptual model orders the construction of a literature review, identifies the pertinent literatures, guides the composition of the research questions and hypotheses, and defines the appropriate method, sampling, measures, and analysis. Crafting a conceptual model is an important preliminary to writing. It may not be all that easy to complete; it's not suppose to be.

In much of my own writing I construct outlines that detail the content and order of ideas. The outline often includes references to my notes file or samples of text. In a sense, the processes of note taking (and reading), outlining, and writing begin to merge in actual practice. Reading and taking notes on those readings promotes some initial writing of text.

---

**BOX 7.1 BEST PRACTICE: LOGGING DAILY WRITING GOALS**

Prewriting activities include logging brief notes on the goal(s) for each session. For instance:

- Map outline of chapter using notes file as a reference. [Need not be perfect today! Just a rough start will do.]
- Write 200 words on previous research.
- Revise yesterday's work.
- Continuing reading on generativity theory.
- Read the manuscript for tone, and edit accordingly.
- Work on easy stuff today.
- Check references and reconcile text and ref list.

---

One difficulty we all face in this early stage is when to transition from reading, note taking, and modeling to actual writing. For certain, we need to complete preliminaries before rushing to prose. The point is to do this work during your writing session time, to estimate after each session when you expect to write, and then begin writing just before you think you're ready to do so. Write a first draft and see if you don't know more than you think. Typically, you'll be ready to write sooner than you anticipate.

For many writers the initial transition from preliminaries to actual writing is challenging. It requires suspending disbeliefs. When writing *The Forgotten Kin* (2010), I began not knowing whether I had enough material for a book and no real idea what the first chapter might look like, or how the data would be organized conceptually or theoretically. In those first few months, I simply told people I was writing about kin. The first few months produced 70 pages, a somewhat disorganized rough draft, but core ideas were emerging. This initial work suggested the first draft of a table of contents as I began to see a broader conceptual framework and how the material could be arranged in separate chapters. With every project I have my doubts, and with every project I have to suspend disbelief. I never quite know what that first sentence will look like or the precise order of ideas, but I am sure it will only get written if I commit to writing. Butt in chair. If all else fails, write *Somerset Maugham* a few times to warm up.

It's at this early stage of writing that the drunken monkeys are most active and need to be corralled. In the early work on any piece, there are always concerns about reading enough material, learning how to conceptualize or write about a particular issue, worries about being able to write something original, and a seemingly endless array of doubts. In our early work on a project, the chief concern is learning to live with all the ambiguity and continue working.

The process of prewriting, transitioning to writing, and the actual experience of writing is similar for new professionals and more experienced scholars. The only difference is that older scholars are usually more aware of their process and how to manage the various phases of writing.

Like experienced professionals, graduate students and new professionals need to establish regular writing times and develop concrete goals for each writing session. My best advice is to never dwell on the fact that you need to write an article, thesis, or dissertation, but rather to dwell on what you are working on at the moment, which is apt to be a few sentences or paragraphs over an hour or two of writing time. There will be a slew of drunken monkeys; you can just count on it. "I don't know where to begin." "I haven't read enough." "I'll never write as well as Somerset whatshisname." "It's too late, I should have started earlier." "This is never going to work." "My data sucks." I could fill the pages with the endless doubts, and you might want to add to this list, but the point is to write anyway and do so with regularity.

These early drafts are always rough and needing heaps of revision. In fact, the first draft of this chapter had all sorts of issues. Although I began with an outline, I wasn't entirely clear what to include and the order in which to do so. Consequently the first draft was messy and disorganized. Then, too, new ideas emerged as I wrote. As always, the process of writing yields inspirations that are unanticipated, and consequently not included in a previously composed outline. Some of this disorganization was difficult to recognize until I reoutlined what I had written. I ended up reoutlining several times over a period of several weeks. My writing log is filled with entries like: "Worked on Chapter 7 mostly revising and editing. Some sections are done but others need work and some reorganization. About a page written today."

In her wonderful and funny memoir on writing, Anne Lamott (1994) wrote: "For me, and most of the other writers I know, writing is not rapturous. In fact, the only way I can get anything written at all is to write really, really shitty first drafts" (p. 22).

Anne also shares on her Facebook page to, above all else, "remain calm, and share your bananas," which seems like good advice.

## Logging Progress and Setting Goals

Many writers, including myself, monitor their progress in daily logs or journals. They can take many forms but have the overall effect of keeping goals explicit, monitoring progress, and recording the outcomes of each session and the accompanying moods states or other pertinent details. Self-monitoring behavior encourages you to sit down and write, and the log will help to uncover your particular writing process and later inform the design of practical accommodations.

Some authors keep Excel or SPSS files with data entries for pertinent details, like date, start and end times, project, words written, and some sort of cumulative totals like total pages written to date (Goodson, 2013; Silvia, 2007). I keep track of these details in a medium-size, lined Moleskine notebook.[2] In addition to the basics, I include a few comments on how I feel about the writing that day and some notes about what I expect to do in the next session, and perhaps some estimates of the remaining work and the time it will take. The latter has the practical purpose of informing me about where I left off in the last session and guiding my goals and activity for the next session. The comments about mood have several purposes. They help me identify patterns in the experience of writing. From these entries I know that my experience of writing is predictable and passes through a predictable set of stages— heavy on the doubt initially, and leaning more toward pleasantness as the work progresses. From my logs, I know four- to six-hour sessions are about the maximum time I can write productively. Any additional time is better spent in housekeeping tasks like collecting references. I know rising from the screen every 45 minutes for a short break is time well spent.

In addition to a writing log, I keep a separate notebook on my office desk that records the tasks I intend to work on each day and the time assigned to each task. A typical page looks like this:

- Class prep—45 minutes
- E-mail—45 minutes
- Read ms 020 and prepare a decision letter—2 hours
- Work on Faculty Senate material—60 minutes

If I happen to complete the day's tasks with time to spare, that time becomes a "stolen moment" and I spend the time writing. I use a paper notebook for this daily goal setting but you might find one of the many "to do" apps useful. The important point is to commit to a set of realistic goals for the day, set times for each task, and use the remaining time for writing. There will be other tasks needing to be accomplished; they are assigned time on other days. Writing is always a priority.

Elizabeth Sharp uses different notebooks for each of her multiple research projects. They are not simply logs but include musings on the topic at hand. She comments on her notebook preferences:

> I'm very particular. I have to have lined paper. It has to be a smaller, a mid-size. No particular brand but I don't like hardbound ones, because I have to carry them around so much and they get heavy. For my personal journals, I like the Moleskine [brand]. But I don't use them for my professional journals. I'm always looking for inspiration [in my professional work] so I select journals that look like they are going to help with a project. It will be just what catches my eye.

Whether you prefer to record progress in a spreadsheet, a paper notebook, or an app, there are many advantages to maintaining some sort of record keeping. How you do so is less important than finding a comfortable means to keep regular entries.

## Moderation and Working to a Deadline

Successful new faculty work regularly but with some moderation (Boice, 2000). They eschew binge writing or writing at the deadline in preference for a more methodical and constant pace. My own preference is not to work to external deadlines but rather work regularly in weekly sessions. For these sessions I have my own personal deadlines or goals but prefer working steadily toward completion rather than working in binge sessions. For instance, I often write multiple chapters of books before seeking a contract with a publisher, which always involves a deadline. When I do sign a contract, I'm clear about when I will have the book done and negotiate a deadline accordingly. Of course, there are times when we have little choice and deadlines are imposed on our work either by editors and publishers, grant administrators, or peer committees and the requirements of periodic evaluations or tenure and promotion reviews. There are certainly times when commitments to coauthors are helpful in moving a project along, but for the most part I prefer establishing a writing routine and just plodding along writing a few pages each session.

Many of my colleagues prefer to work to deadlines. In my role as editor, authors nearly always expect a deadline for completing a submission. The two questions I am consistently asked are: How long should the manuscript be? and When is it due? As Seinfeld would say, "I'm not saying there is anything wrong with that."

## Managing Criticism

The *rarae aves* of new faculty in Boice's study (2000) were able to view criticism as a means to improve their work. Here again, they are unusual. My first reaction to criticism in any form is surely irrational. With regard to reviews of journal submissions, I rant, complain to friends, question the intellect (or lack thereof) of the reviewers, and, after a week or so, get serious about how I might improve the manuscript and respond to the editor and reviewers. But the rant comes first and is a necessary part of my process, as it is for some other authors as well. I have talked with authors whose initial reaction to reviews is emotional, and some who are not quite so affected.

Harry Reis responded to my queries about his usual experience of reviews.

> My initial reaction is usually to get upset. It will either be anger at the reviewers, irritation, annoyance, or sometimes it will be feelings of inadequacy. Any of those sorts of things, and even if the letter is positive by the way.
>
> I typically will be annoyed at the nature of the changes that are being requested. I am revising one today. The reviews are fairly positive actually, but the changes are substantial and I'm annoyed at having to do it. I always tell students "put it aside until the emotional reaction is sort of washed away, and then start to deal with it."
>
> RM: *How long do you have to put something aside? More than a day?*
>
> Oh, absolutely more than a day. It's typically at least a week.

Sarah Schoppe-Sullivan replied to a similar question.

> When you see those e-mails [reviews] in your inbox. I don't know, maybe when someone has published a zillion papers, which I certainly haven't, it doesn't affect them anymore. But when I see those

e-mails, it's like my stomach drops. [laughs] I still put them away for two weeks, maybe longer if it is a really harsh one. My mentor actually taught me that. What hurts most is you read it, and then think they are kind of right. [laughs]

I don't think I'm very good at handling criticism. I mean I've gotten better over time, but it doesn't just roll of my back.

Anisa Zvonkovic responded:

I hate [reviews] and I put them aside, can't even read them. Or I read them real quick. But to be honest, when I get the reviews back, I may not even read the e-mail the first day. Even though I'm less attached than I was as a new scholar. I'm less attached to the techniques, sentences, and paragraphs, but I'm very attached to wanting to be published.

When I look at [reviews] the next day or so, I am kind of furious at every criticism. I have to kind of go through that process. I've noticed that not everyone is like that. Some of my students are not. They kind of roll up their sleeves and get to work. I have to kind of go through this process, and then when I've cooled down, which may only take a day or a couple of days, I'm ready to work.

I used to think of my initial reaction to receiving reviews as a personal weakness. Now I think of it as a process I have to go through.

Paul Amato responded:

Well when I get a decision letter, I don't open it right away. I need to screw up my courage a little bit because, well, you know, nobody likes to be criticized and reviews are unpredictable. I have no idea what to expect. It's kind of a touchy subject with me.

RM: *How long do you wait to open a decision letter?*

I won't open it up right away. I'll let it sit for an hour or two before I go back to it.

RM: *What are your first reactions?*

Well, it depends on the reviews, of course. I think that there is probably some natural defensiveness. In an ideal world, everybody would love everything that we do, but as academics we are putting ourselves out there for criticism all the time. We get evaluated a lot. So this hour or two delay is kind of psyching myself up to realize that even if the article gets a revise and resubmit, there is going to be a lot of criticism; there are going to be a lot of suggestions that come up and I need to deal with that and think about that objectively. I need to be accepting of this and gracious about it, and think about this constructively, and once I've talked myself into that frame of mind, then I'll look at the reviews. But I can't do without that mental preparation.

---

**BOX 7.2 BEST PRACTICE: RESPONDING TO REVIEWS**

- Rant first. Complain to anyone who will listen or pretend to do so. Strong negative reactions to reviews are normal.
- Get strategic. Once you calm down, think strategically. List every issue raised by the editor and reviews and plan strategy for decommissioning each concern.

---

I am glad these authors shared their experience so openly and honestly. It is comforting to know that my emotional experience of reviews is not that much different from that of some very successful authors. I don't mean to say that there is not some variation, that some experience more fret than others, but the underlying issues are similar. Being criticized is difficult and it underscores the emotional baggage of writing more generally.

All these authors share a similar experience and it includes discomfort. They are clearly aware of their typical experience, anticipate their reactions, and manage to deal with discomfort in a productive way. They all went on to explain what they do after their initial reactions, and all had similar strategies. They mine the editorial letters and reviews for the key issues and decide how to address them. In fact, they are masters at strategizing responses, and I suspect that their ability to respond to reviews and successfully publish is contingent on being aware of their initial reactions and allowing for them. They may be somewhat derailed when receiving a review, but not for long.

The emotional context of writing and the accompanying criticism that ensues is expected and part of the writing process. We simply learn to gauge our own reactions, setting aside the self-doubts but not denying their appearance. And when all else fails, I write *Somerset Maugham* over and over until things start to happen; ideas emerge; words follow.

---

**BOX 7.3 BEST WRITING PRACTICES**

- Make writing a priority with the same regularity as teaching.
- Established bounded daily or weekly writing times.
- Manage distractions like e-mail, phones, and social media.
- Set writing goals.
- Keep a writing log.
- Be adaptable. You may not find a preferred and long writing slot, but you will find briefer moments.

- Don't confuse important with merely urgent.
- You will have doubts and be too critical. This is normal. Keep writing.
- Consider collaborating with someone who writes a lot.
- Prewriting, reading, note taking, analyzing data, and thinking are part of writing.

## Summary

This chapter examined some common themes that emerge in discussions of the routine practices of successful writers. I hesitate to refer to them as "best practices" because there is so clearly variability in the practices that writers find most useful, and to be sure our needs change with the circumstances of lives. As an example, children appear and preferences adapt. Nonetheless, there are important reasons to schedule routine writing sessions and to manage intensive sessions so that we avoid the disadvantages of binge writing while accommodating personal preferences in light of professional requirements and social circumstance. Many faculty prefer longer writing sessions and are quite capable of adapting to their professional and family circumstance. Collaborations with colleagues can improve productivity and are commonplace in the conduct of complex research projects, and, not surprisingly, coauthoring manuscripts is a common strategy among productive writers. Successful writers rely on the routine of writing to find inspiration rather than relying on inspiration to fuel their writing. In the routine of writing regularly they establish pace, time for prewriting (reading and note taking), and, most importantly, throughout this process they learn to manage ever-present criticism and discomfort.

## Activities

1. When do you write? How long is a productive session?
2. How important is inspiration in your daily work?
3. How do you make the transition from reading the literature and data analysis to writing?
4. Keep a log of your progress in writing and thoughts about your work. What patterns emerge, and how can you best accommodate to them?
5. Do you prefer working to external deadlines? What are the advantages of doing so?
6. Where is the most significant criticism of your work likely to emerge? What steps can you take to manage criticism?

## Recommended Readings

Boice, R. (2000). *Advice for new faculty members: Nihil nimus*. Boston, MA: Allyn & Bacon.

Simply the best of this genre of books. Boice uses mindfulness—"calm attentiveness to the present moment" (p. 106)—to organize some basic principles of teaching and writing. Unlike similar books, Boice grounds much of his thinking in more than two decades of empirical research on faculty productivity.

Goodson, P. (2013). *Becoming an academic writer: 50 exercises for paced, productive, and powerful writing*. Los Angeles, CA: Sage.

This book is based on Goodson's experience in teaching writing workshops to new professionals. Many of the exercises are thoughtfully designed and useful.

Silvia, P. J. (2007). *How to write a lot*. Washington, DC: American Psychological Association.

A popular book on writing productively and for good reason. Silvia dispels some of the more common myths about writing and offers tips for new professionals.

Lunsford, A. A. (2010). *The St. Martin's handbook* (7th ed.). New York, NY: Bedford/St. Martin's.

It's a small tome, about 1,000 pages, and has everything you ever wanted to know about the mechanics of writing. This is the place to go if you need a review of some obscure grammatical detail, how to feed a gerund, or how to cite a synchronous communication in APA, Chicago, or MLA style. There is a brief rundown of APA style in 15 pages, and even some useful suggestions for creating PowerPoint presentations.

American Psychological Association. (2011). *Mastering APA style: Student's workbook and training guide* (6th ed.). Washington, DC: American Psychological Association.

This is a useful self-directed set of exercises on issues of writing style, grammar, punctuation, and the typical organization of term papers and research reports. If you are new to writing research reports, this guide is well designed and will answer most of your questions regarding the particulars of style, such as how to set up title pages, arrange headings, order sections of manuscripts, the use of capitalizations and hyphens, and much more. In short, the exercises cover all the details that define a professionally composed manuscript.

Strunk, W. Jr., & White, E. B. (1999). *The elements of style* (4th ed.). New York, NY: Simon & Schuster.

Get this book. It is the classic statement on great writing style in 105 pages. First published in 1959, it quickly became a favorite and remains so. It's a no-nonsense explanation of the rules of composition and great advice on matters of style. There are several newer editions. Take your pick.

Truss, L. (2003). *Eats, shoots and leaves: The zero tolerance approach to punctuation*. New York, NY: Gotham Books.

A panda walks into a bar: eats, shoots, and leaves. Or, a panda walks into a bar; eats shoots and leaves. Who would have thought a book on punctuation could be so entertaining?

"The rule is: the word 'it's' (with apostrophe) stands for 'it is' or 'it has'. If the word does not stand for 'it is' or 'it has' then what you require is 'its'. This is extremely easy to grasp. Getting your itses mixed up is the greatest solecism in the world of punctuation. No matter that you have a PhD and have read all of Henry James twice. If you still persist in writing, 'Good food at it's best', you deserve to be struck by lightning, hacked up on the spot and buried in an unmarked grave."

"Proper punctuation is both the sign and the cause of clear thinking."

"What the semicolon's anxious supporters fret about is the tendency of contemporary writers to use a dash instead of a semicolon and thus precipitate the end of the world. Are they being alarmist?"

## Notes

1. Of the 13 authors interviewed, we know nothing of their parental or familial commitments, their ranks, or teaching and service loads; three were women.
2. Moleskine is a brand of notebooks with a pedigree. The Parisian avant-garde crowd of the late 19th century used heaps of them, including Oscar Wilde, Pablo, and Ernest. They are nicely made with a stiff black cover, a ribbon for marking place, and a sewn spine that permits the ivory pages to remain flat when open. For the more digitally inclined, there is an app.

## References

Boice, R. (2000). *Advice for new faculty members: Nihil Nimus*. New York, NY: Pearson.

Goodson, P. (2013). *Becoming an academic writer: 50 exercises for paced, productive, and powerful writing*. Los Angeles, CA: Sage.

Keyes, R. (2003). *The writer's book of hope*. New York, NY: Scribner.

Kiewra, K. A., & Creswell, J. W. (2000). Conversations with three highly productive educational psychologists: Richard Anderson, Richard Mayer, and Michael Pressley. *Educational Psychology Review, 12*, 135–161.

Lamott, A. (1994). *Bird by bird: Some instructions on writing and life*. New York, NY: Anchor Books.

Marsiglio, W., & Roy, K. (2012). *Nurturing dads: Social initiatives for contemporary fatherhood*. New York, NY: Russell Sage Foundation.

Mayrath, M. C. (2008). Attributions of productive authors in educational psychology journals. *Educational Psychology Review, 20*, 41–56.

Milardo, R. M. (2010). *The forgotten kin: Aunts and uncles*. New York, NY: Cambridge University Press.

Silvia, P. J. (2007). *How to write a lot*. Washington, DC: American Psychological Association.

# 8 How Successful Writers Work: Place and Ritual

To write, we need a place of our own. It need not be palatial; comfortable and free from distractions will do. In this chapter we'll take a look at where writers work and how they manage space to suit the requirements of their writing. We'll explore forms of writing groups and the all-important rituals in which writers engage.

## Writing in Place

Faculty write in their university offices, in home offices, in public places, and in group settings. Some have rather austere requirements. Paul Silvia writes daily at home with a simple desk and chair and no Internet access. "The best kind of self control is to avoid situations that require self-control," he says (2007, p. 22). His desk is uncluttered and more like a table without drawers. The walls are unadorned. Paul speaks of his early years writing a slew of journal articles from a folding chair and matching folding table. I recently asked him whether his writing place has changed, particularly after becoming a parent to two children. He responded:

> My writing space has actually become more Spartan over the years. When I got babies, they took over the writing room and turned it into a museum of sorts for dinosaur and truck toys. We don't have an extra room, so I put an old lounge chair and ottoman at the end of a big passageway that links two parts of the house. So now there isn't even a desk or a door to shut.
>
> When I'm writing at work, it is in a grim, half-abandoned lab room that was left vacant and forgotten when a senior faculty member retired. It feels like the old days: I have a particleboard table with a 70s fake wood grain top, an old plastic chair, and a printer on the floor.
>
> One change, though, is that my last couple of computers came with built-in wireless cards—this has been a blessing and a curse. Grrr.
>
> Overall, I really think people put too much stock in finding the right place, the right spot, the right tools. We have all that we need.[1]

For Paul, a room with a view is not at all essential; a printer on the floor is nice. Not all writers are quite so Spartan in their space requirements (or nearly as productive). Successful writers characteristically select comfortable writing spots, often facing a window with a view (Boice, 2000). They frequently display favored objects or art in their writing spaces. My colleague Denise displays pastoral watercolors by a local artist we both admire. I write from a home office. The room has a desk (with drawers), comfortable seat, bookcases, comfortable reading chair, photos of friends, some art (including a mounted Great Spangled Fritillary—a gift from a friend), and heaps of stuff. The view is of forest, snippet of lawn, and, off to the southeast, a field with a blanket of snow in the winter and by summer a riot of black-eyed Susans. I have a small bird feeder for seed-eaters affixed to a window by my desk, and, once the warmer weather rolls around, a small feeder for hummers. There are plenty of potential distractions, but somehow I find the space all the more comforting. It's an easy place to work. More recently, I have been writing from my campus office and from unoccupied seminar rooms, which I scheduled for this purpose simply because there are no distractions and no objects in the spaces imbued with emotional ties. Sometimes Spartan surroundings, or at least surroundings in which we have no particular emotional attachments, are a very good idea.

While working on this book, I spent time talking with many authors. Bill Marsiglio and I spoke via Skype for well over an hour. Bill was at his home office, where he does most of his writing. At the end of interview Bill turned the camera linked to his computer around so I could witness the Floridian view from his window. The same view he has while writing. The picture was of a rural countryside including a barn, a lawn interspersed with native plants like palmetto and surrounded by a copse of flora common to north-central Floridian landscapes. Perhaps Bill, like me, found a room with a view comforting.

A few weeks ago I was talking with Patti, who regularly cuts my hair. I'd guess Patti is about mid-50's, lives with her partner, and has a small dog. As we chatted between snips, she asked what I was doing. I told her I was writing daily and working on a new book. She asked if I went down to the coast to write. The Maine coastline is dramatic, pristine, and with a national park just down the road. I assume she thought writers search out inspiration, and what better place to do it than at the open expanse of sky and wave. The comment surprised me, but maybe it shouldn't have. We tend to think that writing requires inspiration, and I suppose it does in some ways, but mostly it just requires lots of time, concentration, a library, a passel of data, and some hard work. It's nice to have a comfortable place to do it, and a wee bit of distance from the wind and wilds with walls, windows, and a place to plug in. I do find the coast of Maine inspiring, but it doesn't really help with the writing. "Serious writers write, inspired or not. Over time they discover that routine is a better friend to them than inspiration" (Keyes, 2003, p. 49).

Oddly enough, nearly all the writers I spoke with prefer writing from places other than their university offices, although there were exceptions. Harry Reis writes from his university office and never before 10:00 A.M. He prefers late afternoons and early evenings, when child-care responsibilities permit. Faculty who typically write from home offices or in some cases public venues are far more typical. Paul Amato shared:

> I have a complete division between my home and university office. My home office is for my writing. I have everything set up here. I have all my books, files, data files. My office at the university is for teaching, committee work, and meeting with students. That works well for me.

The reasons faculty preferred writing at home were simple enough. A university office was associated with too many distractions, interruptions, and, in some cases, an unpleasant atmosphere. Heather Helms explained, "I need to go to a place where my mind feels clear and uncluttered." When I asked if that was ever her university office, she just laughed. Given that writing is part of our professional assignments, it is a bit peculiar that so many find such work impossible at our places of employment.

Not all faculty write from offices or desks. Anisa Zvonkovic prefers to write from spaces in her home. She recently moved from Texas Tech to a position at Virginia Tech.

> When I work at home I really am a kitchen table person, and I like that, but the downside is that I am kind of messy. I think writing is messy; I have stuff out all over the place.
>
> I only had one house with a [home office] and it was a horrific mess always. As a result I don't really look for homes with a home office, and I think that is different for my colleagues here at Virginia Tech and my colleagues at Texas Tech. Pretty much everybody had a study room in their house. That never really worked for me. I'm from a big family. I had three brothers and we had a very loud house, very verbal, people talking all the time. We would have multiple conversations going at the same time. I get really nervous when I'm in a quiet space, and isolated from interaction. Actually a lot of noise is good. My friend Elizabeth is like that as well. She had five brothers, and we talked about how we do better [working and writing] in a public place where people are moving around us. A coffee place or whatever is good because I just like to have action going on around me.

Rachelle Brunn-Bevel prefers to write from her dining room table, where, as she says, "I can spread out more." She then paused and added:

> But I think really it's that I feel less confined, because the kitchen is right there and the living room is close by and I can see all that.

Whereas when I'm in my home office I kind of feel limited and I think that is why I like to go there to proof because then I definitely don't want any kind of distraction.

Sarah Shoppe-Sullivan writes from her home, usually in the mornings after seeing her daughter off to school. "I just sit on my couch with my laptop. I curl up and write. Occasionally I'll go to a local coffee shop."

Elizabeth Sharp prefers writing in a coffee shop and has a clear preference for the type of shop and where she positions herself in that space. When I spoke with her, she was on an extended leave from her home at Texas Tech and working abroad and writing daily. She tries to get to the coffee shop by 7:30 each morning but sometimes doesn't arrive until 8:00. I asked her why she preferred coffee shops for writing.

> The coffee is a treat for me and especially when I'm writing. I like to have coffee, and sometimes if I am really struggling I'll get myself a cappuccino, but usually just a coffee with cream. The coffee shops are a way to help me focus with just one paper, one task in mind. In the coffee shop, it is really important where I sit and so I have to have my back against the wall. I have to have a big table or two tables together, and I have to be able to see everything in the space, and the space has to be kind of big. I don't like small coffee shops.
> RM: *Why big?*
> I'm not really sure. I'm just much more comfortable.
> I like public spaces because there are distractions but I don't have to attend to them. At [Texas] Tech there was always someone at the door visiting or an e-mail to answer. So my use of coffee shops was partly to decrease all these distractions because I would tell myself not to touch an e-mail while at a coffee shop. In one coffee shop I can't get on the Internet, so it's built in that I can't access those distractions. I would also work at my home office in the early morning before the coffee shops open or late at night when I'm feeling inspired.

Some authors write in plain old peculiar places. The social psychologist Zick Rubin is said to have written in a McDonald's restaurant, perhaps one near Harvard Yard, where he worked, and therefore intellectually supersized. Novelist Jay Parini wrote in Lou's Dinner, of which he said: "What I liked about Lou's was the distant clatter of plates, the purr of conversations and the occasional interruption of a friend" (Keyes, 2003, p.154). Sounds charming.

## Structuring Time and Place

Elizabeth prefers to write in bounded sessions comprised of a minimum of 25 minutes of concentrated writing followed by a 5-minute break, during which she refreshes her beverage, checks her e-mail, or simply stretches. She executes a minimum of four 25-minute sessions before taking a longer break. The system actually has a name—*Pomodoro*—and of course an app for smart phones. It is essentially a time management strategy and means to establish priorities and act on them. Elizabeth finds the structure helpful in focusing and prioritizing her writing, particularly since she typically works on several projects at any given time. By the way, although I don't actually time my writing sessions, I typically write for about 45 minutes before taking a short break, and this has nearly always been my preferred style. Twenty-five-minute sessions are too brief, and anything longer than 60 minutes is likely a bit too long. You may find a slightly shorter or longer session suits your particular style. Incidentally, I did try the *Pomodoro* app and found it unhelpful. My body seems to self-regulate well enough without the helper.

Perhaps more importantly, Elizabeth's use of the *Pomodoro* technique is her response to a need. She has multiple writing projects, all challenging, and all competing for her time. This method is her current attempt to meet the challenges her writing presents while being responsive to her personal preferences and, in doing so, maximize her productivity. Productive faculty are generally well aware of their challenges in writing and are willing to experiment in finding ways to meet those challenges and alter their common practice to meet current circumstance.

## Managing Comfort

Some writers have preferences for their writing attire, a complete surprise to me. Pajamas are commonly preferred, or, in one instance, a particular writing *leisure suit*. One very productive scholar shared: "Shall I say I'm usually in my pajamas when I do this [write]? [She laughs.] I love pj's." She was quick to add, "if I'm not at work or going out." She then offered, "I have a colleague who also writes in her pajamas." My contemporaries are in good company. The Canadian author and Nobel Prize winner Alice Munro wrote in her nightclothes, as did the prolific and immensely popular British author Beryl Bainbridge (Keyes, 2003). Martha Grimes, best known for her mystery series involving Richard Jury of Scotland Yard, wrote in bed with 14 fountain pens with 14 shades of ink to foster different perspectives and keep boredom at bay. I guess if you write 20-plus novels about Richard Jury, Scotland Yard, then boredom might be an issue, and who doesn't like a change of hue now and again?

None of the men I spoke with have particular sartorial preferences when writing, nor do I ever recall a male colleague sharing with me what he wears when he writes, even the few (and now dwindling number) who are pretty new-ageish. Nonetheless, there are exceptions: Tom Wolfe is said to write in a turtleneck and khakis, attire in which he would be loath to appear in public and thus anchoring him to his desk. J. D. Salinger wrote in overalls in a cabin reserved for writing. It is curious how gender creeps into the most mundane of issues, and paradoxically demonstrates just how interesting the ordinary can be. Incidentally, I usually wear blue jeans when writing, but then I generally wear them at home for just about everything. So I guess I can't say I have a writing outfit per se, but I can say I currently own eight pairs of jeans, all in working order.

A good friend shared with me that when she was about to take a year-long research leave she shopped for a comfortable set of writing clothes. She found something and later recommended the outfit to colleagues who were also planning leaves to concentrate on writing. She referred to the outfit as "lounge wear, something between jammies and workout wear." She said she wore the outfit every day when writing. I forgot to ask about the hue. If you are interested, give me a shout and I can put you in touch.

## Creating Meaning: Matching Place, Ambiance, and Purpose

Although productive faculty varied in the precise details of their preferences for writing times and places, they shared some essential qualities. Faculty were, in all cases, very aware of their preferences. They knew where they preferred to write and why. They understood their personal needs, however quirky or idiosyncratic, and they acted on them without much question. The spaces in which they worked sometimes varied quite intentionally with the needs of the task at hand. Rachelle preferred writing from her dining room, but editing from her home office. Anisa preferred writing at home, but at times vastly preferred a public venue, particularly when rewriting. "A different place helps to put on a different perspective," she says. And when she is writing grants, yet another element comes to play.

> When I'm grant writing, I'll have a CD or collection of music that I play. Because my work on grants is a little different from my other writing, there is a deadline, and I've got to work on it every day, and if not, then almost every day, and I have this Celtic punk band [I like]. And for some reason it has really worked for me. I found that I had high energy and worked really quickly when I had it on. It really helped me to focus.
>
> Amadan is high-energy music and a little angry. And I had a certain anger at the whole grant process and how unfair it is, and few people ever got funded, and I just had a kind of head of steam about the whole endeavor and for some reason this music really helped me. Other than that, I usually listen to instrumental music [when writing], because lyrics can be distracting.

In this instance, the music is matched to the nature of the work and the writer's temperament regarding that work. Purposeful manipulations of writing environments require an awareness of individual preferences or needs, the special requirements of the work, and one's attitudes or interpretations of that work. Productive faculty are aware of these issues at some level and act accordingly.[2]

Some masterfully regulate their comfort levels by manipulating place and personal attire, or reward themselves for noteworthy or even daily accomplishments. These instances of active self-monitoring recognize the inherent difficulty of writing and are designed to ease the burden and facilitate productivity. The masters are exceptional in the work they do and how they arrange completing that work.

Writing spaces are imbued with meaning, and therefore can serve different purposes. Rachelle prefers the open space of her dining room with an open view of other parts of her home for writing and the development of ideas, but she moves to a separate room with a more restricted view to edit. Elizabeth—and, to a certain extent, Anisa—find comfort writing in socially active settings.

All the faculty were keenly aware of the need to manage distractions, and chief among such distractions were e-mail, visitors, and other tasks that compete for attention. They arrived at different solutions—for instance, working off campus—but they clearly recognized the issue and the need to manage distractions. A colleague shared with me her recent view of e-mail and the kind of distraction it presents.

> Yes, I check e-mail all the time. I remember when I thought it was really great, a quick way to get things done, but I don't feel that way at all anymore. It's definitely a time sink. You almost never think it's going to be that way, but it is.

I typically start the working day with a check of e-mail but then turn it and the phone off while writing.

## The Company We Keep: Writing in Groups

In the end, writing is between you and the page, an inherently asocial activity, but it can be helpful to have companion travelers and to write in a neighborhood of other writers. I recently spoke with a bright assistant professor of child and family studies who prefers writing in public settings like libraries and coffee shops, and often with a colleague. She says,

> I make a date with one other person to set up our computers in the same place (usually a coffee shop) and work on different things while we are in the same space. We usually don't talk to each other very much except when we greet each other and break for a meal or to

walk back to our offices. The point is to heighten external pressure to write at a particular time rather than actually share ideas, though sometimes it's nice to ask or answer a quick question!

David Brunsma has taken the idea of writing in groups to a new level. David organizes weekly writing sessions with an open invitation to faculty to attend. He refers to these sessions as **write-ins** where faculty come together to write for two hours with the expectation that the group atmosphere will enhance everyone's productivity.

> I started these [gatherings] I call "write-ins" so it is kind of a takeoff on sit-ins. I kind of like the political association. The idea behind it is to get a group of people sitting around a table in the same space, kind of feeding off of each other's collective energies. In academia we all have to write.
>
> So I set up this structure so that I could both send the message to the people I was mentoring that writing is fundamental to what we do, fundamental part of scholarship and teaching. . . . Writing has to be a habit, a practice that you get into. As I thought about how to construct a space or some sort of approach that would send that message while also allowing me to continue my writing. So I created these things called write-ins. Right now I'm doing three per week [each session is two hours].
>
> It is just a basic time that anybody can come and we sit down, and when nine o'clock starts we just start working on our projects. We don't really talk. That's not completely fair to say; at times we do, but by and large the goal is to turn off e-mail and Facebook. You can keep Internet for Google Scholar and other things you might need, but nothing else.
>
> Some people put on headphones to kind of drown out the environment a little bit. But what is really happening is there is a kind of collective camaraderie, a kind of collective energy, even a collective soft, but important, accountability system that is built in there too. The people who have ended up being regulars, because it doesn't work for everybody, say this is the way to do it.
>
> The other thing that is as important, if not more important, is simply the idea that one needs to set aside blocks of time to write, and sometimes that means that you will sit in front of a blank screen, but at least you are in that good pattern. You are not going to wait for the inspiration. You're going to get in the habit of writing a little bit at a time.

David's approach is unique among social science writers and clearly principled. As a senior faculty member, he understands the importance of writing and the need to establish a routine writing schedule, and he pairs this with a sense of social responsibility for the success of his junior colleagues. Rachelle Brunn-Bevel participates in the weekly write-ins; I asked her how she liked writing in a group setting.

> I actually like it quite a bit because—David uses the term *collective energy*—but there really is something about seeing other people working that makes you want to write more, especially on days when you may be struggling on a particular piece and you might be tempted to just say: "I'm just not going to write today; I'm going to do something else." But the pressure of being around other people who are also struggling with writing is for me helpful, so that is really why I like going to those groups.
>
> We usually talk for a few minutes at the very beginning as we are setting up our computers and plugging in, usually about whatever it is that we are going to work on that day, and then again as we are packing up, something about what we accomplished as we were writing.

---

**BOX 8.1  WRITER'S RESOURCE: HOW TO ORGANIZE A FACULTY WRITE-IN**

Arrange for a room with a view, dedicate some time, and send this message (or something similar) to your colleagues.

### Faculty Write-In Sessions

Host: Professor Moriarty, Professor Emeritus of Nonesuch

Writing is an important part of what we all do as academics. Sometimes we need encouragement, accountabilities, and cultures to support that activity. It is about developing good practices and habits.

The Write-In is an idea about accountability, collegiality, and a collective energy devoted to writing.

Twice per week, for about two hours, we will meet with our laptops and accessories, sit down, and write. End of story. No talking. No e-mail. No Facebook. Come to as many or as few sessions as you wish. We take a coffee or beverage break about midway through a session.

Graduate students are welcome.

Feel free to contact me should you have questions: rhd360@maine.edu or 581-3128

*Spring Sessions*
Wednesdays and Thursdays 1–3
229 Merrill Hall

*NB*: Kudos to David Brunsma at Virginia Tech for developing and sharing this method.

Some faculty develop writing groups where participants share details on their current projects, and perhaps reading material and other resources on productive writing strategies. Often graduate students are included, and the sessions become a way for participants to share experience and support and mentor one another. Cheryl Logan and Paul Silvia began a writer's group for faculty in which participants share short-term goals, celebrate accomplishments, and generally provide a forum to discuss writing (Silvia, 2007). Tanya Golash-Boza developed a Facebook page entitled "Daily Writing Updates" to use as a platform to support members' writing, by posting short-term (e.g., daily, weekly) writing goals and pairing them with progress reports. Elizabeth Sharp schedules writing retreats with colleagues, usually in highly desirable settings (e.g., a favored city or rural setting). These are multiday sessions in which participants work on their joint or individual writing projects. In all of these instances, faculty actively seek out ways to support their writing by creating or joining writing communities.

One common strategy is to share drafts with colleagues to invite feedback. This is certainly a fine tactic. Having a trusted colleague read a draft can help identify areas needing attention and lead to significant improvements, and it is far better to discover inadequacies—even relatively minor issues like lapses in grammar, typographical errors, or missing references—before submitting an article for review. I recently received an article for review with grammatical errors in the title and abstract. This is not an ideal way to impress your editor or reviewers. In this case, having a colleague review the manuscript before submission probably would have revealed the simple shortcomings, and the colleague might have added more substantive suggestions as well. I would not recommend asking a former advisor to comment on a new manuscript unless you previously discussed the issue. It is well to recall that reading and editing a manuscript is time-consuming, easily a multihour session that could be spent on writing. Consider asking a peer to read your work and offer to return the favor.

## Ritual

Writing often feels chaotic, nearly impossible, and just plain ornery as we try to wrestle ideas and words into some semblance of meaningful prose. Perhaps for these reasons writers seem to quickly develop rituals in their writing habits that are well defined and purposeful. When asked, my colleagues easily and immediately respond to my questions about their use of computers, paper, and writing implements. Nearly all have very particular preferences, some are a bit self-conscious about sharing the details of their preferences not wanting to appear "silly" or all that peculiar.

On writing mediums, nearly all use large screens or laptops. I have one colleague who writes all her drafts longhand on lined paper, only later transcribing the draft onto a laptop, at which point she edits her work.

Most use laptops, and some use large monitors or multiple monitors. As usual, there are occasional exceptions. One colleague shared: "Recently I had to give a talk to a developmental group, and even though it was based on some [of my own] recently published work, I had to write out the talk by hand on a legal pad. For some reason, I couldn't do it on a computer." Sometimes it's just a good idea to go with the flow wherever it takes us. Faculty use lined or scrap paper to jot down notes or sketch conceptual drawings as they work. Some carry conveniently styled notebooks wherever they go to quickly record ideas as they come.[3] One colleague uses a smart phone for this purpose, which seems like a great idea. For many, the routine of moving from writing on a screen and sketching notes on paper is an integral part of the process. Paul Amato commented:

> Usually I write at a screen. I take notes to myself on paper. It might be outlines or diagrams or sometimes it's keywords when I'm trying to think things through. If I'm trying to think through how a series of ideas are logically related, I'll write down a couple of words or a brief idea and draw arrows between them, and make little pictures like a Venn diagram to help my thinking. Those diagrams don't appear in an article, but I've used them to help me think through how things are related. I'll have a pad of paper next to my computer screen. I'll write for 15 minutes, then stop and scratch on my pad, then go back to writing again.

For Paul and perhaps other writers, the physical process of moving from one medium to another helps to formulate and organize ideas. Nearly all writers I spoke with take notes as they write, but none used note-taking software or created an ephemeral digital notes file. Typically I keep a brief outline and relevant notes in a manuscript or chapter file, usually immediately following the section I'm working on. As I complete writing on a particular issue, the relevant notes are erased. (A separate and permanent file contains notes on readings.)

On writing implements, nearly all the writers I spoke with have clear preferences for a pencil or a pen, but typically not both. Within the general categories of pen and pencil are some more particular preferences. I've not encountered any especially predictive personality attributes or links to early developmental experiences, but the preferences are clear.

- I don't use mechanical pencils. We have them lying around [the house] but I prefer lead pencils. I didn't have a lot of pencils until I had kids. With kids you've got pencils littered all over the place.
- RM: Do you prefer writing with a pen or pencil?
  Pen.
  RM: *Never a pencil?*

No.

RM: *Any reason?*

No. I just like pens.

- I always use a pencil, sharp with a good eraser. My daughter has this whole caddy of pencils, so I usually just pick up her pencils and use them.
- A pen with purple ink. They are the Pilot brand, very fine, rolling ball pens. I buy them by the bunch.
- Always a pencil.
- I have a real fondness for fine point pens, and oddly enough I feel like I can write better and think better if I have the appropriate instrument. I have a distinct preference for these extra fine point pens. [He'll use others if the preferred type is unavailable, but not for sketching.] I suppose an artist wants a certain kind of brush; [with the right pen] I feel comfortable and I feel my mind works better, more relaxed, and the words are more likely to flow or the diagram I'm working on will seem better. When I go to a store, if they have [a pen] on display I'll go test it out to see if I like it. There have been times when I accidentally bought the wrong one and have been very annoyed.
- I almost always use a pen. The only reason I might use a pencil is if my pen is missing.
- I'm very particular about this. It's a pen, and I usually have a favorite pen that I have to have and usually it's purple or black but not always. I don't like fine points; I like more of a mid-point, a thicker line. I have to have my special pen at the time [when I'm writing in a notebook]. My partner has bought me pens, and he knows which ones to get and which ones I like.

I use pencils, and not just any old pencil. I vastly prefer Palomino Blues with a white eraser; I also like a Blackwing 602 (with a black eraser). Both are nominally a number 2 lead (HB), but the Palominos are a bit harder lead and the Blackwings a bit softer but smoother writing, and the erasers are exceptional. Indispensable is a fine sharpener. There you have it. The ultimate truth is revealed.

---

**BOX 8.2 BEST PRACTICE: WRITING ROUTINE**

- Identify your preferred writing places and times.
- Consider starting or joining a writing group.
- Learn your quirks.
- Adjust place and ritual as needed.

## Summary

This chapter explored the importance of place and where faculty typically conduct their work. Some use university offices for writing, but most prefer home offices or more social spaces in the home such as kitchen tables. A surprising number write in social, public settings, and coffee shops seem to dominate here. None mentioned writing in a pub or similar venue, although I imagine surely some do. All seemed well aware of their particular writing process and what it required. Occasionally they matched place and ambiance with the requirements of the writing. Anisa prefers writing at home on the spread of her kitchen table, but writing grants requires an entirely different venue with musical accompaniment in the form of a punk Celtic band. Some wrote independently, but they did so in group settings either with another colleague or with an established writers' group. In these cases, authors were quick to note the benefits in the spillover of public demonstrations of commitment to writing and the accompanying benefit of establishing social comparisons as they viewed others engaged in writing. In their selections of place, writers engage in fairly well-established sets of rituals that include wonderfully particular choices in their selection of writing dress, implements, and platforms.

## Activities

1.   What kind of rituals do you engage in when writing? How do they serve (or fail to serve) your needs in completing a document?
2.   Interview a few colleagues about their writing practice. How do their practices serve the needs of their writing?
3.   In what ways does gender influence the practice of writing? Do any of your colleagues have preferences for what they wear when writing?
4.   How does parenting influence writing?
5.   How long is a productive writing session, and how do you know when to end a session?

## Recommended Readings

### *Finding Your Muse*

King, S. 2000. *On writing: A memoir of the craft.* New York, NY: Simon & Schuster.

Stephen aims to write 2,000 words per day. I'm happy with 250, and that's a good day, but still there is similarity in our experience, and maybe with yours. Here are some of my favorite quips, but then I love to read about writing.

"When you write a story, you're telling yourself the story. When you rewrite, your main job is taking out all the things that are not the story."

"You must not come lightly to the blank page."

Lamott, A. (1994). *Bird by bird: Some instructions on writing and life.* New York, NY: Anchor Books.

Few write about the craft with more insight, humor, and exceptional metaphor. Although written by a novelist for other novelists, the commentary on the essentials of writing applies to all writers, fiction and nonfiction alike.

## Notes

1. A photo of Paul's office is on the *Crafting Scholarship* Facebook page, as well as other office photos. Feel free to add your own. There are no prizes, but . . . well, we are all a bit curious.
2. Boice (2000) reported that productive faculty in his research rarely, if ever, played music while working. The faculty I interviewed occasionally did so. Julie preferred classical, Rachelle and I jazz, and Anisa matched musical style to the nature of the work. Stephen King, by the way, prefers the ilk of Guns N' Roses.
3. I have posted photos of writers' notebooks on the *Crafting Scholarship* Facebook page. Please consider adding to the collection.

## References

Boice, R. (2000). *Advice for new faculty members: Nihil Nimus.* New York: Pearson.

Keyes, R. (2003). *The writer's book of hope.* New York, NY: Scribner.

Silvia, P. J. (2007). *How to write a lot.* Washington, DC: American Psychological Association.

# Part III
# Reviewing and Editing

# 9   Crafting Effective Peer Reviews

*In general, I prefer the term "blended" rather than "reconstituted" when referring to stepfamilies. Reconstituted sounds too much like orange juice.*
Anonymous reviewer

Writing masterful reviews is an important skill and a central part of the peer-review process. This chapter details the peer-review process with journal submissions and, to a lesser extent, other applications of peer review such as evaluating grant applications. Masterful and effective reviews have the dual purpose of informing an editor's decision about the disposition of a manuscript and a more generative intent to help authors improve their work. We describe the core elements of writing masterful reviews, including the evaluation of content and the tone or delivery of that critical commentary. We approach the topic with the implicit belief that writing effective reviews benefits the profession and the quality of published work in addition to informing the reviewer's own success in writing for publication. Quite simply the skills involved in writing great reviews are center stage in writing great articles, books, and grant applications.

## Purposeful Reviews

Peer-reviewed journals vary widely in their specializations, although the core principles of peer review remain the same and serve as the foundation for publication in the sciences, behavioral, social, and otherwise. An editor receives a submission from an author, or team of authors, who wishes to have a manuscript considered for publication. The editor in turn calls on reviewers who have the appropriate expertise to review the submission; usually two to four reviewers are assigned to each submission, including at least one member of the journal's editorial board. Typically the identity of authors and reviewers are not shared with one another, and the process is blinded, at least in principle. There is some variation in the process. For instance, some journals employ deputy editors who solicit reviews and have full decision-making responsibilities regarding the disposition of manuscripts, and others rely on editorial teams to make final decisions. For some journals with high submission rates, an editorial team selects only a portion of manuscripts for full peer review and many are rejected without review. All these organizational structures and practices share the same purpose of introducing the expertise and counsel of peers in the decision to publish a manuscript.

Peer review serves to inform an editor's decision and more generally advise authors and help to improve their work. Reviewers play a major role in both purposes. By virtue of their expertise, which editors may not share, reviewers inform the decision to pursue the development of a manuscript. Reviewers also play an important part in helping to craft an article by offering authors suggestions for improvements and thereby elevating the potential contribution. This dual function of informing the decision-making process for editors as well as guiding authors in the development of their work defines the essential elements of high-quality reviews. This dual function suggests that reviews should be both critical and generative, identifying the strengths and weakness of a manuscript (cf. Tesser & Martin, 2006).

---

**BOX 9.1  WRITER'S RESOURCE: HOW REVIEWERS VIEW THEIR CRAFT**

Over 1 million articles are published in peer-reviewed journals annually. That's a lot of reading and requires a yeoman's effort of the part of reviewers, who essentially volunteer their time and expertise. In 2009, approximately 4,000 scholars, who review for a wide array of journals in the sciences, responded to questions about the importance and utility of the peer-review process (Sense About Science, 2010).

Reviewers are surprisingly positive about their experience. The vast majority, about 80% or more, report being satisfied or very satisfied with their experience of reviewing, and those in the social sciences are no exception. There appears to be little dissatisfaction. The "very dissatisfied" group represents about 1% of respondents.

Reviewers are speedy; 86% complete their reviews in a month or less. Editors report a bit longer completion times, averaging about four to six weeks for the journals published by the National Council on Family Relations.

Scholars overwhelmingly believe peer review improves the quality of published papers (77%) and that the process selects the best manuscripts for publication (61%). They also agree in large measure that the formal training of reviewers should improve the quality of reviews (67%), which is rather encouraging.

Reviewing an article can mean reading complex material that requires considerable specialized knowledge, and can consume several hours, about six on average. So why do scholars donate their time? When asked why they review, responses fall into two camps. Scholars report completing reviews for generative reasons. They wish to reciprocate the benefits they have gained from having their own work reviewed, and otherwise help to improve the work of their colleagues and science more generally. In addition, scholars report they review manuscripts because they may accrue some personal benefit.

*Table 9.1* Why Scholars Complete Peer Reviews

| | |
|---|---|
| It will increase the likelihood of my future papers being accepted. | 16% |
| I believe it will increase my chances of being offered a role on the journal's editorial team. | 30% |
| It is an opportunity to build a relationship with an editor. | 33% |
| I will gain personal recognition from reviewing. | 34% |
| I believe it will enhance my reputation or further my career. | 46% |
| I want to reciprocate the benefit gained when others reviewed my papers. | 70% |
| I enjoy seeing new work ahead of publication. | 72% |
| I enjoy being able to help improve a paper. | 85% |
| I like playing my part as a member of the academic community. | 85% |

*Note.* Data retrieved from *Peer Review Survey 2009: Full Report*, by Sense about Science, 2010, London, UK: Author.

As a new professional, I submitted an empirical report on my dissertation research to the *Journal of Personality and Social Psychology*, an ambitious undertaking, or so I thought at the time. A few months later the editor's decision letter appeared, asking for a revision and resubmission, which for most journals is the best possible response. Of course I was delighted at first but then a bit flummoxed. The reviewers' comments were nearly as long as the paper, one review was eight single-spaced pages. I was to learn later, after the paper was published, that the reviewers were well-established social psychologists Ellen Berscheid and Ladd Wheeler. They had clearly read the paper carefully and suggested sensible revisions to each section. Based upon their commentary, I completely reanalyzed the data, added secondary analyses to bolster the core findings, and in general considered each of their recommendations in turn. The paper was accepted after one revision (Milardo, Johnson, & Huston, 1983). In this instance, the reviews were thoughtful, germane, and reasonable. They were important in helping to improve the paper, and presumably helpful to the editor. It doesn't always go this well.

Much later in my career, I sent a paper to a leading journal for review. The reviews included a mix of sensible and not-so-sensible criticism. For instance, one reviewer took issue with my use of the term "uncling" (the paper was indeed about uncles and their relationships with nephews), and the other reviewer quite remarkably recommended a slew of additional references to the work of one individual, which he believed should have been included in the manuscript. Normally such a suggestion is reasonable. In this instance, it was just plain odd. Most of the suggested citations were included in the original submission. I wondered whether the reviewer had actually read the paper, a fair question, I thought, given the circumstance. Nonetheless, the reviews included a mix of useful and quite insightful suggestions for improving the paper as well as some that I thought were unhelpful. Without a doubt, the manuscript benefited from the more germane commentaries of the reviewers. The original manuscript was substantially revised, resubmitted, and accepted for publication (Milardo, 2005). The entire process was not ideal in that some of the reviewers' comments where unhelpful and a bit distracting. Ideally, it is the responsibility of an editor to guide an author in separating the chaff from the wheat, but in the end successfully responding to reviews falls upon authors.

Imperfect review cycles are to be expected, although I hope they are not routine. Developing a comprehensive and well-tempered approach to reviewing manuscripts is an important skill that can be helpful to authors and editors. Successful authors become skilled in responding to reviews, recognizing the important material, benefiting from that commentary, and communicating with editors and indirectly with reviewers. As an editor, I rely on skillful and thorough reviews, and I am keenly aware of the importance of my role in directing the efforts of an author to the necessary and more important elements of reviewers' commentaries.

## The Elements of Masterful and Ineffective Reviews

To better understand the components of masterful reviews, and not-so-effective reviews, I analyzed the content of reviews received over a one-year period by the *Journal of Family Theory & Review*. Reviewers for this journal, as is the case for many journals in the behavioral and social sciences, are typically members of the journal's board and a legion of scholars who have volunteered to review for the journal. For each review, the editorial office maintains records on the time it takes a reviewer to complete a review, and I rate the quality of each review, with 1 denoting substandard quality, and 3 for a superior review. Reviewers who consistently receive ratings of 1 to 1.5 are rarely invited to complete reviews in the future, whereas reviewers with consistent ratings of 2 to 3 are highly regarded and make important contributions to editors and authors. Many journals use similar systems to effectively manage the enterprise. For the present purpose, I selected 111 reviews randomly, stripped any identifying material, and compared reviews with high ratings to reviews with low ratings. The ratings are consistently applied subjective evaluations that permit a means to compare reviews, identify common characteristics, and quantify the elements of effective reviews based upon a systematic analysis.

Masterful reviews differ from the not-so-useful reviews in several ways. The best reviews are detailed and, as a result, fairly long. Quality reviews—in this instance, reviews with ratings of 2.5 to 3—average 865 words and some exceed 3,000 words. In comparison, reviews with low ratings (1–1.5) are substantially shorter, averaging 250 words and sometimes significantly shorter. Our current record is a scant 15 words. Brevity may be the soul of wit, but it is not the substance of masterful reviewing.

## Scant Reviews

Reviews that fall short are of two varieties. One variety begins with an overall comment about the quality of the manuscript, which may be very positive, or very negative, and little else.[1]

> From my perspective, this manuscript is very useful and interesting. I think it is a contribution to the field about what we might usefully be doing in incorporating same-sex parenting into our research, our theorizing, and our teaching. For me, among the many strengths of the article is the review of the etymological history of the terms like heterogamy. The review not only makes it easier to disinvest from common current usages of the terms in the field, it also helps the reader to recognize that usage of the terms has been historically diverse and culturally embedded.
>
> I also like the piece as a teaching piece. Not only did I learn from it but I think it is well written and succinct and no doubt will be useful to students as well as more established scholars.
>
> I did not see any technical errors in the paper except that the reference list is not in APA style.

There is nothing inherently wrong with this review. The reviewer states what she or he likes about the manuscript and how it will be useful to readers. The problem is the lack of commentary that would help the author to improve the manuscript. The review simply lacks depth, and this is certainly the most common feature of reviews viewed (and rated) as less than useful.

Let's take another example. In this instance, the review is longer and includes more direct commentary, but the substance focuses on editorial issues, the use of language, and matters of grammar or style.

This was a well written and comprehensive manuscript. I highly recommend it for publication with some changes:

(1) The first sentence of the abstract misuses the term risk factor and is likely to confuse readers.
(2) Page 3, 1st paragraph: Consider changing the two uses of the word "adolescent" to "youth."
(3) Page 3, 2nd paragraph: Please elaborate more on what specific confounding variables you are referring to.
(4) Page 3, 2nd paragraph: Spell-out the Smoker et al. (2009) reference since it is the first time that it is being presented.
(5) Page 3, last paragraph: Spell-out the Beatrix et al. (2013) reference since it is the first time that it is being presented.
(6) Page 4, end of page: Please elaborate more on the contextual issues you are referring to.
(7) You tend to use the word "plurality" a lot throughout the manuscript.
(8) Page 7, last paragraph: revise the word "incomprehensible" to read "comprehensible," which is more in keeping with your meaning.
(9) The implications of your research are potentially broad and could apply to other minorities. Consider adding a sentence related to this point.

Overall, this manuscript will make a wonderful contribution to the field.

Like the previous example, this review begins with a **positive start-up**, a statement that compliments some aspect of the manuscript at the outset; not all do. The reviewer concentrates on relatively minor issues regarding word choice and the style of citations. Suggestions regarding word choices and other comments that increase the clarity of an idea are useful, but such comments should not replace an evaluation of the core conceptual model faming the paper, the core theory or hypothesis, the choice and interpretation of analyses, the integration with pertinent literature, or other critical elements of any theoretical paper, review, case study, or empirical report. Incidentally, there were seven spelling errors in the original review. An occasional error is not an issue. A pattern of errors influences my confidence in the content of the review and the care with which the reviewer approached the assignment. In addition, all the comments referred to the first 7 pages of a 30-page manuscript. Our confidence in the thoroughness of the review is further eroded.

This example is possibly one of the briefest we have received to date. "This is an excellent piece of work. I look forward to seeing it in print." In fact, there were four reviewers assigned to this manuscript: Two recommended rejection, one suggested a major revision, and one was ready to accept as is. Perhaps this latter reviewer presaged the potential of the manuscript, because after several revisions, the paper developed substantially and was eventually accepted and published. The purpose of the editorial process is to provide authors feedback that will help them achieve excellence. Kudos are fine, but we need to go farther if our reviews are to be helpful.

---

**BOX 9.2 BEST PRACTICE: SETTING THE TONE WITH START-UPS**

Reviews can begin in several ways. The following are the types of start-up phrases reviewers most typically use. As an author, which do you prefer?

**Harsh Start-Up:** "I have read better papers written by undergraduates."
**Woeful Start-Up:** "I found this paper disappointing."
**Neutral or Descriptive Start-Up:** "This is an important topic."
**Descriptive Start-Up:** "This paper addresses the issue of mothers' influence on fathers' participation in routine child care."
**Descriptive Start With Double Entendre:** "This paper addresses the issue of mothers' influence on fathers' participation in routine child care, which is really interesting because I didn't know there was any."
**Positive Start-Up:** "This manuscript has a number of strengths."
**Positive Start-Up With Take-Back:** "This paper is impressive in many regards, but unfortunately reads rather like third-rate journalism."

I prefer a review that begins with a positive statement or a neutral start-up if the former is not possible. There is nearly always something positive to acknowledge, even if it is only the selection of topics. My goals are always to simply acknowledge the work of authors and, most importantly, motivate them to improve their work. As a reviewer or editor, I am more like an uncle (or aunt) than a parent.

---

## Reviewing Elementary or Substandard Submissions

Occasionally, editors receive manuscripts for consideration that seem to have little chance of being published. Such manuscripts lack a clear understanding of the available literature, lack the data appropriate to the intended purpose, contain misinterpreted analyses, or are otherwise substandard in fundamental ways. In some instances, an editor or editorial team will review submissions and reject a substantial percentage outright and without further review that appear substandard or otherwise inappropriate. Many journal editors rely on the peer-review process for informing nearly all decisions, including instances where at first glance a manuscript appears substandard. The following is an example of such an instance. The review begins with a **neutral start-up**, a statement that simply describes the focus of the manuscript being reviewed.

> This manuscript discusses the socio-cultural ecosystems of Asian couples and families. Overall, the manuscript does not achieve its goal for several reasons: (1) the literature review in the beginning sections is insufficient and several generalized statements are made without appropriate citations; (2) the scope of the article ranges from concerns about individual development, family relationships, and a variety of additional social and cultural factors without providing an umbrella to bring these distinct areas of research together. While the last section of the article adds new insight into understanding contemporary roles of mothers, fathers, and children, it selectively reviews empirical work by a limited number of scholars and does not adequately or fairly represent the relevant empirical literature.

The content of this review is fine. The reviewer believed the manuscript was lacking in important ways, and consequently recommended rejection. The review does little in the way of informing the author how she or he might go about improving the manuscript or otherwise mentoring the author. In this way, the review serves the first function to inform an editor's decision making, but it does little in the way of informing the author how to improve the manuscript, which we earlier defined as the second purpose of reviewing.

Reviewers vary in how they approach manuscripts that they judge as clearly inappropriate for the journal. Some reviewers provide substantial feedback to authors and, in doing so, invest much of their time. Others, as in the case above, are rather to the point and more conservative in their investment. Either approach is appropriate when the recommendation is to forgo pursuing a manuscript. The only clear responsibility of the reviewer is to distinctly state the reasons for his or her evaluation.

In most instances, I and many reviewers prefer to provide more substantial feedback to authors when I suspect the authors are new professionals. Substantial feedback benefits authors and potentially the field more generally. Sarah Schoppe-Sullivan shared a story that demonstrates this. I asked her if she had recently had an especially positive experience in having her work reviewed.

> Yes, recently my students and I submitted a paper to a journal that was rejected quickly, but the reviews were so helpful and constructive that we used them to completely revise the paper. When we sent it to the next journal, it got a very positive response and request for a revision and resubmission. The first resubmission was accepted [by the *Journal of Family Psychology*]. So even though the original submission was rejected, the reviews were so helpful, and it was a great experience for the students. They could clearly see that the paper was so much better after we made the revision. That's not the only positive experience I've had, but it's one of the most positive. It was the way things are supposed to work.

In this example, the initial reviewers were not obliged to provide suggestions for improving the manuscript, but having done so, Sarah and her colleagues took advantage of the suggestions, revised the paper, and sent it off to a second and very well-regarded journal, where it was finally accepted. Although the first submission was unsuccessful, the review process was distinctly generative, the manuscript improved and was eventually published. Both the authors and the field were served well.

Of course, the process is not always quite so helpful, and sometimes reviewers simply give authors terrible advice. For instance:

> I also advise the authors to eliminate references to articles, chapters or books in press or unpublished as yet. It can be very frustrating for readers when they don't have access to these references.

Although I would be reluctant to cite unpublished work or to recommend an author do so, I would encourage citing work near publication or in press for the simple reason that it may be several months or years before the article, and it's once in press citation, reaches a reader. Given the time between the writing of an article (and assembling references) to eventual publication and discovery by a reader can be sufficient time by which a work once in press will likely be published and available.

Sometimes reviewers just get confused. The editorial office of the *Journal of Family Theory & Review* received this review recently: "In short, this article does not meet the standards of the *Journal of Family Relations*." The other reviewers agreed with the overall sentiment, as did the editor, and the paper was eventually rejected; however, we prefer not to be confused with our sibling journals.[2]

## Precision of Voice and Refining the Contribution

Reviewers, like readers, expect some precision in the use of language. For instance, the statement that "social psychological theory suggests a certain relational outcome in family communication" is unhelpful. Just what is social psychological theory? Quite possibly the author had something specific in mind. The reviewer's mission is to encourage the full development of the underlying argument, the degree of precision in the use of language, writing at a level of specificity appropriate for the intended audience, and ultimately the contribution of the paper.

In this way, great reviews help to push advancements—for instance, pushing theory through a series of challenging questions, as in the following example. "Can you move beyond Erikson's fairly simple notion of stages? Are the developmental trajectories of secure and avoidant children likely to be unique? Can you extend these arguments?"

Great reviews often request refinements to existing arguments or analyses. "I would like to see the author buttress her arguments with some mention of the earlier work by Larry Kurdek on gay and lesbian couples." Reviews frequently call for more nuanced argument, and in this way encourage authors to advance their thinking, and perhaps their underlying theory or the complexity of design, measurement, or analyses. For example, in a literature review an author noted how cohabitation before marriage increases the risk of later divorce, relative to couples who do not cohabitate before marrying. True, but more recent work adds nuance to this long-standing finding in that the effect is not consistent across all cohabiting couples (Teachman, 2003).

### Prioritizing Commentary in Effective Reviews

The most useful reviews center on a few core issues, and the overall clarity of the presentation is among the most important. Reviewers expect a clear, unambiguous statement of the purpose of a manuscript, and they expect this within the first few paragraphs. Stating the purpose of a review article or empirical report is simple enough in principle, but often difficult to achieve.

Great reviews look for the clarity of the breadcrumb trail. All elements of the manuscript need to be clearly linked: the data and analyses pertinent to the questions being asked, and the conclusions clearly derivative of the analyses. There should be a "clear conceptual pathway through the thicket of ideas," as one reviewer noted. Often this is evidenced by the author's selection of headings.

Reviewers may usefully question the scope of a manuscript and in this way question the overall contribution. For instance, in a paper on intervention programs for violent adolescent offenders, a reviewer might question the exclusion of programs directed at adults, or the importance of distinguishing programs that are designed specifically for young women rather than young men. For authors, this suggests anticipating the issues a reviewer is apt to raise and providing explanations for the overall design and any likely concerns.

The clarity of any paper is largely contingent on the clarity of key concepts. Oddly enough, for instance, the term *family* is used imprecisely, sometimes referring to spouses and their children or the individuals living in a single household and sometimes referring to multiple households and a wider tracing of people related by birth, marriage, or strong positive sentiments (e.g., fictive kin). Reviewers can benefit authors when they read rather literally for clarity and consistency of language. In this case, even the most common term like *family* may need clarification. Authors can assemble manuscripts with an eye toward clearly defining and consistently using key concepts.

## Identifying Matters of Style

Additional issues in reviews include minor concerns that are relatively easy to remedy. As an editor I am not terribly concerned with minor lapses in style, the occasional typographical or grammatical error. This is especially true if I know the authors are new professionals or their first or primary language is not English. Once a manuscript is accepted, editors of major journals have professional copy editors review the manuscript for all these issues. Editors vary in their concern about such issues and the degree of support they receive from their publishers (e.g., to pay for expert copy editing). Journals sponsored by professional organizations are typically well supported in this regard, and editors and reviewers can focus on substantive issues where their expertise resides. In contrast, significant lapses in the preparation of a manuscript raise questions about the things that really do matter: How carefully did the author construct this particular study, case study, review, or theory paper? A manuscript replete with simple errors invites questions from editors and reviewers regarding more substantive issues such as the character of the literature review, design, measurement, analysis, and interpretation. Reviewers at their own discretion may include suggestions for authors regarding issues of style, and such comments are typically included at the end of a review.

## Missing Citations

Reviewers often suggest additional work they regard as relevant that was not cited originally by authors. This can be quite helpful when it serves our mutual goal to produce the best possible scholarship. Given the complexity of publishing and the breadth of sophistication needed to assemble an article, it is not surprising when an author misses what could be a useful source. The simple omission of a few pertinent publications is important to note but has little impact on the editorial outcome, and it shouldn't. There are exceptions.

More significant are occasions when substantial work is omitted and, in particular, work that might have informed an initial research design or the development of a theoretical model or policy implication. In these cases, the omission can figure prominently in the reviewer's recommendation and eventually that of the editor. Given the sophistication of methods for searching literatures, authors can avoid such problems with a bit of effort. But what if a scholar—for instance, a developmental psychologist—is working in the area of adolescent siblings and in an otherwise talented report misses pertinent material published in an education journal? This kind of omission happens quite regularly and the questions are: Was the theoretical modeling or the manuscript's research design affected? and Can the omission be corrected easily? In journals representing multiple disciplines and diverse readerships, there is an expectation that authors will be familiar with work in neighboring disciplines. The journals sponsored by inherently multidisciplinary disciplines such as education, social work, communications, and family studies are unique in that there is an expectation that authors write for multidisciplinary audiences, at least to a point. Some disciplines are implicitly regarded as too distant. We would not expect someone writing on kinship to cite work in comparative biology (e.g., sisterhood in rodents). In fact, animal studies, including work with primates, is rarely addressed in fields that regularly publish work on human relationships and families, although it would be useful if there were more cross-disciplinary fertilization (Milardo & Allan, 2000).

At times, reviewers face thorny ethical concerns. A reviewer might recommend work to an author including the reviewer's own publications. A reviewer may prefer a more conservative position and communicate the potential relevance of a self-citation to the editor, and let her decide whether it is appropriate to pass the recommendation along to an author. In nearly all cases, a light touch is appropriate, and authors should have the prerogative to include suggested references or to not do so. In the case of the latter, authors can communicate the rationale for their decision to exclude a reference. At the very least, the editor and reviewers need to know the issue was considered thoughtfully.

---

## BOX 9.3  BEST PRACTICE: WRITING REVIEWS

For editors and authors alike, the best reviews include an evaluation of the core content:

- The adequacy of the literature review.
- Clarity of the hypotheses, research questions, or program objectives.
- Strength of the underlying theory and any causal inferences.
- Appropriateness of the method and measurement.
- Appropriateness of the analysis.
- Appropriateness and depth of the interpretation of findings.
- And how all these elements fit together.

Additional issues may be pertinent, but these are the core concerns in my view, and they apply to most disciplines. Journals vary in their emphasis on other issues such as the overall contribution to the field, uniqueness or novelty of the contribution, or the applied implications. The most useful reviews provide a clear evaluation of the core issues, and, where needed, they provide authors with suggestions for improvements. Comments about style or clarity of the writing, suggestions for additional references, and so on are useful and welcome, but they do not replace a careful evaluation of core content.

## The Tone of Reviews

The issue of tone, and in particular off-tone, is a major concern of authors. A colleague recounts an instance of a less-than-desirable review.

It was a paper first authored by a student. We submitted it, got three reviews back, and two of them were pretty positive. The reviewers had suggestions that we had to address but overall they seemed to like the paper. The third reviewer had a very negative reaction and the negative reaction was not very specific. This reviewer thought that we were not appreciating the serious limitations of the study. So we revised and resubmitted the paper. The same reviewers looked at it again and we got their feedback. The first two reviewers were very positive; their additional comments were minor issues easily addressed, but the third reviewer was even angrier. The reviewer accused us of academic misconduct. The reviewer had an issue with the sample. [The sample was middle-class people with incomes averaging around $80,000.] So I certainly understood the criticism and we tried to address it the best way we could. But one of the other reviewers suggested some reanalysis with a measure of income included, and this required recoding the variable. This led to a slight difference in the mean income we reported, a difference of about $500. The third reviewer seized on this and basically said we were trying to make the sample look less wealthy. That was just the worst experience I've had.

We revised the paper a third time and tried to address what that reviewer was really saying. That was the hard part, trying to interpret the review. [audible sigh] What could we do? We thought maybe what the reviewer was saying we were using a language that was too causal for a correlational study. So we went back through and reread the paper with that idea in mind.

I contacted the editor about the review. I had never done that before, but this person was basically saying we were cheating. I thought the review was inappropriate and had crossed the line. And the editor just kind of put it out there with no guidance. When I contacted the editor, he said he had struggled with what to do, and said he had already had a conversation with the reviewer about the review. That made me feel better. My argument was that regardless of whether the paper gets published, I didn't think this was appropriate behavior. [The paper was eventually accepted and published.]

In this case, if the reviewer was concerned about the sample and some variation in the mean incomes reported in the first relative to the second submission, then he or she should simply and directly state the concern. Implying a nefarious motive or action to the authors is inappropriate. It seems an overdramatic response to a fairly minor issue. If a reviewer has concerns about the integrity of the data or analyses, such concerns are best shared with the editor directly. My colleague's experience also raises the issue of whether an author should ever quibble with a reviewer. My advice is to respond directly to content issues raised by the reviewer. Make any changes suggested, offer compromised solutions where you don't entirely agree with the suggestion, and if no compromise is possible, state clearly your reasoning. You are responding to the reviewer as well as the editor and other reviewers. If you have any comments regarding the tone of a review, share them directly and privately with the editor.

Other core issues in my colleague's recounting of her experience concern the responsibility of editors and the importance of well-crafted decision letters—issues we will revisit in Chapter 10 on editing.

Occasionally off-tone commentary can take the form of what seems like shouting. For example:

> It is truly bizarre to say that methodological individualism was adopted as a central, or even minor construct by Doyle. Is there some obscure paper where Doyle used a methodological individualistic approach? Certainly not in any of his books!

The tone feels like one is being scolded. Dad just walked into the room and he's seriously miffed. You've incorrectly cited basic sociological theory yet again!

Comments need to clearly note the problem in a more neutral tone and, just as importantly, serve to motivate the authors. In short, model the kind of comments you would like to hear if you were the author. In her insightful commentary on the content and production of quality reviews, Lynne Cooper (2009) suggests ways to adjust tone by setting a review aside for some time and rereading it for emotional tone. If necessary, check your pulse rate before and after completing a review, and if needed turn on some Coltrane, or whatever calms your spirit.

Masterful reviews have a supportive tone and, just as importantly, treat authors as peers. Subtle and not-so-subtle put-downs are to be avoided and are simply inappropriate regardless of whether you think they are reasonable comparisons. For instance, any reference to the work of unskilled students, or simply undergraduates, lawyers, or any other group is unhelpful. Critical commentary such as "This is the kind of comment we would feed to an undergraduate in a survey course" is unhelpful. I recall an instance (actually more than one) in which a reviewer made such a statement. The authors were senior scholars, well regarded, not accustomed to having their work treated so, and seriously disturbed by the tone of the review. Perhaps this particular paper was not their best work. Nonetheless, the point is to provide authors with fair-minded and useful feedback that is likely to motivate them to improve their work in the future. Railing an author is not in keeping with the purpose. If you feel the need to hurl the slings and arrows of outrageous fortune, bring out the surrogate dolls you should have stashed somewhere for just this purpose and sling away privately.

Occasionally a review will read more like a rant than a well-reasoned bit of scholarship. The best rant is a litany of everything the author did wrong and how you, the reviewer, are personally offended. A rant can be content rich in the sense of providing exceptionally insightful commentary on a manuscript, but the tone has the character of an attack based upon some personal affront. In the midst of all the useful commentary, the reviewer has essentially personalized the review and is saying, or shouting: "I am incredibly offended by the conceptualization, method, conduct, analysis, and interpretation of findings." Sometimes we need to remind ourselves that authors are not trying to personally annoy us or anyone else; in fact, we may never have met. The tone should frankly state the problem, what is lacking, and how you recommend the author might resolve the issue if possible. A reviewer might at times receive a manuscript with multiple issues, in which case the reviewer might focus on a few of the more central issues and note he or she is doing so.

## Midstream Kudos and Soft Landings

One other issue regarding tone deserves mentioning. Reviewers rarely do so, but including midstream kudos are quite appropriate. You don't need to get all gushy, but the occasional comment acknowledging a fine argument or insight is worth mentioning. For instance: "I appreciate the author's insightful analysis of the working models of caregiving." If the goal is to inform authors and motivate them to search out excellence, the occasional nod can't hurt. Clearly noting the contributions of a manuscript is important information for editors as well and is critical in their deliberations.

In closing a review, some reviewers introduce **soft landings**: "Overall this paper is coming together nicely. The introductory and concluding sections are most in need of polishing and I would like to see the author refine these sections as I noted above." Or, "my goal in this review was to provide feedback that might aid you in clarifying the meaning of your manuscript for the reader. I hope you found the comments of some help." I think authors appreciate encouraging commentary. In the midst of a critical analysis, an acknowledgement of a paper's strengths is entirely appropriate.

### Taking Ownership

We all have preferences and sometimes it can be appropriate to share them, and possibly useful to authors. When a personal preference is just that—one of several valid positions—it is important to acknowledge the personal preference and take ownership of it. For instance, I vastly prefer authors use the word *how* rather than the phrase *the ways in which*, but I'm not sure there are any laws involved. Here is an example where a reviewer shared a personal position and clearly takes ownership for it. "I am a little uncomfortable with any discussion of trust as an epiphenomenon. I admit that this is my own ox, so to speak, but I do wish the authors would reconsider their position." Taking ownership for personal preferences invites the author to consider an issue but not necessarily abide by it. Science is served in this instance by communicating ideas that foster innovative thinking rather than insisting adherence to a singular position.

Sometimes authors can truly test our patience and wisdom in these regards. In one instance, I was working with two coauthors on an early draft of their paper. The submission was invited, the authors senior, and there was no question the paper would eventually be published. There was a point in the paper where the authors, at least in my view, misrepresented a literature and a key concept in that literature. It happened to be an area I knew well and about which I had written. In the decision letter to the authors I summarized the important elements of the reviewers' comments as customary, included a copy of the manuscript with my own comments embedded, which I typically do, and noted that I thought they had misrepresented a key concept and it's definition and treatment in the empirical literature. I was surprised they elected to not make a correction or offer a compromise. I thought their position untenable; they thought otherwise. Science is served well when we allow for open dialogue, take full ownership for our positions, and allow for differences. Secretly I hope no one agrees with their position and I'm vindicated, but then that's a bit petty of me.

## Communicating With Editors

A few issues are best directed to editors rather than authors. Examples include any potential bias a reviewer might have, believing you know the author of the work being reviewed, having reviewed the work previously for another journal, or any concerns about academic integrity. Any of these issues should be shared with editors.

Please don't sign your review. Reviews are intended to be blind, with the identity of the author and reviewer unknown to each other. This is not always possible but it is our starting position.

Reviewing templates for many journals allow reviewers to include the body of the review for authors as well as separate comments to be shared confidentially with the editor. In addition to the issues mentioned above, a reviewer might share an overall evaluation of the manuscript in a few sentences. Such comments can be helpful to editors, but they do not replace writing a thoughtful review or a careful reading of that review by the editor.

## Reviewing and Writing for an Audience

Authors can reasonably expect some level of expertise on the part of readers. We *write to the genre,* as my colleagues in compositional studies might say. An author need not define terms we can be reasonably assured that most readers will know, but we do need definitions of terms that might be unfamiliar to a fair number of readers. For example, *stochastic* may not need a definition in a specialized statistical journal, but it may need some definition for a more general or random audience. This can be difficult to judge when writing for a journal new to you, which is yet another reason to establish some familiarity with a target journal. Keeping the likely audience of an article in mind is important. For some readers and journals, an explanation of *hierarchical linear modeling* (HLM) might be completely unnecessary; readers are familiar with the technique. For other readers and journals, HLM might be an unfamiliar procedure. Jennifer Rose, a research professor at Wesleyan University, shared her experience on writing to an audience.

> In my own experience as a social scientist my target audience is most often other social scientists, but sometimes my work may be more relevant to epidemiologists or physicians. Just recently I was working on a manuscript with some collaborators, some of whom are social scientists and some of whom are physicians. I was talking to one of my physician colleagues about the study because I was really excited that we had used a complex statistical method that I had used before, but was particularly novel in the area of medical research. He asked me how the method differed from standard regression. Despite

having published studies using this method in the past, this was the first time I had gotten this question. I gave him an answer he was satisfied with, and didn't think much more about it. But, after circulating a draft of the manuscript to my coauthors, I actually got the same question from two other physicians, and that made me realize that this method, which is typically well understood by social scientists, was foreign to medical researchers. Since the target audience was going to be physicians and researchers in the medical field and we were going to submit to a more medically oriented journal, I realized that I had to provide more details about the statistical method than I would usually provide. The funny thing is that after revising the manuscript to provide more detail and recirculating it to my coauthors, one of the social scientist coauthors edited the material out because she felt it wasn't necessary. Needless to say, I put it back in and explained to her why it was there. This experience drove home to me the understanding that the target audience can have a significant impact on how a manuscript is written.

As important as it is to write for an audience, it is also important to review with the article's intended audience in mind. For an audience of early childhood educators, a definition of *secure attachment* is probably not essential; for an audience in another field, it may well need a simple definition. Reviewers continually make judgments about the level of explanation necessary to communicate effectively with an audience. Journals develop their own cultures or norms regarding the pool of concepts representing common knowledge and therefore not needing definition or citation. Reviewers, and authors, must make their own judgments, and they will do well when recognizing the needs of a likely audience.

### BOX 9.4 WRITER'S RESOURCE: HOW TO BECOME A REVIEWER

There are three main pathways to becoming a reviewer. Once you publish in a particular journal or become known for a particular area of research, you can expect to be invited to review manuscripts. Another pathway might be through one's professional affiliations. I often have called upon former students working in university positions or colleagues I meet at conferences to review. Finally, you can simply volunteer. To do so is a straightforward matter of visiting a journal's website and providing the requested information. Typically you will be asked to select keywords (e.g., adolescence, attachment, marital communication, divorce) representing areas in which you have expertise and in which you are willing to review manuscripts. If you select only a few keywords or keywords representing areas that receive few submissions, then, not surprisingly, you won't be asked to review very often. Generally, editors call on ad hoc or volunteer reviewers no more than a few times per year. Don't hesitate to decline an assignment if you can't meet the deadline or if the manuscript is about an unfamiliar topic. If you are entirely new to reviewing, you might share this with an editor. On occasion, but rarely, new professionals have requested feedback on the quality or content of their reviews. I am happy to do so, but in practice editors will not have the time to mentor new professionals, although they certainly have an interest in doing so. Once you complete a review, you can expect to receive a copy of the editor's decision letter to authors as well as copies of the other reviews. This is important information by which you can measure the quality of your review.

How does one get on an editorial board? There are two ways: You might be invited by the editor, or you might simply share your interest in serving with an editor. If you have reviewed for a particular journal for several years, completed quality reviews, and returned your reviews promptly, you are in line for a position on the editorial board. If any one of these elements is missing, you're not quite ready for prime time.

A few years ago I was speaking with my colleague Katherine at the annual conference of the National Council on Family Relations. I was, at the time, editor of the *Journal of Marriage and Family* (JMF). I related to Katherine how often people approached me in the hallways asking to be considered for the JMF board; I shared with Katherine that they were always men who made such requests, to which Katherine responded, "Well, I'd like to be on the board." I was quite familiar with Katherine's work and the quality of her reviews, and I added her to the board. She soon became a deputy editor of the journal and a trusted advisor. If you've met all the requirements noted above, don't be afraid to ask. You might ask an editor to be considered for a journal board in person at an appropriate time or by a brief e-mail to the editor.

## Reviewing Grant and Contract Proposals

Grant and contract proposals can vary widely in their purpose: for instance, complex multiyear research proposals, proposals for developing and testing intervention programs, and community development grants (Gade, Costanza, & Kaplan, 2006). Reviewing proposals is in some ways similar to reviewing journal articles and in some ways quite unique. On the one hand, issues central to the review of journal articles apply, such as the clarity of the purpose, design, and execution as well as issues of appropriate tone. On the other hand, funding agencies have specific interests, evaluation criteria, and other requirements not typical of journals.

Funding agencies have very specific interests and typically spend a good deal of time in writing formal requests for proposals (RFP). RFPs detail the specific interests of the agency and how proposals need to be prepared, typically with strict page limitations for each section of the proposal and strict submission deadlines. Proposals may undergo an initial screening, and those deemed suitable are sent out for peer review. Proposals and their accompanying reviews may be evaluated in house by agency staff, or the package may be assigned to a team of experts who evaluate proposals and their reviews, and then recommend a small proportion for funding. Many proposals that are evaluated favorably are left unsupported because of a simple lack of adequate funding.

Reviewing proposals requires attending to the RFP and any special requirements of the granting agency. Reviewers may be asked to provide an overall impression of the proposal relative to the RFP or a more technical analysis of the proposal's components (literature review, method or program delivery, and so on). In either case, there are typically additional issues of concern to granting agencies, including an evaluation of the project from the funding agency's point of view, which is often quite narrow, and an evaluation of the researchers and their qualifications, expertise, and experience. These latter issues further distinguish reviewing grant proposals from the more typical fare of peer review. Nonetheless, the core elements of evaluating content remain the bedrock of grant reviewing.

Granting agencies and foundations are always in need of skilled reviewers. Established scholars, especially those who have been previously funded, are routinely called upon to review grants. If you are interested in learning more about how agencies evaluate proposals and make decisions on funding, it can be very helpful to gain experience in reviewing proposals. Rather than wait for an agency or foundation to invite you to review a proposal, you might simply volunteer, or ask a senior colleague to recommend you.

## Summary

This chapter described the submission process and the track a manuscript takes when submitted for review. We defined the dual purpose of peer review: to inform an editor's decision on the disposition of a manuscript and create a generative standard to assist authors in improving their manuscript. With these foundations in mind, we compared the characteristics of effective or masterful reviews to those that are less helpful. In the end, masterful reviews are:

- Based upon soft or neutral start-ups.
- Comprehensive and push for the advancement of knowledge.
- Content rich, clearly detailing the issues of concern.
- Suggestive of ways to improve a manuscript.
- Able to prioritize issues.
- Fair-minded and unbiased, taking full ownership for personal preferences.
- Well toned and generative, denoting a paper's areas needing attention as well as strengths.
- Tactful and treat authors as peers.

## Activities

1. What features of a useful review are most helpful to you as a writer? How should a review begin? Are comments about style or the use of language important and an element of a review you find useful?
2. Ask a colleague to share reviews she or he found especially useful or perplexing. How would you rewrite the review?
3. Each of the following scenarios presents an issue that reviewers commonly confront in reviewing manuscripts. How would you respond to each scenario?

   a. You are asked to review a manuscript that you think was written by your former advisor.
   b. You receive a manuscript on a topic you've often written about, and yet the author cites none of your work.
   c. A manuscript includes text you believe was previously published.
   d. In an otherwise well-designed and -executed study, the authors cite current literature in social psychology but seem to be unaware of important contributions in neighboring disciplines such as communication studies.
   e. In what appears to be a well-executed study, the stated purpose and hypotheses don't seem to entirely match the variables measured.
   f. The authors have elected one form of analysis but you and some of your colleagues prefer another form of analysis.
   g. The journal requires manuscripts under 30 pages in APA style. The manuscript you receive is much longer and in a different style, with numbered headings and citations appearing as footnotes.
   h. It seems a manuscript was written by a non-native English speaker and consequently there are errors throughout the manuscript in grammar and syntax.
   i. The manuscript includes a useful if not stellar literature review, a set of binary hypotheses, and an analysis based on first-order

correlations. You suspect it was written as an undergraduate research project.

j.    You clearly do not understand the core analyses or the accompanying tables, but you are unsure whether the average reader of the journal would have the same difficulty.

4.    This exercise was suggested by an anonymous reviewer of this chapter. The goal is to learn the craft of reviewing by reviewing the work of a colleague and having one's own work reviewed. In a seminar where written assignments are required, participants share their written work and each participant pens a review of another's work. The reviews are circulated in the seminar, discussed and critiqued for their merits, and, from the point of view of authors, they are evaluated in terms of their helpfulness.

## Recommended Readings

McInerney, D. M. (2001). *Publishing your psychology research*. Los Angeles, CA: Sage.

Chapter 7 on the "Review Process" provides another take on reviewing and the expectations of several key psychological journals.

Roediger, H. L. (2007). Twelve tips for reviewers. *APS Observer*. Retrieved from http://aps.psychologicalscience.org/index.php/publications/observer/2007/april-07/twelve-tips-for-reviewers.html

A brief yet entirely useful depiction of the basics of a fine review. Highly recommended; but please don't sign your review, as the author suggests.

Tesser, A., & Martin, L. (2006). Reviewing empirical submissions to journals. In R. J. Sternberg (Ed.), *Reviewing scientific works in psychology* (pp. 3–29). Washington, DC: American Psychological Association.

A useful chapter on the core elements of reviewing empirical work written by psychologists for those new to the task of writing reviews.

Warren, M. G. (2000.). Reading reviews, suffering rejection, and advocating for your paper. In R. J. Sternberg (Ed.), *Guide to publishing in psychology journals* (pp. 169–186). Cambridge, UK: Cambridge University Press.

This chapter presents an excellent discussion on writing strategically from an understanding of the review process and responding to critical reviews.

## Notes

1. The examples are not direct quotes but rather reconstructed from actual reviews to preserve the more important and instructive matters of tone and

content, while altering the less important issue of the specific topics being addressed. In this way, the privacy of all parties is preserved.
2. Our sister journal is called *Family Relations*.

# References

Cooper, M. L. (2009). Problems, pitfalls and promise in the peer-review process: Commentary on Trafimow & Rice (2009). *Perspectives on Psychological Science, 4*, 84–92.

Gade, P. A., Costanza, D. P., & Kaplan, J. D. (2006). Reviewing grant and contract proposals. In R. J. Sternberg (Ed.), *Reviewing scientific works in psychology* (pp. 101–123). Washington, DC: American Psychological Association.

Milardo, R. M. (2005). Generative uncle and nephew relationships. *Journal of Marriage and Family, 67*, 1226–1236.

Milardo, R. M., & Allan, G. (2000). Social networks and marital relationships. In R. Milardo & S. Duck (Eds.), *Families as relationships* (pp. 117–133). London, UK: John Wiley.

Milardo, R. M., Johnson, M. P., & Huston, T. L. (1983). Developing close relationships: Changing patterns of interaction between pair members and social networks. *Journal of Personality and Social Psychology, 44*, 964–976.

Sense About Science. (2010). *Peer review survey 2009: Full report*. London, UK: Author.

Teachman, J. (2003). Premarital sex, premarital cohabitation, and the risk of subsequent marital dissolution among women. *Journal of Marriage and Family, 65*, 444–455.

Tesser, A., & Martin, L. (2006). Reviewing empirical submissions to journals. In R. J. Sternberg (Ed.), *Reviewing scientific works in psychology* (pp. 3–29). Washington, DC: American Psychological Association.

# 10 Editors and How They Work

This chapter describes common editorial practices such as the calculation of **acceptance rates, impact factors** and their interpretations, and general issues concerning the **reliability, validity,** and **fairness** of reviews. We detail the responsibilities of editors and authors, how editors make decisions, and the typical operations of editorial offices. Among the more important issues are the composition of decision letters on the part of editors and how authors can best respond to requests for a revision and resubmission. By understanding these issues, authors can avoid unnecessary errors in the preparation of manuscripts and improve the chance of favorable outcomes.

## Acceptance Rates

Journals pride themselves on the exclusivity of membership, not unlike country clubs or salmon clubs. Those with low acceptance rates are viewed as more desirable venues in which to publish, and to a certain extent they are more influential, with higher citation rates. Such journals are thought to publish the very best work, and their low acceptance rates are regarded as prima facie proof. In the world of scholarship, low acceptance rates are a measure of success. This results in some curious circumstance. We could take another position entirely.

If an editor's responsibility is to mentor, to create generative environments in which great work is created, then the measure of a journal's success is a higher acceptance rate. Journals with low acceptance rates are simply failing in their mission. We might also usefully question the implicit assumption that editors and reviewers are able to consistently distinguish between the top 10% or 20% of manuscripts submitted as well as the assumption that the top 10% represents the best work. It might not in a number of ways. For instance, it's possible the top 10% is largely comprised of the most conventional and least innovative work. Let's dig a bit deeper into the issues.

---

**BOX 10.1  WRITER'S RESOURCE: CALCULATING ACCEPTANCE RATES**

*Acceptance rates* are calculated in several ways. A method used by the *Journal of Family Theory & Review* and many other journals is a straightforward ratio of the number of manuscripts accepted in a year divided by the total number of manuscripts on which decisions were made in that year. For instance, imagine a journal accepts 20 manuscripts for publication in a given year, and rejects 80 with or without review. The acceptance rate is 20%. Manuscripts currently under review or revision and for which no final decisions have been made are not included in the calculation for this particular year, although they would be included in future annual reports once final decisions have been made. Invited manuscripts or commentaries are typically excluded from the calculation because they are rarely rejected. This method of computing acceptance rates has the advantage of a very straightforward calculation and interpretation. It represents one method endorsed by the National Council on Family Relations and is often used by other professional organizations.

---

In a now classic study, Peters and Ceci (1982) selected 12 previously published articles and resubmitted them to the original source journals 18 to 32 months after their publication. All 12 articles had been published in prestigious psychology journals with acceptance rates of 20% or less. We might expect editors or reviewers to discover the ruse and recognize a fair number of the resubmissions, and if not so recognized, we might expect most of the resubmissions to be accepted. Neither outcome occurred. Of the 38 editors and reviewers included in the study, a scant 8% detected the resubmissions as previously published work. This meant 9 of the original 12 articles were fully reviewed; contrary to expectations, 8 of the 9 were rejected. For editors this is a nightmare scenario. The review process has a distinctly capricious tenor, or so it seems. In the next several pages we can shed some light on these remarkable findings.

## Reliability, Validity, and Fairness in Decision Making

Editors are immediately confronted with three core issues in shepherding the peer-review process: the reliability of the evaluation process, often viewed as the extent of agreement between reviewers; the validity of the process in identifying the highest quality work; and the overall fairness of the process. Of course, as in many arenas, the devil is in the details.

Editors depend on the commentary and recommendations of reviewers, and editorial decisions are highly correlated with reviewers' ratings (Bornmann, 2011), which is entirely in keeping with the purpose of peer review. Reviewers and authors alike rate the process favorably in that the vast majority (85%) believe the peer-review process helps scientific communication, that the comments of reviewers lead to improvements, and that overall reviews are executed competently (Bornmann, 2011; Sense About Science, 2010). There is consistent and strong support for peer review across disciplines; there is also criticism.

Reviewers may disagree on the disposition of a manuscript, suggesting poor reliability of the peer review process, which the classic work of Peters and Ceci (1982) revealed. There is little agreement across reviewers, or so it is argued. Others suggest the commentary of reviewers is often biased and based on trivial issues such as the personal attributes of authors or the prestige of their affiliations rather than the scientific merit of a manuscript or grant proposal.

On the issue of reliability there is only moderate inter-reviewer agreement, at least when comparing overall recommendations to reject, encourage a resubmission, or accept a manuscript (Kemp, 2005), although reviewers are far more likely to agree on the decision to reject a manuscript than any other outcome (Weller, 2002). But perhaps too much agreement is undesirable; if reviewers are selected for their complementary perspectives and different areas of expertise, then we could expect some unreliability but greater validity in the process (i.e., a greater likelihood of selecting excellence). Evaluations of reliability based upon the agreement of reviewers to reject, invite revision, or accept a manuscript are on shaky ground. At the risk of introducing a personal bias, the ruminations of a former editor, reviewers are more likely than not to agree in the substance of their recommendations. Although ratings of whether to reject a manuscript may differ, the core substance of reviews shows less divergence. When divergence does appear, it may be welcome from the perspective of an editor. I suspect many editors select complementary reviewers with different areas of expertise, and this is likely to be especially true of journals that service multiple disciplines and diverse audiences (e.g., any of the journals of the National Council on Family Relations).

Some have questioned the predictive validity of the process because there is little relationship of reviewers' judgments to the later value of the work to the scientific community as evidenced by citation rates. Others argue the process is inefficient because it delays publication and inhibits the publication of innovative and unconventional theory, method, or analysis. Finally, the process can be personally damaging or at the very least distressing (Day, 2011). An abundance of literature and several comprehensive reviews address this topic (Bornmann, 2011; Weller, 2002).

When we evaluate the fairness of the review process or the degree to which evaluations are based on scientific merit rather than functionally irrelevant criteria, there is little consistent negative bias. Issues of seniority, gender, race, and institutional affiliation seem to have little consistent effect on the outcomes of reviews, at least in regard to journal submissions. In grant or fellowship applications, there are indications of a gender bias favoring male applicants (Bornmann, Mutz, & Daniel, 2007). Inappropriate biases certainly influence editorial decisions at times. For this reason editors, their journal boards, teams of reviewers, and institutional sponsors need to periodically assess the integrity and fairness of the review process and take appropriate steps to minimize the influence of unwanted biases (Bornmann, 2011; Weller, 2002).

---

**BOX 10.2 WRITER'S RESOURCE: IMPACT FACTORS AND RELATED MEASURES**

Several indices access a journal's influence and most are based on some measure of the rate of citation for individual articles. The most commonly used measure is the **impact factor**, which is simply the average number of citations to articles published in a particular journal. Impact factors are calculated for each volume of a journal and based upon the number of times all articles (called source material) published over a two-year period are cited in the following year. An impact factor of 2 means that articles published in 2012 and 2013 were cited an average of two times in 2014. Impact factors are calculated annually by Thomson Reuters for journals that are indexed in the *Journal Citation Reports* (Garfield, 1994). Citations made in indexed journals are counted; citations in books or nonindexed journals are not counted. Journals with high impact factors have higher average citation rates and are deemed to have more influence on a field. The *Journal of Family Psychology* and the *Journal of Marriage and Family*, for instance, have high citation rates, or impact factors, relative to other family studies journals and are often viewed as more influential. Journals sponsored by professional organizations, especially large organizations with many members such as the American Psychological Association or National Association of Social Workers, generally evidence higher impact factors (see Sternberg & Sternberg, 2010, for citation rates for a selection of psychology journals).

Several issues influence impact factors. Journals that are published by organizations representing large memberships generally have higher impact factors than journals published by organizations with smaller memberships. For this reason impact factors are bested viewed relative to their peer group, other journals serving the same discipline.

Impact factors are influenced by issues unrelated to the quality or importance of the work being published. For example, publishing more articles or a large proportion of literature reviews increases citation rates (Garfield, 1994; *PLoS Medicine* Editors, 2006).

Editors can influence citation rates modestly by including popular topics, authors, or literature reviews early in a given year. Given how impact factors are calculated, publishing a literature review early in an annual volume increases the time for readers to find the article and cite it. Literature reviews are cited more often than empirical articles. A literature review on a popular topic (e.g., attachment theory or the effects of divorce on children) will attract more readers, and this leads to more citations. Curiously, there is a neighborhood effect. Articles published in the pages immediately preceding or following a popular review also garner more citations. Themed issues or special collections of articles on topics that are apt to attract interest are cited more and can be published in the first issue of a volume to maximize annual citations.

In contrast, publishing many short articles or commentaries on lead articles can lower a journal's impact factor because short articles and commentaries are less likely to be cited. For instance, if the 25 articles published in a two-year period receive 100 citations in the subsequent year, the impact factor is 4. If 5 of those articles were commentaries on lead articles, which are rarely cited, such commentaries have the effect of lowering the impact factor. Without the commentaries, the impact factor would be 5 (i.e., 100/20). Although the field may be better served by the publication of short articles, case studies, commentaries, or debates on particularly thorny topics, these sorts of publications may have a negative effect on impact factors and a journal's perceived influence.

Other measures of a journal's importance or influence are available. A **five-year impact factor** reports on the average number of citations over one year for each article published in the previous five volumes. A journal's **cited half-life** refers to the median age of the articles that were cited in *Journal Citation Reports* each year. For example, if a journal's half-life in 2010 is 5, this means that 50% of citations to that journal's content appeared in the last five years. The **immediacy index** refers to the average number of citations to articles in the year they were published.

**Eigenfactors** are an attempt to improve on the simple calculation of impact factors. Journals are evaluated relative to the number of incoming citations, with citations from highly ranked journals weighted to make a larger contribution to the eigenfactor than those from poorly ranked journals (Bergstrom, 2007).

Publishers can now monitor media views or downloads of each article published and continue such monitoring over time. This kind of data is useful to editors as a means to monitor the popularity and, to a certain extent, the influence of recent articles immediately following publication. Authors may also find media views useful to immediately assess the impact of their work. It's nice to know if you're being read, or at least peeked at.

Finally, there is the curious **twimpact**, which is the number of tweets on an article within the first seven days of publication. I think a view or peek more satisfying than a tweet, but maybe that's just me.

## Editorial Decision Letters

Making well-reasoned decisions on manuscripts is by far the most important and difficult element of an editor's duties. Ideally, editors will compose informative and instructive decision letters to authors; this is not always possible. In the best of circumstances, the most informed decisions are based on the recommendations of the reviews as well as the editor's reading of a manuscript. Not all editors have the time to carefully read manuscripts, especially if they are receiving multiple submissions per day, in which case they may rely on the commentary of reviewers. In some instances, I do as well. If the reviewers are in agreement that a manuscript is inappropriate for the journal, and if their concerns appear reasonable, in the interest of time management, I am not inclined to read the manuscript. In these cases, my decision letters tend to be brief; I rely on the comments of the reviewers to inform authors. In nearly all other cases, I prefer to read manuscripts and often include comments directly in the manuscript that I then share with authors.

Whether an editor is able to carefully read a manuscript or not, his or her responsibility is to delineate, prioritize, and summarize the issues that need to be addressed. Decision letters ideally provide a road map for authors in shaping their future revisions, a road map that is rooted in a clear understanding of the manuscript and the comments of the reviewers. Authors certainly appreciate the service and often mention clarity as well as timeliness, helpfulness, and demonstrated respect in rating the quality of service from editorial offices (Adler & Liyanarachchi, 2011).

Sarah Schoppe-Sullivan comments directly on the issues of clarity and helpfulness:

> I think a good letter from the editor is very helpful in terms of summarizing what the key issues are. That can be very helpful. I guess I feel like if I can get a clear picture of what the editor and reviewers think are key issues that need to be addressed, that can help me with the revision, or if it is a reject, I usually revise the manuscript before I send it someplace else because I feel like the feedback is valuable. It doesn't mean I am going to take every suggestion, but especially if there is some consensus and the editor agrees, I am not going to send that paper out to another journal without addressing those issues.

Anisa Zvonkovic also commented on the importance of decision letters from editors. I asked her what made for a positive or helpful experience in the review process. She recounted a recent experience in having her work reviewed:

> In a recent submission one of the things that was helpful was that it was really clear what needed to be changed and what didn't. When the action editor provides specific guidelines, I find that really helpful. I usually do a document where I kind of summarize and bunch up similar comments [of the reviewers], kind of a content analysis. Then I look at what the editor says to see if there is some direction. So definitely if the action editor provides clear guidance that is really important. I don't know if I ever got reviews where the reviewers agreed on everything, usually there is kind of an outlier. My mentor taught me reviewers are very good detectors of problems but not so good at suggesting what to do. So it's helpful if an editor can highlight where a problem came from. An editor doesn't really have to say how to solve an issue, but some guidance is nice.

---

**BOX 10.3 BEST PRACTICE: DECISION LETTERS**

Editorial decision letters are most effective when they include the following attributes:

- A clear explanation of the issues needing the most attention
- Helpful suggestions for attending to the core issues
- Prioritized issues
- Demonstrated respect for the authors

Detailed decision letters are time-consuming and sometimes difficult to write, but they can be quite helpful to authors. In the case of work submitted by new professionals, editors may be inclined to provide additional or more detailed feedback when time permits. I asked Harry Reis if he provided added commentary in his decision letters to new professionals. "Absolutely! Even today when I write reviews I frequently will write it in a more detailed way if I know it is a young author or a less established colleague."

In my experience, authors rarely specifically ask for additional feedback. When they do I am happy to provide it, but there is a catch or two. First, I have to have the time to do so, which means a reasonably manageable workload at that particular moment. Second, the author has to demonstrate a minimal degree of competence and seriousness of intent. If a manuscript is lacking in fundamental competencies, the commentary of an editor is not likely to replace the need for additional training and effort.

An editor's job is far easier when there is considerable agreement between reviewers, when they identify similar issues needing attention, somewhat less so when they raise different issues, and decidedly challenging when the reviews are disparate. In the latter case, editors may not always be entirely certain how to proceed or whether to favor one set of suggestions offered by one reviewer, or an entirely different set of suggestions offered by another. At the very least, editors need to acknowledge whatever differences exist, offer direction or compromise positions if possible, and otherwise let the author establish priorities and so argue his or her case. An editor's failing to acknowledge significant differences in the commentary of reviewers and provide guidance is one the most common complaints among authors (Cooper, 2009; Street, Bozeman, & Whitfield, 1998).

Editors can be further challenged by off-tone or hostile reviews. On the one hand, we don't want to antagonize reviewers by chastising them for inappropriate tone. On the other hand, authors deserve to be treated with respect and our goal is to encourage the production of quality contributions. An editor may decide not to use a hostile review, but the choice brings its own set of issues. We do not want to interfere with the peer-review process, especially when an off-tone review also includes useful substantive comments, which they often do. Negotiating off-tone reviews means separating the unbecoming chaff from the wholesome wheat by delineating the useful criticisms from the less useful, and clearly communicating this with authors. Just as midstream kudos can serve generativity in writing reviews, an editor can remark on the current and potential importance of a manuscript and thereby encourage authors. As was explored in Chapter 9, regardless of the tone of a decision letter or review, authors often, if not typically, find decision letters and accompanying reviews a bit disturbing. Decision letters and their accompanying reviews commonly elicit an emotional response from authors, and editors need to be mindful of that response. Hostile reviews are simply not helpful. Hostile reviewers, even when their reviews are otherwise skillful, are not apt to be invited to the next party.

On a manuscript that is judged to be inappropriate for a journal, how much feedback can an author expect? Ideally, a decision letter will at minimum state the primary reason or reasons for a rejection, but this is not always the case. Rejection letters may not be terribly informative and authors need to attend to the comments of the reviewers. Although an editor may prefer writing helpful and informative rejection letters, the difficultly and time required to do so is prohibitive.

My favorite decision letter, received after I submitted an article to a journal, read: "No thanks. The editor." The letter could not have been more exacting. It was handwritten, which added to the personal touch, yet without exclamation points, I thought a bit disingenuous.

---

### BOX 10.4   AN INTERVIEW WITH KELLY RALEY, EDITOR OF THE *JOURNAL OF MARRIAGE AND FAMILY*

RM: *In your own writing life, have you ever had a paper accepted without revision?*

[laughs] No, not without revision.

RM: *Have you ever accepted a paper without revision?*

I have accepted a commentary with rather minor revisions. [Commentaries are usually brief invited responses to a feature article.]

RM: *In writing decision letters to authors, would you personalize a rejection letter?*

I do. I don't spend as much time crafting rejection letters as I do on requests for a revision and resubmission. How much I put in a rejection letter will depend on the quality of the reviews. If I feel the authors have three very good reviews, I really don't feel like I need to add even more. I am also reluctant to pile on a whole bunch of reasons why I'm rejecting an article, but I do try to point out the two main reasons, and sometimes I'll say these things might be addressable but the paper is just too far from being ready for me to invite a revision. Or sometimes I'll say these are the issues that I don't think can be addressed.

RM: *What is important to include in decision letters to authors, especially for an invitation to revise and resubmit a paper?*

The first thing is to go through the reviewer's comments and highlight those issues that I think are most important. I'm really focusing on what is the contribution and are the methods appropriate. So my comments focus on what I see as the core of the paper. I don't systematically tell authors what they need to do in each section. I try to focus on the key points and combine the advice of the reviewers. I often have additional points that I see as problematic and I will bring those up too. For example, if I feel like they are missing a literature or something, then I'll bring that up. I'm not usually doing a whole lot in terms of style or presentation.

RM: *What happens when you disagree with the recommendation of a reviewer?*

If a reviewer makes a really strong recommendation that I disagree with, then I will tell the author I'm not convinced that [the recommendation] will improve the paper, but whatever you [the author] decide, make it clear why you made that decision.

RM: *So that means you give authors some discretion to decide how they will respond to reviewers?*

Sure. Yeah. Absolutely. Throughout my letter I make sure that authors feel like they can do something different.

RM: *Would you do the same thing when reviewers give contradictory advice?*

I try and do it in a very soft way. Here is what the problem is, and there are a variety of ways you can resolve that.

I do try and provide direction. I don't want to leave authors confused about what they should do.

RM: *How to you deal with offensive reviews?*

I think the most offensive reviews I've received have been comments on people's writing ability because they are not native English speakers. I don't edit the reviews. To me it feels like a slippery slope. It feels like if I start editing reviewers' comments, where do I stop?

RM: *If a review had a truly offensive tone, would this influence how you write your decision letter?*

I absolutely would say Reviewer XXX makes some helpful suggestions, but I found the tone inappropriate. I would call out the issue.

RM: *Would you contact the reviewer?*

I might not invite the reviewer again.

RM: *What is fun about being an editor?*

Oh, I wish I knew, but it is fun. [laughs]

RM: *You responded immediately, so there must be some joys to it?*

Oh yeah. I enjoy it. Yeah.

RM: *What is it about it that you enjoy?*

For a paper where I can see the contribution and the [paper] is on the way [to being published], being able to suggest improvements is for me actually rewarding. If we can tighten this up and remove these distracters, it's there. It's a good paper. I like polishing.

RM: *Do you like the management parts of being an editor?*

There are some parts of the day-to-day work, like dealing with potential authors asking about whether something is a good fit with the journal. I don't enjoy that. I don't enjoy most of my interactions with the [publishing side].

RM: *Does it feel like it's endless, like editing could take all of your time?*

Absolutely. It will take every bit of time I give it. And that is part of the struggle for me, and so when I get involved with a paper, and trying to be measured and careful, I don't want to give a lot of advice, I just want to give the best advice. That just takes a lot of time to get right. I could spend all day editing and often do.

Currently the *Journal of Family Theory & Review* rejects about 5% of submissions without review. These are nearly always manuscripts that are clearly inappropriate for the journal. For instance, the journal does not publish empirical reports or case studies, and such submissions are rejected outright with a simple note stating this reason.

In some cases, a manuscript is submitted that an editor may feel is very unlikely to engender a favorable review. This situation presents a dilemma. On the one hand, I do not wish to rely too heavily on my own preferences and thereby supplant the peer-review process. On the other hand, I am concerned about the workload of reviewers and do not wish to overburden them. Occasionally, I will reject a manuscript that appears entirely unlikely to receive favorable reviews, but this is a rare occurrence.

For some journals the sheer volume of manuscripts received prevents accepting all or even most manuscripts for review, and some triage is required. For instance, *Psychological Science* receives about 3,000 submissions per year and about 66% are rejected without review by the editor and deputy editors. The *Journal of Marriage and Family* and *Family Relations* reject about 15% of new manuscripts without review. Incidentally, in a survey of more than 3,000 reviewers across multiple disciplines, 68% of respondents thought rejecting manuscripts without review was appropriate (Sense About Science, 2010). A triage system is necessary for some journals given the volume of submissions and the work needed by editors and reviewers to complete comprehensive reviews, but it is not entirely in keeping with the objectives of peer review. Triage practices need to be carefully designed, and editors need to be accountable for their decisions while being mindful of overburdening reviewers.

## Heavenly Decision Letters

> *Dear Author,*
> *As you will note, the reviewers believe your recently submitted manuscript is brilliant and I am inclined to agree. I am accepting your manuscript without revision. Best wishes, The Editor.*

This sort of letter will never happen, at least given the current state of reality, but perhaps it may in an alternate universe. Nearly all the editors and authors I've spoken to indicate that outright acceptance without revision is very rare and has never happened to them personally. My colleagues occasionally share stories of people they know, or people they have heard about, who have had a paper accepted outright. This circumstance likely means that some professionals have the ability to visit alternate universes where heavenly events occasionally happen. In my experience, perfection is not of this world.

The editor Julie Fitness laughed heartily when I asked her if she had ever accepted a manuscript outright without revision. Then she went on to explain how a request for a revision and resubmission is a distinct opportunity and one to be welcomed.

> People shouldn't be offended—or upset at all—by being asked to revise a paper. Put your emotions to one side. It is good to get feedback. If you get a revise and resubmit, that is a fantastic outcome. It means that you've got a piece of work in which people can see worth and value, and now you can polish it and make it something beautiful.

## Earthly Experience

Even the most experienced and talented authors on occasion find a less than enthusiastic response to their work and the occasional rejections ensue. Some authors suggest this is a common experience and to be expected. "The really successful authors of social work research articles have something in common: they all have had their work rejected at various points in time" (Thyer, 2008, p. 72). In the field of economics, Gans and Shepherd (1994) similarly report nearly all leading scholars report instances of having their work rejected: "In the big leagues, even the best hitters regularly strike out" (p. 165). They acknowledge that some senior economists report no instances of having their work rejected, but they discount this unusual experience by noting that these are players who submit few journal articles, preferring to publish books.

Among the senior scholars I interviewed the results are mixed. Some very prolific scholars report never having their work rejected and some do report rejections. Although an initial rejection is disappointing and can lead authors to question the value of their work, the vast majority find publication elsewhere (Belcher, 2009; Gans & Shepherd, 1994; Rotton, Foos, & Meek, 1995).

More importantly, authors can increase the probability of favorable outcomes by selecting appropriate journals; fully understanding the review process, including the issues editors and reviewers typically attend to and consider critical; and soliciting pre-reviews by trusted colleagues prior to a formal journal submission.

Less common is when an invited revision undergoes a new round of review and is subsequently rejected. I recall a case where an author submitted three revisions of a paper, each with substantial changes in response to the reviewers' and editor's recommendations. The third revision was sent out to the original reviewers, and again the reviewers called for additional revision. It was not that the authors were unresponsive to the earlier rounds of review, but rather that they just hadn't gone far enough. Once the critical reviews of the third revision arrived, I had to make the very difficult decision whether to issue yet another invitation to revise the paper. I decided that, however well intended the authors, they were simply not making sufficient progress, and I rejected the manuscript.

Rejecting revisions is among the most difficult decisions for editors and to be avoided if possible. Issuing an invitation for a revision is a major investment of scarce resources, and authors rightfully have an expectation of a high probably of seeing their work eventually accepted. This is not always the case.

Revisions are rejected for several reasons. Two common circumstances are situations in which reviewers believe an author has not sufficiently addressed the issues raised in an earlier review, or the revision may raise new concerns for the reviewers and editor. A third scenario, and one more difficult to contend with, is a situation where the reviewers identify concerns in the second round of review that they failed to mention in the first round, but could have.

Another point of concern, and a matter of fairness, is the assignment of reviewers to revisions. Typically editors try to use some of the original reviewers. That's not always possible. Adding a new reviewer is some-times required because one or more of the original reviewers is unavailable. In addition, an editor might add a new reviewer to provide a fresh perspective on a difficult manuscript or because a particular brand of expertise was absent on the first round. Editors must balance the issue of fairness and the reasonable expectations of authors with the need to meet the mission of the journal in publishing high-quality work.

## Responding to Decision Letters

Typically authors are asked to provide along with their revised manu-script a summary of how they have responded to a round of review. Such response letters should briefly summarize how they have dealt with each recommendation of the editor and the reviewers, and the letters should demonstrate common sense. Provide more detail about how you responded to a call for new analyses, but only briefly acknowledge how you responded to the dozen or so modest stylistic errors. Julie Fitness comments on this issue:

> When authors are sending in a revised paper, they need to articulate in their cover letter that they have considered and dealt with each of the issues raised, even if they think the point is trivial. For the editor who is going through and wants to match up the issues raised and the author's responses this can be very important and helpful.
>
> RM: *How long should that cover letter be?*
>
> It depends on the reviewers' comments. It doesn't have to be so long . . . you don't have to repeat every change you've made, it should be a thoughtful letter that demonstrates the author is engaged with reviewers' suggestions and acknowledges those issues.
>
> RM: *Would you ever expect the letter to be more than three single-spaced pages?*
>
> Oh, I've had them longer. [laughs] I've seen eight or nine pages. They are not really welcome. They are often tedious, or argumen-tative. Say what you've got to say clearly and concisely and get on with it.

I completely agree with Julie. The most important part of a response letter is to communicate with the editor and reviewers that your revision has been thoughtful and responsive. If you disagree with a particular sug-gestion, try to find a compromise; if this is not possible, then briefly state your case. Anything longer than two or three pages is unnecessary and not likely to be read. I would rather spend my time reading the actual manuscript than an especially long response letter.

Of course some writers may be reluctant to openly disagree with the recommendations of an editor or reviewer. As an author, I can recall instances when I did not fully agree with a reviewer's or editor's recommendation, and in nearly all cases I sought some sort of middle ground that would satisfy my critics but not necessarily compromise my own values. I assume a reviewer's response to a manuscript is apt to mirror the response of some future readers of a published article. A thorough and thoughtful response to initial criticism is a wise long-term investment.

One on occasion as a new assistant professor I was not quite so confident in frankly responding to a suggestion. A senior faculty member was editor of a prestigious book series published by a professional organization. I had a book under review and after several drafts the senior editor suggested the inclusion of some new material. I was certain this was not a helpful suggestion and in fact would detract from the purpose of the chapter in question. I wanted the book published; I was soon to be applying for tenure and promotion; I didn't regard the editor as terribly reasonable or approachable (rightly or wrongly), and I made the changes as requested. There will be times when dilemmas appear and you'll need to decide on the most appropriate course of action. This experience and many others over the years remind me as an editor of the potential to exert more influence than I might intend or think appropriate. The experience is also a reminder that the essential purpose is to promote the development of great scholarship, and doing so requires editors, reviewers, and authors to work together thoughtfully, respectfully, and mindful that power dynamics are ever present and a bit of a nuisance.

Sometimes an author may believe a rejection is unwarranted. You may believe, for instance, that you can successfully meet the objections of the editor and reviewers. The question is, should you consider writing the editor and requesting reconsideration. Such requests, in my experience, are rare, and editors vary in how they handle them. Before sharing some of the views of editors, let me share one story of such a request.

When I served as editor of the *Journal of Marriage and Family,* I occasionally received a request to reconsider a decision to reject a manuscript—not often, but a few each year. In all cases, I considered the author's request, and in perhaps half the cases, sided with the author and accepted a resubmission. In one such case, the outcome was stunning. An author had submitted a paper that received very critical reviews and, although I knew the author's previous work was of very high quality, I could not see a way to negotiate the criticisms of the reviewers. The paper was rejected. The author wrote back and asked for reconsideration. He made a straightforward and sound case; I accepted the challenge, and the paper was substantially revised and resubmitted. As you might guess, it was eventually accepted after revision and published. The next year, the paper was short-listed for a prestigious award for the best article published in that period. In the end, it was an important lesson in the need for the review process to be permeable and open. Editors and their decisions are fallible, and authors sometimes make less than perfect judgments in the preparations of initial submissions that they are fully capable of correcting. Not all editors view requests for reconsideration in the same way.

I asked Julie Fitness if an author should ask for reconsideration in response to a rejection. Julie is a former deputy editor of *Psychological Science* and, at this writing, editor of *Personal Relationships,* published by the International Association for Relationship Research.

> Well, people certainly do. Sometimes it happens a couple of months later and the authors will say they've corrected the paper and would you take another look at it. That's a bit irritating. If the editor rejects that particular paper, then I think that [an author needs to accept that decision]. If you really believed and could demonstrate that a serious misunderstanding occurred, then I think you should leave it alone. I think you should go on.
>
> I think that it is important for authors to note too that if the editor is really feeling unequivocal about a paper [the editor] should signal that. The editor might say, "If you collect more data or otherwise revise the paper I'd invite you to think about resubmitting as a new submission."
>
> If you've collected new data or otherwise substantially revised the paper, there is no harm in writing to an editor and asking about the possibility of submitting the revision as a new paper given that you've got new data to report. There is no harm in communicating with an editor, but you don't want to hassle them. They are busy people.

Harry Reis, a former editor of *Current Directions of Psychological Science,* published by the Association for Psychological Science, and the *Journal of Personality and Social Psychology,* published by the American Psychological Association, responded to a similar question and, as you will note, had a somewhat different response.

> When an author requested reconsideration, I almost always let people resubmit, with the possible exception when there was some other issue that I wasn't mentioning [in my original decision letter] that was also a factor, but that was rare. If an author wrote and said, "I understand your criticisms and I really think I can address them," and what they said made sense, I would almost always allow them to resubmit.
>
> RM: *Do you have any idea how many were accepted?*
>
> No, but some of them clearly were. And I've had that happen myself as an author.
>
> RM: *In your experience are editors uniformly responsive to those sorts of requests?*
>
> I've never had an editor say "Too bad, you had your chance." Sometimes an editor says, "I understand you could fix that but I still

don't think it is enough of a contribution." But I've never seen any-one say "I made my decision; I'm done."

I think the review process is quite permeable. Where I think it is nonpermeable is in the selection of reviewers. Very often it comes down to "Is this a significant addition to the literature or not?" And that can be a tough call.

When you see a letter requesting reconsideration, your heart sinks, but you feel like this is people's lives you're talking about. This is something that could often have a major impact on the person's life, and maybe the field. And I think you have to give it the respect [it deserves].

A paper I accepted won the award for the most cited paper in the last 20 years in social psychology, the Baron and Kenny paper on mediator/moderator models (1986). There were four reviews on the original paper: two were negative and two were positive. Now I had decided to accept it, but with a split vote I could have just as well turned it down.

RM: *So at the time of decision making it is difficult to forecast what is going to be really important.*

It's *extremely* hard to forecast. Look how many papers we accept that have very few citations. I'm sure there are plenty of papers that I published that went nowhere.

Kelly Raley, editor of the *Journal of Marriage and Family* (JMF) also responded to a question about reconsidering decisions. It is worth noting that this journal receives more than 750 submissions each year.

> I have been asked to reconsider a decision to reject a paper, and I have not reversed a decision. Usually rejections are based on a num-ber of different problems. It would really take a strong argument for me to reverse a decision. I really don't want to encourage that. JMF is just one of many journals and I hope that the feedback [authors receive] will help in submitting elsewhere.

Given the enormous task of editing this journal, it is understandable that Kelly is reluctant to encourage requests to reconsider a decision. Per-haps authors understand this, because few request reconsideration. Kelly estimated fewer than five per year.

It is fair to say that editors will respond differently to requests for recon-sideration from authors. Although some journals may have expressed policies in this regard, for most it is up to the discretion of the editor. When editors have substantial numbers of annual submissions, the work-load does not support the possibility of reconsideration. My advice is to consider such requests carefully before penning a letter to an editor, and certainly consult an experienced colleague for advice and perhaps a more objective read of the issues. Requests for reconsideration are apt to be most successful when they focus on the evidence and on the substance of the editor's or reviewers' specific criticism rather than issues of unfairness, tone, or the personal attributes of the players. "Only the most dispassionate of appeals, based on evidence not rhetoric, will win the day" (Belcher, 2009, p. 392). Although I can recall requests that were successful, the likelihood is uncertain and varies among editors. In one empirical assessment of the issue, 13% of appeals were successful in transforming a rejection into a request for a revision (Simon, Bakanic, & McPhail, 1986). In most instances, your time may be better invested in revising and submitting to another journal. There are, after all, many fine journals to consider.

There are other instances when you might consider writing to an editor; in most cases, I would not recommend doing so. For instance, having received a rejection with what you consider an unfair review, or an especially hostile review. It is simply too difficult to judge such circumstances objectively. The editor may have rejected the manuscript for reasons that have little to do with the tone of one review, or even what you consider the unfairness. The best response in such circumstances is to revise the paper using whatever useful commentary the reviewers or editor provided and submit to a new journal.

When you receive an offer to revise and resubmit a paper accompanied by a commentary you believe to be unfair, perhaps the best strategy is to temper your response and focus on the substance of the reviews rather than the tone. Take the high road. In the cover letter that accompanies your revision, clearly note how you have responded to each of the editor's and reviewers' suggestions, state the improvements you've made, and, where you've disagreed with an editor's or reviewer's suggestion, state exactly why. At the conclusion of the process, if you still feel a correspondence was particularly objectionable, you might alert the editor with a brief note. All editors receive complaints at one time or another. Long letters detailing the wrongdoing are not necessary. I asked Harry Reis about his long experience as an editor in the receipt of complaints.

> Oh, sure, I've received complaints. And in almost all of those instances I thought the complaints were unjustifiable.
>
> RM: *Did you respond to such complaints?*
>
> Always. And I always responded in a courteous way but authors didn't always take it that way.
>
> RM: *Is it important to respond in a courteous way?*
>
> I think so. I think the editor's job is to do so. . . . The editor is the face of the organization that is publishing the journal, and I think it is important to be as dispassionate as you possibly can. Of course that is not so easy to do.

Much like Harry's experience, I recall occasions when I sent unfavorable decision letters with a review that was a bit too hostile and received detailed responses by authors. It is entirely understandable, but I think best avoided. Share your first responses with a trusted colleague and then if you truly believe there remains an important issue, post a brief and unemotional note to the editor.

---

**BOX 10.5  BEST PRACTICE: RESPONDING TO EDITORS AND REVIEWERS**

- Keep responses to decision letters brief.
- Summarize how you've responded to the major issues.
- Only briefly note how you've dealt with minor issues or issues of style.
- Offer compromised solutions when not entirely in agreement with a recommendation.
- Where a compromise is not possible, state your case succinctly based on the issues.
- Avoid personal comments and tone the response appropriately. Responses are about the content of the manuscript and not the persons involved.

---

## The Ethics of Editorial Practices

Occasionally I am asked whether as editor I encourage authors to cite material published in the journal I'm representing. My response is straightforward: only if the material in question is clearly relevant, and then I would allow for a good deal of discretion on the part of the author. I prefer a rather light touch in this regard, adding to the author's menu of possibilities and nothing more. Simply suggesting work to be cited is all I wish to do. It is up to the author to make judgments about what is necessary and what is not so essential in this regard. It is entirely inappropriate for an editor to recommend citations to an author simply to elevate the status of the journal or key statistics like citation rates. I know of no editors who do so, although the practice is certainly not unknown. Coercive citation practices have been reported by authors in economics, sociology, psychology, and multiple business disciplines (Wilhite & Fong, 2012).

More difficult are situations where I think my own published work is relevant. Can an editor suggest citation to their own work to an author? This is rather murky waters because editors clearly have a conflict of interest. Authors might feel coerced to include such citations, feeling a favorable editorial decision depends on citing the work of an editor. As an example—and this happens to be something that occurred recently—an author submitted a work that mentions uncling without citing existing empirical work. Because I have recently published a book on uncling (Milardo, 2010), should I mention this to the author? It's a difficult decision because I'm acutely aware of my own potential bias as well as the potential to unwisely influence the judgment of the authors and the unintended consequence of such a recommendation. An author could easily, and quite reasonably, feel coerced or otherwise intimidated. In these cases, I prefer a conservative approach. I make no mention of my own work directly.

---

**BOX 10.6  WRITER'S RESOURCE: COMMITTEE ON PUBLICATION ETHICS**

The Committee on Publication Ethics (COPE) was established in the United Kingdom in 1997 and is now widely viewed as a leader in establishing guidelines for the operation of peer-review journals and a forum for discussing issues regarding publication ethics and the responsibilities of authors, reviewers, and editors. Membership is open to editors, and many international publishers are represented (e.g., Palgrave Macmillan, Routledge/Taylor & Francis, Wiley-Blackwell). The organization provides useful resources such as a training module for new editors, a quarterly newsletter entitled *Ethical Editing*, and model codes of conduct.

## Code of Conduct and Best Practice Guidelines for Journal Editors
### *General Duties and Responsibilities of Editors*
Editors should be responsible for everything published in their journals. They should:

- strive to meet the needs of readers and authors.
- constantly improve the journal.
- ensure the quality of the material they publish.
- champion freedom of expression.
- maintain the integrity of the academic record.
- preclude business needs from compromising intellectual standards.
- always be willing to publish corrections, clarifications, retractions and apologies when needed.

*Relations with Readers*

- Readers should be informed about who has funded research and on the role of the funders in the research.

*Relations with Authors*

- Editors should take all reasonable steps to ensure the quality of the material they publish, recognizing that journals and sections within journals will have different aims and standards.
- Editors' decisions to accept or reject a paper for publication should be based only on the paper's importance, originality, and clarity, and the study's relevance to the remit of the journal.
- A description of peer review processes should be published, and Editors should be ready to justify any important deviation from the described processes.
- Journals should have a declared mechanism for authors to appeal against Editorial decisions.
- Editors should publish guidance to authors on everything that is expected of them. This guidance should be regularly updated and should refer or link to this code.
- Editors should not reverse decisions to accept submissions unless serious problems are identified with the submission.
- New Editors should not overturn decisions to publish submissions made by the previous Editor unless serious problems are identified.

*Relations with Reviewers*

- Editors should publish guidance to reviewers on everything that is expected of them. This guidance should be regularly updated and should refer or link to this code.
- Editors should have systems to ensure that peer reviewers' identities are protected—unless they have an open review system that is declared to authors and reviewers.

*The Peer-review process*

- Editors should have systems to ensure that material submitted to their journal remains confidential while under review.

*Complaints*

- Editors should respond promptly to complaints and should ensure there is a way for dissatisfied complainants to take complaints further. This mechanism should be made clear in the journal and should include information on how to refer unresolved matters to COPE.

### Encouraging Debate

- Cogent criticisms of published work should be published unless Editors have convincing reasons why they cannot be.
- Authors of criticized material should be given the opportunity to respond.

Retrieved from http://publicationethics.org/resources/guidelines and reprinted with permission from COPE. The Publication Ethics website is a treasure trove of useful information.

## Summary

This chapter detailed some common practices in editorial offices to illustrate the perspectives of editors and what authors are likely to experience. The discussion addressed some of the difficult issues and decisions that confront editors as well as the underlying issues of fairness, reliability, and the inherent validity of the peer-review process. Finally, we detailed many of the responsibilities of editors in providing fair, well-reasoned, and responsive decision letters as well as the responsibility of authors in responding to editors and reviewers. An enriched understanding of the peer-review process and the responsibilities of all participants serves authors, their success in publishing, and the advancement of the disciplines represented.

## Activities

1. An editor requests you shorten your manuscript by three pages. You . . .
   a. narrow the margins.
   b. use a slightly smaller font.
   c. delete one and a half pages.
   d. delete three pages.

2. You receive an invitation to revise and resubmit a manuscript. One of the three reviews begins by suggesting you enroll in an elementary statistics class because you misinterpreted a finding, and then proceeds to list several insightful comments. How do you respond?

3.  An editor happens to have recently written a book on absentee fathers, the same topic of your empirical paper. Should the editor recommend the book in her decision letter? What are the ethical issues involved in this situation?

4.  The journal you have submitted to recently published an article on poverty that you do not consider particularly well done or relevant to your current work and hence you don't cite the work. You receive a decision letter and reviews of your manuscript, and the editor suggests you cite the recent work published in the journal on poverty in your revision. How do you respond?

5.  You are editor of a social science journal and have a four-hour block of time during which you must make decisions on four manuscripts. The reviewers are in agreement that manuscript 201 should be rejected. Manuscript 202 has mixed reviews, with two reviewers recommending a major revision and one recommending a rejection. Manuscripts 203 and 204 receive detailed critical reviews, but all the reviewers seem favorable and all recommend a revision and resubmission. Manuscript 203 is written in an area in which you have little personal interest, and not much expertise. Finally, the reviews of Manuscript 204, although largely favorable, are somewhat contradictory. How much time should you spend on each manuscript, including making your decision, writing the decision letter, reading manuscripts, and possibly commenting on them? Which manuscript(s) would you read?

6.  A student of yours submits a paper that is rejected by the editor without review. The editor says in a decision letter the topic is inappropriate for the journal. You notice the journal has just published an article on the same topic. How do you advise your student? [Many thanks to Harry Reis for suggesting this scenario.]

7.  You are editor of a journal and invite an author to revise and resubmit a manuscript. You receive the revised manuscript and send it out for review. Do you assign the original reviewers to the revised manuscript? Do you assign a new reviewer who did not see the original draft? What's fair, and what is apt to yield the best possible review?

8.  In the example above, the reviews for the revised manuscript are returned and two of the three reviewers identify new issues in the analyses that lead them to question the interpretation of the findings. As editor, what do you do? Ask for a second revision or reject the paper outright?

9.  A volume of the *European Journal of Social Psychology* (EJSP) consists of seven issues published annually and with a global interest. In this exercise the objective is to identify the top article published in a given volume of EJSP, or another journal if the class prefers. Each member of a class should independently select his or her choice for

top honors and be ready to defend that claim. Alternatively, the class might select another journal published outside the United States.

## Recommended Readings

Golash-Boza, T. M. (2011, March 19). How to respond to a "revise and resubmit" from an academic journal: Ten steps to a successful revision [Web log post]. Retrieved from http://getalifephd.blogspot.com/2011/03/

Tanya's commentary on responding to an invitation to revise and resubmit your work is brief, insightful, and nicely written.

Gans, J. S., & Shepherd, G. B. (1994). How are the mighty fallen: Rejected classic articles by leading Economists. *Journal of Economic Perspectives, 8*, 165–179.

Major figures in economics recount their experiences, and often they are not pleasant. A few senior economists report unblemished records with no instances of having their work rejected, but they tend to submit few journal articles, preferring to publish books. Almost all leading economists, including those who have won prestigious prizes (e.g., a Nobel Prize), who regularly submit to journals report instances of having their work rejected. Most rejected papers are eventually published in other journals, but in some instances the lag from initial submission to eventual publication spans years.

Cooper, M. L. (2009). Problems, pitfalls and promise in the peer-review process: Commentary on Trafimow & Rice. *Perspectives on Psychological Science, 4*, 84–92.

Written by a former editor, this essay summarizes the requirements of a great review and the special responsibilities of editors. Brief, to the point, and highly recommended.

Bornmann, L. (2011). Scientific peer review. *Annual Review of Information Science and Technology, 45*, 199–145.

A comprehensive review of issues concerning the reliability, validity, and fairness of the peer review process

## References

Adler, R., & Liyanarachchi, G. (2011). An empirical examination of the editorial review processes of accounting journals. *Accounting and Finance, 51*, 837–867.

Baron, R. M., & Kenny, D. A. (1986). The moderator–mediator variable distinction in social psychological research: Conceptual, strategic, and statistical considerations. *Journal of Personality and Social Psychology*, 51, 1173–1182. doi: 10.1037/0022-3514.51.6.1173.

Belcher, W. (2009). Responding to a journal's decision to reject. *IETE Technical Review, 26*, 391–393.

Bergstrom, C. T. (2007). Eigenfactor: Measuring the value and prestige of scholarly journal. *College & Research Libraries News, 68*, 314–316.

Bornmann, L. (2011). Scientific peer review. *Annual Review of Information Science and Technology, 45*, 199–245.

Bornmann, L., Mutz, R., & Daniel, H. D. (2007). Gender differences in grant peer review: A meta-analysis. *Journal of Informetrics, 1*, 226–238.

Cooper, M. L. (2009). Problems, pitfalls and promise in the peer-review process: Commentary on Trafimow & Rice (2009). *Perspectives on Psychological Science, 4*, 84–92.

Day, N. E. (2011). The silent majority: Manuscript rejection and its impact on scholars. *Academy of Management Learning and Education, 10*, 704–718.

Gans, J. S., & Shepherd, G. S. (1994). How are the mighty fallen: Rejected classic articles by leading economists. *Journal of Economic Perspectives, 8*, 165–180.

Garfield, E. (1994).The Thompson Reuters Impact Factor. Retrieved from http://thomsonreuters.com/products_services/science/free/essays/impact_factor/

Kemp, S. (2005). Agreement between reviewers of *Journal of Economic Psychology* submissions. *Journal of Economic Psychology, 26*, 779–784.

Milardo, R. M. (2010). *The forgotten kin: Aunts and uncles.* New York, NY: Cambridge University Press.

Peters, D. P., & Ceci, S. J. (1982). Peer-reviewed practices of psychology journals: The fare of published articles submitted again. *Behavioral and Brain Sciences, 5*, 187–255.

*PLoS Medicine* Editors. (2006). The impact factor game. *PLoS Med 3*, e291. doi:10.1371/journal.pmed.0030291. Retrieved from http://www.plosmedicine.org/article/info:doi/10.1371/journal.pmed.0030291

Rotton, J. P, Foos, L., & Meek, V. (1995). Publication practices and the file drawer problem: A survey of published authors. *Journal of Social Behavior and Personality, 10*, 1–13.

Sense About Science. (2010). *Peer review survey 2009: Full report.* London, UK: Author.

Simon, J. R., Bakanic, V., & McPhail, C. (1986). Who complains to journal editors and what happens. *Sociological Inquiry, 56*, 259–271.

Sternberg, R. J., & Sternberg, K. (2010). *The psychologist's companion: A guide to writing scientific papers for students and researchers* (5th ed.). Cambridge, UK: Cambridge University Press.

Street, M. D., Bozeman, D. P., & Whitfield, J. M. (1998). Author perceptions of positive and negative editor behaviors in the manuscript review process. *Journal of Social Behavior and Personality, 13*, 1–22.

Thyer, B. A. (2008). *Preparing research articles.* New York, NY: Oxford University Press.

Weller, A. C. (2002). *Editorial peer review: Its strengths and weaknesses.* Medford, NJ: Information Today.

Wilhite, A. W., & Fong, E. A. (2012). Coercive citation in academic publishing. *Science, 335*, 542–543.

# Appendices

## 1. Reuben Hill Awards

Each year a large group of volunteers reviews more than 30 behavioral and social science journals that typically publish theory, review, or empirical work on families. From this review of the previous year's journals a list of articles is developed that committee members then evaluate. The article with the highest ratings receives the Hill Award, sponsored by the National Council on Family Relations (NCFR) and named after Reuben Hill, an influential family scholar especially known for championing the development of family theory. Hill was one of the founders of the Theory Construction and Research Methodology Workshop that takes place before and during the NCFR annual meetings.

The annual winners of the Hill Award represent some of the best work published and are well worth study. Selecting an exceptionally well-crafted article and modeling it in your own writing is a very useful strategy and highly recommended. To do so, focus less on the content or substance of the article and more on the structure. How did the author(s) construct the introduction, and where is the core statement of the problem or focus of the article? How long is this section? Is it clear? For each section of the paper, ask yourself similar questions, all while thinking strategically about how an author organized a section and communicated an idea. Is there a consistency in the theme of the article across the different sections of the paper? How would you describe the basic content of the discussion section? Comparing the work of several authors can be quite helpful. In comparing articles, is great work good storytelling? Is the quality of writing important? Ideally you may find an author whose work and writing style you especially admire and can then emulate in your own writing.

In the list below, the year of the award is followed by the names of the authors, date of publication, title of the article, and particulars of publication.

2013 Soehl, T., & Waldinger, R. (2012). Inheriting the homeland? Intergenerational transmission of cross-border ties in migrant families. *American Journal of Sociology, 118*, 778–813.

2012 Schofield, T. J., Martin, M. J., Conger, K. J., Conger, R. D., Donnellan, M. B., & Neppl, T. M. (2011). Intergenerational transmission of adaptive functioning: A test of the interactionist model of SES and human development. *Child Development, 82,* 33–47.

2011 Budig, M. J., & Hodges, M. J. (2010). Differences in disadvantage: Variation in the motherhood penalty across white women's earnings distribution. *American Sociological Review, 75,* 705–728.

2010 Gibson, C. M. (2009). Money, marriage, and children: Testing the financial expectations and family formation theory. *Journal of Marriage and Family, 71,* 146–160.

2009 Meadows, S., McLanahan, S., & Brooks-Gunn, J. (2008). Stability and change in family structure and maternal health trajectories. *American Sociological Review, 73,* 314–334.

2008 Amato, P. R., & Hohmann-Marriott, B. (2007). A comparison of high and low distress marriages that end in divorce. *Journal of Marriage and Family, 69,* 621–638.

2007 Sturge-Apple, M. T., Davies, P. T., & Cummings, E. M. (2006). Hostility and withdrawal in marital conflict: Effects on parental emotional unavailability and inconsistent discipline. *Journal of Family Psychology, 20,* 227–238.

2006 Huston, A. C., & Rosenkrantz Aronson, S. (2005). Mothers' time with infant and time in employment as predictors of mother-child relationships and children's early development. *Child Development, 76,* 467–482.

2005 Brody, G. H., McBride Murry, V., McNair, L., Brown, A. C., Luo, Z., Chen, Y., Neubaum-Carlson, E., Gerrard, M., Gibbons, F. X., Molgaard, V., Spoth, R. L., & Wills, T. A. (2004). The strong African American families program: Translating research into prevention programming. *Child Development, 75,* 900–917.

2004 Wickrama, K.A.S., & Bryant, C. (2003). Community context of social resources and adolescent mental health. *Journal of Marriage and Family, 65,* 850–865.

2003 Simons, R. L., Lin, K., Gordon, L. C., Brody, G. H., & Conger, R. D. (2002). Community differences in the association between parenting practices and child conduct problems. *Journal of Marriage and Family, 64,* 331–345.

2002 Axinn, W., & Yabiku, S. T. (2001). Social change, the social organization of families, and fertility limitation. *American Journal of Sociology, 106,* 1219–1261.

2002 Van Laningham, J., Johnson, D. A., & Amato, P. (2001). Marital happiness, marital duration, and the U-shaped curve: Evidence from a five-wave panel study. *Social Forces, 78,* 1313–1341.

2001 Sayer, L. C., & Bianchi, S. B. (2000). Women's economic dependence and the probability of divorce: A review and reexamination. *Journal of Family Issues, 21,* 906–943.

2000 Amato, P. R., & Gilbreth, J. G. (1999). Nonresident fathers and children's well-being: A meta analysis. *Journal of Marriage and the Family, 61,* 557–573.

1999 Downey, D. B., Ainsworth Darnell, J. W., & Dufar, M. J. (1998). Sex of parent and children's well-being in single parent households. *Journal of Marriage and the Family, 60,* 878–893.

1998 Karney, B. R., & Bradbury, T. N. (1997). Neuroticism, marital interaction, and the trajectory of marital satisfaction. *Journal of Personality and Social Psychology, 72,* 1075–1092.

1997 Matthews, L., Conger, R., & Wickrama, K.A.S. (1996). Work-family conflict and marital quality: Mediating processes. *Social Psychology Quarterly, 59,* 62–79.

1996 Karney, B. R., & Bradbury, T. N. (1995). The longitudinal course of marital quality and stability: A review of theory, method, and research. *Psychological Bulletin, 118,* 3–34.

1995 McLoyd, V. C., Epstein Jayaratne, T., Ceballa, R., & Borquez, J. (1994). Unemployment and work interruption among African American single mothers: Effects on parenting and adolescent socioemotional functioning. *Child Development, 65,* 562–589.

1994 Amato, P. (1993). Urban/rural differences in helping friends and family members. *Social Psychology Quarterly, 56,* 249–262.

1993 Bielby, W., & Bielby, D. (1992). Family ties, gender-role beliefs, and reluctance to relocate for a better job. *American Journal of Sociology, 97,* 1241–1267.

1992 Rusbult, C. R., Verette, J., Whitney, G. A., Slovik, L. E., & Lipkus, I. (1991). Accommodations processes in close relationships: Theory and preliminary evidence. *Journal of Personality and Social Psychology, 60,* 53–78.

1991 Parcel, T. L., & Menaghan, E. G. (1990). Maternal working conditions and children's verbal facility: Studying in the intergenerational transmission of inequality from others to young children. *Social Psychology Quarterly, 53,* 132–147.

1990 Godwin, D. D., & Scanzoni, J. (1989). Couple consensus during marital joint decision-making: A context, process, outcome model. *Journal of Marriage and the Family, 51,* 943–956.

1989 McLanahan, S. S., & Bumpass, L. L. (1988). Intergenerational consequences of family disruption. *American Journal of Sociology, 44,* 130–152.

1988 Sorenson, A., & McLanahan, S. (1987). Married women's economic dependency, 1940–1980. *American Journal of Sociology, 43,* 659–687.

1987 Glass, J., Bengtson, V., & Dunham, C. C. (1986). Attitude similarity in three-generation families: Socialization, status inheritance or reciprocal influence? *American Sociological Review, 51,* 685–698.

1986 Mirowsky, J. (1985). Depression and marital power: An equity model. *American Journal of Sociology, 91,* 557–592.

1985 Mutran, E., & Reitzes, D. (1984). Intergenerational support activities and well-being among the elderly: A convergence of exchange and symbolic interaction perspectives. *American Sociological Review, 49,* 117–130.

1984 Menaghan, E. G. (1983). Marital stress and family transition: Panel analysis. *Journal of Family Issues, 4,* 545–573.

1983 Polonko, K., Scanzoni, J., & Teachman, J. (1982). Childlessness and marital satisfaction. *Journal of Family Issues, 3,* 545–573.

1982 Hornung, C. O., McCullough, B. C., & Sugimoto, T. (1981). Status relationships in marriage: Risk factors in spouse abuse. *Journal of Marriage and the Family, 42,* 675–692.

1981 Acock, A. C., Bengtson, V. L., Reiss, I. L., Anderson, R. E., & Sponaugle, G. C. (1980). Socialization and attribution processes: Actual versus perceived similarity among parents and youth. *Journal of Marriage and the Family, 41,* 501–515.

1980 Gove, W. G., Hughes, M., & Galle, O. G. (1979). Overcrowding in the home: An empirical investigation of its possible pathological consequences. *American Sociological Review, 44,* 59–80.

## 2. Anselm Strauss Awards

The National Council on Family Relations gives this award annually to the best qualitative research article published in the previous year. The process is similar to the Hill Award in that a team of volunteers reviews journals that publish qualitative family research and eventually selects the most highly rated work for the award. Anselm Strauss was a leading proponent of qualitative research designs and developed many of the methods we now consider best practices. Consider reading several articles from the list of award winners and thinking about how the authors crafted their work, organized each section, anticipated potential criticism, described the basic message throughout the paper, and utilized theory. By reading some of these articles, you may discover work you particularly admire and what you'd prefer to avoid, and in this way improve your own writing.

In the list below, the year of the award is followed by the names of the authors, date of publication, title of the article, and particulars of publication.

2013 Weaver-Hightower, M. B. (2012). Waltzing Matilda: An autoethnography of a father's stillbirth. *Journal of Contemporary Ethnography, 41,* 462–491.

2012 Davis, J., Ward, D. B., & Storm, C. (2011). The unsilencing of military wives: Wartime deployment experiences and citizen responsibility. *Journal of Marital and Family Therapy, 37,* 51–63.

2011 Garcia, M., & McDowel, T. (2010). Mapping social capital: A critical contextual approach for working with low-status families. *Journal of Marital and Family Therapy, 36,* 96–107.

2010 Funk, L., & Stajduhar, K. (2009). Interviewing family caregivers: Implications of the caregiving context for the research interview. *Qualitative Health Research, 19,* 859–867.

2009 Oswald, R. F., & Masciadrelli, B. P. (2008). Generative ritual among nonmetropolitan lesbians and gay men: Promoting social inclusion. *Journal of Marriage and Family, 70,* 1060–1073.

2008 Read, T., & Wuest, J. (2007). Daughters caring for dying parents: A process of relinquishing. *Qualitative Health Research, 17,* 932–944.

2007 Matta, D. S., & Knudson-Martin, C. (2006). Father responsivity: Couple processes and the construction of fatherhood. *Family Process, 45,* 19–37.

2006 Beitin, B. K., & Allen, K. R. (2005). Resilience in Arab American couples after September 11, 2001: A systems perspective. *Journal of Marital and Family Therapy, 31,* 251–267.

2005 Edwards, M.L.K. (2004). We're decent people: Constructing and managing family identity in rural working-class communities. *Journal of Marriage and Family, 66,* 515–529.

2004 Wuest, J., Fod-Gilboe, M., Merritt-Gray, M., & Berman, H. (2003). Intrusion: The central problem for family health promotion among children and single mothers after leaving an abusive partner. *Qualitative Health Research, 13,* 597–622.

2003 Fergus, K. D., Gray, R. E., Fitch, M. I., Labrecque, M., & Phillips, C. (2002). Active consideration: Conceptualizing patient-provided support for spouse caregivers in the context of prostate cancer. *Qualitative Health Research*, *12*, 492–517.

2002 No award given.

2001 Oswald, R. F. (2000). Family and friendship relationships after young women come out as bisexual or lesbian. *Journal of Homosexuality*, *38*, 65–83.

2000 Mannis, V. S. (1999). Single mothers by choice. *Family Relations*, *48*, 121–128.

2000 Banister, E. M. (1999). Evolving reflexivity: Negotiating meaning of women's midlife experience. *Qualitative Inquiry*, *5*, 3–23.

# Index

# media
## MANUAL

**The Use of Microphones**

Fourth Edition

# media MANUAL

# The
# Use of
# Microphones

## Fourth Edition

Alec Nisbett

Focal Press
An imprint of Butterworth-Heinemann Ltd
Linacre House, Jordan Hill, Oxford OX2 8DP

A member of the Reed Elsevier plc group

OXFORD  LONDON  BOSTON
MUNICH  NEW DELHI  SINGAPORE  SYDNEY
TOKYO  TORONTO  WELLINGTON

First published 1974
Second edition 1983
Third edition 1989
Fourth edition 1993
Reprinted 1994

© Alec Nisbett 1993

**British Library Cataloguing in Publication Data**
Nisbett, Alec
  Use of Microphones. – 4 Rev. ed. – (Media
  Manuals Series)
  I. Title  II. Series
  621.38284

ISBN 0 240 51365 7

**Library of Congress Cataloging in Publication Data**
Nisbett, Alec.
  The use of microphones/Alec Nisbett. – 4th ed.
  p.    cm. – (Media manual)
  Includes bibliographical references and index.
  ISBN 0 240 51365 7
  1. Microphone. 2. Sound – Recording and reproducing.  I. Title.
  II. Series: Media manuals.
  TK5986.N57  1993                                    93–6236
  621.382'84–dc20                                        CIP

Printed and bound in Great Britain by
Biddles Ltd, Guildford and King's Lynn

# Contents

*Sound is a medium for communication.*
*High-quality sound serves communication; it is not an end in itself.*

# Introduction: On quality

Your end product is sound from a loudspeaker — or, occasionally, head-phones. In the listener's home it may be high-quality sound (hi-fi); more often it is simply appalling by the standards of the sound enthusiast. The immediate source may be radio, CD or vinyl record-player, cassette or open-reel tape deck; or it may accompany pictures on TV or film. In a car, it will compete with engine and traffic noise. A signal recorded or trans-mitted in stereo may be heard with inadequate loudspeaker separation or in mono. The range of possible listening conditions is wide — and we may assume that except in your own home it will generally be out of your control.

But what you can control is the quality of sound that you make available to the listener. Your first responsibility will often be towards the vast majority whose needs are simple: intelligibility and clarity of speech or a concentration on the less demanding rhythmic or melodic qualities of music. Your second responsibility will be towards those who enjoy the wider ranges of frequency and dynamics, and the greater complexity of tonal structure that may be appreciated on good equipment. This aspect of your work will give the greatest satisfaction but it is not your sole task: never forget those whose simpler need is clarity.

It is also well to remember that sound quality comes second to sound content: that what is being said is generally — though not always — more important than how you say it. The sound balancer should help to ensure that the message transcends the medium.

## Recent improvements in quality
In the late 1980s, the advent of compact discs (CD) and promise of digital audio tapes (DAT) heralded a great improvement in the quality of record-ings. Digital technology spread from studio to home. However, this does not extend to the interfaces between sound and electronic signal: improve-ments in loudspeakers and microphones have been more modest. In particular, a small loudspeaker still cannot produce a big, balanced bass sound. The quality of some microphones with very small diaphragms and head amplifiers has improved. But microphone techniques have changed very little and the principles of microphone balance not at all.

I am fortunate in the background that allows me both to describe all this and to practise it: the British Broadcasting Corporation is the biggest of its kind in the world whose contract is not with government or advertisers but directly with the audience. The range of activity that is possible in so vast an organisation, together with the simplicity of its responsibilities, makes the BBC unique both as a place to learn and as a place to do the job. This book reflects the fruits of my own experience together with that of many colleagues who have been generous with both time and advice.

*Aesthetic and engineering aspects of the sound balancer's job may sometimes conflict.*

# Listening to sound

The microphone is the central and crucial item of sound studio equipment. It converts the mechanical energy of sound in air into electrical energy. The original sound consists of a series of variations in air pressure: the microphone turns them into a similar (but not necessarily identical) series of fluctuations in voltage. They may then be frozen in the mechanical form of a record, printed as a pattern in magnetic particles on tape, or coded piggyback on to electromagnetic waves and transmitted at the speed of light. And at the end of all this it must be possible to feed the electrical signal to loudspeakers, which drive the air in a series of variations in pressure which closely mimic the original sound.

Microphones and loudspeakers are, by their nature, analogue devices, faithfully and continuously following the soundwave. Intervening stages may be either analogue or digital, sampling the wave at frequent intervals and encoding it as a series of numbers.

Reproduced sound may be similar to the original sound but it cannot be identical. In monophonic sound (mono) it comes to the listener through a single loudspeaker; in stereo from two; in quadraphonic reproduction it comes from four; in auditoria perhaps from many more. None of these can recreate the original sound field that existed in the studio; the sound is necessarily modified in some way. The results of the changes that inevitably take place can only be judged aesthetically, by ear.

The exercise of this judgement is a craft or, at best, it might even be suggested, an art. It is not a science or an aspect of engineering, although the job is often, for convenience, combined with the engineering side of sound control.

**Microphone balance**

The subject of this book is microphone balance: the placing of the one or many microphones which sample the sound field in the studio, the control of their output, and the aural evaluation of the results. Quadraphonic techniques enjoyed a brief vogue, but are no longer widely used. A brief description is included in *The Technique of the Sound Studio*. (See 'Further Reading', page 177.)

The microphone is treated as part of a system which includes the sound field in the studio, characteristics of microphones themselves and the equipment that is used to mix and control the resulting signals. All of these are discussed in the following pages.

An important objective of audio engineering is to minimise change, to avoid degradation of quality below some chosen level; in contrast the sound balancing techniques that are described in this book actually promote change within certain conventions. The two functions should not be confused.

## THE STUDIO CHAIN

The *sound source* radiates sound as *pressure waves* in the air.

Some of the sound travels direct to the microphone. Some is reflected and arrives later as *reverberation*.

Unwanted sound, *noise*, also travels to the microphone.

The *microphone* converts the variations in air pressure into electrical variations – the *signal*. Imperfections in this process introduce *distortion*. The microphone and all other components also produce unwanted electronic *noise* – hiss, hum, etc.

*Amplifiers* may be introduced at any stage to compensate for loss in *volume* of the electrical signal. There may also be an *analogue-to-digital* converter.

*Equalisers* may be introduced at any stage to compensate for deficiencies in preceding or subsequent components or to creatively modify the signal.

*Artificial reverberation* ('*echo*'), may be added to individual components or to the mixed output. This process is usually digital.

In a *mixer*, electrical signals from microphones, tape reproducers and record players are combined.

A *volume* or *peak programme meter* is used to ensure that the electrical level is within specified limits.

*Headphones* are used only when no suitable listening room is available (e.g. on film locations).

The resulting *sound balance* is judged by ear and *monitoring loudspeaker* in the listening room.

*Studio output* may go to a *tape recorder*; to a *transmitter* (radio or TV); or to a *closed circuit* line.

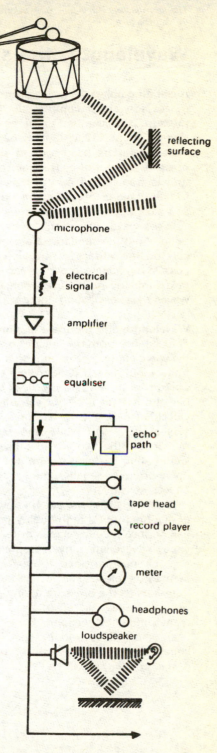

reflecting surface

microphone

electrical signal

amplifier

equaliser

'echo' path

tape head

record player

meter

headphones

loudspeaker

**9**

# Wavelength: the size of sound

A vibrating object such as a drum skin produces pressure variations: as it moves forward it compresses the air in front of it. This increase in pressure is transmitted to the next layer of air, and so on, travelling at a rate of about 1120ft (341m) per second in warm air. Meanwhile the vibrating surface has begun to move backward, creating a region of low pressure in front of it. The natural elasticity of the air is such that this in turn is transmitted outward at the same speed, to be followed by a further wave of pressure and rarefaction as the surface moves forward and back again. A regular series of waves radiates from the source.

These waves are a little different from the waves on the surface of a pond — but the similarities are greater than the differences. If you put a cork on the surface of the water it bobs up and down as each wave passes, but it stays more or less in the same place from one wave to the next. Similarly an air particle dances backward and forward as the pressure waves pass, oscillating about a median position.

### Wavelength and the ideal diaphragm

The distance from the crest of one wave to the crest of the next is called the wavelength. The sounds that we can hear have wavelengths ranging from about 1 inch (2.5cm) to perhaps 40ft (12m). The orifice and diaphragm of an ear is rather less than half an inch (12mm) across, about half the size of the shortest wavelength that we can hear. This is no coincidence. If it were larger some parts of the diaphragm would be subject to pressure while other regions would be sucked outwards by the rarefaction: the two would cancel out. If the diaphragm were smaller it would still register pressure and rarefaction in turn, but the area acted upon would be smaller, the total pressure would be less: the ear would be less sensitive.

By analogy with the ear we now have an ideal specification for the size of diaphragm of a high-quality pressure microphone. It should be about half an inch (12mm) across or less. Because of the difficulty of obtaining enough sensitivity early microphones were very much bigger, but modern microphones are often about this size, and some are smaller, allowing them to sample the shortest audible wavelength with even greater fidelity.

In real life, the pressure at any point fluctuates in a complex manner in response to sound of different wavelengths and intensities and from many different directions. A microphone which measures only pressure hears the total sound irrespective of the direction it comes from. It behaves almost exactly like the human ear. But this is not the only type of microphone, as we shall see.

## SOUND WAVES

A vibrating panel generates waves of pressure and rarefaction: sound. Air is displaced backward and forward along the line of travel.

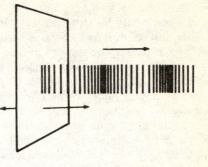

## LATERAL WAVE

Diagrammatically, it is convenient to represent the pressure waves of sound as lateral waves, as though the air were displaced from side to side as the wave passes. In fact, this is a graph in which displacement of air from its median position (vertical axis) is plotted against time (horizontal axis).

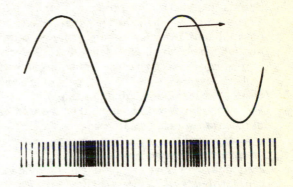

## THE SHORTEST WAVELENGTH

that young ears can hear defines the size of diaphragm that is needed for a high-quality pressure microphone.

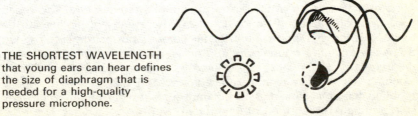

# Frequency: the timing of sound

The frequency of a sound measured in hertz (Hz) is the number of regular excursions made by an air particle in one second.

The range of human hearing is sometimes quoted as being from about 16Hz to 16 000Hz, the upper limit depending on age and health. Young ears tend to hear higher frequencies, but 16 000Hz is often taken as a reasonable upper limit required of engineering systems. Even so, the diaphragm of a full-range high-quality microphone must be capable of responding faithfully to very rapid changes of pressure. This means that it must be very light, or, more precisely, that it must have a very low inertia. Such microphones may be both expensive and delicate, so they are used only where absolutely necessary, e.g. for individual instruments like cymbals and triangles which have a strong high-frequency content. For many combinations including the human voice, a frequency response up to 10 000Hz is satisfactory.

At the other end of the scale the lowest frequencies that can be heard as musical notes merge into those that are perceived as separate puffs of air pressure. We shall see later that a perfect low-frequency response is not essential: even for the fullest range of music a frequency response that is level to about 50Hz is all that is needed.

In practice, electronic components can easily go well beyond these limits, while mechanical components may be subject to radically increased cost or reduced durability if they have the same full range. The available audio range may also be limited by external factors such as the capacity of electromagnetic or line transmissions.

### Frequency and wavelength

Frequency and wavelength are closely related. The speed of sound in air can, for rough calculations, be treated as a constant. A rapidly vibrating source (high frequency) produces sound of short wavelengths; a source vibrating relatively slowly (and a hundred excursions per second is slow enough to be called low frequency) produces long wavelengths.

Large objects are necessary to radiate low-frequency sound efficiently. The sound-board of a piano is suitable, but not so efficient as the larger pipes in the lower register of an organ.

### The effect of temperature

A factor that does affect the speed of sound is temperature. The speed rises gradually as temperature goes up. The strings of violins can be tuned, but the vibrating column of air some wind instruments cannot. So, when air temperature goes up and wavelength remains the same, the frequency that we hear also rises. A flute, for example, sharpens by a semitone as the temperature goes up by 15°F (8°C). This is a daily problem for orchestral musicians: they tune (to the oboe) when they start and again when the instruments are warm.

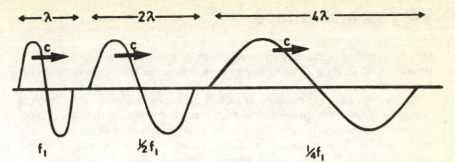

$\lambda$     $2\lambda$     $4\lambda$

c     c     c

$f_1$     $\frac{1}{2}f_1$     $\frac{1}{4}f_1$

**FREQUENCY AND WAVELENGTH** All sound waves travel at the same speed, c, through the same medium, so frequency, f, is inversely proportional to wavelength, $\lambda$.

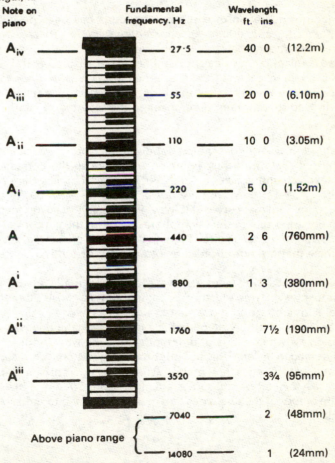

| Note on piano | Fundamental frequency. Hz | Wavelength ft. ins | |
|---|---|---|---|
| $A_{iv}$ | 27·5 | 40 0 | (12.2m) |
| $A_{iii}$ | 55 | 20 0 | (6.10m) |
| $A_{ii}$ | 110 | 10 0 | (3.05m) |
| $A_i$ | 220 | 5 0 | (1.52m) |
| $A$ | 440 | 2 6 | (760mm) |
| $A^i$ | 880 | 1 3 | (380mm) |
| $A^{ii}$ | 1760 | 7½ | (190mm) |
| $A^{iii}$ | 3520 | 3¾ | (95mm) |
| | 7040 | 2 | (48mm) |
| | 14080 | 1 | (24mm) |

Above piano range {

**MUSICAL NOTES: FREQUENCY AND WAVELENGTH** Some examples. Frequency multiplied by wavelength equals the speed of sound, which is 1100ft/sec (335m/sec) in cold air. (The speed is a little faster in warm air.)

**13**

# Waves and phase

*Particle velocity* is the rate of movement of individual air particles. It is proportional to air pressure: where one has a peak in its waveform so has the other.

*Pressure gradient* is the rate at which pressure changes with distance along the wave. Where pressure is at a peak its rate of change is zero, and where pressure is that of the normal atmosphere, its rate of change is maximum. The pressure gradient waveform is similar to that for pressure, but lags a quarter of wavelength behind it.

*Particle displacement* is the distance that a particle of air has moved from its equilibrium position. Displacement is proportional to pressure gradient.

The mode of operation of some microphones has been described as *constant-velocity*, and others as *constant-amplitude*. These confusing terms actually mean that the output voltage is equal to a constant multiplied by diaphragm velocity or amplitude (i.e. displacement) respectively. Of more practical importance are the terms *pressure operation* and *pressure-gradient operation*, as these characteristics of a microphone's action will lead to important differences in the way that it can be used.

### Adding sounds together

*Phase* is a term used in describing subdivisions of one wavelength of a tone. The full cycle from any point on the wave to the corresponding point one wavelength further on is a 360° change of phase. Here the two points are *in phase*; they are fully *out of phase* (or '180° out of phase') with the point on the curve half way in between. The mathematical jargon is not important to the microphone user, but the concept of waves being in or out of phase is vital. Signals that are in phase reinforce each other; those that are out of phase subtract from or tend to cancel each other.

Complex sounds with complex waveforms are made up by adding many simple waveforms together – adding, that is, those parts that are in phase, and subtracting those that are out of phase.

The ear is not as a rule interested in phase. Two sound-waves can be added to give a whole range of different composite waveforms which all sound the same to the ear. This has important implications for microphone design and use. It does not matter whether a microphone measures pressure (like the ear) or pressure gradient which is 90° out of phase with it. And the output of the two types can usually be mixed together without problems.

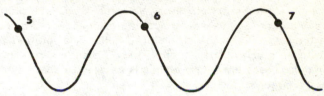

**WAVEFORM RELATIONSHIPS** 1, Pressure wave. 2, Displacement of air particles. 3, Pressure gradient. 4, Air particle velocity. Note that: (a) pressure is proportional to particle velocity, (b) pressure gradient is proportional to particle displacement, (c) the pressure gradient 'wave' follows a quarter of a wavelength behind the pressure wave. Pressure gradient is said to be 90° *out of phase* with the pressure wave; to lag 90° behind it.

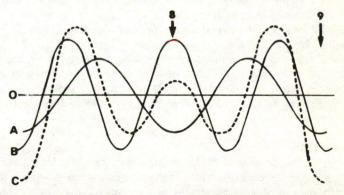

**PHASE** This is the stage that a wave has reached in its cycle. The points 5, 6, 7 are said to be *in phase* with each other.

**ADDING SOUND PRESSURES** At any point and at any time the sound pressure is the algebraic sum of all pressures due to all waves passing through that point, i.e. everything above normal pressure is added; everything below it is subtracted. It does not matter what direction the wave is travelling in. If the simple waves A and B are summed the result is shown in the complex waveform C. At 8 there is partial cancellation as pressure in wave A coincides with rarefaction in curve B. At 9 the rarefactions coincide; they reinforce each other.

**15**

# Energy, intensity and resonance

The energy of a sound source depends on the amplitude of vibration: the broader the swing the more power (energy output per second) it is capable of producing.

The sound intensity at any point is the acoustic energy passing through unit area per second. According to the inverse square law which applies to *spherical waves*, the intensity of sound radiated from a point source diminishes as the square of the distance.

In practice, however, if the source is a large flat area the waves are not at first spherical: for a distance comparable to the size of the source they, too, are flat or *plane waves*, and in this region there is little reduction in intensity with distance. As we shall see, the different conditions that are met in plane and spherical waves affect the operation of pressure gradient microphones.

### How a sound source works
To convert the stored energy of the vibrating sound source to acoustic energy in the air, the two must be efficiently coupled. Objects that are small or slender compared with the wavelength associated with their frequency of vibration do not radiate sound at all well. For example, the prong of a tuning fork and the string of a violin slice through the air without giving up much of their energy: the air simply slips round the sides. So in these cases the sound source is coupled to a wooden panel (or box) with a larger surface.

A freely suspended panel has natural frequencies at which it 'rings' if you tap it. If it does this at the frequency of the tuning fork or string, the panel quickly absorbs energy from the source and so can transmit it to the air. The panel is said to *resonate*.

The violin has panels which must respond and resonate at many frequencies. To achieve this it is made very irregular in shape. Such a panel does not ring or resonate to any particular note: if you tap it it makes a dull, unmusical sound. But if the strings are connected to it (through the bridge of the instrument) the panel oscillates in forced vibrations. Energy is transferred from string to panel, and from this to the air.

### Cavity resonance
Another sort of resonance is found in the *cavity* or *Helmholtz resonator*. If the panel becomes part of a box with a relatively small opening, the air inside resonates at one special frequency (as when you blow across the mouth of a bottle). This is useful for the sound box of a tuning fork, but in a violin it causes a 'wolf tone' which the violinist treats with particular care.

16

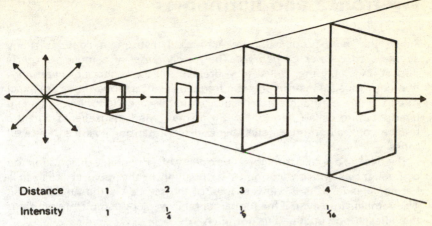

| Distance | 1 | 2 | 3 | 4 |
|----------|---|---|---|---|
| Intensity | 1 | $\frac{1}{4}$ | $\frac{1}{9}$ | $\frac{1}{16}$ |

SOUND INTENSITY is the energy passing through unit area per second. For a spherical wave (i.e. a wave from a point source) the intensity dies off very rapidly at first. The power of the source is the total energy radiated in all directions.

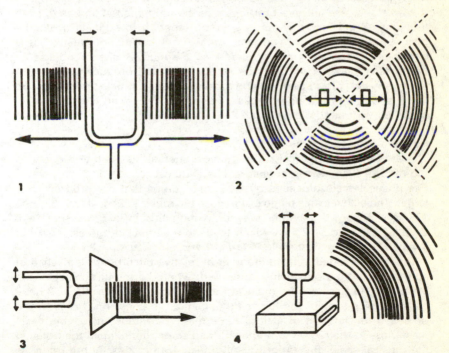

TUNING FORK   1 and 2, Each fork vibrates at a specific natural frequency, but held in free air radiates little sound. 3, Placed against a wooden panel, the vibrations of the tuning fork are coupled to the air more efficiently and the fork is heard clearly. 4, When the tuning fork is placed on a box having a cavity with a natural resonance of the same frequency, the sound radiates powerfully.

**17**

*When a single note is played on a musical instrument, many frequencies are produced at the same time.*

# Overtones and harmonics

Any single *note* produced from a musical instrument contains many separate *pure tones* or *partials*. The *fundamental* of a musical note is almost invariably the lowest tone present; all the others are *overtones*. For many musical instruments the frequencies of the overtones are exact multiples of the fundamental frequency. In this case the fundamental and overtones are called *harmonics*. String and wind instruments and the human voice all produce notes that consist of harmonic series of related tones.

The *pitch* of a note is the subjective quality of a frequency or combination of frequencies which determines its position in the musical scale. In a harmonic series it is the lowest tone of the series, i.e. the fundamental. This remains true even if the fundamental is weak or completely missing: this affects tone quality, but not pitch.

### Pitch and percussion instruments
Many percussion instruments produce notes of indefinite pitch: most of the overtones are not exact multiples of the fundamental. In some, such as tympani, the fundamental is powerful enough to suggest a definite pitch even though the overtones are without harmonic quality. Many percusion instruments are arranged as a series of similar objects of progressively decreasing size, so that the notes they produce when struck form a musical progression; but in others such as cymbals or the triangle, there is such a profusion of tones present that the sound blends reasonably well with almost anything.

### How we hear sounds as music
The ear (and brain) perceive the musical interval between two notes as the ratio of their two frequencies. The simplest ratio is 1 : 2, an octave. The musical scale proceeds by frequency jumps that get progressively larger. The octaves on a piano progress in the ratios 1 : 2 : 4 : 8 : 16 : 32 : 64 : 128 (see page 13). Another way of writing this is in powers of two, $2^0 : 2^1 : 2^2 : 2^3 : 2^4 : 2^5 : 2^6 : 2^7$, which leads to a simpler progression: 0,1,2, 3,4,5,6,7 — the musical scale is *logarithmic*.

The brain is aided in its judgement of relative pitch by the presence of harmonics in the notes being compared; where harmonics coincide, the brain hears a harmonious musical interval. Notes in the ratio 1 : 2 have all harmonics (except the lower fundamental) in common. Notes in the ratio 2 : 3 (an interval of a fifth) have many harmonics in common, as have those in the ratio 3 : 4 (a fourth); and so on, defining all the notes in the musical scale. But unfortunately these are not exactly the intervals you get if you divide an octave into twelve equal ratios. The equal or 'well-tempered' scale that we use today is a compromise: it is imperfect musically but makes it easier to change key.

**18**

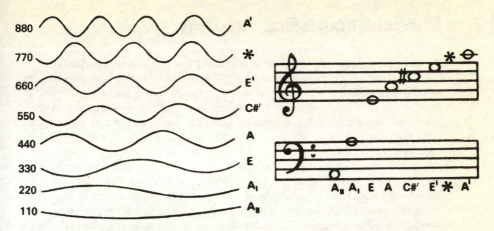

**THE FIRST EIGHT HARMONICS OF THE MUSICAL NOTE A₁₁ (110Hz)** The fundamental is the first harmonic, the first overtone is the second harmonic and so on. They are all notes in the key of the fundamental except for the seventh harmonic which is not a recognised musical note at all: it lies between G and G♭.

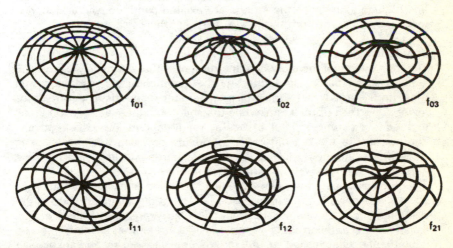

**VIBRATION OF A DRUMSKIN** The suffixes indicate the number of radial and circular lines (nodes) where there is no motion. The first circular node is at the edge where the membrane is clamped. The overtones are not harmonically related. If $f_{01} = 100$Hz the other modes of vibration shown here are: $f_{02} = 230$; $f_{03} = 360$; $f_{11} = 159$; $f_{12} = 292$; $f_{21} = 214$Hz.

# Musical acoustics: strings

If a string is bowed, struck or plucked in the middle, the fundamental and the odd numbered harmonics, which all have maximum amplitude in the middle of the string, are emphasised; while the even harmonics, which have a node in the middle of the string, are lacking. Exciting the string anywhere near the centre produces strong lower harmonics; exciting it near the end produces strong upper harmonics. The tone quality of the harp is varied in this way.

A violin string is bowed near — but not too near — one end, so that a good range of both odd and even harmonics is excited. But some will be weaker than others. For example, if a string is bowed or struck at approximately one-seventh of its length it does not produce the seventh harmonic, an advantage because this is an overtone that is 'out of tune' with those of other notes that are being played.

**Attack and envelope**
The method of excitation helps to give an instrument its particular quality. The way that a note starts is called the *attack*, and a microphone must be capable of responding to the rapid and erratic transients that may be present in this part of a note. Early keyboard instruments where the string is plucked are very different in character from the piano, where the string is struck by a felted hammer.

Another quality which defines the instrument is the way in which the note changes in volume as it progresses, i.e. its *envelope*. Here the violin and its family, in which the strings are excited continuously, are characteristically different from the piano, harp and harpsichord.

**Tone quality**
The tone quality of the individual instrument within a family — e.g. violin, viola, 'cello or bass — is defined by the qualities of the resonator; and most particularly by its size. A large resonator responds to and radiates lower notes than a small one, while the sound box of a violin is too small to radiate the fundamental of its lowest note (the low G) effectively. There is also a marked difference in quality between the lowest notes (very rich in harmonics), and the highest (strong in lower and middle harmonics, but relatively thin in tone colour).

As we have seen, the point at which the string is excited emphasises some frequencies at the expense of others; and the shape and size of the resonator modifies this still further. This characteristic of a resonator is called its *formant*. Formants are obviously a virtue in music, but in audio equipment they are called 'an uneven frequency response' and are usually regarded as a vice.

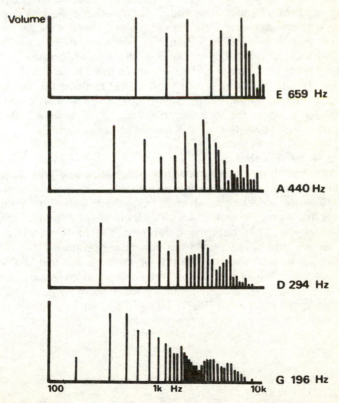

SAWTOOTH WAVEFORM   The first three harmonics add together to produce a first approximation to a 'sawtooth', the waveform that is produced by drawing a bow across the string of a violin. The string is dragged and then slips, repeatedly.

Volume

E 659 Hz

A 440 Hz

D 294 Hz

G 196 Hz

100          1k  Hz          10k

THE OPEN STRINGS OF THE VIOLIN: the relative intensity of the harmonics.

**21**

# Musical acoustics: wind

The air column inside a wind instrument may be excited by the vibrations in turbulent air at the edge of an orifice (as in the flute), by one or two reeds in the mouthpiece (clarinet, oboe) or by the player's lips (brass). The note that is produced depends on the dimensions of the resonator itself, and on the formation of standing waves within it.

The progressive waves of radiating sound are converted into stationary waves by reflection at a boundary. At a solid, rigid surface there can be no air movement perpendicular to it: the incident and reflected waves add together in such a way that air displacement at the wall is always zero. This is called a node in the standing wave: there will be further nodes at the first, second, and each successive complete wavelength from the wall; while at the intervening half wavelengths there will be antinodes, places where there is maximum air displacement.

## Behaviour of standing waves

In practice, not all of the wave is reflected: the surface absorbs some of the sound, and transmits some through to the other side, but in the air column of a wind instrument the standing wave dominates the pattern. In fact, one or both ends of the air column of a musical instrument may be open, but reflections still occur because the pipe is narrow compared with the wavelength of most of the sound in the column: the air pipe forms a piston which is simply not big enough to drive the outside air efficiently. In this case the energy has to go somewhere: it is reflected repeatedly back along the column, building up a powerful standing wave, whose pitch is defined by the length of the column.

## Harmonics in an air column

Some instruments have air columns that are open at one end; some are effectively open at both. A column that is open (or closed) at both ends has a fundamental wavelength which is twice the length of the pipe, and produces a full harmonic series. An air column that is open at one end and closed at the other behaves differently: the fundamental is four times its length, and only the odd harmonics are produced.

In orchestral instruments the length of the column may be varied continuously (as in the slide trombone), by adding discrete extra lengths (trumpet and French horn) or by opening and closing holes in the body of the instrument (woodwind). The formant of an instrument depends on the shape of its body and bell (the open end).

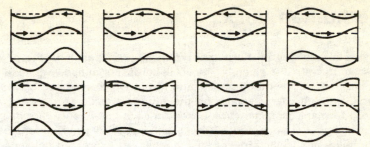

STATIONARY WAVE formed as two progressive waves move in opposite directions, successively reinforcing and cancelling each other. The combined wave has twice the amplitude of the original waves.

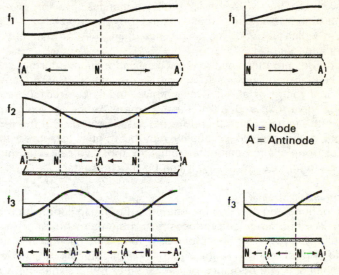

N = Node
A = Antinode

VIBRATION OF AIR COLUMN   *Left*: for a pipe open at both ends the fundamental frequency $f_1$ is approximately twice its length. The overtones are multiples of the fundamental: $f_2 = 2f_1$; $f_3 = 3f_1$ and so on.
*Right*: for a pipe that is closed at one end the fundamental frequency $f_1$ is four times its length. The even harmonics are absent: the first overtone is $3f_1$ the next $5f_1$ and so on.

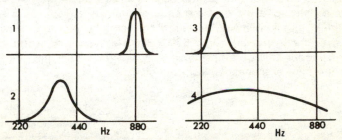

INSTRUMENTAL FORMANTS   1. Oboe. 2. Horn. 3. Trombone. 4. Trumpet. The formants, imposed by the structural dimensions of parts of the instruments, provide an essential and recognisable component of their musical character.

# The human voice

The special qualities of the human voice lie – in part – in the precise control of pitch that is given by the vocal cords, combined with flexibility of the cavities of the mouth, nose, and throat which are used to impose variable formant characteristics on the sounds already produced.

These formant characteristics, based on cavity resonance, are responsible for vowel sounds and so make an important contribution to the intelligibility of speech. Most of this variability is expressed between 200 and 2700Hz, the range of telephone transmissions.

Other characteristics of speech include sibilants and stops of various kinds which, together with the formant resonances, provide all that is needed for high intelligibility. These extend the range to about 8000Hz. A whisper, in which the vocal cords are not used, may be perfectly clear and understandable.

The vibrations produced by the vocal cords add volume, further character, and the ability to produce song. For normal speech the fundamental varies over a range of about twelve tones and is centred somewhere near 145Hz for a man and 230Hz for a woman. As the formant regions differ little, the female voice therefore has less harmonics in the regions of stronger resonance; so its quality may be thinner (or purer) than a man's. For song the fundamental range of most voices is about two octaves – though, exceptionally, it can be much greater.

### Microphones for speech

For a microphone and other sound equipment that can cope with orchestral music, the human voice produces no problems of frequency range, nor of volume except for the plosive 'p' that can blow a diaphragm beyond its normal working range when some people talk directly into it.

As we shall see, the demands of intelligibility require that there must be less indirect (reverberant) sound than for musical instruments; and this in turn may create further problems due to working close to a directional microphone. But apart from this, the main question with microphones for speech is whether a very wide frequency range is desirable: this adds not only to the cost of the microphone but also to the noise picked up at the extreme ends of the range.

Sometimes intelligibility is increased by using a microphone with a peak (a stronger response) in the 6000–8000Hz frequency range. Some older or cheaper microphones have this anyway. But this may also enhance the natural sibilance of some voices.

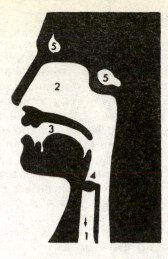

VOCAL CAVITIES 1, The lungs. 2, The nose. 3, The mouth (this is the most readily flexible cavity and is used to form vowel sounds). 4, The pharynx (above the vocal cords). 5, Sinuses. These cavities produce the formants which are characteristic of the human voice, emphasising certain frequency bands at the expense of others.

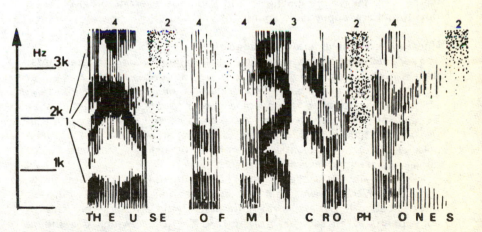

THE USE OF MI CRO PH ONES

HUMANS SPEECH analysed to show formant ranges. 1, Resonance bands. 2, Unvoiced speech. 3, Vocal stop before hard 'c'. There would be similar break before a plosive 'p'. 4, Voiced speech. These formants are unrelated to the fundamentals and harmonics, which would be shown only by an analysis into much finer frequency ranges than have been used here. This example is adapted from a voiceprint of the author's voice. Each individual has distinct characteristics.

25

# Sound volume and the ear

Every time you *double* the intensity (or the energy) of a sound your ear hears the *same* increase in loudness. Intensity is a physical characteristic of sound in air. As intensity goes up in progressively increasing jumps, $1:2:4:8:16:32$ and so on, the ear hears this as equal increments of loudness, $1:2:3:4:5:6$. Because of this special characteristic of the human ear, it is not very convenient to think in terms of intensity or energy, so instead a new measure of sound volume is defined. This is the *decibel* (dB).

In mathematical terms: the volume in decibels is ten times the logarithm of the ratio of intensities. For non-mathematicians it is enough to know that a regular increase in volume $1:2:3:4:5:6$ described in decibels will sound like a regular and even increase in volume. And a decibel is a unit of a convenient size: it is about as small an increase in volume as we can hear in the most favourable circumstances.

## Intensity and volume

As it happens, the ratio of intensities in 3dB is about $2:1$. This is convenient to remember, because if we double up a sound source we double the intensity (at a given distance). So if we have one soprano bawling her head off and another joins her singing equally loudly the sound level will go up 3db (not all that much more than the minimum detectable by the human ear). But to raise the level by another 3dB two more sopranos are needed. Four more are needed for the next 3dB — and so on. Before we get very far we are having to add sopranos at a rate of 64 or 128 a time to get any appreciable change of volume.

## Human hearing at different frequencies

The ear does not measure the volume of all sounds by the same standards: the ear is more sensitive to changes of volume in the middle and upper frequencies than in the bass. So loudness (a subjective quality) and the objectively measurable volume of a sound cannot be the same at all frequencies. Loudness in *phons* is taken to be the same as volume in decibels at 1000Hz. The expected loudness of a sound can then be calculated from the actual sound volume by using a standard set of curves representing 'average' human hearing.

The lower limit is called the threshold of hearing. It is convenient to regard the average lower limit of human hearing at 1000Hz as zero on the decibel scale. (There is no natural zero: the arbitrary zero chosen corresponds to an acoustic pressure of $2 \times 10^{-5}$ newtons per square metre.)

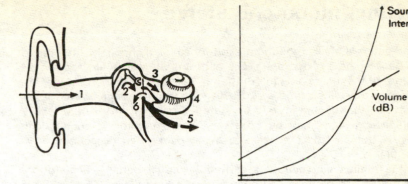

THE EAR *Left*: 1, Sound enters via the outer ear and the auditory canal. 2, The sound is transported mechanically from the eardrum across the middle ear via three small bones. 3, It is then pumped via the oval window into the inner ear (cochlea). 4, The cochlea has two channels along it, becoming narrower until they join at the far end. Distributed along the upper channel are elongated cells, 'hairs', which respond to particular frequencies: when one of these is bent, a nerve impulse is fired. 5, A bundle of 4000 nerve fibres carries the information to the brain, where it is decoded. 6, Pressures in the cochlea are equalised at another membrane to the inner ear; the round window. *Right*: As sound intensity rises exponentially the corresponding volume in decibels (as heard by the ear) rises linearly.

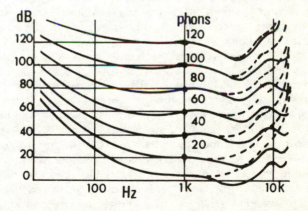

EQUAL LOUDNESS CONTOURS (Robinson and Dadson). Intensity (decibels) equals loudness in phons at 1kHz. *Right*. The curves take age into account and show marked peaks and dips in young hearing. The unbroken lines are for age 20; the broken lines show typical loss of high-frequency hearing at age 60. The lowest line in each case represents the threshold of hearing. The threshold of feeling lies somewhere between the top two curves.

# Hearing, mono and stereo

Sound enters the ear through an auditory canal, a channel with a resonance peak in the 3−6kHz range. The eardrum vibrates in air, and the airpressure of the inner ear is intermittently matched to that outside via the Eustachian tube. If this tube is blocked and pressure changes with weather or altitude, the diaphragm will be stiffened resulting in hearing loss. A nasal decongestant may be necessary when monitoring sound while suffering from a cold (and also to avoid pain when descending from altitude).

In the middle ear, sound is carried by small bones which form a system of levers, in effect an impedance-matching device. The inner ear, or cochlea, is a small spiral shell-shaped structure containing a fluid with tiny 'hairs' along its length. Each 'hair' (actually an elongated cell) responds to a narrow frequency band, and in the middle and upper range they are spaced at equal musical intervals (i.e. at equal spacing on a logarithmic range of frequency). At low frequencies there are fewer 'hairs' and our capacity to distinguish pitch is corresponding poorer.

Some directional information comes from masking by the head, aided by slight movements which change the high-frequency response. There is therefore some stereo effect even for a single ear. Further information comes from a comparison of the sounds reaching the two ears, which (except at high frequencies) differ in phase and for close sounds also differ in volume. Transients from the side will also reach one ear before the other. Although the ears sample air pressure at only two places in a complex acoustic field, the brain can detect and concentrate on events at a particular point, by tuning in to one conversation among many (the 'cocktail party effect'). It can also de-emphasise room resonance, which comes from all directions.

## Loudspeakers and stereo

A single, mono loudspeaker offers little positional information: only distance. This is given partly by how much reverberation there is for each component: the more, the farther away. In addition, the brain will make allowances for expected loudness; an intrinsically quiet source (such as a whisper) that is loud must be close. Contradictory information such as that in a loud, reverberant whisper will change the apparent size of a source; in this case to make it sound big. Because direct and reverberant sound all comes from the same direction, the ear (and brain) tolerates less reverberation than in a two- or three-dimensional soundfield, particularly if intelligibility or musical clarity is diminished.

In two-loudspeaker stereo, only a limited two-dimensional effect is restored, but this provides much of the information required by ear and brain to establish position and to separate direct from reverberant sound. Quadraphonic sound does not add enough further information to have achieved commercial success.

**28**

**HEARING STEREO** The position of apparent sources is perceived by time, amplitude and phase differences between signals received by the left and right ears, and (at high frequencies) by the effects of shadowing due to the head.

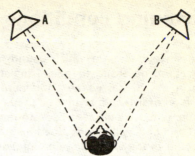

**TWO-LOUDSPEAKER STEREO I.** Here the signals from A and B loudspeakers are equal; the B signal takes longer to reach the left ear, and the A signal takes longer to reach the right. But the combined signal C is exactly in phase: the image is in the centre.

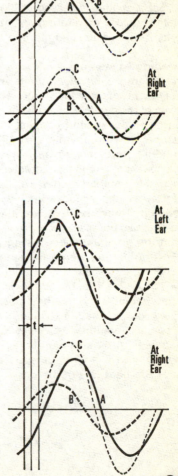

**TWO-LOUDSPEAKER STEREO II.** Here signal A is increased. The effect is to make the peak in the combined signal C arrive at the left ear a little earlier, and that at the right ear, later. There is therefore a slight delay (t) between the two signals C; this phase difference is perceived as a displacement of the image to the left of centre. In these diagrams it is assumed that the listener is on the centre line between A and B, and facing forwards. If, however, he turns his head this will cause the phase difference at his ears to change – but in such a way as to keep the image roughly at the same point in space. If the listener moves away from the centre line the image will be distorted but the relative positions of image elements will remain undisturbed. These arguments apply in their simplest form only to sound derived from a coincident pair of microphones, and to frequencies below about 700Hz, at which the head itself causes shadowing effects.

**29**

# Listening conditions

The surroundings in which sound is heard range from the controlled conditions necessary to monitoring at source; through high-fidelity listening in the home, where equipment may be of good quality, but the position of listeners cannot be predicted; to include the effects of poorer equipment, acoustics or background noise. Here arrangements for the first two only will be described – though the sound balancer should take account of the likely range of conditions in which the production will be heard.

For monitoring mono sound, the loudspeaker may be placed at a distance of 3–6ft (0.9–1.8m). Closer than this, the field may be distorted by the standing waves near any large cabinet; at more than 6ft (1.8m), the acoustics of the listening room begin to dominate. These acoustics should be similar to those in many homes: a reverberation time of 0.4sec at 250Hz, falling to 0.3sec at 8kHz has been found satisfactory. At this relatively close monitoring distance, it is possible to distinguish between faults in the original sound and those of the listening room itself.

**Listening to stereo**
The difference between monitoring in the studio and listening at home is likely to be greater for stereo. This is due to the Haas effect whereby a delay of a few milliseconds (a longer sound path of some 3ft, 0.9m) causes all the sound to appear to come from the nearer loudspeaker. To hear stereo with anything like the spatial resolution of the original, it is therefore necessary to be fairly close to the median line between the loudspeakers, though the greater the distance from the loudspeakers, the greater the spread within which the stereo image is heard. This is also affected by the distance between the loudspeakers and here there is a trade-off. The closer they are, the greater the freedom of movement for the listener, but also the narrower the image that is heard. For reverberation the original wider spacing is better.

For monitoring stereo the sound balancer will be on the median line and if the loudspeakers are about 8ft (2.5m) apart he or she could be at the apex of a triangle some 6ft (1.8m) from each, with the producer sitting behind – not the best position for close communication and quite unlike companionable seating in the home. To monitor a wider range of audience conditions (especially for television sound) it should be possible to switch to small ('near-field') loudspeakers at lower volume. These should be in line with, but closer than, the main loudspeakers, perhaps set at the back line of the desk.

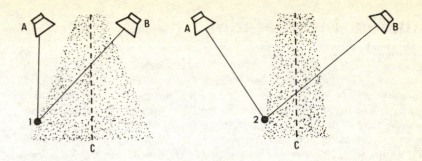

**STEREO LOUDSPEAKERS:SPACING** With the closer loudspeakers, *left*, the spread of the stereo image is reduced, but there is a broad area over which reasonable stereo is heard. With wider spacing, *right*, the stereo image has more spread, but a relatively narrow region in which it can be heard at its best. For listeners off the centre line C, the growing difference in distance rapidly 'kills' the stereo, due to the Haas effect. Position 1 (with a narrow spacing of speakers) has the same loss of stereo effect as position 2 (with the broader spacing).

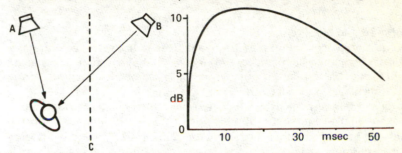

**HAAS EFFECT** For a listener away from the centre line C, the difference in distances means that the sound from the farther loudspeaker arrives later. The delay is one millisecond for every 13.4 inches (34cm) difference in path length. For identical signals coming from different directions, a difference of only a few milliseconds makes the whole sound appear to come from the direction of the first to arrive. The effect can be reversed by increasing the volume of the second signal: the curve shows the increase in volume required to recentre the image.

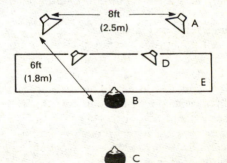

**MONITORING STEREO** A, High-quality loudspeakers. B, Balancer. C, Producer, also equidistant from loudspeaker. D, 'Mini-speakers' offering a distinctively different lower quality. E, Desk.

**31**

# Studios: reverberation and coloration

Sounds in an enclosed space are reflected many times, with some (great or small) part of the sound being absorbed at each reflection. The rate of decay of reverberation defines a characteristic for each studio: its reverberation time. This is the time it takes for a sound to die away to a millionth part of its original intensity (i.e. through 60dB). Reverberation time varies with frequency, and a studio's performance may be shown on a graph for all audio frequencies. Or it may be simply given in round terms for, say, the biggest peak between 500 and 2000Hz; or at a particular frequency within that range.

Reverberation time depends on the number of reflections in a given time, so large rooms generally have longer reverberation times than small ones. This is not only expected but also, fortunately, preferred by listeners.

### Coloration and eigentones
In some studios coloration may be heard. This is the selective emphasis of certain frequencies or bands of frequencies in the reverberation, caused by successive absorption of other frequencies at each reflection. This is most noticeable in smaller rooms.

Parallel walls also give rise to eigentones, resonance at frequencies corresponding to the studio dimensions. If the main dimensions are in simple ratios to each other these may be reinforced. Adequate diffusion is an important quality of a good studio. The more the wave front is broken up, the more smooth the decay of the sound becomes, both in time and in frequency content.

A hand clap can be used as a rough guide to both reverberation time and studio quality: for example in a speech studio, the sound should die away quickly but not so fast that the studio sounds muffled or dead. And there must certainly be no 'ring' fluttering along behind it.

### Reverberation times for music studios
For a music studio, listening tests show that the preferred reverberation time depends on size: the larger the studio, the longer the time, but the number of sound reflections remains about the same. For monophonic radio and recording work the preferred ideal reverberation time seems to be about a tenth of a second less than for music heard 'live'. Some authorities suggest a slight rise in the bass.

An acoustic control system (which does not employ acoustic feedback in the hall itself) can now be installed in a relatively dead studio to give it a wide range of simulated live acoustics (see pages 104–105).

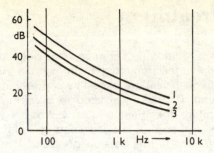

PERMISSIBLE BACKGROUND NOISE IN STUDIOS   1, Television studios (except drama and presentation). 2, Television drama and presentation studios and all radio studios except those for drama. 3, Radio drama studios.

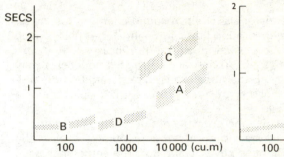

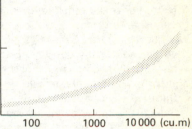

RADIO STUDIOS   Typical reverberation times for:
A, Programmes with an audience.
B, Talks and discussions. C, Classical music. D, Drama, popular music.

TELEVISION STUDIOS   Typical reverberation times for general-purpose studios.

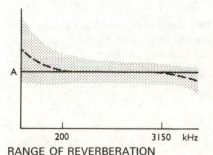

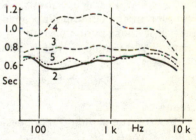

RANGE OF REVERBERATION TIMES   A, Median for any particular type. Below 200Hz the reverberation in talks studios and their control rooms may rise; above 3150Hz, for most studios it should fall by 10−15%. For a large music studio the tolerance is about 10% on either side of the average; for other studios and control rooms it may be a little wider.

FOUR TELEVISION STUDIOS: FREQUENCY RESPONSE   Variation in reverberation time with frequency. BBC Television Centre Studios 2 and 5 are both 116000ft$^3$ (3280m$^3$); Studios 3 and 4 are 357 000ft$^3$ (10 100m$^3$). Studio 4 was designed primarily for musical productions.

**33**

# Acoustic treatment

A sound studio is a room with designed − or defined − acoustics. The reverberation time and the frequency response (the amount of reverberation at different frequencies) are varied by controlling the reflection and absorption of sound. Diffusers are used to break up the wave fronts; plenty of hard furniture does this quite as well as irregular wall surfaces. But the main means of control is absorption in various forms.

*Absorption coefficient* is the fraction of sound that is absorbed at a particular frequency. It takes a value between 0 and 1 and unless otherwise stated is for 512Hz at normal incidence.

### Types of absorbers

Soft absorbers are porous materials in which sound energy is lost by air friction. For really efficient absorption it has to be 4ft (1.2m) thick, which takes up a lot of space. So it is usual to lay it in thicknesses that absorb well above 500Hz. Excessive absorption at very high frequencies may then be reduced by overlaying the absorber with perforated hardboard. With 0.5% perforation much of the 'top' is reflected; with 25% perforation a high proportion is absorbed.

Damped cavity absorbers use the principle of the Helmholtz resonator, in which the mass of air in the mouth of a bottle vibrates against the 'spring' of the air inside. Damped cavity resonators are sometimes used to cut down sharp peaks in studio reverberation − such as may be caused by dimensional resonances.

Membrane absorbers are often used to reduce low frequencies: a panel with a broad middle- to low-frequency response is driven like a piston by the sound pressure, and as the movement is damped the energy is lost. In practice they do not always work well.

An all-purpose combination absorber has been used by the BBC with success. It consists of standard 2ft (60cm) square units that are easy to construct and simple to install without supervision (see opposite).

The best − and cheapest − sound absorber on the floor is a thick carpet.

### Screens

Screens are free-standing diffusers or diffuser-absorbers, typically about 3ft (0.9m) wide × 6ft (1.8m) high. They are not very efficient absorbers, as the padding is usually too thin. In the dead pop-music studio, Perspex screens provide local high-frequency reinforcement. This helps musicians hear their own sound, helps to separate instruments for easier control of levels, improves diffusion and may also reduce low-frequency resonance in the studio as a whole.

**SOFT ABSORBERS** Padding applied close to a reflecting surface is efficient only for sufficiently short wavelengths. The thicker it is the wider the range of frequencies that it will absorb. Thin padding (or, for example, heavy drapes) is more effective over a wide range of frequencies if it is away from the reflecting surface.

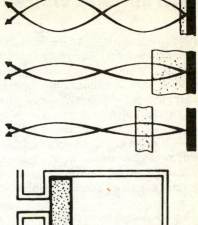

**DAMPED CAVITY ABSORBER** This employs a Helmholtz resonator responding to a particular frequency, which is then absorbed.

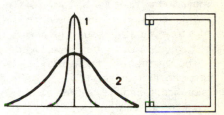

**MEMBRANE ABSORBER** A panel over a box. Unlike the cavity resonator (which has a single sharply tuned resonance), 1, the panel which is fixed at the edges has a very broad response, 2. If it is damped by weighting it with a material such as roofing felt, it will absorb sound.

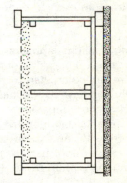

**COMBINATION ABSORBER**, size: 2ft × 2ft × 7in (600 × 600 × 180mm). The back and sides of the box are of plywood. The interior is partitioned by hardboard into cavities of 1ft × 1ft × 6in (300 × 300 × 150mm). On the front is 1in (25mm) of heavy density rockwool, covered by perforated hardboard. With 0.5% perforation the peak of absorption is at 90Hz. With 20% perforation there is wide band absorption, with less at low frequencies.

**STUDIO SCREENS** A dead music studio has a supply of full and low screens with absorbers about 4in (10cm) thick that are easily moved on rollers to provide acoustic separation without loss of visual contact. Vocalist's screen may have a window of stiff transparent plastics.

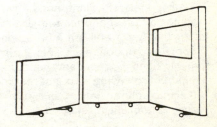

**35**

# Microphone characteristics

A microphone is a device for turning the acoustic energy of sound into electrical energy. The main types are condenser (electrostatic), moving-coil and ribbon, which have all been used for high-quality work. An electret is a condenser microphone in which an electrostatic charge is permanently implanted in one of the plates.

For normal sound levels a microphone should produce an electrical signal which is well above its own electrical noise level, i.e. it should have a good signal-to-noise ratio. Sensitivity is the voltage produced per unit of sound pressure: see table opposite. An 'equivalent noise level' is a lower limit to the sound pressure level that can be distinguished from electrical noise in the microphone.

### Distortion and frequency response

For normal sound levels the signal must be substantially undistorted, i.e. the electrical waveform must faithfully follow the sound waveform, and it must do this over a wide range of volumes. Distortion caused by overloading depends on the use to which the microphone is put: close to the bell of a trombone the sound level may be 60dB higher than that met in use elsewhere. Moving-coil types withstand overload very well.

The microphone taken together with its associated equipment should respond almost equally to all significant frequencies present. What is 'significant' depends on the sound source: different microphones may be used for speech and for various musical instruments. Sometimes deviations from an even frequency response are desirable, and can be used constructively.

### Handling qualities, appearance, cost

Robustness and good handling qualities are other essentials. Moving-coil types in particular stand up well to the relatively rough treatment a microphone may accidentally suffer outside a studio, to handling by interviewers or pop singers, or to rustle when attached to clothing. Condenser microphones are also used for all of these purposes and may be preferred for an extended, smooth frequency response; and electrets also for their unobtrusiveness in vision.

Ribbon microphones rate lowest in sensitivity to wind noise. In windy conditions all microphones may benefit from the use of a windshield.

Simple electret microphones can sometimes be cheap, and good moving-coil microphones may be relatively so. Condenser microphones (other than electrets) are more expensive.

Some microphones are sold with a choice of impedances. Nominally, the microphone impedance should be matched with the input to the equipment following it, but sometimes a mismatch — low into high, e.g. $200\Omega$ microphone impedance into a mixer input rated at $1200\Omega$ — is permissible or even required.

## RIBBON MICROPHONE

1, Corrugated light alloy foil diaphragm. 2, Permanent magnet with pole-pieces above. 3, Transformer. The output voltage is generated as the ribbon diaphragm vibrates in the magnetic field.

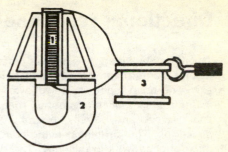

## MOVING-COIL MICROPHONE

1, Diaphragm. 2, Coil fixed to diaphragm. 3, Permanent magnet. Movement of the coil over the fixed centre-pole produces the output voltage. A robust microphone.

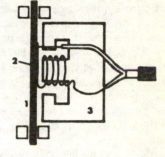

## CONDENSER (ELECTROSTATIC) MICROPHONE

1, Light, flexible membrane diaphragm. 2, Rigid backplate. 3, Cable to head amplifier and polarising voltage supply. Air pressure varies the capacitance between diaphragm and backplate. This is converted to an output voltage in the amplifier. Expensive, but can give very high sound quality. Electret microphones are similar, but require no polarising voltage.

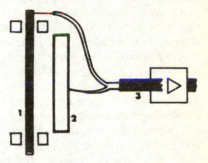

## MICROPHONE SENSITIVITIES

Usually given in dB relative to 1 volt per pascal. This corresponds to a (linear) scale of millivolts per pascal, as shown in table. Other units that may be encountered are dB relative to 1 volt per dyne/$cm^2$: this gives figures which are 20dB lower. One mV/Pa is the same as 1mV/10μbar or 0.1mV/μbar.

| dB rel. to 1 V/Pa | mV/Pa |
|---|---|
| −20 | 100 |
| −25 | 56 |
| −30 | 31.6 |
| −35 | 17.8 |
| −40 | 10.0 |
| −45 | 5.6 |
| −50 | 3.16 |
| −55 | 1.78 |
| −60 | 1.00 |
| −65 | 0.56 |

One of the most critical factors in the selection and use of a microphone.

# Directional response

The directional response or field pattern of a microphone is illustrated in a polar diagram, in which sensitivity is plotted against the angle from the axis. The main types are as follows:

Omnidirectional microphones measure the pressure of the air in the sound wave and, ideally, respond equally to sound coming from all directions. The simpler moving-coil and condenser (including electret) microphones work in this way. The diaphragm is open to the air on one side only.

Figure-eight microphones are bi-directional. The diaphragm is open to the air on both sides: it measures pressure gradient (the difference in pressure at two successive points along the path of the sound wave). If the microphone is placed sideways to the path of the sound, it compares the pressures at two points on the same wave front and, as these are the same, there is no output. The microphone is therefore 'dead' to sound coming from the side and 'live' to that approaching one face or the other. The simplest form of ribbon microphone works in this way, responding to the difference in pressure on the two faces of a strip of foil.

**Cardioid and switchable types**
Cardioid and supercardioid microphones are unidirectional in the sense that they are live on one side and relatively dead on the other, but the live side is very broad and undiscriminating. A heart-shaped polar response can be obtained by adding the output of a pressure (e.g. simple moving-coil) microphone to that of a pressure gradient (e.g. simple ribbon) microphone. Indeed, some earlier types of cardioid did just that, with a ribbon and a moving coil in the single case. Today, many cardioids still have two diaphragms (most commonly in condenser microphones) or a single diaphragm with a complex acoustic network behind.

The cardioid microphone is a special case of the combination of pressure and pressure gradient principles. By varying the proportions, a range of polar diagrams is possible. Where a combination of microphones has been used in a single case, it has been possible to add a switch so that one or the other could be switched off. Twin-diaphragm condenser microphones can be even more versatile, as a whole range of different responses can be obtained by varying the polarising current of the diaphragm. The supercardioid response discriminates most strongly against reverberation; between this and the pure cardioid lies the most unidirectional response (see page 51). For an even more highly directional response, one of these is used in combination with a device to focus or otherwise modify the sound field (see page 53).

## POLAR DIAGRAM: PERFECT OMNIDIRECTIONAL RESPONSE

The scale from centre outwards is sensitivity, measured as a proportion of the maximum response (which is taken as unity).

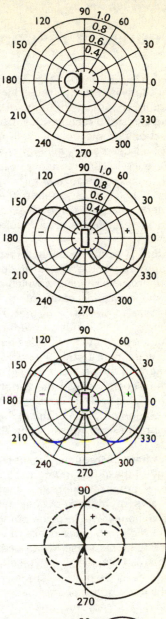

## PERFECT FIGURE-EIGHT RESPONSE (BI-DIRECTIONAL)

The response is similar in the plane through the 0°–180° axis; that in the plane of the 90°–270° axis is always zero. At 60° off axis the output is reduced to half. The response at the back of the microphone is opposite in phase. The two diagrams above have a linear scale, reducing to zero at the centre.

## FIGURE-EIGHT WITH DECIBEL SCALE

The apparent distortion of the perfect response is due to the use of a scale which does not reduce to zero.

## PERFECT CARDIOID RESPONSE

This is the sum of omnidirectional and figure-eight pick-up when the maximum sensitivity of the two is equal. The front lobe of the 'eight' is in phase with the omnidirectional response and so adds to it; the back lobe is out of phase and is subtracted.

## TYPICAL SUPERCARDIOID RESPONSE

This is a more directional version of the cardioid microphone. It is one of a continuous range of patterns that can be obtained by combining omni- and bi-directional response in various proportions.

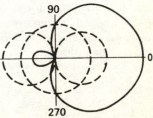

# Frequency response in practice

Even when a microphone has a response that is almost flat on its main axis there is usually some degradation at the sides or back: the polar diagram changes with frequency. These changes are most marked on the dead sides of directional microphones, but they also matter least in these directions as the output is so low. In the intermediate ranges between live and dead sides a slight change of direction can make a substantial difference in the frequency response to direct sound, as a study of the diagrams on the following pages will show. This can often be used to help a balance by angling the microphone to reduce high-frequency content where it is obtrusive, or pointing it directly at the source when increased intelligibility is required in a noisy background.

### Factors affecting frequency response

In addition to the mode of operation (pressure or pressure gradient), there are several factors which affect frequency response. These inlcude: the shielding effect of the microphone body, which reduces high-frequency response to sound from that direction; reflection within the diaphragm housing, which tends to produce an erratic response at high frequency; resonances of the air cavities between casing and diaphragm, which may produce a high-frequency peak; resonances in the cavity behind the diaphragm or in pressure equalisation channels; cancellation of extreme high frequencies over the surface of a diaphragm when wavelengths are comparable with its size; a tendency to form standing waves in front of the diaphragm, also in the highest frequencies; and the resonance of the diaphragm itself (on a ribbon this is at a low frequency).

### The effect of frequency response

Many of these factors are used constructively in the design of the microphone, often resulting in a slight increase in sensitivity along and near the axis at high frequency (at, say, 4000Hz and above). Antiquated microphones with large diaphragms, e.g. of 1½in (38mm) diameter, show these high-frequency peaks to excess. Many microphones have a somewhat spiky response in the octave from 5000 to 10 000Hz. Microphones with small diaphragms, typically less than ½in (13mm) diameter, have a more even response. Among these, condenser microphones can be particularly good, as the diaphragm is so light.

The frequency response of one sample of a particular high-quality microphone may vary by several dB from another, but (except for stereo pairs) this may not matter very much. In the complexity of sound received by a microphone – including reverberation – such small variations are barely perceptible.

**40**

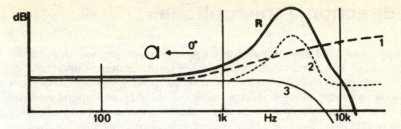

HIGH-FREQUENCY EFFECTS on a large microphone diaphragm. The response R at 0° (i.e. on axis) is the sum of several components including: 1, Obstacle effect (which sets up standing wave in front of diaphragm). 2, Resonance in cavity in front of diaphragm. 3, Inertia of diaphragm as its mass becomes appreciable compared with high-frequency driving force. These are improved by making the diaphragm smaller and lighter, and by careful design of the case.

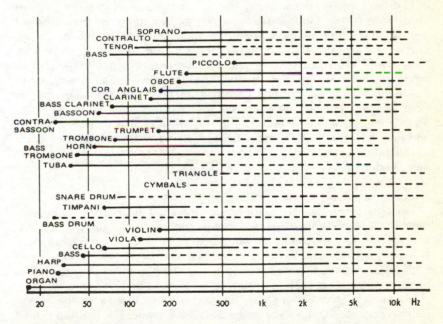

FREQUENCY RANGES  A microphone with a frequency response which matches that of the sound source will not pick up noise and spill from other instruments unnecessarily. The lowest frequency for most instruments is clearly defined, but the highest significant overtones are not. At high frequencies, an even response is usually considered more valuable than a matched one.

# Bi-directional microphones

Over the years the popularity of bi-directional microphones such as the single ribbon has diminished as the cost of both condenser and moving-coil microphones has come down; as the condensers have become more versatile and more reliable; and as more complex combinations within a single casing have come into use. As a result of this increasing flexibility in the availability and use of directional microphones there has been a move away from the operational procedures that employed bi-directional microphones, and a tendency towards using one microphone for each source. In addition, the quality of response of the ribbon microphone itself has been overtaken by the improvements in cardioids using other principles: the response of the ribbon is neither so smooth nor so extensive. Nevertheless it remains valuable for a limited but important range of uses such as the human voice and certain musical instruments (notably strings) whose frequency characteristics happen to fit in with those of the ribbon microphone.

**Control of acoustics**
In bi-directional use the working area is wide – including about 100° on either side of the microphone – which allows room for a number of people (four sitting or six standing) at about 2ft (0.6m) from the microphone. The directional response allows the use of studios or rooms with fairly lively acoustics without these becoming too dominant. To an omnidirectional microphone, reverberation comes from all directions; to the bi-directional microphone it comes only from the double cone at front and rear. For the same acoustic the speakers must be much closer to an omnidirectional microphone to achieve a similar balance of direct and indirect sound; slight movements then have a much greater effect on the ratio. The bi-directional microphone therefore allows more flexibility and greater subtlety in the use of acoustics.

**Avoiding phase problems**
When two bi-directional microphones are used near each other they must be *in phase*. If they are not, there is cancellation of direct sound for sources which are at similar distances from the two. To avoid this there is usually some visual indication of which side is the 'front'. When two bi-directional microphones are used for separate sources they can often be arranged so that each is dead-side-on to the other's source.

The polar response of a ribbon microphone that is set with the ribbon upright approaches the ideal in the horizontal plane, but is more erratic in the vertical plane, due to phase cancellation. As with most such variations in response this, if known, can be used constructively.

## FIGURE-EIGHT MICROPHONE
Working areas. An arc
of approximately 100° on each side is
'live'.

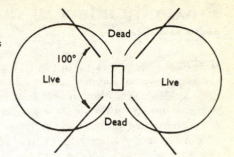

## RIBBON MICROPHONE
Much of the casing is taken up by the
magnet system, which in early ribbon
microphones had to be substantial in
order to provide reasonable
sensitivity. The stem contains
a transformer.

## FREQUENCY RESPONSE OF
## RIBBON MICROPHONE
The response at 60° to the
axis is 6dB down, as
predicted by theory, but
begins to depart from the
common curve at about
2000Hz, where high-
frequency effects begin.
Those for variation in the
vertical plane (v) are more
pronounced than those for
variation in the horizontal
plane (h).

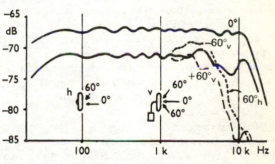

## RIBBON AT AN ANGLE
At an angle to the length of a ribbon
there is partial cancellation of short
wavelengths (high frequencies).

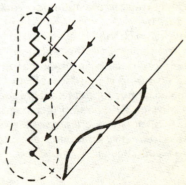

43

*There is an increase in bass response when a sound source is within about 2ft (0.6m) from a directional microphone.*

# Proximity effect in directional microphones

Proximity effect (bass tip-up) is a direct result of the pressure gradient mode of working, which in turn is fundamental to the directional response of bi-directional, cardioid and similar microphones. It is found in its most extreme form with the figure-eight response, less with cottage-loaf, less still with cardioid and so on – in proportion to the diminishing importance of the figure-eight component in comparison with the omnidirectional component of their polar diagrams.

The following description is for a ribbon microphone, which is pure pressure-gradient in operation and exhibits the effect in its strongest form.

Tip-up occurs when the pressure gradient microphone is in a field of spherical waves and if it is close enough to the source for there to be a substantial reduction in intensity within the distance that the wave has to travel to get from front to back of the diaphragm. This loss of intensity creates a pressure difference which is added to the normal pressure gradient that is due to the phase difference. The effect is only appreciable at low frequencies where the phase difference is small compared with the fall in sound intensity.

**Uses of bass correction**
The response of some directional microphones falls off below 200Hz; in these, bass tip-up may be used to restore a level response. In cases where the response is more nearly level, 'bass-cut' (actually bass-correction) is required. This may be applied either in the control channel following the microphone or sometimes by switching in a filter built into the microphone itself. One result of bass-cut is a reduction in studio reverberation at low frequencies, which may be used to compensate for small-room resonances or 'boominess'.

**Working distance**
Without bass correction the minimum working distance may be as much as 2ft (0.6m) or as little as 1ft (0.3m) or less, depending on the microphone. With correction the optimum working distance is reduced, but any movements backward and forward of more than a few inches then produce a noticeable change in bass response even if the actual volume is controlled to compensate for the change in intensity. There is also (in this case) a variation in the ratio of direct to indirect sound.

Bass tip-up is more troublesome on some voices than others. Women, with a higher fundamental frequency, can often speak at less than the recommended working distance without distortion becoming apparent. For whispers it is often possible to speak very much closer, because the main frequency content of a whisper is generally much higher than that of voiced speech.

44

**PRESSURE GRADIENT OPERATION** The sound wave travels farther to reach the back of the ribbon, 1, than it does to the front. The effective path difference d is roughly equivalent to the shortest distance D round the pole-piece, 2.

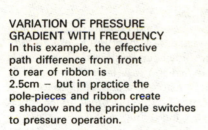

**VARIATION OF PRESSURE GRADIENT WITH FREQUENCY** In this example, the effective path difference from front to rear of ribbon is 2.5cm – but in practice the pole-pieces and ribbon create a shadow and the principle switches to pressure operation.

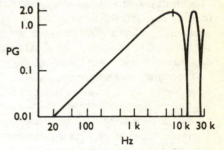

**PROXIMITY EFFECT: VARIATION WITH DISTANCE** This increases as a directional microphone approaches a sound source. For a bi-directional ribbon the curves 1–4 may correspond to distances of 24 to 6in (60 to 15cm).

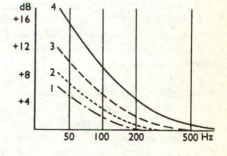

**COMPENSATION FOR CLOSE WORKING** Some microphones have a reduced bass response which automatically compensates for close working: with the microphone at a certain distance from the source, its response for direct sound is level.

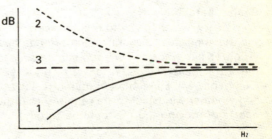

**45**

*Microphones that are live on one side only.*

# Cardioid microphones

With true cardioid microphones the working area lies within a broad cone including about 160° on the live side. At the sides the response diminishes rapidly, and at the back, where the output is low, the frequency response is erratic. Bass tip-up occurs with close working, though less than for figure-eight microphones. Some cardioids tend to degrade to omnidirectional response at low frequencies, and this considerably reduces the tendency to bass tip-up. However, the degradation may itself depend on distance as well as frequency; so it is necessary to study the manufacturer's details first, and then learn the possibilities and eccentricities of each model from actual use.

### Combination and phase shift microphones
In early cardioid microphones the response was produced by combining a moving coil and a ribbon in a single case, but most modern cardioids are even more complex. The most commonly used method today employs a condenser with two diaphragms – of which more later.

Directional microphones may also, in principle, contain a pair of moving coils back to back, or even two ribbons, one behind the other. By connecting them electrically through networks which change the phase of the signal, a response intermediate between omnidirectional and figure-eight can be achieved. In these cases the second diaphragm, behind the first on the main axis, has a slightly different response; and the polar diagram must also depend on the relative sizes of the two signals. There is so much scope for variety of design detail that it is impossible to generalise; it is better to study the characteristics of individual types as they are produced for particular specialised purposes.

A cardioid response can also be obtained in a single diaphragm microphone, such as a condenser or moving coil, by allowing sound to reach the back of the microphone through an acoustic labyrinth so that it arrives with a change of phase.

The diaphragm or diaphragms may be mounted in the microphone casing in two main ways. One, 'end-fire', has the main axis in line with that of the microphone itself; in the other, more commonly employed in switchable microphones, the axis is at right-angles to it.

### Boom operation
With their low sensitivity to rapid movement, the double moving-coil and the moving-coil phase-shift microphones have both been used on television or film booms. They are satisfactory for following speech but for music it is generally better to use a condenser microphone on the boom. Experience will show how vibration-resistant the mounting needs to be; and whether windshields are required to protect the diaphragm from the effects of moving the microphone through the air.

**46**

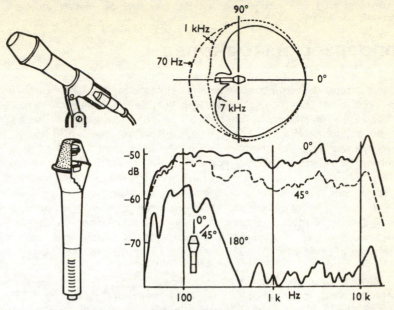

DOUBLE MOVING-COIL CARDIOID MICROPHONE  This is an example of an 'end-fire' microphone: the 0° axis of the diaphragm is along the axis of the casing. Inside, a forward diaphragm responds to high frequencies, while that behind it is more sensitive to low frequencies. Entry ports lower down the stem allow sound to reach the rear of the second diaphragm: this partially compensates for any increase in bass owing to proximity effect.

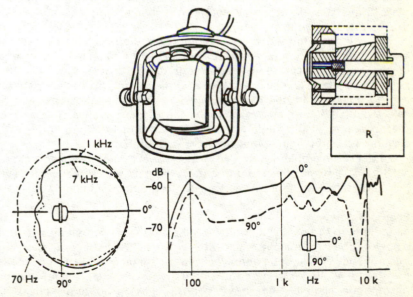

A MOVING-COIL CARDIOID MICROPHONE that has been used on a television boom. A complex system of acoustic labyrinths is built into the microphone housing. The air reservoir R (shown in the simplified sectional diagram) provides the damping for one of three resonant systems used to engineer the response.

# Condenser microphones

In their simplest form, condenser (or electrostatic) microphones are omnidirectional. They have a single thin flexible diaphragm close to the surface of a rigid backplate. There are changes in capacitance between the two, as the diaphragm vibrates in sympathy with the sound pressure. These are converted to changes in voltage in a small amplifier that is either within the same housing as the capsule or nearby. The diaphragm itself may be of very thin metal, perhaps in the form of a gold-sputtered plastic membrane. The backplate has small cavities in it: without these the thin layer of air would be too 'stiff' and would prevent the membrane moving freely. To make the microphone work a polarising voltage has to be applied between diaphragm and backplate, or alternatively may be introduced permanently in manufacture as in an electret (see page 60).

**Double-diaphragm condensers**
Some condenser microphones in use today are more complicated. They have two diaphragms, one on either side of the backplate. If the polarising voltage is the same on both diaphragms, the microphone continues to be omnidirectional in operation. With no polarising voltage applied to the second diaphragm, it can be arranged that the microphone has a cardioid response. In this case, the cavities in the backplates are designed as a phase shifting network: as the acoustic pressure travels through the plate to the back of the main diaphragm it changes in phase sufficiently to generate the cardioid response.

Going a stage further, if the second diaphragm is polarised in the opposite direction, a figure-eight response can be obtained. The double diaphragm then acts as a pressure gradient capsule. Finally, if the polarising voltage is made variable, a whole range of response patterns can be obtained. In one example, any of nine polar diagrams can be selected at the turn of a switch. In these microphones, the axis of response is at a right angle to the body of the microphone, in order to accommodate the figure-eight mode of operation.

Condenser microphones may include a variable filter for bass cut, and a filter to eliminate the radio-frequency signals which are very easily picked up in the stage from the capsule to the head amplifier.

**Phantom power**
In addition to the polarising voltage, all condenser microphones require a power supply. Nominally this is often rated at 48V, but in practice many microphones will accept a supply within the range of 9−52V: this allows the use of a 9V battery or the phantom power supply available on microphone channels on many control desks. The term 'phantom' originated in telephony, when a two-way circuit was added to a distribution system by a single extra wire, with the return balanced within existing wires.

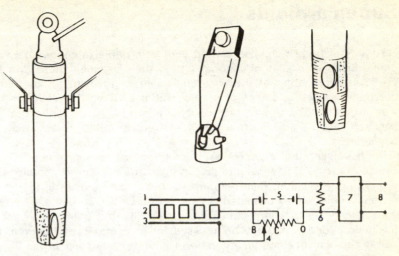

SWITCHABLE CONDENSER MICROPHONE  *Left*: the early version of a mono, high-quality variable-response condenser microphone, and *centre* a later smaller version that has replaced it. Its side-fire operation is more obvious. The circuit diagram shows how the response is changed by varying the polarising voltage to one diaphragm. 1, Front diaphragm. 2, Rigid centre plate (perforated). 3, Rear diaphragm. 4, Multi-position switch and potentiometer. 5, Polarising voltage. 6, High resistance. 7, Head amplifier. 8, Microphone output terminals. When the polarisation is switched to position O the voltage on the front and back diaphragm is the same, and above that of the centre plate: the capsule operates as an omnidirectional (pressure) microphone. At B the capsule measures pressure gradient and is bi-directional. At C the polar response is cardioid. *Top right*: two such capsules in a single casing, making a co-incident pair.

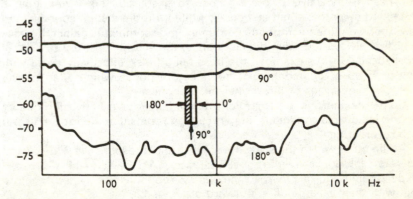

CARDIOID RESPONSE OF HIGH-QUALITY CONDENSER MICROPHONE  The axial response is substantially flat to 15 000Hz and the response at 90° almost so. The irregularities in the 180° curve are at low level.

**49**

# Supercardioids

Flexibility of polar response started with being able to choose between omnidirectional and bi-directional types; then between these and the cardioid combination of the two, and so to the switchable condenser microphones with a choice of nine conditions. Given the choice in this way, users rapidly discovered the special value of the range that lay between cardioid and figure-eight: the response called supercardioid or hypercardioid.

We have seen that a directional microphone can favour one particular source or group of sources and discriminate against others, and also that it picks up less studio reverberation so that it can be used further back, giving a more evenly-balanced coverage of a widely spread source. The figure-eight has excellent directional properties, but unless the back of the microphone is actually being used for a second sound source, the size of the rear lobe can be an embarrassment: it may pick up an excess of reverberation or sound from other, unwanted sources. In these circumstances, where much of the forward directivity of the bi-directional microphone is required, but *not* its full rear pick-up, the supercardioid response is a distinct improvement. It may be particularly valuable for individual instruments in a multi-microphone music balance, or for single sources in a lively acoustic. For such purposes microphones with a fixed supercardioid response have been specially designed, seeking for each use the best compromise between directivity, discrimination against ambient sound, and bass tip-up.

**Bass tip-up turned to advantage**
It should be noted that bass tip-up is to be expected with close working, but this too can be turned into a virtue. If a supercardioid with a fall-off in the bass from 200Hz is placed close to a source, this lower limit is extended by perhaps half an octave, while for more distant sources (and reverberation) the microphone continues to discriminate against the bass which is always the most difficult part of the sound spectrum to control acoustically. In this example, the bass fall-off also effectively deals with the problem of degradation of frequency response which often affects the low frequencies of directional microphones.

Some inexpensive supercardioid microphones give fairly high-quality sound in adverse conditions, in particular in rooms that are too small and too reverberant.

At the other end of the scale the supercardioid response is widely used in very high-quality stereo music balance — in the form of a 'crossed supercardioid'. In this, two switchable microphones are placed together but with their axes pointing outward at about 120°.

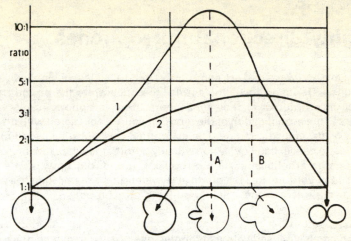

DIRECTIVITY as a microphone ranges from pure pressure operation (omnidirectional) to pure pressure gradient (bi-directional). Curve 1 shows the ratio of sound accepted from the front and rear. The most unidirectional response is at A, for which the microphone is, essentially, dead on one side and live on the other. Curve 2 shows discrimination against ambient sound. With the supercardioid B, reverberation is at a minimum. In the range between omnidirectional and cardioid, direct sound from the front and sides is favoured, so a microphone of this type can be placed close to a broad source.

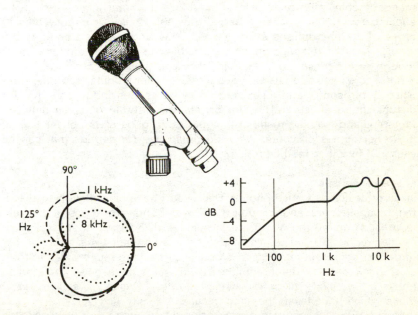

SINGER'S MICROPHONE   The supercardioid response with unswitchable bass roll-off makes this suitable for close working only. The moving coil is rugged and will withstand high sound pressure levels. The double peak is designed to give strong presence on some voices.

**51**

# Highly directional microphones

There are two ways that are commonly used to achieve a highly directional response. One is to focus the sound: to concentrate the sound from the direction of interest at the point where the microphone is placed. This results in the amplification of the required sound, compared with unwanted noise from other directions. The second method is to cause sound from the side to cancel itself out automatically before it reaches the microphone. There is no amplification of the required sound, but unwanted sound is reduced in volume. Both degrade at wavelengths greater than the physical size of the microphone's field-modifying attachment.

**Focused sound**
Sound can be focused with a parabolic reflector. This may be of fibreglass, metal, or of transparent plastics (to see action through it); it may be segmented to be folded like a fan for easy transport or storage.

In practice a reflector can give a gain of about 20dB for distant, high-frequency sounds along its axis. For faint sounds this results in a significant improvement in the ratio of signal to microphone and amplifier hiss. And the angle of acceptance for high frequencies is very narrow: no more than a few degrees. But the practical limitations are severe: a reasonably manoeuvrable reflector of 3–4ft (0.9–1.2m) diameter loses much of its effect below 1000Hz. At low frequencies the response degenerates to those of the microphone itself – which may be a cardioid pointing the wrong way. Also the microphone is still subject to close unwanted noises – though where these are in the bass they can often be cut.

Reflectors have been used very successfully for wildlife recording (particularly birdsong), and, because they work as well indoors as out, for distant sound effects in the film or television studio (e.g. the dancers' footsteps and clothing rustle in ballet). But, in general, the sheer bulk of the reflector has prevented its widespread use for sounds that can be captured by other methods.

**Phase cancellation**
In early designs of microphones that used phase cancellation to discriminate against unwanted sound there were bundles of tubes of different lengths, sampling the wavefront at a series of points in the direction of the desired sound source. Noise coming at an angle travels by a number of paths of different lengths. When these signals are recombined in front of the microphone diaphragm, some of them have been changed in phase by the extra distance travelled, and will therefore tend to cancel those which have taken the shorter path.

Later it was discovered that a long single tube with a slot (in practice, a series of perforations along its length) could be made to work as well: this is the principle now employed in the gun microphone.

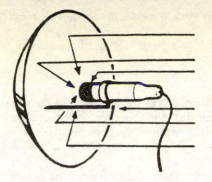

PARABOLIC REFLECTOR High-frequency sound is concentrated at the focus. The contribution from the rim is important, so the microphone should not be too directional. For low-frequency sounds of wavelengths greater than the diameter of the bowl the directional qualities degenerate.

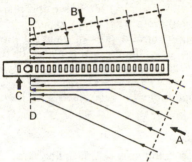

PHASE CANCELLATION Wave A approaching a gun microphone from a direction close to the axis reaches the front of diaphragm D by a range of paths which differ only slightly in length. There is cancellation only at very high frequencies. Wave B reaches the diaphragm by a much wider range of path-lengths. Cancellation is severe at middle and high frequencies. Normal sound reaches the back of the diaphragm via port C. The polar diagram of the capsule without the acoustic delay network is cardioid; with the interference tube it becomes highly directional.

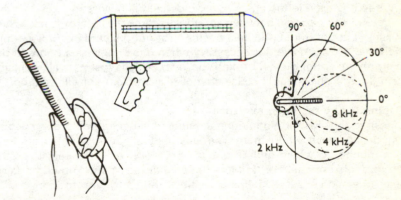

SHORT INTERFERENCE MICROPHONE Overall length about 10in (25cm). At 2000Hz and below, the response is cardioid. The minimum distance from capsule to mouth is controlled by the length of the tube, so that there is little proximity effect (bass tip-up) even when held close to the mouth. Cancellation due to the interference tube makes the microphone highly directional only at high frequencies. It has excellent separation from surrounding noise when hand-held by solo singers or reporters, or when used as a gun microphone for film sound.

*Shotgun (or rifle) microphones are used on outdoor locations and for specialised jobs in the studio.*

# Gun microphones

The interference tube, which depends on phase cancellation of sounds approaching from the side, has two important limitations. One is common to all highly directional microphones: its response degenerates to that of the microphone capsule at wavelengths below its own physical size. A gun microphone with an interference tube about 16in (400mm) long has an angle of acceptance of about 50–60° from 1500Hz upwards, but at 250Hz it is substantially cardioid (this being the response of the capsule without the tube). It is therefore sensitive to such noises as low-frequency traffic rumble, although some degree of bass cut may reduce this. When used for effects – e.g. a tap dance – or the sounds that accompany most sports (to which it adds great realism) it is often best to use bass cut at, say, 300Hz.

Shorter interference tubes are also used, and have higher switch-over frequencies.

**Effect of reverberation**
The second limitation is that it is not directional for reverberation. This is because reverberant sound arrives at the microphone by many different paths and so the phase cancellation effect does not work. In live interiors a comparable directional response with better quality might be expected from a good cardioid or supercardioid microphone. A television or film studio may be dead enough for this not to matter too much, though even here it is better to use it only where the subject always faces forward – e.g. in some discussion programmes, but not usually in drama.

When it is used in the open air a windshield is necessary: this is bulky so careful co-operation between sound and camera operator is necessary to keep it out of frame (the best position for good sound is often *just* out of frame). No windshield is necessary when it is on a studio boom (if the microphone is not moved around too fast). This is just as well, because such a large object could cause shadows even from soft-fill lighting.

**Pinpointing voices in an audience**
One special use is for pinpointing a single voice in a large group such as a studio audience, where there is already general coverage with a cardioid microphone, to which high-frequency presence is added selectively by the gun microphone. For this it is better that the studio should be fairly dead (the audience itself helps to achieve this) and not too big.

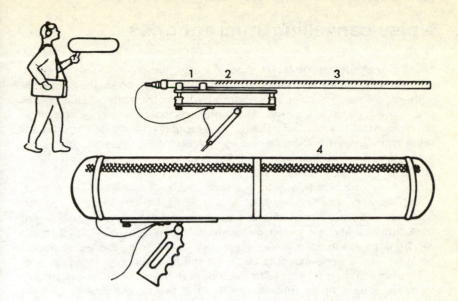

GUN MICROPHONE  1, Head
amplifier of condenser microphone.
2, Electrostatic capsule (cardioid
operation). 3, Acoustic interference
tube (with entry ports along upper
surface). 4, Windshield for open air
use. Overall length of microphone
and interference tube, 22in (560mm)
(windshield, 26in × 4¼in,
660 × 110mm). For location recording,
the user listens to playback on
headphones.
*Centre*: The response depends on
frequency, but for high frequencies
the cone of acceptance encloses
about 50°.
*Below*: The axial response is
reasonably level, but only within a
narrow angle. The erratic response to
the side is unimportant.

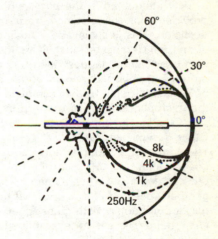

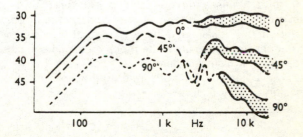

55

*The best ways of discriminating against heavy background noise.*

# Noise-cancelling microphones

Microphones often have to be used in noisy places: at sporting events, for example, where (for radio) the time of loudest noise may coincide with the greatest need for explanation by the commentator. One way of dealing with this is to give him an omnidirectional microphone and allow him to control the ratio of voice to background himself. The results are often satisfactory for short items – in particular for news reports – but for long, continuous commentary it is better to separate voice and effects and mix them later in the chain.

One way of doing this is to put the reporter into a soundproof box, a commentary booth. But this also has limitations. Noise – even whispers – from other people speaking nearby becomes obtrusive, and the sound quality due to the dimensional resonances of a small booth can be unpleasant. So a useful alternative is the noise-cancelling microphone – and a good example of this is the lip-ribbon microphone.

This has a ribbon very close to the mouth of the speaker, and is subject to extreme bass tip-up (proximity effect). If the microphone is given a reduced bass response to compensate for this, background noise is heavily attenuated in the bass, while the voice has a level response – provided that the distance from mouth to ribbon is controlled with precision. This is achieved by having a mouthguard, fixed to the microphone, which must be touched against the upper lip when the microphone is in use. The model described has a distance of 2⅛in (45mm) between mouth and ribbon. The low-frequency discrimination against background noise is additional to that achieved at *all* frequencies simply by having the microphone close to the mouth.

## Other design features
The choice of a suitable high-frequency response also helps: if it has a peak at about 7000Hz and then tails off, it will cover speech adequately but cut down on noise at higher frequencies. The overall response is generally designed for the normal to loud speech which mixes well with background noise. With quiet speech it may sound a little bassy; if so, it will require bass cut, for example when it is used for very quiet speech in a public concert hall.

A particular difficulty that always arises in close working is a tendency for breath noises to be noticeable, and for 'p' and 'b' sounds to 'pop' the microphone (the ribbon is particularly susceptible to this). In the lip ribbon this is avoided by a design that cups the ribbon *behind* the magnet, and by having a fine-mesh breath screen on top of the microphone to shield it from the nose.

The appearance of this microphone makes it unsuitable for use in vision.

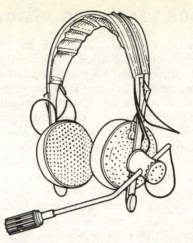

**HEADPHONE/MICROPHONE COMBINATION** The omnidirectional electret has a frequency response that is engineered to suit the direction of the mouth. Discrimination is otherwise by distance, but loud nearby voices will still be audible and may be distracting. Loud sound effects may be satisfactory if the speaker projects to balance them.

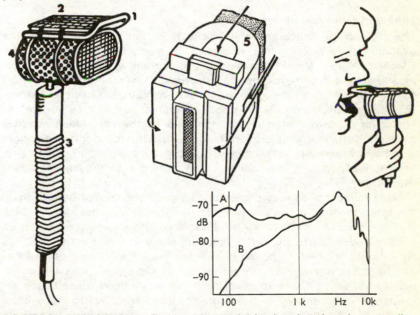

**LIP-RIBBON MICROPHONE** The mouth guard 1 is placed against the upper lip and the stainless steel mesh 2 acts as a windshield below the nose. The handgrip 3 contains a transformer. Within the housing 4 the microphone assembly is mounted with the yoke of the magnet 5 towards the mouth. The sound paths are marked. A, Response to spherical wave at approximately 2½in (76mm) (i.e. the user's voice). B, Response to plane wave (ambient sound) on axis. This effect is achieved by equalisation, without which B would be flat and A would be very high at low frequencies, owing to extreme bass tip-up at this working distance.

*A microphone in picture must be treated as an important visual element.*

# Microphones for use in vision

Everything within a television or film picture, as much as everything in the sound, contributes to the total effect. Accordingly, some microphones have been designed specifically for good appearance as well as high-quality performance; others have simply evolved into a suitable shape. Indeed, one of the criteria for a microphone is that it shall be reasonably small and neat, so that it does not unduly disturb the high-frequency component of the sound field it is sampling. It should normally be mid- or light-toned, perhaps silver-grey, with a matt finish to diffuse reflection of studio lights.

The condenser microphone lends itself to suitable visual design. Characteristically, a pencil shape about ¾in (20mm) in diameter has room for a diaphragm about ½in (13mm) across, usually arranged in the end-fire configuration, with a head amplifier inside the tube behind it. A moving coil unit can also be fitted into the same shape; though with so small a diaphragm sensitivity may be lower. An electret, smaller still, may be attached to clothing below the neck, or (for singers) to a headset.

A microphone will usually look better projecting into frame from the bottom, rather than the top.

**Floor and table mountings**
The problem of stands is more difficult than that of microphones. The evolution of their design has not carried them so easily towards unobtrusiveness. A floor stand must be solid, heavy and with a sizeable base-area to ensure that the microphone it carries is not knocked over; it must cushion the microphone against shocks and may also have to be telescopic. The design problem extends to connectors and cables, to the knobs for securing extension fittings, and to the clip which attaches microphone to mounting (the clip should be neat but easy for the performer to release in vision). But whatever else can be achieved in a long shot there is likely to be a vertical line in the picture – so the cleaner this is the better.

Table microphones may sometimes be partly concealed by designing the table to have a sunken well for the stand, but the capsule itself should be above the level of the table top, and should be away from solid surfaces which will form a standing wave at high frequencies. The well should not be fully boxed in or it will generate its own resonances (see page 87). Alternatively, a neat stand and microphone may be acceptable in full vision. Sometimes microphones have been concealed in set dressing – e.g. in flower arrangements. In an ideal world this will be done only if the flowers themselves serve an important visual purpose in a suitable place for the microphone and the microphone itself is definitely not wanted in vision. But on a heavily cluttered desk or table it may be better to hide the microphone behind one of the objects, rather than to add an inconsistent element to the scene.

Microphones with slender, 'swan-neck' extensions may also be useful.

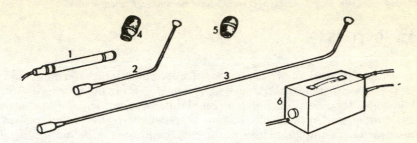

CONDENSER MICROPHONE KIT WITH 'SWAN-NECK' EXTENSIONS FOR USE IN VISION and alternative capsules for cardioid and omnidirectional operation. 1, Head amplifier and capsule (5in, 13cm). 2, 3, Extension pieces which may be fitted between head amplifier and capsule (1ft, 30cm, and 2ft 3in, 68cm). 4, 5, Windshields. 6, Power supply unit.

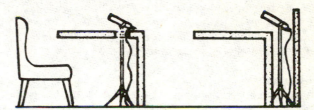

FLEXIBLE 'GOOSENECK' extension for floor or table stand. It is stiff enough to allow precise positioning of the microphone, with a clean line that makes it suitable for use in vision.

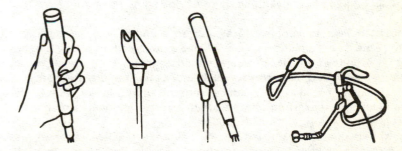

TELEVISION DESK AND MICROPHONE   To avoid bumps, the microphone is on a floor stand; *left*, emerging through hole; *right*, behind false front.

EASY RELEASE CLIP (*left*) on floor stand allows the microphone to be taken from the stand while in vision. Alternatively (*right*), the performer may wear a lightweight headset (without headphones) which is designed for minimal disturbance of hairstyle. This holds the microphone in a fixed position, and at this distance it must be positioned beyond the corner of the mouth in order to avoid 'popping'.

# Electrets

An electret is a variant of a condenser microphone in which the diaphragm has an electrostatic charge sealed within it during manufacture. This eliminates the power supply that would otherwise be required to charge the condenser. A small d.c. battery or phantom power supply is still needed for an amplifier close to the diaphragm, either within the head itself or nearby. Early versions have suffered some loss of high-frequency response as they aged, so this may need to be checked. Later variants have been designed to hold their polarising charge better, and the technology (of sealing the surface) continues to improve.

In this application of the electrostatic principle, both size and cost can be reduced dramatically, as the electronics are simplified and the polar response is limited to a single pattern. It is commonly used for the cheap microphones built into domestic recorders.

For the more carefully manufactured and tested electrets, one professional use is in personal microphones, where the small size of the capsule allows it to be both inconspicuous and extremely light. Another is on musical instruments, to which it may be clipped, usually on a small arm or 'gooseneck' arranged to angle in towards the source. So close to it, the reduced sensitivity and therefore higher noise level associated with a smaller diaphragm is acceptable.

## Personal microphones

At one time personal microphones were hung on lanyards around the neck, and some examples may still be encountered. In America this arrangement was called a lavalier, presumably after Madame de la Valière, who wore her pendant jewellery in this manner. However, for most purposes the suspended moving coils are now replaced by tiny electrets, which can be fixed to the clothing, in much the same position, below the neck.

Lanyard and lapel microphones (as they are commonly called) discriminate to some extent against noise. They also allow freedom of movement, and give a uniform quality of sound in close shots. They benefit from good reflected sound, but are also satisfactory out of doors. Response is omnidirectional, because the distance from the mouth is not completely predictable, and there is normally a smooth extended frequency response, perhaps with some top-lift (2500−8000Hz).

The sound quality is affected by the electret's position close to the chest, the lack of high frequencies under the chin and by the filtering effect of any thick clothing used to conceal it. In practice, it is better to allow the microphone to be in vision, as this also reduces the danger of clothing rustle. The effect is neater if the colour or tone matches clothing.

If it must not be seen, an electret can be taped to the skin under a shirt, or to the clothing itself, perhaps with double-sided tape, in order to avoid rubbing or bumping it.

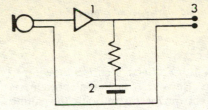

ELECTRET CIRCUITRY Compared with earlier condenser microphones this is very simple. 1, Integrated circuit amplifier. 2, Low voltage d.c. power supply and resistor. Phantom power may also be used. 3, Output (cable).

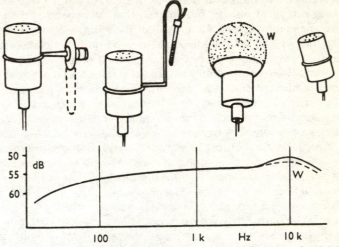

SMALL PERSONAL MICROPHONE Size: 0.7 × 0.42in (19 × 11mm). Weight of condenser capsule 0.16oz (4.5g), plus cable permanently attached to supply unit. The microphone can be used with one of several clip attachments or a windshield. W, which very slightly affects the high-frequency response. A more recent version (*far right*) is even smaller, and deterioration of the electrostatic field with age has been reduced; it is also more resistant to temperature and humidity impairment.

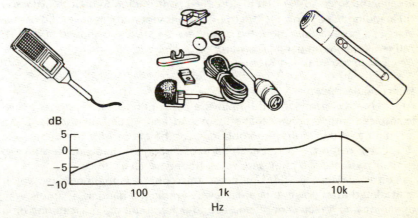

VERSATILE, TINY PERSONAL ELECTRET Half an inch long (13 × 7 × 44mm), this is supplied with a moulded connector and a range of holders — clip, tape-down strip, tie-bar and tie-pin — in black, grey, tan and white, or with a small windshield or pressure-zone adaptor. The response is level in the mid-range, with a smooth, extended presence-peak of 3—4dB in the 5—15kHz range. Its relatively large power supply can be clipped to a waist-band or go in a pocket.

*A microphone close to a hard, extended surface has special properties.*

# Boundary microphones

Generally, microphones are kept away from reflective surfaces owing to the interference fields these produce. However, as the diaphragm is moved closer to the surface, this effect moves up through the sound frequency spectrum, until at a distance of 1in (25mm) it occurs only in the highest octave of human hearing, so that on speech and song the effect becomes unimportant. As a result, if the surface is solid enough to reflect sound well at all frequencies, a good-quality balance can be obtained by a microphone placed within an inch of it.

For a sound wave approaching a rigid solid reflecting surface at a right angle to it, a microphone near the surface registers only pressure variations, not the pressure gradient. On the other hand a sound wave travelling parallel to the surface can be detected either by its pressure or by its pressure gradient. A directional microphone is effective therefore only in directions parallel to the surface. A common arrangement is to place an end-fire cardioid microphone parallel to the surface and directed towards action at a distance. It may therefore be well-suited to opera performed before an audience. Sightlines are not obstructed by the small, neutrally coloured, and felicitiously named 'mice'.

The formal name for this arrangement is *boundary microphone*. (One proprietary name is *pressure zone microphone*, or *PZM* – which sounds better with the American 'zee' pronunciation.) The pressure zone itself has one practical advantage. Close to any rigid boundary, there is a pressure-doubling effect, which results in a 6dB increase in the signal.

A microphone which is specially designed to operate in this regime can look very different from a normal microphone. Some have been engineered to be so flat that the greatest contribution to their thickness is the padding used to protect them from floor vibration. In several designs, stereo pairs have been mounted on either side of wedge-shaped housings, rather like binaural pairs. The hard, reflective surface should, if possible, be clear for several feet around.

### Home-made mice
An alternative arrangement employs a conventional microphone, which is inserted into a polyurethane-foam pad and placed on the floor. An advantage of this is that microphones can be chosen for frequency and directional response to suit each particular source – and can be returned to their normal uses after service as boundary layer 'mice'.

A disadvantage of a floor-mounted microphone is that however well it is insulated from noise, this must always remain a danger. A simple way of minimising directly conducted sound is to mount the microphone on a stand in the orchestra pit, with the capsule on a flexible 'swan-neck' bending over the edge of the stage and angled slightly down, almost to touch the surface. As before, the directional response will be horizontal. The final limitation will be noise radiated from the stage surface and travelling through the air to the microphone.

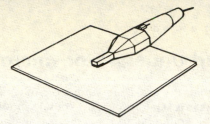

PRESSURE ZONE MICROPHONE ON PLATE   This is easily fixed to a surface by tape (on top) or double-sided adhesive (below). The tiny capsule, very close to the surface, broadens out to allow for a conventional connector. The hemispherical polar response does not change with distance, a benefit when the distance of the source is unpredictable.

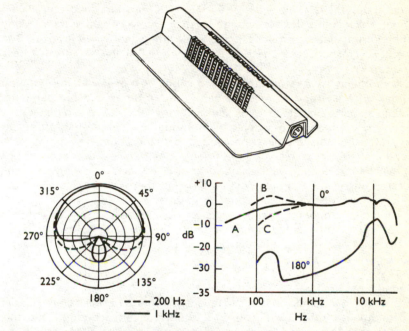

PRESSURE ZONE MICROPHONE WITH FLANGES   These may be fixed to a stage surface by tape of a matching colour, or by double-sided adhesive tape or adhesive putty. In this case the response is near-cardioid, and the response at low frequencies depends on the distance of the source. Spaced at intervals of 3–4m along the apron of a stage, these have been used successfully for opera. The polar response (for a source at an angle of 30° above the stage) is unidirectional. There are controls to boost bass, B, and to cut it, C.

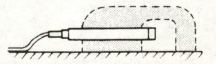

MICROPHONE MOUSE IN SECTION   Polyurethane foam is moulded with a tubular slot for the insertion of the microphone, and a cavity for the capsule. It is placed on the floor. Alternatively, tape the microphone loosely over a foam pad.

# Contact and underwater microphones

Many solids and liquids are excellent conductors of sound – much better than air. A device that is used to pick up sound vibrations from a solid material such as the sound-board of a musical instrument is called a *contact microphone*. In addition to this, a variety of scientific instruments originally developed for other purposes can be adapted to produce a signal carrying sound information – though not always with the fidelity required of a professional microphone.

Contact microphones sold for use with 'electric' instruments include a strip about 1in (25mm) wide, 3–8in (75–200mm) long and only 0.04in (1mm) thick that is flexible enough to stick onto a curved surface. Made of barium titanate, it produces a piezo-electric signal when it flexes. The frequency response emphasises the mid-range at the expense of bass and top.

In another type, the whole microphone housing moves with the vibration of the surface – and so must be very light, in order to avoid damping. Inside, an 'active mass' remains still by its own inertia, so can generate a signal by a variety of principles. A high-quality example has a broader response than the strip described above, but still requires a separate conventional electret to pick up high frequencies (above 4kHz) acoustically. (Typically the electret will be close and directed towards strings – on an electric guitar, for example, just underneath them, in the air hole, from which it will receive an additional component.)

Contact microphones can be attached with adhesive putty, or in some cases with double-sided adhesive tape: find a compromise between security of attachment and the need to get the transducer off without damage after use.

### Sound from liquids

To pick up sound under water, a simple technique is to seal a conventional microphone (often moving-coil) in a rubber sheath (condom), but this means that the sound must cross the barrier from water to air, an acoustic impedance which reduces sensitivity and distorts the frequency response (totally apart from causing embarrassment, hilarity, or both).

In principle, it is better that the water is separated from the transducer only by a material such as chloroprene rubber, which is of matched impedence. One miniature hydrophone has a frequency range of 0.1Hz to 100kHz or more, which may seem excessive in terms of human hearing, but not for that of whales and dolphins. By recording and replay at changed speeds, or through a harmoniser to change frequency independently of time, the extended frequency-range of underwater communication and sound effects can be matched to our human perception.

However, in practice, few recordists will use a true hydrophone: the sheathed microphone will pick up a signal that is adequate for most purposes. After all, the human eardrum is rarely used to pick up sound directly from water (and never from solids!).

## CONTACT MICROPHONE
This can be attached to the soundboard on a guitar or other stringed instrument. The principle is electrostatic but is unusual in having a rubber-coated diaphragm, in order to give it relatively large reactive mass. Polar response is figure-eight.

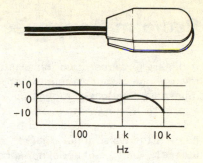

## ELECTRIC GUITAR
In this example a contact microphone close to the bridge is combined with an acoustic microphone clipped to the edge of the air-hole.

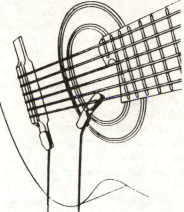

## SOUND FROM SOLIDS: ACTIVE
MASS 1, Contact microphone. 2, Vibrating surface. 3, The mass of the suspended magnet holds it relatively still. For a reverberation plate or similar source in a fixed position, the microphone assembly can be mounted on a rigid arm, 4.

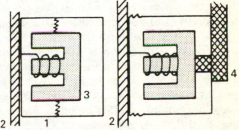

## MINIATURE HYDROPHONE
The ideal underwater microphone, 0.37in (9.5mm) diameter, with a rubber compound bonded directly onto a piezoelectric ceramic. This allows an excellent sound-transmission path from the water, and permits a frequency response which extends far beyond the range of human hearing. The response is flat over the normal audiofrequency range, in directions at right angles to the axis; there is a very slight reduction in some other directions.

# Radio microphones

A battery-powered radio-transmitter and aerial is used with a personal microphone (whether hand-held or attached to clothing) when its user must have freedom of movement or where a cable could drag, tangle or appear distractingly in vision.

The transmitter pack should be small enough to go in a pocket, or be hung at the waist under a jacket, or possibly in a pouch at the small of the back. The type of aerial depends on waveband. A VHF aerial, approximately a quarter-wavelength long, may be allowed to hang under outer clothing; or the screen on the microphone lead may serve, if it is made the right length. A VHF aerial is shorter and on some hand-held microphones may be fitted as a flexible stub, projecting from its base.

The receiving antennae (often two) are usually simple dipoles placed where one or both will always have an unobstructed electromagnetic path from the transmitter. Television and film studio sets made of wood and non-conductive materials should be transparent to the signal, but metals, predictably, will cause problems. So, when setting the aerials, it may be advisable for a sound assistant to walk and talk in all sound-source locations, so that the supervisor can check for dead spots.

In a television studio, existing monitor circuits can often be used to carry the signals from the dipoles to a radio receiver in the sound gallery. The transmitter controls must be preset, with a consequent danger of overload or undermodulation. This can be minimised by a compander – compression at the transmitter compensated by matched expansion at the receiver. (Otherwise use a modest amount of automatic gain to smooth out variability in the signal, but with care so as not to conflict with performance values.)

The transmitter should be free from frequency drift, and it should not audibly 'bump' if tapped or jolted. Battery power generally drops suddenly when the power is exhausted. Watch for automatic early-warning signals if available; otherwise log hours of use and replace the batteries early. The transmitter will have a radio-frequency power of 100mW or more – substantially more, if distances extend beyond those of a normal studio.

## Standby arrangements

Wavebands are allocated by national regulating authorities; in particular, equipment carried across the Atlantic will have to be reset. Interference may come from other studio equipment: to safeguard against last-minute problems, have standby packs ready to operate on different frequencies, and before live broadcasts also run out a cable and make it ready for use in case all else fails.

Radio microphones are widely employed in documentary filming and news reports; by the roving hosts of studio shows, and for many other purposes. But although the quality of the radio link may be high, it may be compromised by the unfavourable position of a personal microphone. So always consider using a studio boom, fishpole or gun microphone.

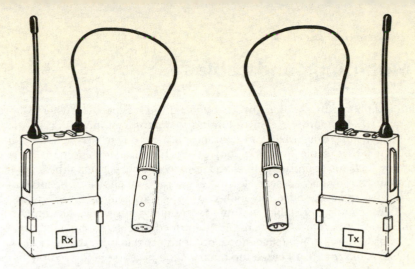

**A RADIO MICROPHONE TRANSMITTER PAIR** Externally, the appearance is similar, although the controls on top are slightly different, and the connector pins or socket reflect the direction of the signal.

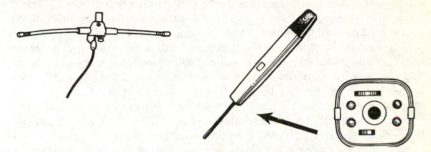

**RADIO MICROPHONE AND RECEIVER DIPOLE** The microphone contains its own UHF transmitter and has a stub aerial emerging from the base. Capsules are available for either omnidirectional or end-fire cardioid operation. The base of the stick has switches including on/off, tone, and base roll-off (for cardioid close working) and LED condition and warning lights. Aerials are mounted nearby.

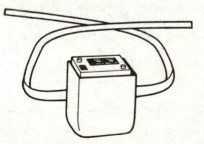

**COMMUNICATIONS POUCH** A radio microphone transmitter or talkback receiver can be carried in a specially-made pouch held by a tape in the small of the back. For a television performer with tight clothing, matching or blending material is used, and the tapes are taken through splits in the side seams.

# Mountings and cables

In addition to the equipment for television, described elsewhere, there are many standard ways of mounting microphones, including a variety of booms. In concert halls, most microphones may in principle be slung by their own cable from the roof of the hall, but for additional safety many halls insist on separate slings, and in any case guying (by separate tie-cords) may be necessary for the accurate final choice of position and angle. A radio-operated direction-control is also available.

Floor stands and table mountings should have provision for shock insulation, to protect the microphone from conducted sound, vibration or bumps. Where appearance does not matter, this may be a cradle of elastic supports; in all cases the microphone must be held securely in its set position and direction.

### Microphone cables

Three wires (and therefore three pins), one being earthed, are sufficient for most purposes, including both the signal (mono or stereo) and the power plus polarizing voltage for electrostatic microphones. For phantom power supplies to condenser microphones both of the live signal wires are raised to a nominal 48V above ground. The difference in voltage between this pair and the (grounded) third wire also provides the polarization for electrostatic microphones that need it (any but electrets).

More complex systems have more wires − for example, for switching polar response or bass-cut, and also for radio microphones. Old designs of electrostatic microphones containing valves (vacuum tubes) − collectors' items or working replicas that are treasured by some balancers for their distinctive sound quality − require an additional 12V supply to the heater.

Trailing or hard-wired audio cables will usually have substantial but flexible, colour-coded conductors, with braided or lapped shielding to protect against electrical interference, and with a strong outer sheath. The more complex 'star-quad' cables have higher noise rejection: in a studio it will soon become apparent if these are needed. For longer distances, multichannel cables (with additional coding colours) will terminate in a junction box for the individual microphone cables that lead through a multipin connector to the control desk.

In order to minimise induction, sound wiring should be kept away from power cables (to lighting or other equipment) and should cross them at right angles. This is necessary also for wiring built into the studio structure.

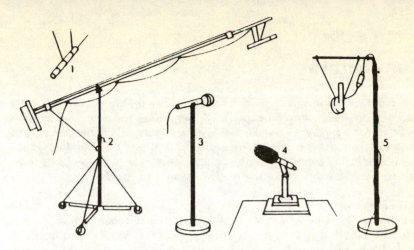

STANDS AND SLINGS   Methods of mounting microphones (used in radio studios). 1, Suspension by adjustable wires, etc. 2, Boom (adjustable angle and length). 3, Floor stand (with telescopic column). 4, Table stand (but 1, 2 or 5 are better for table work if there is any risk of table-tapping by inexperienced speakers). 5, Floor stand with bent arm. Most methods of mounting have shock absorbers or straps.

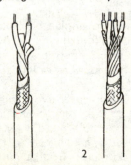

CONTROL OF MICROPHONE POSITION   1, Tie-cord. 2, Microphone cable. 3, Guy-wire giving fine control of position.

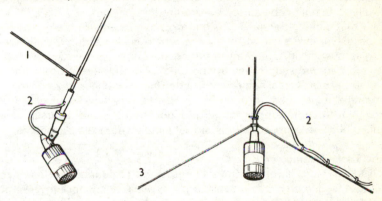

CABLES   1, Screened pair. 2, Multichannel cable. 3, 'Star-quad' cable.

# Connectors

The most common types of connectors for microphones are XLR, DIN, Tuchel, Lemo and simple jackplugs. A minimum of three conductors is required for a balanced signal: two are for the signal circuit and a third, earthed (grounded), shields them from hum. If just two conductors are used, one inside the other ('unbalanced'), this may pick up mains hum, so can only be used where there is no danger of this.

### XLR connectors
XLR plugs are widely used in studios, and the number of pins is indicated by a suffix: XLR 3, for example, has three. Typically, a cavity in the base of a microphone contains three projecting (i.e. male) pins: they point in the direction of signal flow. A cable therefore has a female socket at the microphone end and another male plug to go into the wall socket. Other arrangements are available, including right-angled plugs and other numbers of pins. Non-standard arrangements are sometimes encountered (more often in connectors to monitoring loudspeakers), so female-to-female cables may be required.

All XLR connectors have a locating groove to ensure the correct orientation. Some are secured by a latch which closes automatically when a plug is pushed in. The way in which the pins are wired is also nearly always standardised. If they are connected in a different order, this may lead to phase reversal, which should therefore be checked when installing unfamiliar equipment in a studio. Phase can usually be reversed in the desk, but to avoid a non-standard layout there, phase-reversal adaptors (and other accessories such as signal splitters) are also available.

### DIN, Tuchel, Lemo, etc.
The XLR system is robust and will withstand accidental bumps or rough use, but is also rather too massive for applications where low weight or small size are required. In such cases, another common standard is DIN (the German Industry Standard). The pins are more delicate, and the plugs and sockets smaller. For connectors that must be secure, a screw collar may be provided.

Among others: Tuchel plugs have three flat pins angled on radii from the centre and are rather bulky; Lemo connectors (much smaller) overlap inside a sleeve; jackplugs have either 3.5mm or 6.3mm (mono or stereo) central pins – take care not to plug these into a headphone or loudspeaker socket, and replace them by XLR if possible.

A radio studio may be hard-wired to offer a choice of two sockets for each channel, one on each side of the studio. The complicated layouts for television require many more, mostly distributed around the walls in groups, but with some in the studio ceiling, so that cables can be 'flown', or microphones suspended from above. In addition, from a multiway single-socket output at the studio wall a cable can be run out to a terminating box for, say, ten microphones on the studio floor.

XLR PLUGS *Left*: XLR 3 M *Centre*: XLR 3 F *Right*: XLR 7 F   The figure is the number of pins. 'M' is 'male', with pins pointing in the direction that the signal travels. The output from a microphone would normally have 'M' pins, the feed to control desk would go into an 'F' connector.

XLR 3 F WALL MOUNT with latch to lock plug firmly in place.

DIN 7 F   The German industry standard connector is less robust than the XLR, but the pins can be protected by a screw collar.

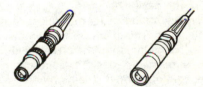

LEMO PLUGS *Left*: Lemo 3 M *Right*: Lemo 3 F   Here the inner connectors overlap: the 3 M has two pins and the 3 F has one.

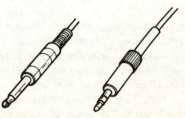

JACKPLUGS *Left*: Mono jack (6.3mm) *Right*: Stereo jack (3.5mm).

*An acoustically transparent screen can protect the microphone with little effect on its response.*

# Windshields

The term *windshield* (or *windgag*) covers several distinct functions, for which different devices are used. The first use, as the name implies, is to reduce noise due to wind turbulence at sharp edges, or even corners that are too sharply curved. To reduce wind effects proper, a smooth airflow round the microphone is required.

The ideal shape, if the direction of the wind were always known and the same, would be a teardrop, but in the absence of this information practical windshields are usually made either spherical or a mixture of spherical and cylindrical sections typically of 2in (5cm) radius. For outdoor use gun microphones have a shield of this size. The framework is generally of metal or moulded plastic, with a fine and acoustically transparent mesh, often of wire and foamed plastic, covering it. This should reduce noise by more than 20dB.

For studio operations, the shield radius is often less. Note that where there is also a rear-entry port, this too may require a shield – usually a tube of foam.

A second purpose is to reduce the effect of gusting breath or the puffs of air that accompany plosive 'p' or 'b' sounds, which may displace the microphone diaphragm beyond its working range. This may often be countered by a small, general-purpose windshield that is supplied with the microphone and consists, typically, of two layers of acoustic mesh with a thin layer of porous material between. Slipped snugly over the tip, this has little effect on the frequency response, changing the curve marginally only at high frequencies. Where a shield is already fully integrated into the microphone body, its effect on frequency response should have been calculated in the design.

Alternatively, shields made of foamed plastics can be stretched to fit over a variety of shapes. The effect on frequency response will again be small; even so, windshields should be removed when not required, in order to restore the optimum, desired response.

For a radio talk studio, foamed shields may be supplied in a variety of colours, so that a speaker can be directed to sit at a clearly identified microphone, and will be reminded by its colour to work to that and no other.

### Pop-shields

An alternative is the pop-shield, a gauze screen on a supporting ring, which protects only from breath effects and is open to the sides. 'Popping' may also be controlled by suitable microphone techniques, without the use of screens. Experiment by projecting 'p' sounds at your own hand: you will feel the blast of air which would push a microphone diaphragm beyond its normal limits. Then move the hand a little to one side. This will demonstrate one solution: to speak past the microphone, not directly into it.

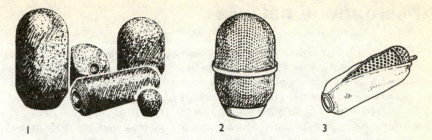

1                 2            3

**WINDSHIELDS** These come in a variety of shapes for different sizes of microphones and may be made of 1, plastic foam; 2, foam-filled wire mesh; or 3, mesh with an outer protective cover and air space between the mesh and the microphone.

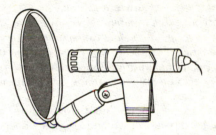

**POP-SHIELD** A framework covered with gauze protects a microphone from gusts of air caused by plosives, etc., in speech and song.

**POPPING** 1, Speaking directly into a microphone may deflect diaphragm beyond its normal range. 2, Speaking on-axis but to the side of the microphone may cure this without changing frequency response. 3, Speaking across and past the microphone may cure popping and also change frequency response. 4, Speaking across the microphone but still towards it may still cause popping. 5, A simple screen of nylon mesh over a wire obstructs the puff of air.

73

# Microphone balance

The most modest requirement of any microphone in use is that it must convey sufficient information – whether this be in terms of the intelligibility of speech, or the content of musical sound or effects. When a microphone is used to pick up speech in difficult acoustics or noisy conditions, this need may override all others. But where more than one limiting position of the microphone is possible, there is a series of choices that we may make. The exercise of these choices, the selection and placing of each microphone in relation to sound sources and studio acoustics, is called microphone balance.

## The objectives of balance

The first objective of microphone balance is purely technical: to pick up the required sound at a level suited to the microphone and recording set-up, i.e. to convert the acoustic energy of sound to a corresponding electrical signal with a minimum of irreversible distortion. The next objective is to discriminate against unwanted noises.

In professional practice this means that we must decide whether to use one microphone or several, and select those with suitable directional and frequency characteristics. For stereo we must choose between different ways of picking up positional information and also set a scale of width. In many cases we may also be able to arrange the position of the source or layout of several sources.

These decisions depend on the next and, some would say, most important aim of a good balance, which is to place each microphone at a distance and angle which produce an aesthetically satisfying degree of reinforcement from the acoustics of the studio. That entails controlling the ratio of direct to indirect sound picked up by the microphone, and making sure that the indirect sound is of a suitable quality.

Acoustic reinforcement may, however, be replaced by artificial reverberation which is mixed into the final sound electrically. In this case each individual sound source can be individually treated. For this reason, and because picking up a sound on a second more distant microphone reintroduces the effect of the studio acoustics, an alternative aim of microphone balance is to separate the signals from different sound sources so that they can be treated individually. For pop music the term balance means a great deal more than microphone placement. It includes treatment, mixing, and control, all integral parts of the creation of a single composite sound.

## Balance tests

Good balance can only be judged subjectively, and the best way of achieving it is by making direct comparative tests in good listening conditions between two (or more) microphones and moving one at a time until the best sound is achieved.

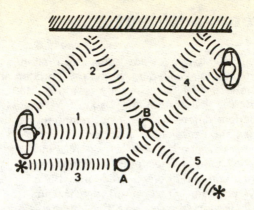

**BALANCE TEST:** Compare the sound from microphones A and B by switching between the two. The microphones lie in a complex sound field comprising many individual components. For simplicity, the illustration shows monophonic microphones. In stereo, the principles are the same, but the sound paths are more complex.

*Listen for:*
1. Clarity and quality of direct sound.
2. Ratio of direct to indirect sound. Does this add body, without being obtrusive or heavy (or otherwise unpleasantly coloured)?
3. Unwanted sound from the source or close to it. Can this be prevented or discriminated against?
4. The relative volume of other (required) sources, direct or indirect.
5. Unwanted sound from other sources.

*and, in stereo:*
6. Scale of width (the width of image, compared to distance between loudspeakers).
7. Location of individual components within stereo image.

*The variables:* Change only one of these, or as few as possible, between successive comparison tests.
i.   Distance from the source.
ii.  Height and lateral position (at a given distance).
iii. Angle of directional microphone.
iv. Directional characteristics of microphone (either by internal switching or by changing the microphone).
v.  Frequency response (by changing the microphone or its equalisation).
vi. The use of additional microphones.

If sufficient microphones are available for adequate balance tests, trial recordings may be made, and replayed one after the other, 20 seconds or so at a time.

*To prevent phase distortion place both microphones of a stereo pair at the same distance from all sources.*

# The stereo coincident pair

The most obvious way to convey positional information is by means of a spaced pair of microphones, feeding the output from left and right to the corresponding loudspeaker. This is done (see page 108), but creates a problem. For sources that are not equidistant from them, there will be a frequency-dependent difference of phase, resulting in reinforcement at some frequencies and cancellation at others.

Fortunately, there is another way of establishing the direction of a source. A matched pair of directional microphones is placed close to each other, but pointing in different directions: it is arranged that on the centre line between them, direct sound is picked up on each at a level such that the sum is much the same as that obtained along the main axis of each individual microphone. A coincident pair may consist of two mono microphones side by side, so that phase cancellation occurs only at very high frequencies. Better still, with the capsules one above the other in a single housing there wil be no significant cancellation.

The pair should be matched, but the balancer can choose their polar diagrams, angle of separation, and distance from the source. This allows control over the width of the image compared with the distance between loudspeakers, and also the reverberation (always full width): this affects the apparent size and distance of the subject.

A coincident pair changes the apparent shape of a spread image: a source at the front but towards one side may be as far away from the microphone as those at centre-back. Within the stereo image, it will stay on the same side but further back than in the original layout. It may be possible to correct this by changing the layout.

**Lining up a coincident pair**
Here is a simple way to check that the output of both elements of a coincident pair is the same:
1. Check that the monitoring loudspeakers are balanced. If the signal is fed to both together, it should appear to come from the centre.
2. Make sure the microphone elements have identical polar diagrams and visually set them at 90°. Identify left and right in turn.
3. Then visually set the pair along the same axis (i.e. at 0°, not back-to-back) and listen to the *difference* (signal A − B). If this cannot be done, reverse the leads on one capsule and *add* the output, which will have the same effect.
4. As one person speaks into the pair, another adjusts their relative output for *minimum* volume.
5. Restore to normal stereo output, but still keeping the capsule on the same axis. The speaker walks and talks all the way round the microphone: the image should stay in the middle, whatever the volume. This completes the check.
6. Restore the direction of the capsules to the normal working angle.

**76**

STEREOPHONIC MICROPHONE The method of picking up stereophonic sound that will be recommended in this book is the coincident pair: two directional microphones very close together, 1, or in a common housing, 2. The second symbol (as 2) will generally be used. The microphone elements will not necessarily be at 90° to each other. 3, 'dummy head' with directional microphones mounted on either side of a baffle. This arrangement is most successful when the two signals are heard on headphones.

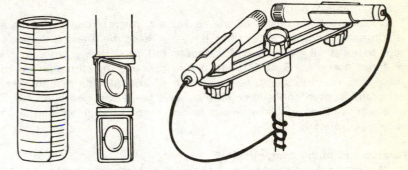

STEREO COINCIDENT PAIRS *Left:* Suspended within a single housing. *Right:* Two monophonic microphones on a bar. For nearby sources such as voices (particularly in drama) this arrangement avoids distortion of the image due to height.

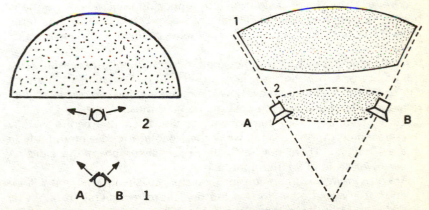

CONTROLLING REVERBERATION WITH A COINCIDENT PAIR *Left*: studio layout. *Right*: the resultant image. 1, A distant pair picks up strong reverberation, so that when the signal is fed to the loudspeakers A and B, it sounds as though the subject is set back behind them. 2, With less reverberation, the subject is set forward between the loudspeakers. Reverberation normally fills the full width between loudspeakers.

*The stereo signal can also be thought of as the sum of middle and side components.*

# Stereo field patterns

The coincident pair should be matched, but the balancer can choose their polar diagrams, angle of separation and distance from the source. These permit control of the scale of width (width of image compared with the distance between loudspeakers) and also the ratio of direct sound to reverberation (which is always full width): this affects the apparent size and distance of the subject.

For the figure-eight response, the microphone should be placed so that the angle between the axes of the two capsules includes the whole image. Outside this angle, the two elements will be out of phase and will begin to cancel out.

So far we have described stereo signals, microphone elements and loudspeakers only as left or right. If we call these the A and B signals and add them, $A + B = M$ where M is middle and also effectively mono. If we subtract them, $A - B = S$ for side. S also contains the stereo information (but note that full stereo requires both M and S). The M and S polar diagrams shown opposite could also have been obtained by combining the output of two different microphones – one omnidirectional and the other figure-eight.

**Stereo and mono compatibility**

A stereo signal is described as compatible if it is transmitted or recorded in a form from which normal mono processing automatically extracts a good mono signal M, which is the sum of A and B. On analogue tape, the A and B signals are recorded side by side: the broader mono reproducing head scans both thereby adding them. A vinyl disc has a V-shaped groove with the A and B signals cut in opposing angled walls: a mono needle, designed to track a lateral groove, picks up $A + B$. On stereo radio, M is broadcast on the normal mono channel and S is encoded separately.

Artistic compatibility is another matter: something is necessarily lost from a stereo production if it is heard in mono. Sometimes the stereo can be modified a little to make sure the mono version is more satisfying. Here are some hazards, with possible counter-measures:

1. Loss of volume from components at the sides; the centre is fully represented in the S signal, while the sides are represented partly in the M signal. There may also be phase distortion at the sides. A narrower scale of width might help.
2. There is more reverberation in S, so the remaining M signal will be drier. If it would otherwise be too dry, more reverberation might be added to M at the expense of S.
3. Sources that are spatially separated in stereo may be less distinct in mono: it may help to boost them – one way being to bring them closer to centre stage. However, unwanted noises which may be spatially distinct in stereo may be less obvious in mono.

**78**

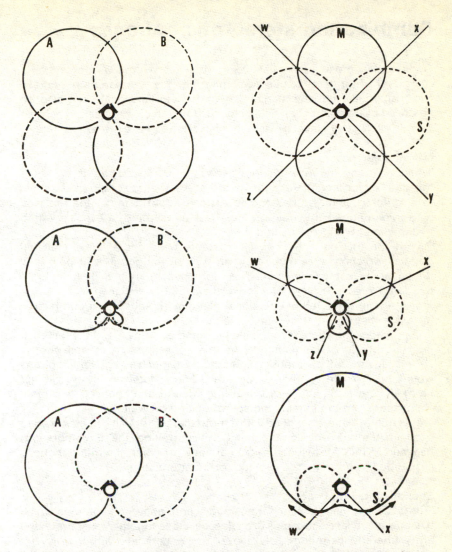

STEREOPHONIC FIELD PATTERNS Polar diagrams for coincident pairs of microphones at 90°. *Top left*, Crossed figure-eight. *Centre left*, Crossed cottage-loaf. *Bottom left*, Crossed cardioid. M and S diagrams for the same coincident pairs of microphones are shown on the right. *Top right*, For crossed figure-eight the useful forward angle (W-X) is only 90°. Sound from outside this (i.e. in the angles W-Z and X-Y) will be out of phase. The useful angle at the rear (Y-Z) will (for music) be angled too high for practical benefit. *Centre right*, Crossed cottage-loaf microphones have a broader useful angle at the front (W-X). *Bottom right*, The crossed cardioid has a 270° usable angle (between W and X, forwards) but only about 180° is really useful, as to the rear of the elements the response is erratic. Note that although the subject of crossed microphones is introduced here in terms of elements set at 90°, a broader angle is often better for practical microphone balances. 120° is commonly used.

# Combination stereo microphones

Traditionally, most stereo has been obtained by the use of either a coincident pair or a range of spaced microphones – or a mixture of these two techniques. But the standard A and B stereo signals can also be produced by combining the field patterns from the directional microphone capsules in several other, specialised microphones. Here are two examples.

## MS microphones

When recording stereo sound for a series of pictures that are to be edited together, or for a continuous television scene that is composed of shots from different angles, the standard AB coincident pair is often replaced by a microphone containing an end-fire hypercardiod M capsule with a bi-directional S capsule behind it.

With the MS pair, there is no absolute need for a finely matched frequency response (as required in an AB pair), although it helps if they do have the same character. This, for speech, may include a high-frequency presence peak. The forward capsule is designed to capture a mono signal, while the bi-directional element spreads the sound picture to match that on the television screen.

In principle, the same result could be obtained from A and B signals; in practice, MS is easier to handle in this application. A master shot is chosen, and the MS microphone pointed into it, much as a gun microphone would be. To allow coherent picture editing, cutaway shots will not normally 'cross the line' – a visual line which often connects two main characters – and this helps the sound editing as well.

This microphone is supplied with a matrixing unit which can be switched between various MS combinations by controlling the S component; between MS an AB (with reversed versions for when the microphone is suspended); and may also provide for LF attenuation.

## Soundfield microphone

This is the proprietary name for an exotic combination microphone which has four identical electrostatic capsules, set close together in a tetrahedral array, thereby permitting 2-D stereo to be derived from a truly 3-D combination of signals. The four axes are designated W, X, Y and Z (different from the WXYZ directions within a plane shown on page 79), and these are combined by using a remote control box to select azimuth (horizontal angle), elevation and 'dominance' (directivity).

The response can be altered during a live event to favour a source from some unexpected direction, or after recording the four separate signals may be remixed through the same control box to improve the coverage. The static microphone can be controlled to track a moving source. Again, there is a control to change the signals appropriately when the microphone is inverted.

This specialised microphone requires familiarisation before use.

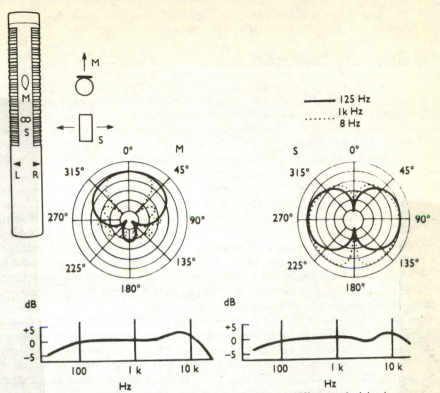

125 Hz
1 k Hz
8 Hz

M

| 0° | M |
| 315° | 45° |
| 270° | 90° |
| 225° | 135° |
| 180° | |

S

| 0° | |
| 315° | 45° |
| 270° | 90° |
| 225° | 135° |
| 180° | |

dB

+5
0
-5

100    1 k    10 k

Hz

dB

+5
0
-5

100    1 k    10 k

Hz

**MS MICROPHONE**   This combines capsules employing two different principles in a single housing. The forward M or 'middle' microphone is end-fire with short interference tube to narrow the high-frequency response. Behind this is a bi-directional S or 'side' microphone. The M response has a presence peak which is suitable for speech or actuality; S is flatter, but matches the effect of the peak. This example has an XLR 7 connector cable to its control box (matrix unit) which has XLR 5 output.

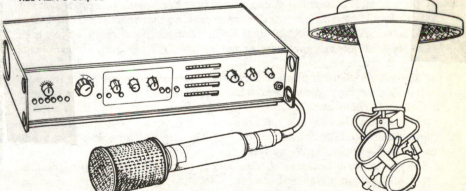

**SOUNDFIELD MICROPHONE AND ITS CAPSULES**   The variable polar response is switched remotely, as are azimuth (horizontal response) and the angle up or down. A control for 'dominance' narrows the response, giving a zoom effect, within the usual limits (i.e. there is no highly-directional response available). The signals from the four capsules can be recorded separately, then fed back through the control box so that the directional response can be modified later.

**81**

*The three factors on which speech balance depends are the voice, the surrounding acoustic conditions and the microphone.*

# Speech balance

In a good speech balance, the voice is clear and natural-sounding, perhaps reinforced to some degree by the room acoustic.

In mono, the two are combined as though from a single point in space; in stereo, each voice comes from a single point but the reverberation is spread. Many of the criteria for good mono balance apply equally to stereo. Microphone type and distance are important. A deep voice is over-emphasised by close working on a microphone that is directional at low frequencies and therefore subject to bass tip-up (proximity effect). Electronic correction (in the microphone channel) may be used to compensate for this, and does not affect voices that are less bassy, but it does limit movement backward and forward. Clarity of speech may be enhanced by a modest peak in the high frequency (5000–8000Hz) range, but a sibilant voice is made worse by it. In this case, a microphone with a smooth response is better, but it is not essential that this be extended into the extreme high-frequency range.

For many purposes, some acoustic reinforcement is good. Smaller studios are, however, likely to introduce coloration which can be reduced only by electronic filtering or closer working. Film commentary usually requires a fairly dead acoustic, in order to avoid conflict with picture, and to separate narrative from action – but this can make it difficult to match the same voice recorded on location.

### Using directional microphones

Directional microphones are generally used for speech. In mono a response which is cardioid over most of its working range, but which degenerates to omnidirectional in the extreme bass, can be used for a single voice at 12in (30cm) or less. Unless the studio is unusually dead an omnidirectional microphone would have to be placed much closer, so that balance between voice and acoustics is impracticable: such a microphone is therefore more likely to be used only for very close working, to eliminate acoustics and unwanted noise as much as possible.

Bi-directional microphones (ribbons) have been widely used in radio studios, even for single voices. Unless corrected for close working, balance is at a minimum of 18in–2ft (0.5–0.6m), depending on the bass content of the voice. This gives a full account of the studio acoustics and these must therefore be of good quality, i.e. without marked coloration. Small studios are not generally suitable for this type of balance.

In stereo, an announcer is often, by convention, placed in the centre: this allows the balance between left and right loudspeakers to be checked.

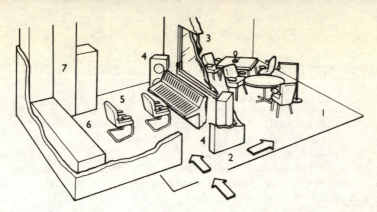

RADIO STUDIO LAYOUT   1, Studio. 2, Lobby. 3, Double-glazed window for acoustic, separation. 4, Control console and monitoring loudspeakers. 5, Producer's position (behind balancer). 6, Recording and replay equipment. 7, Equipment racks.

## INTERVIEWING TECHNIQUES USING DIRECTIONAL MICROPHONE (e.g. supercardioid)

*Position 1:*
Microphone at waist level: sound quality poor to fair. In television, this position may sometimes be used in order to clear the picture, but only if background noises are low, and the acoustic dead.

*Position 2:* Microphone at shoulder level, static. Sound quality is fair to good, provided that both speakers are close together — e.g. standing close and at 90° to each other, or sitting side by side.

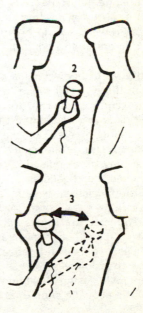

*Position 3:* Moving the microphone from one person to the other. Sound quality is good; but the aggressive use of the microphone may either distract the interviewee or allow him to move closer to it than is desirable. With a stereo end-fire microphone check the directional response with care, first.

**83**

# Two or more voices in mono

Speech balance for two voices can be accomplished by using separate microphones for each voice, or a single static microphone for the two; or by a moving microphone which is directed to each speaker in turn. Further voices may be covered by additional microphones for individuals or pairs; by balancing more voices to a single static microphone; or, again, by directing a movable microphone to individual speakers or groups of speakers in turn.

### Using separate microphones

As more and more microphones are used, the effect is to open up progressively more of the studio acoustics. If many microphones are open at the same time, closer balance or a deader acoustic is required. In principle a more sharply directional response from each microphone would also do the trick, but as we have seen, there are fundamental limits to the directional qualities of small microphones. The alternative is to hold back all microphones by about 6dB except that for the main speaker at any one time: this also tends to improve intelligibility when several people are speaking together. In an informal discussion, the sound mixer needs to see all of the speakers directly all of the time, in order to anticipate each contribution. Where a wide area is to be covered and there is no direct line of sight, place a sound assistant with a sub-mixer close to the action.

Unidirectional microphones may be used for pairs of speakers – e.g. in a panel game. Sometimes, however, one speaker may spend much of his time talking away from the microphone. If this happens, the sound balancer must make up his mind whether that is worse than having an extra microphone to control.

### Advantages of bi-directional microphone

In radio there is still much to be said for the bi-directional microphone which accommodates up to four speakers easily (two sitting on either side at distances of about 2ft (0.6m) or six (three plus three) at a pinch. The position of each speaker may sometimes be adjusted a little to compensate for differences in volume and voice quality, so that minimal control may be exercised by the sound balancer (who again should be able to see the speakers).

A group discussion with, say, six speakers can be balanced on a cardioid above the centre of the group and directed downwards – or below, directed up. This is not an ideal arrangement because the volume will be set for off-axis speech and the microphone is therefore particularly sensitive to noise and reflected sound in the line of the main axis. Another possibility is to use an electret with a foam pad on a hard-topped table, using the boundary pressure-zone effect. In all of these cases, the acoustic should be relatively dead.

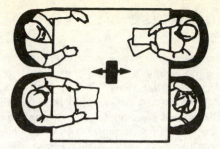

BI-DIRECTIONAL MICROPHONE (usually a ribbon) in layout for studio discussion with up to four speakers.

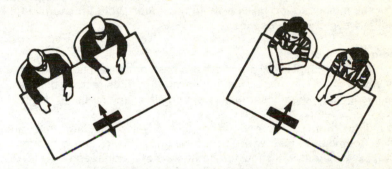

PANEL GAME BALANCED WITH TWO BI-DIRECTIONAL MICROPHONES  Each microphone is arranged so that the other pair of speakers is on its dead side. But any sound from in front of the desks (from the audience, for example) will be picked up on both: the microphones must therefore be in phase to signals from that direction. Supercardioid microphones are likely to be equally satisfactory.

HOSTS AND GUESTS in radio, allowing individual control of each contributor's voice. Guests sit in while records or pre-recordings are played.

ROUND TABLE DISCUSSION with six speakers working to a cardioid microphone, 1, suspended above them, or, 2, sunk into a table-well.

# Background noise

In all natural locations there is some normal level of background noise or 'atmosphere'. It is generally acceptable in films, radio and television reporting, etc., provided that there are no obtrusive, inappropriate or very loud elements. Examples of the most inconvenient types of noise encountered in filming are passing aircraft or unseen traffic; machinery; hammering; or people talking or whistling out of vision. It is difficult to discriminate against these, even with directional microphones; the best safeguard is a suitable choice of location.

Apart from such difficulties, low levels of background sound in a location may help to establish or confirm the character of the place. Whether on location or in the studio an 'atmos' or 'buzz' track should be recorded at the same level and with the microphone in the same position as for the master sound takes to help the editor avoid unnaturally quiet gaps between edited passages.

### Studio noise problems

In a studio, noticeable background noise has no natural place, except in a play where the atmosphere of a 'real' location is to be recreated, in which case it is the deliberately-composed sound effect and certainly not studio noise that is required.

Ventilator hum can sometimes be obtrusive, particularly with quiet voices. Comparative tests with various volumes of voice and with different microphone layouts will show the limitations of a studio and how to keep such noise to a minimum. Plainly, this problem can be minimised by using a close balance and a strong voice. But this, in turn, is a limitation on use both of the natural (or designed) acoustics of the studio and of the quality of speech (or type of speaker) that it is being used for. You may not wish to have an unpractised but naturally quiet speaker change his whole style of delivery for purely technical reasons (though this would be better than his not being heard).

Structure-borne noise is another nuisance. Some studios have complex forms of construction to avoid this (e.g. the whole room is floated on rubber blocks). Steel-framed buildings transmit sound more efficiently (i.e. worse) than older, more massive structures. Building works can be obtrusive. Polite persuasion − or payment − may be necessary to get hammering or other loud noises stopped.

Doors, chairs, footsteps and scripts, all potential offenders, are easily identified and dealt with. Noises due to personal habits or idiosyncracies may be more difficult to spot: a persistent and erratic click may turn out to be a retractable ball-point pen or a loose dental plate. In radio such sounds are more noticeable than in real life.

Where a monophonic balance is to be heard as a component of stereo, discriminate against background sound (as well as reverberation) so that it does not all seem to come from the same point.

**86**

**MICROPHONE POSITION** In a good microphone position for speech the head is held well up and the script a little to one side. The speaker should work to the microphone and not to the script or down towards the table. The script must never be allowed to drift between mouth and microphone.

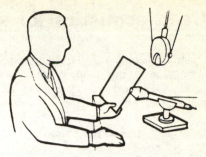

**AVOIDING SCRIPT NOISE** Corners of script are turned up to make it easier to lift pages noiselessly to one side. Stiff paper is used.

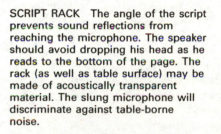

**SCRIPT RACK** The angle of the script prevents sound reflections from reaching the microphone. The speaker should avoid dropping his head as he reads to the bottom of the page. The rack (as well as table surface) may be made of acoustically transparent material. The slung microphone will discriminate against table-borne noise.

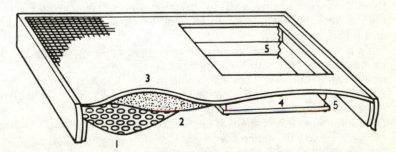

**ACOUSTIC TABLE WITH WELL** The table top has three layers. 1, Perforated steel sheet. 2, Felt. 3, Woven acoustically transparent covering. 4, Wooden microphone platform, suspended at the corners by rubber straps, 5.

**87**

# Dead acoustics for speech

Open-air scenes are frequently required in sound drama, but recordings actually made out of doors are subject to extraneous and often unsuitable noise. It is therefore necessary to simulate the open air — with its characteristic lack of reverberation — in the studio.

**Dead acoustics in the studio**
A truly dead acoustic — as can be obtained by the use of absorbent material a yard or more (1m) thick — has certain advantages:
1. It provides the best possible contrast to other acoustics in use, so making a wider range of sound quality possible.
2. The muffling effect of the treatment causes the performer to lift and edge voice as it really would be in the open air.
3. Effects recorded out-of-doors blend in easily.
4. Voices that are made to appear more distant by placing them toward the dead side of the microphone do not generate parasitic studio reverberation to ruin the effect.
5. There is more space than inside a tent of screens.

But there are also disadvantages:
1. A truly dead acoustic is uncomfortably claustrophobic to work in.
2. Completely dead sound is not so easy to balance: the muffled voices must either be lifted (in which case the peaks may overmodulate), or allowed to appear more distant than interior sound. Alternatively the level of interior sound may be held down.
3. It is not so pleasant to listen to for long periods.
    The first of these is the main reason for finding an alternative. One that has been widely used is a tent of screens in the deader end of the main studio.

**Using screens for drama in mono**
With a double-V of screens round a bi-directional microphone:
1. Keep the screens fairly close to the microphone. This restricts movement a little but keeps sound path-lengths between reflections short, and reverberation low.
2. Set each pair of screens to form an acute-angled V. Actors should not retreat too far back into this angle.
3. Keep 'entry' and 'exit' speeches within the V, but physically move round towards the dead side of the microphone. Do not direct the voices out into the open studio.
4. Off-microphone (i.e. distant) speeches may be spoken across the angle of the V, giving the voice less volume but more edge.
    Such techniques are half-measures, perhaps, but acceptable as a convention. The main thing is to set up a satisfactorily contrasting range of acoustics.

**DEAD ROOM ACOUSTIC TREATMENT** Wedges of soft foamed plastics cover solid walls. In a room to be used for acoustic measurements the floor might also be treated similarly, with a false floor (an acoustically transparent mesh) above the wedges.

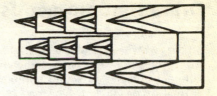

**USE OF SCREENS** Double reflection of sound in a V of screens set at an acute angle. For any particular path there are some frequencies which are poorly absorbed, but these are different for the various possible paths.

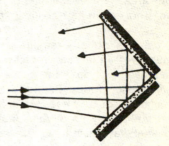

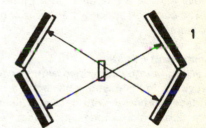

**A TENT OF SCREENS** If there are parallel surfaces, 1, standing waves may form. It is better that sound should be reflected twice on each side, 2. This breaks up and absorbs more of the sound waves.

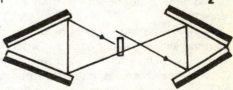

**SPEAKING OFF-MICROPHONE** No actor should go further than this, or turn further into the screens. The effect of greater distance must be achieved by a change of voice quality, or by adjusting the microphone fader.

*Speech balance can be changed creatively by altering the acoustic furniture surrounding speaker and microphone.*

# Drama studio acoustics

Studios with a range of acoustics are still used for radio drama in countries where this survives. These studios have two or three separate areas with different qualities of sound reinforcement. These may be bright ('live'), normal or dead; and they may be varied further by the use of heavy drapes and movable screens. Truly dead acoustics — representing the open air — are difficult to simulate realistically within the studio.

One area — the deader end of the main studio — will, in fact, differ little from a normal indoor acoustic, being deader only by enough to permit normal working distances of 30in–4ft (0.75–1.2m) with a bi-directional microphone (ribbons remain satisfactory for monophonic drama). This layout gives a realistic simulation of the actual conditions it is supposed to represent, as does the live area (which could be also be used for a small music group). But note that a space with lively (and therefore dominant) acoustics has certain built-in limitations. Its size may be registered audibly by its dimensional resonances. A small bathroom and a large hallway may have the same reverberation times but they are recognisably different. The characteristics of the reflecting surfaces (e.g. wood panelling) may also be recognisable, and noticeably different from those of, say, a hall lined with marble.

The confined space within a car can be simulated by the use of padded screens.

### Action and narrative
If action is to be combined with narrative a separate microphone will be provided. In the past this has been a ribbon, near a confining or reflecting surface, and often with bass equalisation for close working; or an omni-directional microphone used close. Better, however, may be a cardioid or similar microphone, still used fairly close: characteristically the narrator should appear to be closer than the action, and with less acoustic 'dressing'.

Ideally the narrator should be in a part of the studio that is well away from the action — but if a participant in it, it is more convenient to use a microphone close to the main microphone, in which case the narrator will either need screens or the microphone should have a characteristically different frequency response. As different kinds of microphone may fall short of the ideal of a level frequency response in a variety of ways, that should not be too difficult.

The layout described here is suitable for continuous recording — a technique that is still preferred by many. But with stop and start recording, the acoustics can be modified in the gaps between takes.

**90**

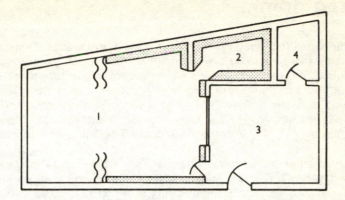

DRAMA STUDIO SUITE   This is typical of the specialised studio layouts adopted for broadcast drama in the days when radio was at its peak of popularity. Many such studios still exist (as at the BBC) and are used for their original purpose. The principles involved in the layout remain valid for many other purposes. The areas shown are: 1, Main acting area – the 'live' and 'dead' ends of the studio can be partially isolated from each other (and their acoustics modified) by drawing double curtains across. 2, 'Dead' room, with thick absorbers on walls. 3, Control cubicle. 4, Machine room. In this example a virtue has been made of the irregular shape of the site. The non-parallel walls avoid standing wave coloration.

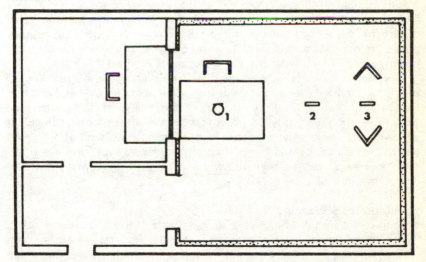

SIMPLE LAYOUT FOR DRAMA   A simple set-up using a hypercardioid microphone, 1, for narrator, near the window, and two ribbons in the open studio for the actors. Microphone 2 is 'open' for normal indoor acoustics and microphone 3 is enclosed in a 'tent' of screens to represent outdoor quality. This is a less versatile layout than is possible in a studio that has a built-in range of acoustics, but it may be adequate for low budget productions with small casts, or where the broadcast is likely to be heard in poor listening conditions.

**91**

# Stereo drama

The acting area for stereo drama takes up much more space than that for mono, so if there are to be live and dead areas, a much larger studio will be required. Alternatively, record all the scenes which take place in one acoustic first and then move drapes, screens, etc., to suggest the next. The 'dead' acoustic is likely to be less satisfactory than that of a specially designed dead area, so it may help if the actor projects more (but with low volume) and also if some bass cut is applied to the microphone output.

Again, the best microphone arrangement is likely to be a coincident pair, and the polar diagram may be crossed figure-eights, supercardioids or cardioids. These give different ratios of direct to indirect sound and will require different layouts of the acting area, which must curve round to the sides — movement in a straight line across the sound stage will be simulated by an arc in the studio. In mono, a long approach can be simulated by a slow, short move from dead to live side of the microphone; in stereo a realistic move must be planned within the space available. A simplified studio layout using supercardioids is shown opposite. The areas will be physically marked out by tapes on the studio floor. In practice, to follow the polar diagram more accurately the limits will bulge out further at the centre and pull in rather more at the side.

For intimate scenes, performers should not work too close or any lateral movement will be exaggerated — but in any case this may also distort the stereo effect if the stereo pair is mounted with one capsule above the other. For a tall actor working closer to the upper capsule, the image will 'pull' one way; for a short actor, the other.

Very lively acoustics may be simulated by adding 'echo', perhaps by means of a spaced pair on the dead side of the working pair and directed toward the dead end of the studio. Alternatively, as for mono (see page 169), the effect may be improved by adding a second coincident pair with the same polar response and a strong echo feed about 3–4ft (0.9–1.2m) above the main pair. Then as performers move out, reverberation increases, but as they move close to the main microphone, it diminishes in a natural manner.

## Stereo drama problems
Note that in stereo drama there is no dead side of the microphone. Also, with a more distant balance of voices, channel settings are higher, and electronic noise from the microphone itself will be higher. Also, unwanted offstage noises which are spatially separated from the actor will be more obtrusive.

It may also be necessary to check whether an effect recorded in stereo has the same meaning when heard in mono.

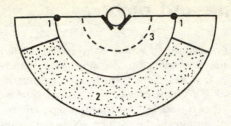

**STAGE FOR STEREO SPEECH** 1, If crossed supercardioids are used, voices in these two positions, roughly opposite to each other in the studio, appear to come from the loudspeakers. 2, Most of the action takes place in this area, at a distance of about 2–3m from the microphones. 3, More intimate speech may be closer.

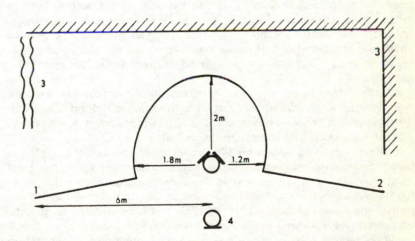

**STEREO DRAMA IN PRACTICE** This layout emphasises extreme side positions and allows long approaches from left (1) and right (2). In many studios (as here) there may be asymmetry in the acoustic treatment, distorting the sound-stage, and minimum working distance around the microphone pair. The positions may be judged by ear and marked on the floor accordingly. 3, Drapes screening live studio area beyond. 4, Announcer, centred.

*In television and film the normal criteria for good speech balance still apply, but the methods used must be visually acceptable.*

# Microphone and picture

There are several conventions which may be consulted on the use of microphones in vision. According to one, close pictures should have close sound, while a wider picture may have rather more open (more reverberant) sound. This can often be satisfied by having a movable microphone just out of frame. But for many programmes, in the case of a subject who always remains in the same place (e.g. in a seated discussion, or quiz) such variations in sound quality add little or nothing to the effect, while making lighting more difficult (because of microphone shadows). Also, in very wide shots intelligibility may be reduced — and the need for adequate intelligibility usually overrides the matching of sound to picture. For many purposes it is simpler to accept that microphones may be placed where the camera sees them.

Where colour-separation overlay (chromakey) is used to provide a setting, it is the background of the composite picture that governs the desired acoustic. Even when the setting is physically present, it may sound different from how it looks, requiring some compensation.

**When microphones may be seen**
This is the subject of another convention: they should not be seen in dramatic presentations (including situation comedy) where they would spoil the attempted realism, or get in the way of the action, but may appear in most other programmes, such as for example news, discussions, quizzes or musical entertainments. This is not to say that microphones should be in vision in all of these. Their very ubiquity is a point against them: there is visual relief in getting rid of them when the opportunity allows.

A further convention requires that unless the microphone is carried by one of the performers, it should not be seen to move. If it did, it would be distracting. The breaking of any of these conventions must be intentional, and for a purpose that is clear to the audience.

In films, including television films, the same conventions apply. But here the use of microphones in vision needs to be more discreet, because most films are shot in places where microphones are less a part of the furniture than they are in television studios: seeing the microphone may remind the viewer of the presence of other technical equipment, together with the director and the camera crew. Also, in film there may be greater variety of picture and faster cutting; in these circumstances a microphone that is erratically in and out of vision can be more intrusive.

The use of table, stand, hand and neck microphones in vision has been discussed (see pages 58–61), also the use of gun microphones (pages 52–55) and the MS microphone (80–81). In the studio there are other techniques: notably *the studio boom*, which serves to place a microphone just out of frame (pages 95–99).

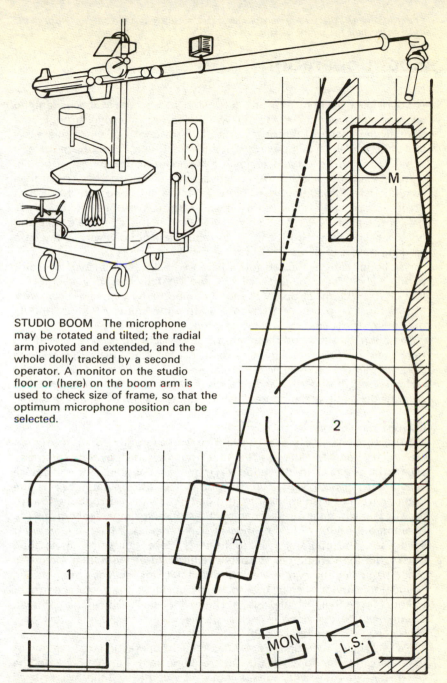

**STUDIO BOOM** The microphone may be rotated and tilted; the radial arm pivoted and extended, and the whole dolly tracked by a second operator. A monitor on the studio floor or (here) on the boom arm is used to check size of frame, so that the optimum microphone position can be selected.

**MICROPHONE BOOM** On studio plan (actual size, using 1:50 metric grid): A, Boom, indicating shortest and fully extended lengths of arm. 1, Small motorised camera crane. 2, Pedestal camera. MON, Monitor. L.S., Loudspeaker. M, Slung microphone to cover speech in a corner inaccessible to the boom when the actors are separated.

*For studio work where the microphone must not be seen, the studio boom is the most important means of picking up sound.*

# Boom operation

A boom used in both film and television has a typical reach, ranging telescopically from about 7 to 17ft (2.1–5.2m). It can swing through 360° (though the shape of the operator's platform does not make this easy) and tilt to angles of 45° upward or downward. The microphone at the end of the arm can be rotated to favour sound from one direction or discriminate against another. All of these movements can be controlled continuously. In addition, the height (of the point about which the arm pivots) can be adjusted over a range of 3ft (0.9m) – in a typical case between 6ft 5in (1.96m) and 9ft 5in (2.9m) – the operator's platform going up and down with it. It is normal practice, however, to preset a working height of about 7ft (2.1m).

The boom can be tracked (on inflated wheels) by a second operator during a shot. There are three wheels and the dolly is readily steerable – though it is a clumsier object to move around than most studio cameras. Moves must be planned in advance so that the line of the dolly and its one steerable wheel are suitably aligned.

The operator stands on the platform to the right of the boom, with the right hand holding the crank to extend or retract the arm (this crank is near the point of balance). With the left hand the operator holds a handle which is pulled round the boom to rotate the microphone; this arm also controls the angle of the boom – which can be locked off in any position.

### Microphone position

The microphone is often a cardioid or supercardioid for mono or an MS microphone for stereo. The ideal microphone position for many scenes is as close to the edge of frame as possible. For maximum separation between signal (voice) and noise, the operator brings the boom in front of each speaker in turn and directs the microphone toward the speaker's mouth. During rehearsal the operator repeatedly drops the boom into the edge of frame, checking on a monitor what the limit is for each shot. The operator's microphone is closer for some shots than others, but the variation is consistent with picture: the tighter picture is accompanied by more intimate sound and the perspectives are right. The sound for exterior scenes has to be as close as the picture permits; interiors may then be allowed a slightly looser balance for contrast. Sometimes the microphone 'splits' between two speakers: in this case each voice is given equal value.

For talk shows requiring greater flexibility of operation and to allow for unrehearsed wide shots, a gun microphone may be mounted on the boom; its high directivity means that it can be held a little further back than a cardioid, but the inertia of the long interference tube makes it clumsy to move rapidly from one angle to another.

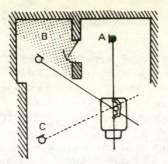

**BOOM OPERATOR IN DIFFICULTIES** If the operator of a boom positioned for use in area A is immediately asked to swing to area B, he or she is blind to all action which is obscured by the wall, and so cannot judge the angle and distance of the microphone. If the action continues to area C, again without movement of the dolly, the operator is supported only by the boom and a toe-hold on the platform. Better provision must therefore be made for coverage of B and C before the position for A is decided.

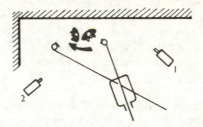

**BOOM OPERATOR IN A HURRY** A simple movement by the performer may require a complex movement of the boom, here swinging it to the left, extending the arm, and turning the microphone to the right. Dialogue which continues during a rapid move may go off-microphone. How tolerable this is depends on the camera position: if the action continues on Cam 1 it may be acceptable; if there were a cut from Cam 1 to Cam 2 it would be unsatisfactory; if the whole action were taken on Cam 2 it would be ludicrous.

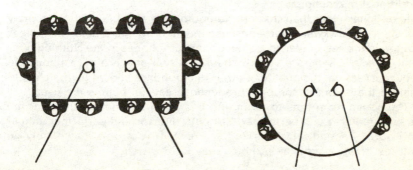

**BOOM COVERAGE** of a large television discussion (e.g. a scene showing a board meeting in a play).

*In television you need good sound coverage that does not get in the way of good pictures.*

# Sound in the television studio

When a boom is chosen as the main instrument of coverage it requires precise co-operation between its operator and the sound supervisor. The boom operator has headphones with programme sound on one phone and director's talkback on the other.

In the talkback circuit to sound staff on the floor, the sound supervisor can override the director's line (in BBC practice there is a tone-pip as the supervisor cuts in on the line) and can warn the operator of changes foreseen on the preview monitor or clear the operator to a new position at the end of a scene: the sound supervisor can follow a script, while the operator has only a card listing the shots and his or her own notes on framing. In cases where the operator cannot easily see a floor monitor (which should be as rare as possible) the supervisor will have to talk the operator through the framing of the shots. Better than a floor monitor, however, is for each sound boom to have a miniature monitor clipped on to the boom arm just in front of the operator.

If at a late stage the director asks for wider shots than have been rehearsed there is a risk of the boom intruding in vision. The alternative is to allow sound to suffer by adopting a looser balance. Good sound demands co-operation and self-discipline all round.

### Cables
The sound cable is multicored, to carry the microphone output and the various communication circuits. The front of the boom pram is a good place from which to point a loudspeaker into the set, so this too may be fed by the same route. The sound cable may be dropped from the lighting grid (where several microphone points will be available) at a place where it does not get in the way of lights or cameras. The cameras must be able to move rapidly from one set to another without running over sound cables, and the cables should not be visible in shot.

### Additional microphones
Microphones other than that on the boom may also be used; these may be slung in awkward corners, suspended from hand-held 'fishpoles', hidden in the set, or placed as personal microphones in the clothing of or near to actors. Where a voice is heard on two or more microphones in rapid succession, the quality of other microphones should be matched to that on the boom. In complex productions several booms are used.

The sound team tries to accommodate all of the movements that the director requires of a performer. But both director and performer should be aware of sound problems and so consider what may reasonably be accomplished: again, compromise may be required.

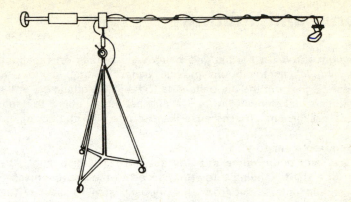

SMALL STUDIO BOOM (about 5ft, 1.5m, high) in which the arm can be swung and the microphone angled by gripping the handle at the back of the boom with one hand and the body of the tripod stand with the other. The extension of the arm is preset, but the whole stand can be rolled bodily toward or away from the action.

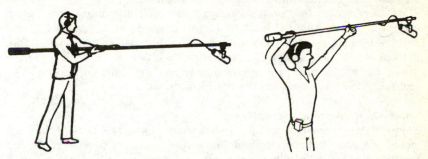

FISHPOLE   This provides a highly mobile microphone, but held underarm the rod may cross too low and get into the picture of a second camera, or cause a shadow. A second position in which the operator balances the boom overhead is even more tiring.

LAST RESORT   Short gun microphone on hand-held camera picks up loud effects in the field of view. For speech, this should if possible be supplemented by a microphone giving a closer balance.

*Lighting and sound in a television or film studio must be planned together.*

# Booms and lighting

A key light throws a hard-edged shadow. If it falls on the boom the shadow moves as the boom moves. Other lighting includes the fill (a diffused light from the opposite side to fill in the shadows) and rim or back lighting that shines from above and behind a subject to separate it from the background. These cause less trouble with the boom.

### Avoiding boom shadow
If the key and boom come into the set from a similar angle, there is danger of a shadow being thrown down on to the main subject. So the boom should enter a set from the opposite side to the key (the two forming an angle of say, 90–120°). The shadow is then thrown to the side of the subject. But it may still be visible in any wide shot taken from the same side of the set as the key light. Wide-angle shots should therefore be taken from an angle well away from the key light; the camera taking them will be close to the boom.

In order to allow for boom shadows to fall on to the floor rather than a wall, it is best to allow at least 5ft (1.5m) between any important action and the backing (in fact, this makes back lighting easier too). In addition, the boom arm should not be taken close to any wall or vertical feature that is likely to appear in vision at that time. Take it too close, and even soft-fill lighting from a wide source forms a shadow.

### Shadows from static microphones
Slung microphones can also cause shadows – and especially if they are close to a wall; but such a shadow may be easier to conceal (provided that the surface is not plain and evenly lit) because it does not move. It follows that if a boom shadow is unavoidable, it may similarly be concealed in some feature of the background provided that it does not move while in shot.

Where lighting and sound are at odds, this should be discovered long before a production reaches the studio. The director will arbitrate or may find a solution by changing the action or asking for a change of set layout or design. In practice, boom-shadow problems rarely result from bad planning. They are such a headache that everyone makes an effort to avoid them. But they can arise from a succession of minor changes and compromises which finally snowball into a bigger problem.

**100**

**LIGHTING, CAMERAS AND MICROPHONE** The ideal situation. The close-shot camera has near-frontal key lighting (from K). The microphone shadow is thrown on to the backing at point A where it appears in neither picture.

**LIGHTING, CAMERAS AND MICROPHONE** The actor has now moved 18in (0.5m) closer to the backing, and the microphone, to get good sound, has followed. With the key light and long-shot camera in the same positions there is now a shadow visible at B in the long shot.

**BOOM SHADOW** With a boom close to a long wall there is a danger of a shadow along it (C) in wide shots. If the boom is very close, even soft-fill lighting casts a shadow.

**101**

# Balance checks for music

The simplest 'natural' balance uses the acoustics of the studio, blending these with direct sound by the judicious placing of either a stereo pair or a single monophonic microphone. Additional microphones are added only to remedy faults of internal balance, to cope with difficulties in the acoustics or to bring forward individual instruments, voices or groups (particularly soloists) which are felt to require a higher proportion of direct to indirect sound. Characteristically this type of balance is used for classical music.

The alternative is electronic, or multi-microphone balance. Each instrument or small group has its individual microphone. Many of the instruments are acoustically separated from each other, and the studio is dead, so that little of the reflected sound from one instrument is picked up on the microphones set for the others. The microphone's own frequency response together with equalisation (i.e. filtering) and dynamic compression – all forms of distortion – are used as positive elements of the finished sound. Artificial reverberation is added individually to each channel. This type of balance is generally used for pop music.

The differences between these two approaches are at their greatest when there is a large number of instruments. For smaller groups and single instruments, the techniques overlap: here the characteristics of individual instruments dominate the choice of balance. In the following pages the techniques for music balance are considered first for the full orchestra, then instrument by instrument, building up to successively larger combinations of microphones.

### Checks for music balance

In music balance (of all types) listen for:

1. Wanted direct sound, i.e. sound radiating from part of the instrument where the vibrating element is coupled to the air. It should comprise a full range of tones from bass to treble, including harmonics, plus any transients which help to characterise and define the instrument. For each individual instrument or group, these components should all be in the same perspective.
2. Unwanted direct sounds: e.g. hammer (action) noises on keyboard instruments, pedal operation noises; piano-stool squeaks, floor thumps, page turns, etc.
3. Wanted indirect sound: reverberation. In mono this should be rich, but should not obscure direct sound. In stereo there can be a little more than in mono, as it is spread across the entire audio field. If so desired, different instruments may be in different perspectives.
4. Unwanted indirect sound: severe coloration.
5. Unwanted extraneous noises.
6. Stereo layout: adequate placing and spread, allowing for any compression of the scale of width.

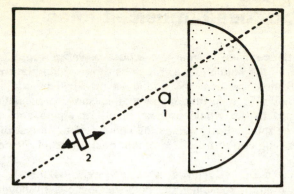

MONOPHONIC ORCHESTRAL BALANCE USING NATURAL ACOUSTICS  1, Gives a tight, brilliant sound, discriminating against acoustics that may be over-bright, but may distort the balance in favour of the nearer instruments. 2, With a bi-directional microphone set back on a diagonal gives a well-blended and evenly balanced sound in which the acoustics play a generous part. Coloration due to dimensional resonances is minimised by having the microphone off centre line.

STUDIO LAYOUT FOR MULTI-MICROPHONE BALANCE (on same scale as studio above). This contains the same number of musicians in a much smaller space. The walls have acoustic treatment to minimise reverberation, and the sources are separated and sound diffused by the many screens. Screens are arranged so that all players can see the conductor or leader.

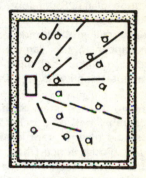

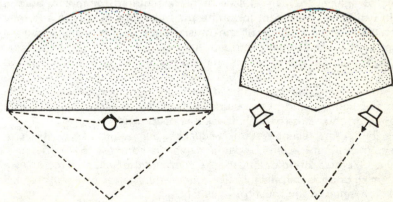

COMPRESSION OF SCALE OF WIDTH  A sound source that might be spread over 90° or more in real life (*left*) may be compressed on the audio stage to 60° or less. Adding reverberation may make it seem further back.

**103**

# 'Live' and 'dead' music studios

In a music balance using normal live acoustics we are reproducing the characteristics of the studio just as much as those of the players. With a stringed instrument we hear the sound as modified by the sounding board. The studio is a further stage in this same process: it is the sounding board to the whole orchestra and its shape and size give character to the music. But whereas the characters of all instruments of any particular type conform to a common ideal, those of music studios differ widely.

A studio that is too live requires a narrow, close balance. In a studio that is deader than the ideal, a wider polar response is employed, or the microphone is placed at a greater distance from the source. Most music is balanced in stereo. Stereo orchestral balances are shown on the following pages.

*Air humidity* strongly affects acoustics. There is usually little attenuation in air below 2000Hz. But at 8000Hz, air at 50% relative humidity has an absorption of 0.028 per foot, resulting in a loss of 30dB at 100ft (30m) (or rather less if the air is very damp). In very dry air, however, absorption is greater still and extends down to lower harmonics (400Hz) as well. Performances in the same hall on successive days may sound very different; and close-balanced sound in a dead studio will have different instrumental quality as well as different acoustics.

### Enhancing the acoustics of the dead studio

An assembly hall or a general-purpose television or film studio is the dead studio on the grand scale: its size may be similar to that of a live music studio or concert hall, but if it is to be used for purposes other than music it is much more dead. Typically it has a reverberation time of 0.7sec as against, say, the 1.8sec or more required for music. Such a studio would be unpleasant for orchestral musicians to play in and may affect the internal balance of the music, because the players can no longer evaluate their own contribution by ear.

In such a studio the acoustics may be enhanced. In a method called ambiophony, the sound was picked up on microphones 6–8ft (1.8–2.4m) from the source, delayed, and fed back through loudspeakers on the walls and lighting grid of the studio to simulate reflected sounds. In a variation on this, electronic feedback has been used.

In a third, more recent system, feedback is avoided: an array of microphones over the musicians feeds the signal via complex digital mix-and-delay circuits to a string of loudspeakers around the hall. This recreates a field which sounds surprisingly like a good musical acoustic, but which can be changed at the touch of a switch.

All these enhanced acoustics circuits are kept completely separate from those used for any recording or broadcast.

## TELEVISION STUDIO WITH AMBIOPHONY LOUDSPEAKERS

A, scattered around the walls; B, at lighting grid or gantry level. C, The orchestra below. The loudspeakers (0–4) feed delayed sound back into a studio which would normally be too dead for the acoustic balance of music. The balancer treats the result as a normal live music studio, but keeps his or her microphones well away from individual loudspeakers.

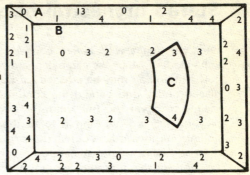

## ACOUSTICAL CONTROL SYSTEM

(ACS) Signal from microphones above the performers is fed to a complex digital system which mixes, delays and feeds the recombined signals to loudspeakers (more than shown here) around the hall. Feedback between loudspeakers and microphones is kept as low as possible. The aim is to simulate the soundfield of a good music studio, but with variable reverberation time.

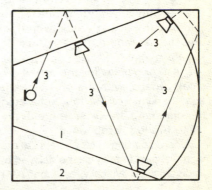

## 'ACOUSTIC HOLOGRAPHY'

In this example, the original walls, 1, carry speech rapidly to the back of the fan-shaped auditorium, so that people at the rear can hear individual speech syllables clearly. 2, Ideal music auditorium simulated by the acoustical control system. 3, Simulated sound path using three of the many loudspeakers lining the walls at sides and rear.

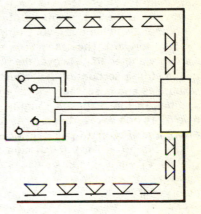

**105**

# Stereo orchestral balance

Here we begin with a live concert-hall acoustic (whether natural or enhanced) in which we can balance the orchestra using a coincident pair.

The main pair may be crossed cardioids or similar and will be centrally placed above and behind the conductor at a distance that is designed mainly to cover the full width. In a studio performance, the layout of players may be rearranged to fit the polar response: this may entail pulling the forward sections closer round the sides.

To add (and separately control) reverberation, further microphones are set, and for this there are several possibilities. One is to place a second coincident pair on the median line but set back in to the hall and directed away from the orchestra. Another employs a spaced pair pointing back along the sides of the hall. In both cases, the two components of the reverberation must be steered to their correct sides, as some direct and short-path reverberation will reach them. These balances have also been used to feed the four channels of quadraphonic sound.

Another two-channel layout employs two coincident pairs with both directed forward. The rear pair is set to figure-eight responses with the elements angled to just cover the full width of the orchestra: this pair will give a strong account of the acoustics. The forward pair has broad polar responses and is set fairly close, again covering the full width so that all sections of the orchestra roughly coincide. The output is combined to give more or less reverberation as required, or to handle extreme changes of volume. The extra pair also provides redundancy in case of faults or failure during a live transmission. All of these balances give sufficient control to allow for changes in the acoustics which occur when an audience arrives for a performance which has been rehearsed in the empty hall.

### 'Spotting' microphones

Mono microphones are often added. For a concert hall, where orchestral layout is dictated by the shape of the stage, it may help to place microphones near the outer corners to bring these forward in the stereo image. Similar 'spotting' microphones placed close to instruments or sections (particularly woodwind) can be faded up just enough to add presence as required; these must be panned to their proper places in the stereo image.

These principles for the use of a coincident pair can also be applied to small groups, with the provision that the width may be controlled to be less than that of the full audio stage. Individual instruments other than the piano are, however, more easily balanced and are usually controlled using mono microphones.

Where spotting microphones are much closer than the main stereo pair, their signal should in principle be delayed by an amount equivalent to the difference in distance – typically, by about 10–16msec.

**106**

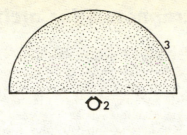

ORCHESTRAL BALANCE IN STEREO   1 and 2, Two stereo pairs with different polar diagrams but giving the same stage width to the orchestra, 3. Microphone 1 is double supercardioid; microphone 2 is double cardioid: a mixture of the two can be used to control and change reverberation where there is such a wide dynamic range that a great deal of volume compression is necessary.

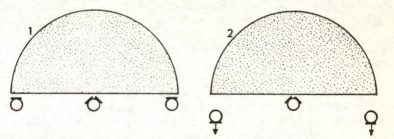

STEREO ORCHESTRAL LAYOUTS   1, With a spaced pair to 'pin down' the corners of the orchestra (e.g. harp on left and basses on right). 2, With a spaced pair used to increase reverberation. This layout can be readily adapted for use in four-channel stereo.

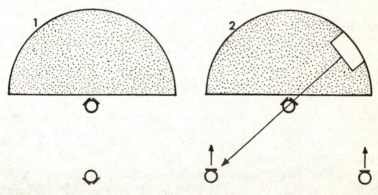

REVERBERATION IN STEREO ORCHESTRAL LAYOUTS   1, A second coincident pair with reversed output used to control reverberation separately: can also be used for four-channel stereo. 2, Wrong: A forward-facing spaced pair set back into the hall may give false information from the brass, which, directed towards the microphone on the opposite side, may suddenly appear to be in the wrong place.

*Alternatives to coincident pairs.*

# Spaced microphones for orchestra

The simplest multi-microphone balance still uses a coincident pair, but with reinforcement of the forward left and right corners; and probably also the woodwind and such other sections as require additional presence. If all sections have their own microphones, the main pair can be moved back to pick up more reverberation, or alternatively this can be added via echo feeds from the individual channels or the mixed signal.

The argument in favour of using a coincident pair is that it avoids phase cancellation, but it does distort the shape of the audio stage, especially at the forward corners. Some balancers prefer to use spaced microphones throughout, on the grounds that this gives greater control of positional information and internal balance. They point out that when additional microphones are used for individual instruments we do not hear substantial phase distortion (because this occurs only where output is picked up on two microphones at comparable levels), so surely spaced microphones can be used for the whole balance.

The simplest balance on a close spaced pair was, however, found to have a disadvantage: the region at the centre of the front, including the leaders of the string sections, was more distant. This 'hole-in-the-middle' may be corrected by an additional central microphone from which the output is divided equally to the two stereo channels. A spaced pair can, however, still be used when set back above and behind the conductor's head. Two omnidirectional microphones on a bar 16in (40cm) apart gives a rich, spacious sound. Their axes are angled slightly outwards to allow for high-frequency reinforcement normal to the diaphragm. The faders must be locked rigidly together, as any slight difference in level will swing the layout to one side. Greater control is obtained if the 'space-bar' is combined with a closer curtain of microphones.

### A 'curtain' of microphones

In a further shift towards a multimicrophone, spaced balance, we can use a curtain of microphones along the front. If these are all omnidirectional microphones, this will add much more reverberation than if they were directional. It will, however, give a poor account of the centre-rear, which will sound disproportionately distant. This may not matter for most brass and percussion, but the woodwind and horns (at least) will require additional microphones. The use of omnidirectional microphones for the main balance avoids any possibility of cancellation by out-of-phase lobes of adjacent microphones.

Is the spaced microphone balance truly rich or just muddy? Does the coincident pair sound clean or could it be called 'clinical'? Plainly it is a matter of taste — and vigorous debate.

Where spotting microphones are much closer than the main stereo pair, their signal may be delayed by an amount equivalent to the difference in distance. Typically, this may be around 10–16msec.

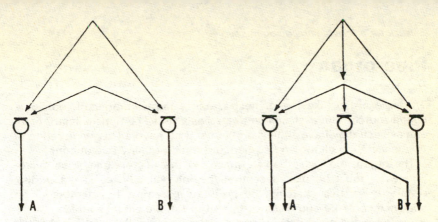

**SPACED PAIR: HOLE IN THE MIDDLE** *Left.* For subjects along the centre line the apparent distance from the front of the audio stage is greater than for subjects in line with the microphones; and the further forward the subject is, the more pronounced the hole. *Right.* The introduction of a third microphone in the centre does much to cure this.

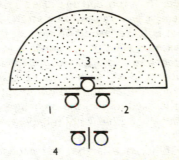

**MICROPHONE TREE – OR DUMMY HEAD** 1–3, A spaced pair of omnidirectional microphones, with a third to fill in the middle, has been used for many years by one recording company. Alternatively, 4, a dummy head layout, with omnidirectional microphones on either side of a disc, has been favoured for its spaced effect – but the space-bar (10, *below*) may be preferred.

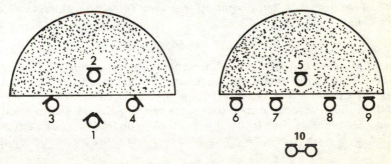

**MULTIMICROPHONE TECHNIQUES** 1, Stereo pair. 2–4, Directional spotting microphones about 6ft (2m) from string and woodwind sections, adding presence and strengthening positional information. 5, Favours woodwind. 6–9, 'Curtain' of four microphones. 10, Space-bar. Curtains of five along the front of the orchestra and three over the central region have also been used to complement a space-bar.

**109**

*Balance for a widely spread sound source.*

# Pipe organ

The pipe organ, like the orchestra, has a large number of individual sound sources. But each can be treated as a single composite instrument, and as such they have similar problems. Both have a very wide range of frequency and volume and so demand a high-quality microphone.

The organ, too, is spread in space, so the microphone – or microphones – must be placed so that the internal balance is not unduly distorted. But this need not be taken to extremes: no member of an audience could be equidistant from all of the individual sources.

Again like the orchestra, its sounding board is the hall itself, so that the main problem of microphone placing is to balance direct with reflected sound. But this may be more acute in the case of the organ, as many are built into the vast stone vaults of cathedrals or churches with reverberation times of 3–6sec, where it may really help to have acoustic treatment in the form of an audience. They, too, can be treated as part of the instrument: their number and placing can sometimes be arranged with the balance in mind. A recording that is to be issued on tape or disc would be marred by coughing, but for a broadcast performance a live audience is good.

Historically, both orchestra and organ have been fashioned by the very nature of the surroundings in which they are likely to be heard, but differ in that the combination of organ and the dominant characteristics of its acoustic environment is fixed, unlike the orchestra, which can be varied in layout and size, and even physically moved – in the final resort to another hall.

A further possible difference is that the acoustics surrounding the organ may be more subject to echoes. In these circumstances the acoustic effects of the absence of an audience and even of the humidity or dryness of the air is more noticeable than in the concert hall.

In searching for a satisfactory microphone position the balancer needs not only technical skill but also an attitude of mind. Test for ways, not of beating the acoustics, but of making them work for you as effectively as possible.

**Organ with orchestra**
Where a pipe-organ is heard with orchestra, a coincident-pair balance can make its stereo image too narrow: additional microphones may be required to give some separation to the various voices. On the other hand, in some layouts it can sound far too broad: the sound should always blend rather than be completely broken up into obvious sections. In this case, a coincident pair may help to counter the excessive width.

**110**

CURVED SURFACE Concave
architectural features focus sound,
selectively emphasising particular
components (and often noise).
Microphones should not be placed
within the radius of a vault such as this.

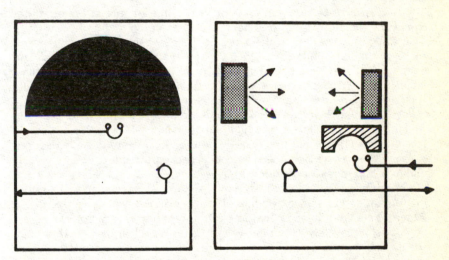

HEADPHONES Neither the orchestral conductor, *left*, nor organist, *right*, is
ideally placed. The conductor is too close, and the organist may be in an awkward
corner or out of line of sight of some of the sections of pipes. When they are
producing sound specifically for the microphone, headphones *may* possibly help
them to modify their performance for the better.

*With stringed instruments we relate the microphone to the sounding board, not to the strings themselves.*

# The string family: the violin

Vibrating strings do not radiate sound directly: they slice through the air without moving it much. They are coupled through a bridge to a wooden panel — a resonator or sounding board — which radiates the sound.

The rear panel of the irregularly shaped box that constitutes the resonator of instruments of the violin family is shielded and sometimes also damped by contact with the body of the performer; and the sides of this box are fairly stiff. The high-frequency radiation is therefore emitted most strongly nearly at right angles to the front panel, a little off-axis towards the E string. Only the lower frequencies, whose wavelength is comparable to the size of the body of the instrument, are radiated in anything approaching an omnidirectional pattern, and even for these the more directional upper harmonics are important.

**Microphone position**
The audience does not normally sit in the line of this strongest high-frequency radiation: from the violin, it travels upward and outward over their heads to resonate in the body of the hall itself, and to soften and blend with the sound of its fellows and with other instruments. The sound of a solo violin — including much of the original harshness, squeak and scrape that even a good player emits — is substantially modified before it is heard by an audience.

In positioning a microphone for the violin, the sound balancer may prefer the extra brilliance of a high, close balance — though not usually less than 3ft (1m) — but this is not how the violin is supposed to sound. An extremely close balance would be used only for a special effect or within a pop-music convention.

For a concert violin balance the microphone is set well away from the instrument and usually off its line of maximum high-frequency radiation. Experiments with balance can be made by the usual technique of direct comparison tests, switching between two (or more) similar microphones set in trial positions, the better balance being retained and the other changed for further comparison tests. For stereo, a mono microphone is used for direct sound, and spread reverberation is added.

**Microphone frequency response**
The lowest string of a violin is G, of which the fundamental at 196Hz is weak because the body of the instrument is too small to radiate this efficiently (although the overtones are strong). Very high frequencies (say, above 10 000Hz) are also not so important. So a microphone should have a smooth response over this range, and ideally it should have a slightly greater range than the instrument, but if it is very much greater it also picks up unwanted sound either from other instruments or simply as noise. A ribbon microphone can be satisfactory for strings. In a close balance, the excessive high-frequency response must be corrected.

**VIOLIN BALANCE** 1, Low frequency radiation. 2, High frequencies. 3, Move along this arc for more or less high frequencies. 4, Move closer for clarity: more distant for greater blending.

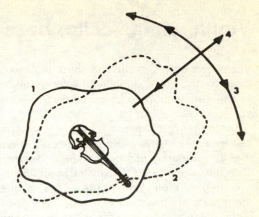

**CLOSE BALANCE FOR THREE DESKS OF VIOLINS** The microphone is above and a little behind the first desk. For very clean separation between violins and other instruments it may be necessary to work closer, with a separate microphone for each desk, but this produces a very strong high frequency response which must then be corrected.

**EXTREMELY CLOSE BALANCE IN POP MUSIC** The player has encircled the microphone stand with his bowing arm. A directional microphone is not subject to much bass tip-up, as the lowest frequency present is a weak 196Hz. In fact, a filter at 220Hz may be used to discriminate against noise and rumble from other sources.

**113**

# Violin, viola, 'cello, bass

Violas can be treated in the same way as violins, except that in a very close balance on a directional microphone (e.g. when used as a novelty instrument in popular music) there is some bass tip-up that requires correction.

The larger instruments are progressively more omnidirectional in their patterns of radiation, but still have a forward-radiating lobe of upper-middle frequency components. For deeper-toned body from a mass of stringed instruments, a sideways balance is satisfactory; for richness of tone a position closer to the axis is required. For a group in which all of the strings are present the microphone position is largely conditioned by violin balance, although the microphone should be able to 'see' all of the instruments: with the 'cello in the second row of a string quartet the body of the instrument should not be shielded from the microphone. Listen to each instrument in turn as though it were a soloist. Aim to combine clarity and brilliance of individual instruments with a resonant, well-blended sonority for the group as a whole.

In a fairly close balance for a 'cello or bass the microphone is in front of the body of the instrument, perhaps slightly favouring the upper strings. For the 'cello the response of the microphone should be substantially level to below 100Hz at the working distance – or equalised for this – and lower still for the bass. In an orchestral balance, basses may need an additional close microphone, set at about 3ft (1m) from the front desk.

### The double bass in popular music
When the double bass is used in the rhythm section of a jazz, dance, novelty or pop music group, a very close balance discriminates against other instruments of the group. Be aware that the music stand may act as a reflector. The following positions are all possible:
1. A cardioid, supercardioid or figure-eight microphone set a few inches in front of the bridge and looking down at the strings.
2. A similar microphone near the f-hole by the upper strings.
3. An electret suspended from the bridge.
4. A contact microphone near the bridge.
5. Exceptionally, an electret, wrapped in foam and suspended by its cable *inside* the upper f-hole.

Balance number one, probably the best, picks up the percussive attack quality as the string is plucked, and the ratio of this to the body resonance can easily be controlled. Balance number five gives maximum separation, but a heavy hanging quality which has to be held to a lower level when it is mixed with the other instruments.

Some supercardioids have a response which falls away in the bass, so that correction for close working is automatic, but other close directional microphones require low-frequency equalisation.

**STRING QUARTET** Typical mono balance for the two violins, viola and 'cello on a single microphone which for this frequency range may be a bi-directional ribbon. The rich upper harmonics of the 'cello lack the harshness of those of the violin, so the microphone should be in the 'cello's radiating lobe.

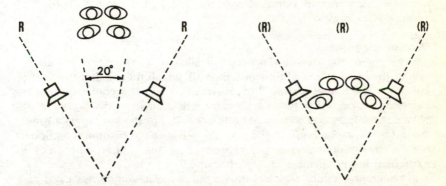

**A QUARTET IN STEREO** *Left*, The quartet uses only a third of the audio stage, but reverberation fills the whole width. *Right*, The quartet occupies the whole of the space between the loudspeakers. Here the reverberation must be low in order to avoid the players appearing gross: such reverberation as there is appears from behind them.

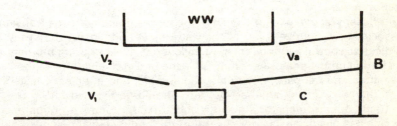

**ORCHESTRAL LAYOUT** The most common layout for the strings of an orchestra is based on current ideas on internal balance. The second violins ($V_2$) were formerly at the front of the orchestra on the right – but radiated their high-frequency sound away from the audience. Here, the 'cellos and basses have more body and presence. A further possibility is to have the 'cellos behind the violas.

**115**

*For the piano too, the microphone is balanced to sound from the soundboard.*

# The concert grand piano

The radiation pattern from the soundboard of a piano allows the balancer control over the proportions of treble and bass. The bass is strongest if the microphone is placed at a right-angle to the length of the piano; and from this same position the extreme top is clearest if the axis of the microphone is directed towards the top end of the soundboard.

From this position we may imagine an arc extending from top to tail of the piano. As the microphone is moved along this arc, the bass is progressively reduced until it reaches a minimum at the tail. For very powerful concert pianos this tail position may be the best, but with a slight disadvantage in that with reduced volume there is also a loss of definition in the bass. For most purposes, a point somewhere in the middle of this arc is likely to give a good balance. This is a good starting point for comparison tests. For stereo a coincident pair may be used, or a spaced pair at two points along the arc and a broader spread of reverberation may be added.

**Microphone placing**
The height of the microphone should allow it to 'see' the strings (or rather, the greater part of the soundboard), which means that the further away it is, the higher it should be. However, if this is inconvenient, other balances are possible: for example, by reflection from the lid, as in the balance which an audience hears at a concert. For the very lowest tones, the pattern of radiation from the soundboard tends to be omnidirectional: but for the middle and upper register, and the higher harmonics in particular, the lid ensures clarity of sound.

In twentieth-century classical music the piano is sometimes used as a percussion instrument. In this case, it is set well back in the orchestra, often with the lid removed. Unless percussion transients need to be enhanced, no microphone is necessary for the piano, even when other sections of the orchestra are picked out.

**Action noise**
The closer you get to an open piano, the more apparent are the transients associated with strike tone; at their strongest and closest they may be difficult to control without reducing the overall level or risking momentary distortion on the peaks. Action noise − the tiny click and thud as the keys are lifted and fall back − may also be audible, and in balance tests this and the noises from pedal action, etc., should be listened for.

The frequency range of a piano is such that, for mono, a ribbon microphone has given satisfactory coverage: the bi-directional response gives fine control of the ratio of direct to indirect sound. However, because of its size, the piano often benefits from stereo coverage, even when part of a larger group. Except for very close balances, a coincident pair may be used.

**116**

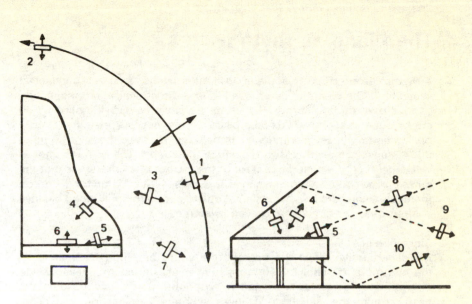

PIANO BALANCE   The best balance for a grand piano is usually to be found somewhere along the arc from the top strings to the tail. A close balance gives greater clarity; a distant balance gives better blending. Of the positions shown: 1, Often gives a good balance. 2, Discriminates against the powerful bass of certain concert pianos. 3, Picks up strong crisp bass (a mix of 2 and 3 can be very effective). 4, Close balance for mixing into multi-microphone dance band balances (with piano lid off and microphone pointing down toward upper strings).
5, Discriminates against piano for pianist/singer. 6, (angled down towards pianist) as 5. 7, One of a variety of other positions which are also possible. 8, Concert balance 'seeing' the strings. 9, By reflection from lid. 10, By reflection from floor: remember that microphones set for other instruments may inadvertently pick up the piano like this.

PIANO AND SOLOIST ON ONE MICROPHONE   Balance for the piano first, and then balance the soloist to the same microphone. The piano lid may have to be set in its lower position. For stereo, a coincident pair is used.

**117**

# The piano as rhythm

A rhythm group consists of piano, bass and drums, each being balanced separately. The piano lid is removed, and a directional microphone suspended over the top strings – perhaps as close as 6in (15cm). A cardioid or supercardioid will usually be preferred but, surprisingly, even a bi-directional ribbon microphone can be used, because the bass tip-up at this distance actually helps to rebalance the sound. The position chosen will depend on the melodic content of the music: one criterion is that the notes played should all sound in the same perspective. Listen for distortion (particularly on percussive transients) due to overloading. A mono balance is often used for direct sound even in stereo.

**Close balance**
For a percussive effect the microphone could be slung fairly close to the hammers. If action noise is obtrusive, use directional response to discriminate against it. A second microphone may be added over the bass strings; this can have its own separate equalisation and echo. Another possibility (in which action noise can be completely avoided) is to place one or two microphones a few inches above holes in the frame. The quality of sound from individual holes can be sampled by ear. It has been known for a baffle – perhaps a piece of hardboard – to be fastened to the upper side of a ribbon microphone in order to further emphasise and harden the higher frequencies and transients.

**Upright pianos**
Lift the lid and try the microphone somewhere on a line diagonally up from the pianist's right shoulder – a good balance can generally be found in this position. But remembering that it is the soundboard that is radiating, an alternative is to move the piano well away from any wall and stand the microphone on a stool or box at the back (for a close balance), or diagonally up from the soundboard (for a more distant one). At the back, the sound will have body but will lack percussive transients.

Alternatively, try two very close microphones, with one for the bass clamped to the frame at the top of G2 and the other somewhere between one and two octaves above middle C. Experiment for the best position. Where separation is a problem, try a contact microphone for the bass. Use equalisation to emphasise h.f. percussive transients and perhaps also to add weight to the bass.

One of these arrangements may also be suitable for a 'jangle-box', a piano which has leaves of metal between hammer and strings (to give a tinny strike action) and in which the two or three strings for each note of the middle and top are slightly out of tune with each other.

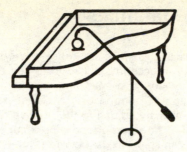

**CLOSE PIANO BALANCE** Directional microphone suspended over the top strings – but not too close to the action.

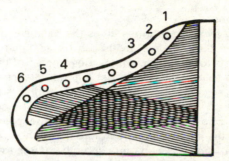

**PIANO HOLES** Some pianos have holes like this in the iron frame, and their focusing effect can be used for a pop music balance. A microphone 2 or 3in (5–7cm) over hole 2 probably gives the best overall balance, but those on either side may also be used, as also can mixtures of the sound at hole 1 with 4, 5 or 6.

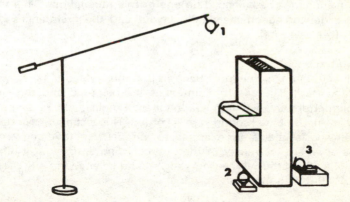

**UPRIGHT PIANO** Position 1, microphone above and behind pianist's right shoulder. Position 2, to right of pianist below keyboard. Position 3, at rear of soundboard.

**119**

# More piano balances

The piano is intrinsically very much more powerful than the human voice, so it is part of an accompanist's job to see that a singer (or any other soloist) is not swamped by the piano sound.

Balance on a single microphone or coincident pair can often handle this adequately – simply by adjusting the relative distance between the second performer and the microphone. For a concert given before an audience the soloist can stand in the curve of the piano, facing outward: this has the piano and soloist on the same axis of the microphone, but in this position the soloist cannot see and react to cues from the pianist. In a studio performance it may be better for the two players to be on opposite sides of a bi-directional microphone.

**Two microphones**
A balance using two microphones gives the balancer separate control of the two sources: their relative levels can be adjusted precisely without repeated requests to the musicians or movements of the microphone. In carrying out the balance tests, first get a good balance of the soloist and then fade in the second microphone until it just brings the piano into the same perspective. This minimum setting will often be quite loud enough.

A performer who is singing or talking at the piano needs a close microphone for the voice. A supercardioid microphone with its dead side toward the piano often picks up quite enough volume from the instrument for an accompaniment. This requires a microphone with smooth polar and frequency characteristics. Without that, the sound quality will be better if a second microphone can be used for the piano. It may be worth comparing this with an older type of balance: a ribbon at about 20in (50cm) with its dead side towards the piano soundboard.

Two pianos may be balanced on one or two microphones in a variety of ways, depending on the studio layout and the preferences of the players (see opposite).

**Backing track**
A technique that is sometimes used in pop-music recording is to make a backing track. The accompaniment is pre-recorded and the singers (or other performers) listen on headphones to replay, adding their contribution as the combined sound is re-recorded. This technique can be used to obtain special effects: for example, to combine very loud and very soft sounds or where the replay of the pre-recording is to be at a different speed. Note that artificial reverberation should be added to any speeded-up sound if it is to match the original.

**PIANO AND SOLOIST ON TWO MICROPHONES – I** 1, Covers both instruments and provides the studio reverberation. 2, Adds presence to the soloist's sound: here a bi-directional microphone has its dead side to the piano. 3, For stereo, a coincident pair is used together with microphone 2 for presence on soloist.

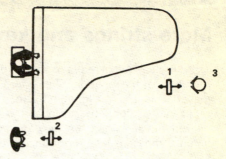

**PIANO AND SOLOIST – II** A second version of two-microphone layout. Here the pianist and soloist can see each other well.

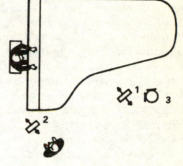

**TWO PIANOS – I MONO** Here a single microphone is used, giving an adequate if not perfect balance. The players can see each other's faces.

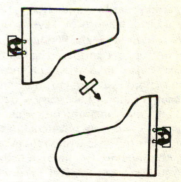

**TWO PIANOS – II** Balance is on a single microphone or stereo pair, 1, or individual microphones, 2 and 3. The players can see each other's hands.

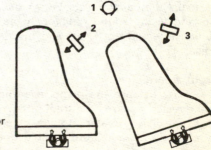

**121**

*The principles already described can be extended to other stringed instruments.*

# More strings and keyboards

The classical guitar radiates sound in much the same way as the middle members of the violin family, so a microphone forward of and above the player achieves a reasonable balance. Noises arising from the fingering — rapid slides along the strings and so on — are characteristic of the instrument and need not be eliminated entirely, but in a more distant balance they are less pronounced. For the electric guitar see pages 65 and 130—1.

The folk guitar, banjo and ukulele are all used as accompaniment to the player's own singing. In these cases the first step is to balance the voice: often, with little adjustment, this will give adequate coverage of the instrument as well. If an additional microphone is required it may be placed either close to the body of the instrument (in which case the same stand may be used), or further back to give a somewhat more distant coverage to include both singer and instrument.

Other instruments of the same general class are the viol, lute, etc.; the harp; and also the balalaika and the mandolin. The mandolin often benefits from added perspective; in a group of instruments its penetrating tone and continuous sound overlay the reverberation and make it seem more forward than it actually is.

### Other keyboard instruments

For a close balance on keyboard instruments such as the harpsichord, clavicord or virginals, first identify the sound board (or box) and balance the microphone to that, discriminating, where necessary, against mechanical noise. In a wider balance that includes other instruments the harpsichord may be too loud and penetrating. Its position should be chosen so that if necessary a directional microphone can be angled to hold the other instruments, while discriminating a little against the harpsichord. The celeste presents the opposite problem: it is rather quiet, and unless the music is written to favour this, an additional close microphone may be required to reinforce its sound.

A good starting point for any unknown instrument is to put a microphone above the position of the audience in the acoustics for which the instrument is designed (some are designed for the open air) and then employ the usual comparison tests. For a closer balance start from first principles, working to the sound radiator, avoiding harsh axial sounds which the audience would not hear, and discriminating against instrusive action noise.

### Piano accordion

In a close balance the piano accordion may require two microphones, one directed towards the treble (the keyboard end) and the other to the bass. To allow greater mobility, stand microphones may be replaced by electrets on miniature flexible goosenecks that are attached to the instrument itself.

HARP  The soundbox is cradled by the player. Parts of the action – the pedals for selecting the key of the instrument – are at the foot, F. A balance from microphone position 1 gives adequate coverage from a distance, but for closer work the less obvious position 2, above and slightly behind the player's head, may be adopted . In a very close balance (e.g. when the harp is used as a novelty instrument in a light-music group) the microphone may be directed toward the soundbox, 3.

CELESTE  As with the upright piano, a microphone near the soundboard and behind it avoids mechanical noise, which can be loud compared with the music in this relatively quiet instrument. A close balance is often needed to get adequate separation from other instruments of the orchestra. An alternative position for the microphone is in front of the instrument, below the keyboard, on the treble side of the player's feet at the pedals – and keeping well away from them.

PIANO ACCORDION  For a popular music balance, the bass and treble may be picked up separately. In this example, an electret on a miniature gooseneck is clipped to a plate attached above the bass, and a stand microphone is directed towards the treble. Alternatively, a second gooseneck may be fitted above the treble. *Left*: Detachable clip with a base-plate that can be stuck to the frame or body of an instrument with double-sided tape.

**123**

# Woodwind

For woodwind, with fingered or keyed holes, the bell radiates relatively little of the sound – and very much less than in the brass. Woodwind sound is emitted largely through the first few open holes. It follows that unless we need to go very close we have considerable freedom of position is balancing woodwind: a microphone placed somewhere in front of and above the players should prove satisfactory. For a special effect in pop music, an additional microphone can be clipped to the bell of, say, a clarinet.

Distance softens the transients that are produced by the initial excitation of the sound by edge tone or reed. These transients are characteristic of instrumental quality, and their exaggeration in a close balance is no great disadvantage – with the exception, perhaps, of the flute and piccolo which can sound like wind instruments with a vengeance at close quarters. But in balancing these, the player's head can be used to shield the microphone from the edge tone.

'Electric' versions of some wind instruments have been produced by fixing a transducer to the body of the instrument. An 'electric' flute has been used for the smooth, mellow tone of the 'Pink Panther' theme.

**Saxophone characteristics**
Woodwind in popular music – particularly in a dance or show band – often takes the form of a saxophone section. (Note that the defining characteristic of 'woodwind' is the method of playing and not, despite the name, the material of the instrument.) Up to five saxophones may be employed, some of the players doubling on clarinet, flute or even violin.

On a stage these would be laid out in a line or arc with a microphone to each desk of players, with an additional microphone for any soloist. In the studio this might become a tight semi-circle round a downward-angled cardioid. An alternative is to group them three and two on either side of a central bi-directional microphone. A ribbon has a suitable frequency response, but its live angles project horizontally and so are in danger of picking up open studio reverberation and the sound of other instruments – particularly from the brass. A pair of downward-angled supercardioid microphones avoids this, and also picks up more radiation from the bell.

To exaggerate the characteristic quality of the woodwind in a popular music balance, and to allow its 'presence' to be heard through other instruments, midlift may be employed. A peak of 5–8dB, centred on 2500–3000Hz, is introduced electronically.

**WOODWIND** *Left*: Orchestra layout. F, Flute. P, Piccolo. O, Oboe. C, Clarinet. B, Bassoon. If the main orchestral microphone is set for a close balance, an additional microphone may be required. This can be bi-directional, pointing down at about 45°, with its dead side toward the instruments in front. Alternatively, set two supercardioids about 3ft (1m) up from the flutes and oboes. *Right*: Flute. Placing the microphone behind the player's head shields it from the windy edge tone from the mouth hole.

**WOODWIND IN DANCE BAND (SAXOPHONES)** Five saxophones grouped for a close balance around a central microphone. *Left*: a bi-directional microphone set at the height of the bells of the instruments. *Right*: C, Two supercardioid microphones set above bell level and angled 45° downwards. This reduces pick-up from outside the woodwind area. S, Solo microphone for player doubling on a second instrument.

**POP MUSIC WOODWIND** *Centre*: 'Electric' flute, discriminating strongly against breath noise and producing a distinctively pure tone. *Left*: 'Electric' penny whistle. *Right*: Clarinet with two microphones, including miniature gooseneck for the bell.

# Brass

In a brass instrument the bell emits the main stream of high harmonics, but the audience will not usually hear these directly unless the music specially requires that trumpets or trombones are directed toward them. Most of the time these instruments are angled down toward the music stands or floor. The tuba is directed upward to the roof, and the horn backward away from the audience. Orchestral horns benefit from the acoustic reinforcement by reflecting screens that are set behind them. A good balance hears the sound much as the audience does – with a microphone forward of the brass and not too high. In the orchestra, with the brass set back and raised behind the woodwind, this is usually accomplished satisfactorily on the main microphone.

Spotting microphones may, however, be required for an unusual reason: to increase presence on a section that, because it is too loud, may be held back or discriminated against in the main balance, so making it appear rather distant. Use delay to resynchronize any signal from a closer microphone.

For a solo in popular music, a miniature gooseneck may be clipped to the bell, with the microphone capsule off-axis.

The balancer should not rely on rehearsal levels of 'big band' brass players he or she does not know, but should allow for as much as a 10dB rise in volume on the 'take'. Failure to do this could preclude an adequate working range on the faders, and face the balancer with new and unrehearsed problems of separation.

A close balance on trumpets and trombones is easier to control if the players are prepared to co-operate by leaning in to the microphone in the muted passages, and sitting back for louder passages.

For the trombones the appropriate height for a microphone conflicts with that of the music stands: the leader of the section can be consulted on whether the microphone should be above or below the stands. For a close balance, one microphone between two will suffice.

In popular music, brass is another group that may benefit from midlift somewhere in the region of 6000–9000Hz. Trumpet formants are at about 1–1.5kHz and 2–3kHz; trombone formants are at about half those.

### Brass band

A brass or military band may be laid out either in an arc or along three sides of a hollow square, with the cornets and trombones facing each other at the sides and the deeper-toned instruments at the back. Balance can be achieved on a single microphone or stereo coincident pair placed a little way back from the band and off the centre line of the studio. Additional microphones may be placed to add presence to soloists and also clarify the tone of the bass tubas.

**126**

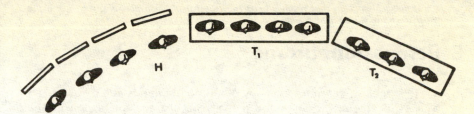

ORCHESTRAL LAYOUT OF BRASS   H, The horns need a reflecting surface behind them. $T_1$, The trumpets need to be raised high enough to see over the heads of the woodwind. $T_2$, The trombones, at about the same level.

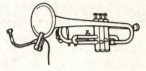

TRUMPET WITH GOOSENECK MICROPHONE   An electret with a cardioid response can be clipped to the horn of a brass instrument for popular music balances.

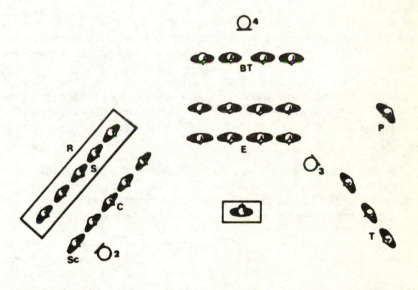

BRASS BAND   Possible layout and microphones. 1, Main microphone: cardioid. C, Cornets. S, Sopranos (ripieni). The rear rank is set on a rostrum R as they tend to play downward into the backs of the line in front, thereby losing echoing figures. Sc, Solo cornet playing to microphone 2. T, Trombones. P, Percussion. E, Euphoniums; soloist comes forward to play to microphone 3, which points downward to separate the musician from other instruments of similar sound quality. Euphoniums and bass tubas, BT, radiate directly upward: on the main microphone the quality sounds woolly unless there is a good reflecting surface above them. If not, use microphone 4 above the bass tubas. This can be a ribbon; the others, condensers.

**127**

# Percussion, drums

It is this department more than any other that demands audio equipment with a full frequency range and a really good transient response. The bass drum produces high acoustic power at low frequencies, while the triangle, cymbals, gong and snare drum all radiate strongly in the extreme high frequencies, i.e. in the octave above 10 000Hz (although 15 000Hz is a reasonable limit for broadcasting).

As the microphone moves closer to the percussion, it becomes necessary to check the balance of each element in turn as it is used, adding further microphones as required. A vibraphone may require a close microphone beneath the bars, angled towards the open tops of the tubular resonators.

At the back of an orchestra, percussion is usually set up on rostra. These need to be solidly built, or reinforced, in order to avoid coloration.

**Balance for pop percussion**
In popular music, percussion shows itself mainly in the form of the drum kit: this includes snare drum, bass drum (operated by a foot-pedal), cymbals, hi-hat (a foot-operated double cymbal), and tom-toms (medium-sized drums).

In the simplest balance for these, a single microphone points down at the snare drum. But any attempt to move in for a close balance from the same angle increases the dominance of the nearer instruments over the bass drum and the hi-hat. (The hi-hat radiates most strongly in a horizontal plane, in comparison with the up-and-down figure-eight pattern of the cymbals.)

For an overall balance try an electrostatic cardioid at the front of the kit and at the level of the hi-hat. For a tighter sound this can be moved in closer to the hi-hat, also favouring the left-hand top cymbal or cymbals and, to a lesser extent, the snare drum and small tom-tom, together inevitably with some pick-up from the bass drum; a second cardioid microphone is then moved in over the other side of the bass drum to find the remaining cymbal or cymbals, the big tom-tom, and again, perhaps, the snare drum. Further close microphones may be added for each component of the kit. Changes of position, angle, polar diagram, or relative level give considerable control over nearly every element – except for the clarity of sound from the bass drum.

For the bass drum, set a microphone close to the edge of the skin where there is a wider and more balanced range of overtones than at the centre of the skin. This is one instrument for which an old heavy moving-coil microphone with a limited top-response is as good as a modern high-quality microphone – which might in any case be overloaded. For a dry thudding quality, remove the front skin (tightening up the lugs to prevent rattling) and put a blanket inside.

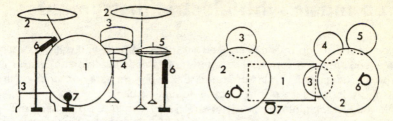

TYPICAL DRUM KIT for dance band or pop group. 1, Bass drum. 2, Cymbals. 3, Tom-toms. 4, Snare drum. 5, Hi-hat. 6, Microphones with good high-frequency response used in two-microphone balance. 7, Additional microphone (moving-coil) for more percussive bass drum effect (used in some pop music). Further microphones may include two above for the cymbals and overall stereo. The snare drum may benefit from midlift at 2800Hz, plus additional bass and extreme top.

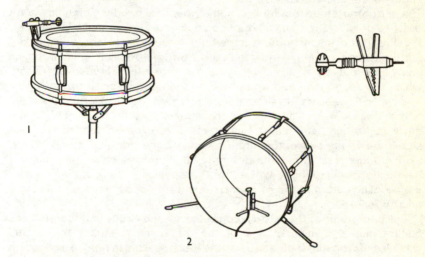

MINIATURE MICROPHONE FOR USE WITH DRUMS   An electrostatic supercardioid, 1, clamped to top hoop or tensioner and, 2, inside shell of bass drum, fairly close to the skin.

# Pop music with electric instruments

Most modern pop music is created by the treatment and mixing of close balanced sound. A common component of this is the 'electric' instrument with a loudspeaker. This sometimes also appears as a composite instrument, as in the case of the electric/acoustic guitar.

In the electric guitar each metal string vibrates in the field of a coil. The vibration induces an alternating signal which is amplified within the body of the instrument. Sometimes there are several rows of signal generators. To obtain a signal from a conventional guitar or from a violin or bass, a contact microphone (transducer) is fixed, perhaps by double-sided adhesive tape, to the body of the instrument (see page 65).

**Loudspeaker characteristics**
The performer's loudspeaker is usually capable of handling high power (in order to provide strong bass) but need not necessarily be of high quality: the character of the instrument as a whole includes that of the loudspeaker. For the most flexible balance, the feed from the guitar is split, with one line going directly to the mixer and the other to a loudspeaker from which the sound is picked up by microphone and also fed to the mixer. The two components have separate equalisation and reverberation.

The loudspeaker of an 'electric' instrument may be balanced like any other instrument: for fullest high-frequency response the microphone should be on the axis of the high-frequency cone; for less, it may be off-axis. A supercardioid microphone may be used for a close balance, or a bi-directional microphone where the loudspeaker is to be balanced with the acoustic output of the same instrument on opposite sides of a single microphone.

The pop group of the 'sixties consisted of one drum kit, three electric guitars plus the voice of one of the guitarists. A studio layout that achieves reasonable separation has the loudspeakers in line on a common axis each with a close directional or supercardioid microphone. The guitarists are on one side of this line and the drummer is on the other, on the dead side of the loudspeaker microphones and with as much screening as proves necessary.

**Equalisation and compression for singer**
The microphone for the vocal line may be equalised for very close working, with presence added by midlift at 2000–3000Hz and perhaps compression as well if the voice is supposed to blend into the backing. If the vocal is compressed this means that the backing can be brought up higher behind it. The backing may in turn be limited to hold back any excessive peaks: this will therefore result in a high common level for all of the sound.

STUDIO SAFETY  The power supplies to electric instruments should be fed through isolating transformers.

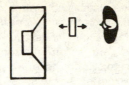

ACOUSTIC/ELECTRIC GUITAR balanced on a single bi-directional microphone. The amplifier-loudspeaker unit is set on a box opposite the player, with the microphone between loudspeaker and instrument. The player can now adjust the overall amplifier level, comparing it with the direct, acoustic sound and controlling the loudspeaker volume from moment to moment by means of a foot control. If separate microphones are used, they can be treated individually, e.g. by 200Hz bass roll-off on the acoustic guitar channel.

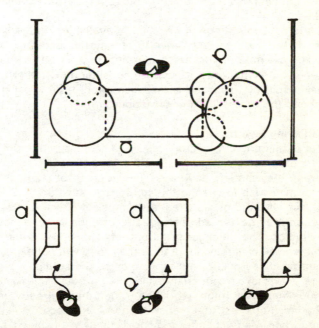

POP GROUP with three electric guitars, drums and singer. Maximum separation has been achieved by screening the drummer heavily: there are two low screens in front, high screens at the sides, and a further screen bridged across the top. The two main microphones for the drums are at the rear, and the bass drum microphone is separated from the skin only by a layer of foam plastic or stands inside it. Other microphones may be added for stereo and are steered to suitable positions on the audio stage. Blended and spread artificial reverberation is also added.

**131**

# Rhythm group and small band

We have already seen how piano, bass and drums are balanced individually (pages 114, 118 and 128). We may now put them together, and add further instruments: a guitar (acoustic/electric), brass, woodwind (primarily saxophones), a vocalist, and so on. Instruments used for particular effects might include celeste, violin, horn, harp, electric piano or anything else that interests the arranger. A low screen helps to separate the sound of bass and drums. Further screens are required, e.g. between piano and brass, and around particularly quiet instruments or singers.

For good sound separation a dead studio is chosen whenever possible. In the dead acoustics of a big recording studio, the various components are often placed in screened booths around the walls. Lead and bass guitar loudspeakers may be directed into half-screened bays and taken by cardioid or supercardioid microphones. An acoustic guitar may require a separate room. Considerable use is made of tracking (sequential recording), particularly for vocals. Good separation allows considerable freedom in constructing a stereo image, to which spread artificial reverberation is added.

When bright surroundings are all that is available some spill may be inevitable. In this case we may have to modify the ideal fully separated balance. For example, if the brass is going to spill on to the singer's microphone come what may, it is worth considering whether to make it good-quality spill by using the same microphone: the vocalist sings at 3in (7cm) and the brass blows at 6ft (about 2m).

**Factors affecting layout**
The layout of instruments, microphones and screens within the studio is affected by the nature and purpose of the group itself:
1. The group may already have a set layout used for stage shows. The balancer may wish to change this to improve separation. Discuss this in advance with the group's leader or musical director.
2. The group may have made previous recordings or broadcasts in the same studios. The balancer finds out what layout was used before, and if it worked well may adopt that: the group will not expect to be in different positions every time they come to the studio. However, the balancer may make minor changes for the purposes of experiment, or to include ideas that might work better than those already used. Consult the individual instrumentalist, section leader or musical director, as appropriate. Major changes may be dictated by the use of additional instruments (of which the balancer should have been informed), or particular new problems created by the music itself (which may only become apparent in rehearsal).
3. The group may be created for the session only, and the balancer – having found out the composition from producer or musical director – can start from scratch, but with due regard for the needs of the musicians.

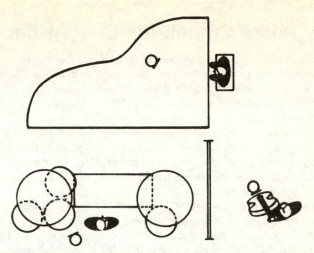

RHYTHM GROUP  This is the basic layout to which other instruments may be added. One low screen is required to separate bass and drums. Various positions are possible for microphones for piano (see page 119), bass (page 114) and drums (page 129), with additional microphones for the drums as necessary.

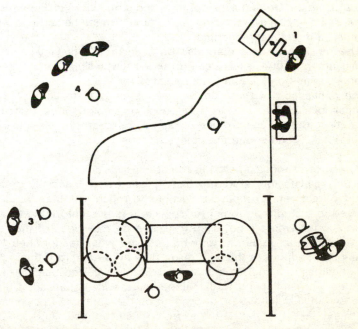

SMALL BAND  To the rhythm group (with microphones in any of the positions already described) are added: 1, Guitar (acoustic/electric). 2, Trumpet (with a full screen to separate this from the drums). 3, Trombone. 4, Woodwind. (This is one of many possible instrumental groups.)

**133**

*Instrumental layout must help the players as well as the balancer.*

# Many microphones for the big band

Where the studio layout is decided or influenced by the balancer he or she is guided by principles which are designed to help the musicians and must achieve the balance within their limits.

1. The drummer, bass player and pianist form a basic group (the rhythm group) which expects to be together.
2. The bass player may need to see the pianist's left hand, to which his music directly relates — and especially when they improvise.
3. When the bass player has fast rhythmic figures he needs to hear the drums, particularly the snare drum and hi-hat; these can be heard well on the drummer's side.
4. In a piano quartet the fourth player can face the other three from beyond the piano: everybody can see everybody else. But a guitar player may have to work closely with the bass: placed at the top end of the piano keyboard, he can see behind the pianist to the bass player.
5. Any other two players who are likely to be working together on a melodic line or other figures need to be close together.
6. Where players double, e.g. the pianist also playing a celeste, the two positions are together.
7. All players, including a saxophone (and woodwind) group which may be split with players facing each other, must be able to see the musical director or conductor.
8. The musical director may also be a performer playing a particular instrument. But if it has been arranged that all players can see each other, condition 7 should still be satisfied.

The application of these conditions may appear to conflict with the original idea of building up a layout according to good principles of separation. But the careful use of directional microphones and screens should make good sound possible.

**The balance cannot be heard in the studio**
The only satisfactory studio is one that has been specially built, with acoustic treatment to reduce reflections to much less than would often be used in a studio designed for speech. It is uncomfortable to work in for musicians who are not used to it, and no clear idea of the result is heard by a leader or conductor who does not wear headphones. Indeed, even with headphones the final result may not be heard if the individual components are being fed to a multitrack recorder, because the final mix is made later, following further experiment with equalisation, artificial echo and mixing (although, depending on the desk and tracks available, there may be a trial mix at the same time as the recording).

A session might start by recording rhythm plus guide vocal, followed by acoustic guitar and piano, and next the lead vocals and backing. Then come solo guitar and riffs; an extra instrumental line may be added by an earlier performer and so on.

**134**

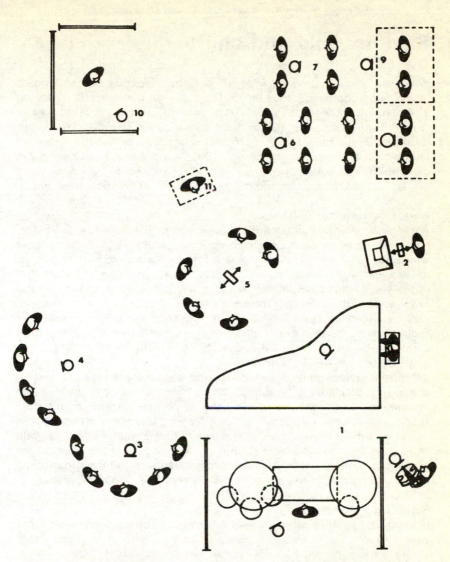

SHOW BAND WITH STRINGS  1, Rhythm group. 2, Electric/acoustic guitar.
3, Trumpets. 4, Trombones. 5, Woodwind. 6, First violins. 7, Second violins.
8, Violas. 9, 'Cellos. 10, Singer. 11, Musical director. Variations must be made for
acoustic difficulties: in one layout it was found necessary to bring the bass
forward to the tail of the piano and separate him by acoustic screens from brass,
drums and woodwind (the trumpets having been moved further away). A wide
range of different microphones is used: see the notes on individual instruments
for details.

# Singers: solo and chorus

What counts as a close balance for a singer depends on the type of music. For a pop song it may be 2in (5cm); for an operatic aria it may be 3–4ft (1m). In either case this is a very much closer perspective than you would hear in the concert hall or theatre. In a public performance with no microphone, the demands of internal balance require that the singer be loud or the accompaniment be soft. But where a close microphone is used, there is full freedom to create brilliant orchestral backings which can be interwoven and contrasted with a subtle and varied vocal line.

### Frequency response
A microphone with a supercardioid (or figure-eight) response is satisfactory, with equalisation for bass tip-up if necessary. With a microphone which has bass roll-off to compensate for close-working, bass may have to be added if the singer moves back. A frequency range limited to that of the voice helps to avoid spill on to this microphone at the upper and lower ends of the orchestral frequency range. In popular music, presence may be added somewhere in the 1500–3000Hz range. Sibilance can be reduced by selection of a microphone with a smooth middle-top response, with high-frequency roll-off if necessary; and perhaps by singing at an angle across the microphone.

Artificial reverberation may be added to a close balance, but clarity of the words (if clarity is required) limits this to less than that of the instrumental backing. For a backing chorus several singers group tightly round a directional microphone. For a larger chorus, the group gathers round a cardioid microphone, which can still be positioned to give good separation from the louder instruments. The singers at the sides of the group can come closer to the microphone than those at the centre, their line following that of the curve of the microphone's polar diagram.

### Balancing a chorus
In balancing a larger chorus for serious music — opera, oratorio or other choral music — aim first for clarity of diction (except in those cases where a more distant balance is specially called for). The microphone must be far enough back and high enough to get a well-blended sound but the limit is generally the lower limit of intelligibility. One or several cardioid, supercardioid or figure-eight microphones are used, depending on the layout of the singers. These may have to be too high up for soloists to work to; for them, separate microphones may be placed in front of the chorus.

There is no particular virtue in separation into registers — except where forces are weaker in one than another, in which case separation may help the balancer to compensate for lack of internal balance. In general, allow the group to follow its established procedure.

**136**

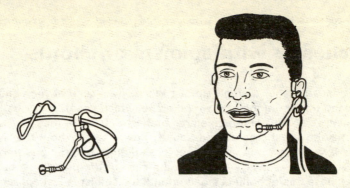

**SINGER'S HEADSET**  This clips over the ears and has a band round the back of the head for minimal disturbance of hairstyle (see page 59). The electret microphone is in a fixed position, and at this distance must be beyond the corner of the mouth in order to avoid popping.

**SCREENED AREA FOR SINGER**  When the voice level is much lower than the volume of surrounding instruments the microphone is screened from them. The live side of the microphone is towards the screens, the dead side towards the open studio.

**CHORUS**  A high, directional microphone favouring the rear singers gives an even balance. A figure-eight or cottage-loaf response (perhaps using several microphones in a line) gives coverage to the chorus while picking up little sound from the area in front of it (which may contain an orchestra).

*For a concerto an additional microphone – or several – will be required.*

# Orchestra with soloists or chorus

In a concert layout a single soloist is usually placed at the conductor's left hand (except in the case of the piano, which will usually be placed at the centre). A coincident-pair stereo orchestral balance may give satisfactory results for the combined sound: again, this is how the audience hears it. However, it is used to set in a spotting microphone to give the soloist more presence – except in the case of the piano (see below).

The close microphone is faded in until the soloist is just appreciably in closer perspective, but beware of other instruments which may also be in its field. In an alternative studio layout, the soloist is separated by being brought out to the front and side of the orchestra, and for stereo is 'folded' back, or steered to the desired position. Where directional microphones are used, each may then be placed with its dead side to the other source: this gives the greatest separate control of the component sounds.

When a second or third microphone is added at much the same level as the first, the apparent reverberation of the hall is increased. Any main microphone or pair therefore has to be moved a little closer, or its directional characteristics changed.

### The piano concerto
In piano concertos there should not be any problem with the level of the piano – unless it is too loud, in which case physical separation (or, alternatively, moving the piano back into the orchestra) may be necessary in order to redress the balance in favour of the accompaniment. If the main microphone is moved back away from the orchestra (and its pick-up narrowed) a second microphone may be placed high above the conductor, and shielded from the full blast of a centrally placed piano by its lid. This microphone favours the orchestra, and in particular the woodwind, the section that is generally most in need of such benefit.

Where a curtain of microphones is used for the orchestra they may be set or their output adjusted to exclude the piano, and the microphones over the woodwind brought up to compensate.

### Further soloists – and chorus
Additional solo instruments or singers may be treated similarly to the first, but for a chorus the traditional layout is behind the orchestra. A line of bi-directional microphones above and dead-side-on to the orchestra adds missing presence and intelligibility. For a monophonic balance an alternative is to bring the chorus to the front and to one side of the orchestra and to balance it separately.

**ORCHESTRA AND SOLOIST** 1, Mono balance with the microphone slightly favouring the soloist, S. 2, Stereo coincident pair with 3, additional microphone for soloists.

**SOLOIST OR CHORUS WITH ORCHESTRA (MONO)** The main microphone, 1, which would hold the orchestra on its own is replaced by a closer microphone, 2, and a solo (or chorus) microphone, 3. S, Soloist. C, Chorus.

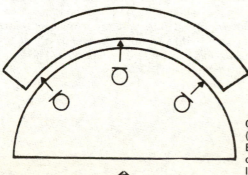

**CHORUS BEHIND ORCHESTRA** (Suitable for mono or stereo). Bi-directional microphones, set high on stands or suspended from above, look down on the chorus at an angle of about 45°.

# Opera – without pictures

Opera may be recorded or broadcast in concert form, i.e. without movement about the stage by the singers; or it may be taken direct from a stage performance.

In a studio performance the simplest layout has the chorus forward of and to one side of the orchestra. There is a row of microphones in front of them, to which the soloists also work. This layout works in stereo, the action being laterally reversed so that the corners of orchestra and the chorus that are closest are on the same side of the stereo sound stage. The left-hand side of the orchestra and the side of the chorus and soloists nearest to it will be picked up on each others' microphones and *must* therefore be arranged to coincide in the audio stage.

For the singers, examples of positioning for particular scenes are as follows:

1. Part of chorus *left*; principals centre; off-stage chorus, *right*.
2. Duet at centre solo microphones; harp figures, *right*.
3. Quartet at four centre solo microphones.

**Separating chorus, orchestra and soloists**
In a more conventional studio arrangement the chorus is placed in a block behind the orchestra. But whereas for a concert performance they will be spread tightly around the periphery in an arc, in a studio they can often be grouped in a separate block. They can usually be on the same centre line but will have a narrower stereo image on any main orchestral microphone, so extra microphones will be set in at the sides in order to spread them to the same scale of width. With sufficient separation their sound can also be steered to one side or the other if a scene so requires.

Soloists can be brought forward to concert-style fixed positions or to a 'stage' area which allows for movement in front of the orchestra. Working to a coincident pair, they would sing (and perform) in an arc rather like that shown for drama on page 93, but further back. On this pair, the orchestra is likely to have a narrower scale of width and sound more reverberant than for a closer balance, which may be an advantage when their role is to accompany the singers. If not, additional microphones may be set to extend the image and add presence. It is convenient to keep the main body of the chorus fixed in the studio and simulate any movement by panning them on the control desk.

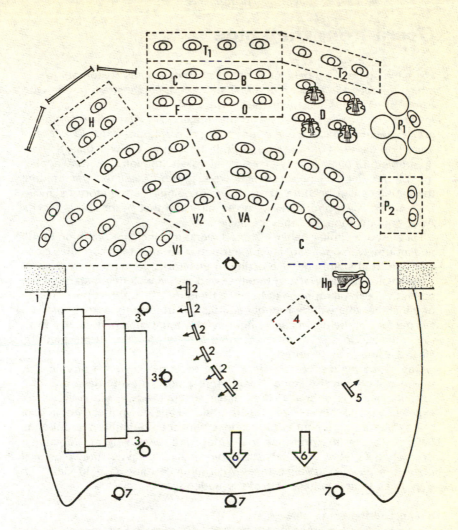

OPERA LAYOUT in which the chorus and soloists are reversed left to right and superimposed on the orchestral stage. A converted theatre is used in this example. 1, Proscenium arch. The stage is extended into the main auditorium. 2, Soloists. 3, Chorus. 4, Conductor. 5, Announcer. This microphone can also be used for spotting effects (e.g. castanets, which can be steered to represent the movement of a dance). 6, An off-stage chorus can be placed underneath the balcony without a microphone. 7, Audience above. Orchestral layout: V1, 1st violins. V2, 2nd violins. VA, Violas. C, 'Cellos. D, Basses. H, Horns (with reflecting screens behind). F, Flutes. O, Oboes. C, Clarinets. B, Bassoons. T1, Trumpets. T2, Trombones. P1, Timpani. P2, Other percussion. Hp, Harp. Note that in this layout the harp is 'in' or near the right-hand loudspeakers. Other orchestral layouts, particularly for harp, horns, basses and percussion are possible.

**141**

# Opera from the stage

For stage opera good balance is not easy. In mono it is customary to use a high microphone to get a good balance on the orchestra together with a row of cardioids just over the forward edge of the stage (dead side towards the orchestra) to pick up the singers. An alternative that gives greater separation is the use of boundary microphones (such as PZMs or 'mice') on the front of the stage itself. If the singers are well back there is no problem of balance between several voices (though they may appear too distant). But if a singer comes down stage very close to a microphone the footsteps can become gargantuan: the singer is therefore balanced on the next microphone along in the direction that he or she is facing. Additional microphones may be necessary.

For stereo, a similar balance should work: a coincident pair high in the auditorium, with boundary layer microphones or mounted cardioids close over the front stage and also acting in effect as boundary microphones.

If two singers are working together and one is well down stage of the other, the best microphone to balance them may be on the opposite side of the stage: this will be roughly equidistant from both, and should still see the face of the downstage singer even when turned partly away from the audience. In stereo, this may give a false position. If this matters, steer the image as required.

One of the main problems here is the excessive distance of voices in most positions on the stage. It is therefore best to avoid having a long row of open microphones: they make coverage easy, but only at the expense of adding even more reverberation. Fade down those not in use.

A similar arrangement is to dispense with the 'footlight' microphones (and, of course, the presence they offer) and rely solely on directional microphone(s) above the orchestra, but angled to favour the singers. If there is a paying audience these microphones may have to clear the sight lines to the highest part of the auditorium.

## Sound and the stage play

The techniques for mono opera from the stage may also be suitable for plays *televised* from the stage. The convention of stage voice projection is thoroughly unsatisfactory for television, but audiences will accept it and especially in comedies where the theatre audience is more obviously reacting. But it is not suitable for plays recorded or broadcast in sound only, as theatre acoustics are far too lively. A recording may be made as a matter of historical record, but there is no method of coverage from fixed microphone positions that is both satisfactory and totally unobtrusive.

In some cases it may be possible to use personal radio microphones, but with these the problem is that coverage is uniformly close, lacking the perspective of the pictures, unless subtle artificial reverberation is added.

**142**

**MICROPHONE POSITIONS FOR THE STAGE** (e.g. for opera)
1 and 2, A pair of cardioid microphones in the footlights. Though very close to the orchestra their response discriminates against it.
3, For mono, a single cardioid microphone placed high but well forward in the auditorium; or, for stereo, a coincident pair.

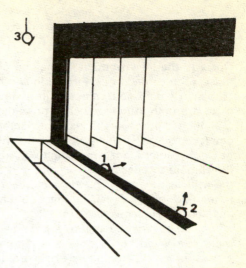

**MONOPHONIC OPERA BALANCE FROM STAGE PERFORMANCES**
Singers A and B, well down stage, are balanced on microphone 3 or 4, but not on 2 which is closer. For stereo such a balance would also be better, but entails reconstruction of their positions on the sound-stage.

**STAGE STEREO PAIR SET IN PIT** with capsules on goosenecks angled slightly down, almost touching the stage. These act as boundary layer microphones, with directional responses that are parallel to the stage surface, which should be clear of absorbers for at least 3–4ft (1m). Additional spaced microphones will be required to cover action to the sides.

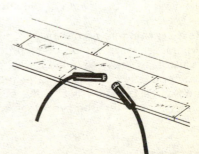

**143**

*In a production employing vast musical resources, the main problems are sound communication and sound spill.*

# Televised opera

Opera in the television studio may be presented with actors miming to music prerecorded or performed in another studio; with the singers in a television studio and orchestra in a sound studio; or with singers and orchestra both in the same hall or studio.

Miming is probably the least satisfactory method, although it has been employed successfully (more so in the more controlled conditions of film or single-camera video recording). Its main advantage is that it permits the camera to concentrate on plot and action without being limited by the artificial convention of opera. Prerecorded sound is fed by loudspeaker to the performers. Provision must be made for picking up sound effects and spoken passages.

The use of separate studios for orchestra and singers generally carries more conviction and spontaneity. The singers are covered by booms, etc., as for a play, but there are new problems of communication between the two studios. The interchange of picture – including that of the conductor, who needs to be visible to the singers or repetiteur – is technically straightforward, but the provision of sound links is complicated by the need to avoid spill.

**Sound links between singers and orchestra**
Orchestral sound is relayed to the action studio floor by means of a vertically mounted line-source loudspeaker on the front of the boom dolly. As this is moved around to cover different action areas, the spatial relationship between loudspeaker and microphone is maintained, and good separation can be achieved. The voices of the singers can be relayed to the conductor by a partly shielded loudspeaker over his head or by a line loudspeaker on the back edge of his music stand. Line loudspeakers used for communication should not be allowed to radiate bass at frequencies below those corresponding to their length: this ensures that their directional qualities do not deteriorate and cause spill at low frequencies.

Where the orchestral and acting areas are at opposite ends of the same hall, similar methods may have to be employed to overcome sound delays due to the length of the studio.

**Post-synching an orchestra**
Where scenes must be prerecorded or filmed before the orchestra is available, a separate guide track of the beat or piano accompaniment is recorded. On videotape it is recorded on to an audio cue track. In the studio the cues are fed to the conductor by headphones, so that the orchestra can then be synchronised to the prerecording.

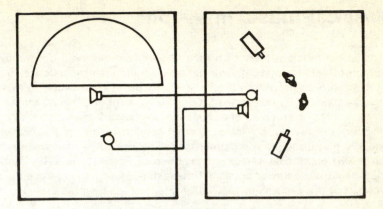

COMMUNICATION between sound and television studios that are used together presents obvious possibilities for the degradation of sound quality. Precautions taken to avoid significant spill include the use of line loudspeakers which are placed so that they do not radiate strongly in the direction of the microphone.

OPERA OR BALLET ON TELEVISION with the conductor and orchestra in a separate studio from the action. 1, Line loudspeaker along the top of the music stand; several small elliptical loudspeakers produce little bass and are adequately directional at high frequencies. An alternative is 2, a loudspeaker in a hood. The 4ft (1.2m) square baffle limits high frequency spill but may also get in the way of lights. 3, Monitors for conductor to see action. 4, Camera to relay beat to repetiteur in television studio.

# Classical music in vision

For classical music a television picture should make little difference to the type of balance sought. The musical values take precedence. But it can be more difficult to achieve a good balance because television studios are generally rather dead; because microphones and their stands should not be obtrusive; and because the layout should be visually satisfying. In practice, however, normal concert layout of the orchestra generally gives adequate pictures; while the use of concert halls rather than television studios solves the problem of adequate reverberation as well. Directors and designers sometimes adopt more visually adventurous layouts, but the success of their attempts is often debatable.

## Picture and sound perspectives
The television camera can take close-ups of individual orchestral players, but it would distort the music if the balance were to be varied from shot to shot to match this. The balance required for television may, however, benefit from more presence than is usual for music presented in sound only: this will justify the close-ups and may sound better on the inferior loudspeakers in so many television sets. If for dramatic rather than musical purposes the balance is modified to match a close-up, it is better to add a close-up microphone to a normal balance, rather than to present the whole sound from the position of the camera.

## Ballet
When ballet is presented on television it may not be easy to get the orchestra into the same studio. In this case it is as well to separate the two entirely and take the orchestra to a concert hall or sound studio where a good balance can be obtained, and then to feed this by loudspeaker to the dancers. Indeed, even if the orchestra is in another part of the same studio loudspeakers may still help them. Sound effects in the form of the dancers' steps or rustle of costume that are occasionally audible through the music will add life and realism to the performance. For these a directional microphone should be placed on the dead side of any loudspeaker array. (A set of small loudspeakers arranged in a line one above another radiates in a horizontal plane, with a dead zone above them.)

## Singer and accompaniment
For singers, the principal alternative to a microphone in vision is a boom with a cardioid microphone just outside of the edge of frame. Where singer and accompaniment are widely separated, there is a slight time lag unless the singer is given a loudspeaker feed of the accompaniment (the conductor hears the combined sound on headphones).

The relative deadness of most television studios can be turned to advantage: singers generally require less artificial reverberation than the orchestra.

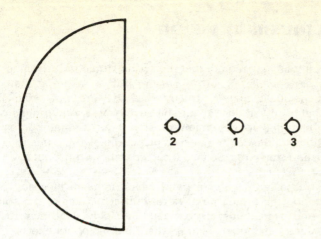

**ORCHESTRA IN VISION**  Where a standard balance for sound only is achieved on microphone 1, a combination of the other two microphones may be more suitable for television. Microphone 2 gives clarity but insufficient reverberation; this is added by microphone 3.

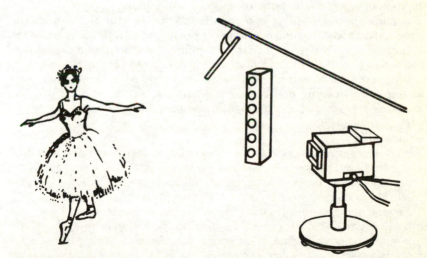

**BALLET: PLAYBACK AND EFFECTS**  The dancer needs to hear the music from reasonably close at hand, so a loudspeaker may be necessary. Here a series of loudspeakers set in a vertical line radiate high frequencies in a horizontal field; a microphone above them receives only low-pitched sound from the loudspeaker array. This can be filtered out, as the main component of the required effects is at higher frequencies. Close microphones are ruled out by the very wide shots that are often necessary in showing ballet.

# Popular music in vision

Visual considerations may require that the sound studio layout cannot be used for musicians appearing on television. But for a group that has been recorded, the quality of the sound by which they are known demands that the principal results of that layout still be achieved. And groups who have not been recorded are dependent on sound quality that must be as close as possible to that of the recording studio if their music is to conform to existing standards. So visual considerations must not override musical quality.

The simplest case is that of the band which appears in vision only occasionally during the programme. Here, the techniques of the sound studio are carried over almost unchanged: the fairly dead acoustic of most television and film studios favours the multimicrophone technique. Low screens may be used to divide the sections, and the conductor wears headphones. This is accepted as a visual convention.

Where the players are more strongly featured, the main change from the sound studio is to avoid microphones or stands that are unduly obtrusive, or which obstruct the line of the camera. But sound still comes first, and again visual conventions permit this. Singers generally work to stand microphones or with hand microphones; but where this is inappropriate a boom can be used, as close as possible, and perhaps with a high-quality gun microphone to improve separation.

A particularly rewarding approach is for the director and designer to accept the needs of sound as a starting point, and to attempt to make the layout visually intriguing. For this to work well, the sound supervisor, too, has to enter into the spirit of the co-operative venture.

Where the visual and musical demands are totally incompatible — for example, an exacting dance routine where the dancer also sings — the sound is prerecorded and the dance performed to playback.

### Filmed music
Film differs from television in that it is usual to take shots one at a time and edit them together afterwards. The whole action of a scene may be repeated several times, taking the sound each time, if only as a guide track. Separate cutaways are shot, often to playback.

Several cameras may be used, as in television, when repetition of the music would be more expensive than the additional equipment and operators, where a unique event cannot be reshot, or where the director feels that there are strong artistic benefits to be obtained. A final possibility is that there will be more music played (e.g. at a public event) than is finally required on film, so that cutaways can be shot during this same performance.

To edit picture to music, the beat can be marked on the guide track, and appropriate actions matched to that of the master sound.

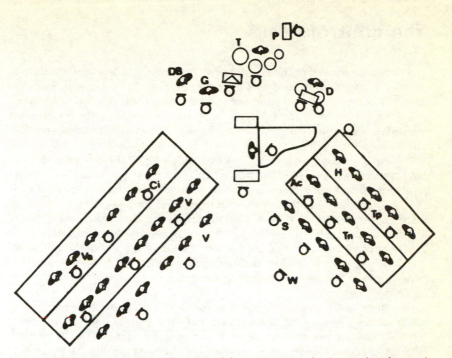

SHOW BAND appearing in vision and giving support to singer or other featured acts. Typical layout: V, Violins. Va, Violas. Ci, 'Cellos. DB, Double Bass. G, Acoustic guitar. T, Tympani. P, Percussion. D, Drum kit. H, Horns. Tp, Trumpets. Tn, Trombones. Ac, Accordion. S, Saxophones, doubling woodwind. W, Overall wind microphone. All microphones may be condenser cadioids except for moving coil on bass drum.

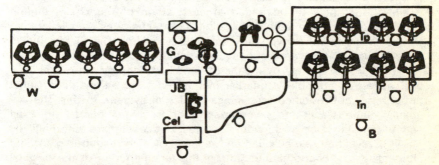

ANOTHER POSSIBLE LAYOUT FOR DANCE BAND   Again the rhythm is in the centre to give the strongest beat in such an excessively spread layout. W, Individual microphones for saxophone (woodwind) section. JB, Jangle box piano. Cel., Celeste. G, Guitarist and amplifier. Tp, Trumpets. Tn, Trombones. B, Brass microphone.

*How the audio signal flows through microphone and other channels in the desk.*

# The control desk

The primary function of the control desk is to combine the various sound sources at appropriate levels. At its most complex, the input may include up to 60 microphones, several disc and tape reproducers, reverberation plates or echo rooms, and, say, 16 outside source lines (from telecine and videotape, other studios, remote locations, overseas circuits and the public telephone system).

The input volume may range over as much as 90dB, grouped as low level sources (such as microphones) or high level (such as lines from remote sources). All signals are raised to a common high level at about 50–70dB above the output level from most microphones. This minimises electrical noise and the effects of induction in the desk itself and in lines to other equipment. Each source is channelled through a separate fader. Where several microphones are likely to be faded up and down together they are preset on individual faders which are then fed to and controlled by a single group fader. The groups are then mixed to a master fader (main gain control).

The desk will usually have provision for modifying the frequency response on a number of channels ('equalisation' and compression) and for adding artificial reverberation in some proportion to each signal. Filters to reduce full-frequency sound to telephone quality for dramatic purposes may be switched in. In television these may be interlinked with picture cut buttons. A press-button 'prehear' facility allows circuits to be sampled on a small auxiliary loudspeaker (see pages 31 and 155). A 'solo' facility allows a single channel to be monitored, suppressing other feeds to the loudspeaker but without affecting the mix that is fed to any recorder.

Other circuits associated with the desk are shown on page 175.

**Noise reduction**
In a recording studio producing commercial records or tapes, there is a potential for noise to be added at each stage of the chain, and in particular at any intermediate recording. Two techniques are available to combat this. One is to convert the (analogue) signal from the microphone to a digital signal at the earliest convenient stage, operate on the signal in the control desk entirely by means of digital technology, then convert it back as late as possible. An earlier method employs an analogue signal throughout, but modified by a noise reduction system. In this, the frequency range is split into several parts. The frequency bands with least energy (and in which noise would be most noticeable) are automatically raised in level before recording, and reduced by a corresponding amount afterwards as a coded signal controls the reconstitution of the original sound.

**150**

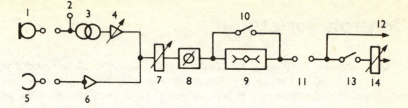

**MONO CHANNEL**   Some of the facilities that may found before the channel fader. 1, Microphone (low level) input. 2, 48V phantom power for electrostatic microphone. 3, Isolating transformer. 4, Microphone channel amplifier. 5, Line (high level) input: in this case, tape replay. 6, Buffer. 7, Fine preset gain (typically ± 15dB). 8, Phase reverse control. 9, Equaliser. 10, Equaliser bypass. 11, Optional 'insert' routing: allows external module to modify channel signal. 12, Prefade-listen. 13, Remote cut, or 'cough key'. 14, Channel fader.

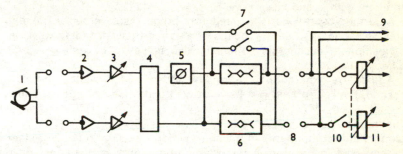

**STEREO CHANNEL**   Some facilities before channel fader. 1, Stereo microphone. 2, Buffers. 3, Coarse channel amplifiers. 4, Channel input switching (to mono). 5, Phase reverse in left leg only. 6, Equaliser. 7, Equaliser bypass. 8, Optional 'insert' for plug-in modules (e.g. graphic filter). 9, Prefade-listen. 10, Remote cut. 11, Ganged channel faders.

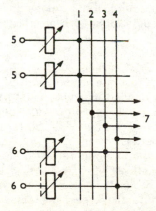

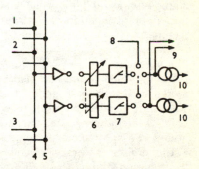

**GROUPS**  1–4, bus bars, wires that cross all channels. Here two mono channels, 5, are both connected to bus 1 and stereo channel, 6, is connected to 3 and 4; nothing is fed to bus 2. The output of each bus (or stereo pair) is fed via group controls to main control. 7, Group outputs.

**MAIN OR MASTER CONTROL**
1–3, Stereo input from group faders. 4 and 5, Left and right main buses. 6, Ganged main control. 7, Limiter and make-up amplifiers, also linked for identical action on left and right channels. 8, Tone input. 9, To monitoring meters and loudspeakers. 10, Stereo output.

**151**

*A stereo image can be altered or built up from mono.*

# Controls for stereo

A stereo channel may have a linked pair of faders for the left and right (A and B) signals. If these are not exactly in step the image will shift sideways. In older, stepped faders where contact with the next pair of studs might not be in perfect synchronisation, this could result in stereo 'wiggle' or 'flicker'.

In principle, the A and B signals can be added and subtracted to create M and S signals, and the faders will act on these. There is no sideways wiggle, but there could be minor variations in image width, which is less objectionable. It is, in any case, necessary to be able to control width: with A and B fader controls, a crosslink fader feeds part of the A signal to combine with B and vice versa.

A further control can be used for image displacement. The entire stereo channel is offset by means of a ganged pair of faders working in opposition to each other. Offset is also achieved by fading A and B differentially.

Artificial reverberation is normally added at full width, although if desired, the return feed can be narrowed and offset for special effects.

**The panpot**
Monophonic components of the stereo image must be guided or steered to their chosen position. A panoramic potentiometer or panpot divides the signal in the proportions required to move the mono signal sideways without making it appear to move forward or backward at the same time.

The panpot is used with spotting microphones in classical music balances, and for all channels in popular music, in order to construct the stereo image. In film or television stereo sound, the panpot matches the apparent position of a mono sound source (of speech or effects) to picture.

**The spreader**
A monophonic sound can also be spread across the whole width of the stereo image. In a spreader, the signal is divided into two equal parts which are passed through delay networks producing differential phase shift. One side only goes through a fader and the two signals are then added and subtracted to create A and B signals.

This is most commonly used to convert monophonic recorded effects to simulated stereo for rain or other weather effects which would surround the action; or for crowd scenes or generalised traffic noise, within which individual components may be panned in order to increase the realism of a scene.

A more complex image could combine spreaders and panpots: for a horse-and-four passing close by, spread horses hooves may be panned across the scene followed by the carriage wheels.

**152**

**STEREO CONTROLS** 1, Preset control to balance output between microphone elements. 2, Ganged channel fader. 3, Image width control. 4, Channel offset control (this displaces the complete spread image).

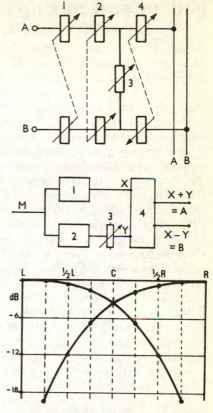

**SPREADER CIRCUIT** The monophonic input (M) is split equally between paths X and Y. 1 and 2, Delay networks producing differential phase shift. 3, Spread control fader. 4, Sum and difference network producing A and B components from the X and Y signals.

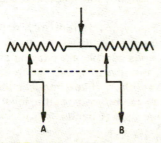

**PANPOT ATTENUATION** Each mono source is split and fed through a pair of ganged potentiometers. Step-by-step, the attenuation in the two channels is matched (*dotted lines*). The apparent volume will then be the same in all available positions across the stereo stage. L, Left. ½L, Half left. C, Centre, etc.

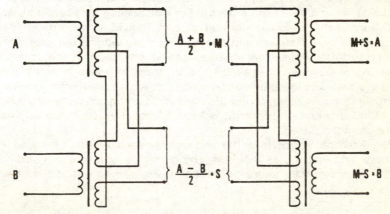

**STEREO SIGNALS** Converting A and B signals to M and S, and vice versa.

*Only a few controls are operated directly: most are preset and sometimes they can be altered later.*

# Fading and mixing

A fader is essentially a variable resistance or potentiometer which is designed to be logarithmic over its main working range. The effect of this is that, measured in decibels, its calibration is linear over perhaps 60dB, below which the rate of fade increases rapidly to a final cut-off. Some desks have two faders in each channel, one of which is used to control relative levels as the sound is mixed, while the other, above it, feeds a separate signal to a multi-track recorder.

Each fader is generally associated with several amplifiers. One compensates for the action of the fader, providing 10dB of 'headroom' above the nominal zero. In some cases the signal does not itself pass through the fader, which instead controls a voltage that operates on the signal (analogue or digital) in equipment which may be remote from the desk itself. Whatever the system used, the layout has many features in common, reflecting the wide range of possibilities for control that is available in most modern desks. These are usually laid out in line for each channel – resulting in a vast and, to the uninitiated, potentially intimidating mass of faders, switches and indicators.

Since most controls on a desk are used rarely or intermittently, digital desks can be simplified in their layout by routing the presets sequentially to a sector where their currently desired values can be laid out one after another. Most of the operation (including the use of group faders) are arranged in this way, so that in, for example, a live broadcast, the seemingly enormous array of possibilities is reduced to the level at which it can be physically controlled by one pair of hands.

**Building sound stage by stage**
Tracking, building up a complete sound by additive recording, is taken a stage further in post-balancing, or 'reduction'. Broad tape is used to record many tracks (typically 16 or 24) in synchronisation so that the recording session itself can be devoted to establishing the broad musical qualities and the basic contribution of each individual instrument. The precise details of treatment and relative levels are worked out later. This is a powerful technique which has been widely used in the creative balancing of pop music. It allows the balancer to concentrate on one thing at a time and to experiment. Begin by checking the treatment given to individual tracks, starting with the rhythm, and then gradually assemble a composite sound. If the result is unsatisfying, try again: the original tracks are not affected.

Digital technology permits the settings for each trial to be saved in memory, and updated as required. The operation of faders can also be stored, allowing many more operations to be carried out at the same time.

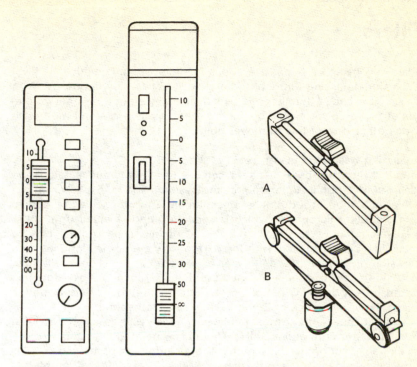

FADERS   *Left*: Short and long throw conductive plastic faders. These may be associated with channel monitoring and group selection controls. Some faders used for line input may also have remote start buttons. *Right*: A. Manual fader. B. Motorised fader.

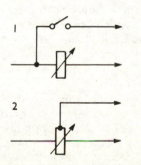

PREFADE-LISTEN (PFL, PREHEAR) 1, Output is taken before channel fader. 2, Symbol for 'overpress' facility: when channel is faded out, pressing the fader knob routes signal to prefade-listen (heard on near-field or studio loudspeakers as selected, or on headphones).

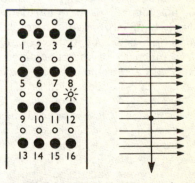

ROUTING MATRIX   At the top of each channel strip on a desk designed to be linked to a multichannel recorder, the mass of press-buttons looks more complex than it is. Press any button to send channel output to selected track.

# Filters

Filters may be active or passive. A passive filter can only reduce the level of the signal passing through it, doing so selectively by frequency. With the simplest circuit the filter passes substantially all of the signal on one side of a chosen frequency and cuts progressively more and more of it on the other side of this turn-over point.

**Simulating telephone quality, etc.**

Simple switchable passive filters can be used to simulate telephone quality sound, public address, intercom systems and loudspeaker output within the action of a dramatic presentation. The original signal comes from a studio microphone which is separated and shielded from other open microphones to avoid spill. For complete separation it can be placed in a closed cubicle, with the performer wearing headphones. In a television play where the performer has to appear in vision in alternate shots, this is not possible: in this case the studio layout must be designed to minimise the possibility of spill. Directional microphones help to only a limited extent, as much of the spill is by reflected sound.

The frequency range of most public telephone systems is some 3000Hz, with a lower limit of about 300Hz. There is no need to copy this exactly: the degree of cut-off used is a matter for the judgment of the balancer, as is the relative level of the 'far' voice in a telephone conversation (meters provide no useful indication of the appropriate level when the bass has been removed from a sound).

**Response selection (equalisation, 'EQ')**

For more complex changes in frequency response an active filter employing amplifiers is used. In inexpensive domestic equipment this can very simply be incorporated into amplifier circuits which are needed anyway, so simple bass and treble controls are widely available. Studio desks have much more sharply-defined controls for lifting and reducing not only bass and treble but also one or more ranges in between, to provide what is called equalisation or EQ.

Nominally, 'equalisation' as applied to microphones means restoring a level frequency response to a microphone that has inherently or by its position an uneven response: it may be used to match microphones with different responses. In practice it may often also mean taking a second step in the creative distortion of sound for a particular effect (the choice of microphone and its position being the first). It is used in this way in pop music — and the result is a matter for the judgment of the balancer.

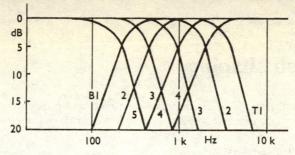

EFFECTS UNIT with four degrees of bass cut (B1–4) and five of treble cut (T1–5).

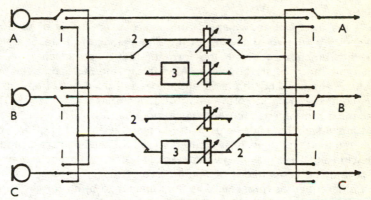

**TELEPHONE EFFECTS SWITCHING UNIT FOR TELEVISION** 1, Pre-selector switches. 2, Switches linked to video cut buttons. 3, Bass and treble filters. Here, microphone A is undistorted only while B is filtered and vice versa.

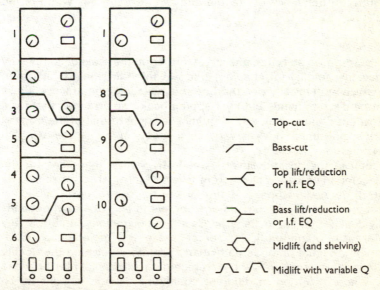

**EQUALISATION MODULES** *Left*: Mono channel. 1, High and low pass filters. 2, HF equalisation. 3 and 4, High and low mid-frequency equalisation. 5, Variable Q (bandwidth). 6, LF equalisation. 7, Routing switches. *Centre*: Stereo channel. 8–10, High, mid- and low-frequency equalisation. *Right*: EQ symbols.

**157**

*More complex filters are used to change the central part of the frequency response curve.*

# Response shaping

Between the extremes of bass and treble controls, a rather more complex form of filter can be used to selectively amplify a particular narrow range of frequencies. Where this is done without affecting the remainder of the sound, the effect is called midlift.

### Midlift
This is the electrical equivalent of the selective emphasis of particular frequencies by the vocal cavities or the dimensions of the resonators of many instruments. In these, the formant that is produced gives the instrument much of its character. Midlift can therefore be seen as a device for emphasising character and, indeed, if used out of any appropriate context can do so to the point of caricature.

The most common use for midlift is in popular music. Here the emphasis of individual character helps instruments that are battling for recognition in a loud and densely structured sound. As we have seen, singers, woodwind and brass may be given peaks of midlift at different frequencies and so may be combined in a single piece of music. These peaks may also be described as 'presence', as they appear to bring forward a particular source without affecting its overall volume. A comparable effect is a mid-range dip or 'shelf'.

Digitally-programmed equalisation can have almost continuously variable control of frequency or volume and can also vary the width of the curve (known as the Q).

### Graphic filter
If we take response selection one stage further up the scale of complexity we reach the graphic (or shaping) filter. In this the signal is split into bands which are typically one-third of an octave wide. In practice, these will not be discrete bands but overlapping peaks, so arranged that for a 'level response' the sum at any frequency is equal to that of the original signal. Visually similar devices vary considerably in the degree to which this is achieved.

Selection of the desired effect is made by setting the slides for the various component bands at different levels to form what appears to be a graph of the new response on the face of the control unit. The actual response that is achieved may differ from this to an extent that depends on individual design and the sharpness of the fluctuations set. But in any case, the result of any particular operation can only be judged by ear.

This type of equalisation is particularly useful in matching the quality from different microphones when rerecording (dubbing) film or video sound. Voices recorded in different conditions cannot, in general, be matched so perfectly that they sound as if they were in the same place. But deficiencies in quality and intelligibility can be made less obtrusive, and unnecessary minor variations can be evened out.

**158**

**SIMPLE BASS AND TREBLE CONTROL**
The effect of early 'tone' controls.

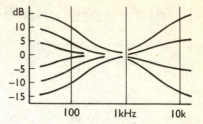

**PRESENCE PEAKS** Typical examples of midlift. Singer S, woodwind W and brass B each have their separate range within which their character is selectively emphasised, so that one does not conflict with or obscure another.

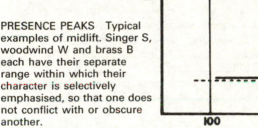

**GRAPHIC FILTER** In the most usual design the slide faders are at third-octave intervals, and control the gain or attenuation in a band of about that width. In principle, the overall effect should match the line shown on the face of the module, but this may not be achieved in practice. The result should be judged by ear.

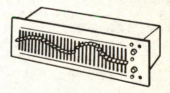

**AUDIO RESPONSE CONTROL** Effect of, A, a single fader and, B, nearby faders set at opposite extremes. In practice, sharp jumps in the response can only be achieved at the expense of a more erratic response when the sliders are set for a smooth curve. Apparently similar units may differ in their capacity to compensate for this.

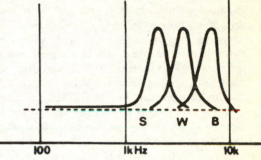

**159**

*Reducing volume range by automatic electrical methods.*

# Compressors and limiters

Compression (reduction in dynamic range) may be used to maintain a high overall level in order to ensure the strongest possible recorded or broadcast signal. In popular music it may be applied to individual components of a backing sound which would otherwise have to be held low in order to avoid sudden peaks blotting out the melody; or it might be used on the melody itself, which might otherwise have to be raised overall, and as a result become too forward.

**How a compressor works**
Below a predetermined level (the threshold or onset point) the volume of a signal is unchanged. Above this point the additional volume is reduced in a given proportion, e.g. 2 : 1, 3 : 1, or 5 : 1. For example, if the threshold were set at 8dB below the level of 100 per cent modulation and 2 : 1 compression selected, it would mean that signals which previously over-modulated 8dB were now just reaching full modulation. Similarly if 5 : 1 had been chosen, signals which previously would have overpeaked by 32dB will now only just reach 100 per cent.

What this means in practice is that the overall level may be raised by 8dB or 32dB, so that relatively quiet signals make a much bigger contribution than would otherwise be possible.

An expander operates like a compressor, but in reverse, allowing further fine control of dynamics; a compander combines the two, first compressing, then restoring the original dynamics.

**How a limiter works**
Suppose now that the compression ratio is made large, say 20 : 1, and the threshold level raised to something very close to 100 per cent modulation. Working like this the compressor now acts as what is called a limiter. A limiter can be used to hold unexpected individual high peaks that would overload subsequent equipment or it can be used to lift the signals from virtually any lower level to the usable working range of the equipment – though this may cause problems with high level signals that may be excessively compressed, and with background noise that will be lifted.

It will be seen that the effect of a 2 : 1 compressor with a threshold at 8dB below 100 per cent modulation is to compress only the top 16dB of signals while leaving those at a lower level to drop away at a 1 : 1 ratio.

The decay time in a typical simple limiter may be set at 0.1, 0.2, 0.4, 0.8, 1.6 or 3.2 seconds. The fastest of these can hold brief transient peaks without affecting background but with a rapid series of peaks could produce an unpleasant vibrato-like effect. For most purposes about half a second is satisfactory, but duration is not critical at low compression.

Compressors and limiters should not be used for classical music. Indeed, where manual control is feasible it is almost invariably to be preferred. The use of compression in pop music is a special case.

**DYNAMICS MODULES** *Left*, stereo: In-line channel controls. 1, Limiter threshold and release (decay time) settings and 'gate' key. 2, Compressor threshold, compression ratio, attack and release settings. 3, Gain reduction due to compressor or limiter. 4, Make-up gain amplifier setting. 5, Switches for compressor, limiter, or external control. *Right*, mono: Useful for fine control of popular music dynamics. 6, Expander controls. 7, Compressor controls.

**LIMITER AND COMPRESSOR** 1. Limiter preventing overload. 2, Limiter used for programme compression 3, Compressor. 4, Lowest level of programme interest. 5, *shaded area:* Range of expected maximum level. 6, Lowest acceptable output level. 7, Maximum permitted level.

**COMPRESSION RATIOS** A, Linear operation: input and output levels correspond. Above threshold level, B, various compression ratios, C, reduce output. In the extreme case, D, the compressor acts as a limiter holding maximum output close to the threshold level.

**LIFTING LOW LEVELS** 1, With the compressor out of circuit, only a small proportion of the input goes into the desired dynamic range (2–3). 4, With increasing compression more can be accommodated. 5, Limiter.

**NOISE GATE** 1, Range of maximum expected input level. 2, Corresponding maximum output level. 3, Lowest level of interest. 4, Lower end of designed dynamic range. 5, Gating level: if level of signal drops below this, the input characteristic falls from level A to level B.

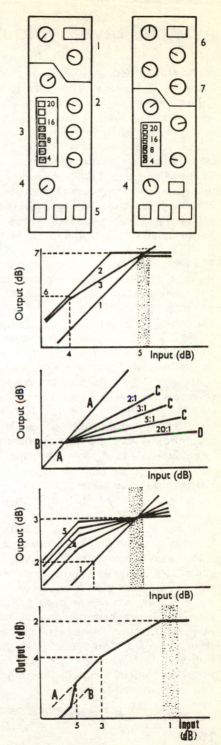

# Artificial reverberation: 'echo'

Artificial reverberation (AR) is often colloquially called 'echo' – an odd name for a device which serves to extend reverberation without, it is hoped, introducing any actual echoes. It is used on occasions when more reverberation is wanted than the built-in acoustics of a studio can supply, or (for music) when a multimicrophone close balance has been adopted.

Most control desks have 'auxiliary send' facilities which can be used to take a feed from each channel to an artificial reverberation device. Since each can be given its own individual setting, this allows greater control than is possible with natural acoustics.

In the past, echo chambers, reverberation plates and even systems of springs have been employed. These all produce a randomised decay of sound by a system of multiple reflections.

**The echo chamber**
An echo chamber may be a room with 'bright' reflecting walls, perhaps with 'junk' littered about at random, in order to break up the reflections and mop up excess mid-range reverberation. A humid atmosphere gives a strong high-frequency response; a dry one absorbs top. An echo chamber linked to the outside atmosphere varies with the weather. The shape and size of the room controls its quality of reverberation. In practice, the volume is often rather small, typically $4000ft^3$ ($113m^3$) or less.

Another disadvantage of the echo chamber is that, once laid out, its reverberation time is fixed. Two seconds may be suitable for music but less satisfactory for speech. A further problem, which may add to the cost, is that echo chambers need to be isolated from structure-borne noise. But at least the decay is natural, because the reverberation is in three dimensions. A plate, with two, sounds more mechanical.

**The reverberation plate**
A metal plate takes up less room than an echo chamber and is less susceptible to structure-borne noise. It can, however, pick up sound from the air, so to avoid how-round it could not be housed in the same room as a monitoring loudspeaker. It is not affected by other plates.

The plate is a sheet of metal with transducers. One vibrates the plate and others, acting as a contact microphones, pick up the signal, reflected many times from the edges. Unlike the echo chamber, its natural reson-ances do not thin out to sharp peaks at the lower frequencies, but are spread fairly evenly throughout the audio range. Damping is also used to vary reverberation times between a nominal 0.3 and 5.3 seconds.

For a given setting the actual duration is longest at mid-frequencies, with a slight reduction in the bass and rather more in the top (15dB at 10 000Hz), thereby simulating the high-frequency absorption of the air of a room of moderate size.

**ECHO AND REVERBERATION** 1, An echo is a discrete repetition of a sound after a delay of some 20ms or more. 2, Delays that are shorter than 20ms, associated with the dimensions of all but the largest halls, are perceived as components of reverberation.

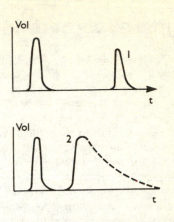

**FLEXIBLE 'ECHO SEND'** 1, Channel fader. 2, Channel output. 3, Pre- or post-fader switch. 4, AR send fader. 5, Bus bar allocated to AR. 6, To AR device, outside control console. On many desks, the feed to AR passes through auxiliary 'send' circuits that may also be used for many other purposes, and in the simplest case may be fed from a point after the channel fader.

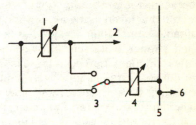

**ECHO CHAMBER** A U-shaped room may be used to increase the distance the sounds must travel from loudspeaker to microphone. A stereo pair would pick up sound from different directions.

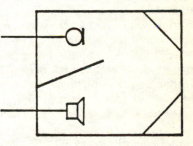

**REVERBERATION PLATE** 1, Tinned steel plate (at least 2m²). 2, Tubular steel frame. 3, Damping plate, pivoted at 4. (Here the spacing is shown as being set by the hand-wheel, but many damping plates are motor driven from a point on the sound control desk.) D, Drive unit. M, Contact microphone. For stereo, two are used, asymmetrically placed.

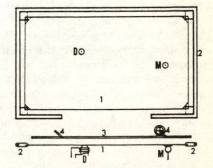

**163**

# Digital reverberation and delay

Reverberation can be mimicked by computer control of a digital signal, but, as in the evolution of the desk itself, this needed the development of relatively powerful techniques of data manipulation and storage (by random access memory). Now that these are available, digital artificial reverberation has largely replaced earlier techniques which, as we have seen, were limited in their flexibility and often had severe coloration or recognisably unrealistic characteristics. Indeed, for those who developed an affection for the plate, its quality can be offered digitally as one special case among many.

A versatile digital reverberation device will simulate a wide range of acoustics, with many pre-programmed and given the reassuringly familiar names of commonly-encountered environments. Such titles do, of course, represent the programmer's concept of what they might sound like, so should be taken only as starting points in the search for something suitable, rather than accepted at face value. Even so, for many balancers such a range will cover most of their requirements.

Beyond them, however, there is far more on offer – at least in principle, for the vast array of separately controlled parameters can at first sight be daunting. With practice, they allow the user to 'fine-tune' existing options or construct completely new, customised effects, should these be required.

A useful facility allows crossover points between frequency ranges to be set so that each can be given its own special quality. In a realistic example, the low frequencies might be assigned a reverberation time that is perhaps half a second longer than the mid-range. Other characteristics might include an initial delay (sometimes confusingly called 'pre-delay'), first reflections, the 'attack' of the main body of reverberation, then its slope and its final decay. There may (though perhaps with some overlap of function), be more: one device offers 22 parameters which can be used to modify reverberation, and a further 13 to produce effects which lie outside the range of natural acoustics.

**Digital special effects**
Sophisticated effects can be obtained, including reverberation times that depend on frequency and unnaturally long times for special effects. Continuous sampling gives a 'spin' effect, which by slightly enhancing part of the frequency range can sound like a rapidly degenerating feedback effect or howl-round (which is normally avoided like the plague). Variable delay is also achieved, and by recombining this with the original signal, 'phasing' and 'flanging' effects can be obtained, a hollow phase-cancellation quality that can be made to sweep through the audio-frequency range. Used as special effects in pop music, this has previously been achieved by manual drag on one of a pair of recordings.

**164**

DIGITAL AR CONTROL UNIT  The
deceptively compact controls for one
'digital signal processor' which offers
a wide variety of AR and other effects.
1, LED display showing a descriptive
name of the selected program, its
main characteristics, and the volume
(including overload warning).
2, Program or register. 3, Number of
program or register selected.
4, Function keys. 5, LED display,
sliders, and keys associated with the
currently selected control 'page'.
Operation is not intuitively obvious:
new users should follow the step-by-
step instructions, guided initially by
the supposedly 'user-friendly'
program names.

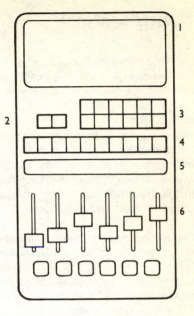

FLANGING AND PHASING  The
change in amplitude (vertical scale)
with frequency. A, The effect of
flanging − here with a delay of
0.5ms − is evenly distributed
throughout the frequency range, but
is not related to the musical scale,
which is logarithmic. B, Cancellation
and enhancement produced by the
use of a phase-changing network: the
dips are distributed evenly over the
musical scale.

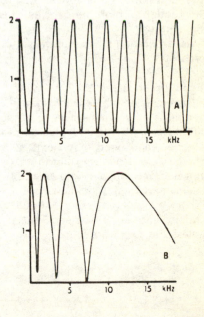

**165**

*How 'echo' is used creatively in pop music, remedially in classical music and for special effects on speech.*

# Using 'echo'

Artificial reverberation (AR) is an integral part of any balance where close microphones are used. As each source has a separately controlled feed, differential amounts of 'echo' can be added, depending on the clarity of line or resonance required. Soloists can be brought forward by lifting the direct component of the sound and reducing AR input. The voice requires less echo (either in volume or reverberation time) if the words are to be heard clearly – though in modern music the marginal audibility of a few key words or phrases may be all that is required to establish subject matter or mood. Here the application of AR is a matter for the balancer. In his interpretation of the composer's or arranger's intention there is scope for skill and versatility.

**Simulating concert hall conditions**
When classical music has been recorded in an acoustic which is too dead (as in most television or film studios), AR may be added in an attempt to improve matters. Because of its size, in a concert hall there is a tiny delay between direct sound and the first reflection arriving at the microphone. What happens in this interval often helps to define the character of particular instruments. A delay of a tenth of a second corresponds to a path difference of 100ft (30cm), as in a big hall. Note that we are already in the realms of true echo, as a delay in excess of a twentieth of a second can begin to separate original sound and reverberation to produce discrete echoes on staccato sounds. Digital delay will have the same effect. The long path of true concert hall reverberation results (in dry air) in the attenuation of high frequencies: this would also be included in a digital simulation.

Reverberation times of different durations may be used for singers and orchestra.

**'Echo' on speech**
In using 'echo' for speech (e.g. in plays) the main problem is one of perspective: moving closer to a microphone produces more feed to the AR device – the very reverse of a realistic effect. A separate microphone for the 'echo' feed may help; so will careful rehearsal of the desired effect. Where differing amounts of reverberation are required on two voices taken on a single microphone, a switch in AR feed (changed between voices) should be used in preference to the AR output fader. Where the latter is varied it should be reset at the start of the new sound and not in the gap between sounds, where the change would be audible unless the gap were long.

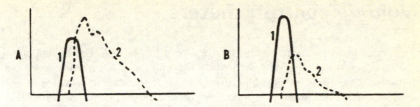

**'ECHO' MIXTURES**   With separate control of the direct feed, 1, and the artificial reverberation (AR) feed, 2, a wide range of effects is possible. A, Reverberation dominates the sound. B, Reverberation tails gently behind it.

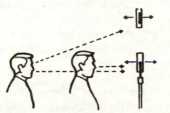

**'ECHO' ON TWO VOICES**   Where differing amounts of AR are needed on two voices, opposing microphones and voices are placed dead-side-on to each other. This layout (using bi-directional microphones) might be adopted in a radio studio; in a television studio there will normally be more space, making separation easier.

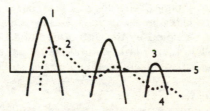

**'ECHO' FOR PERSPECTIVE**   A second bi-directional microphone, suspended above the main and having a stronger AR feed helps to create perspective on crowd scenes. The reverberation effect is automatically reduced as a speaker moves closer to the lower microphone.

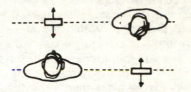

**THE EFFECT OF LEVEL**   1, Loud direct sound. 2, Audible reverberation. 3, Quiet direct sound. 4, Reverberation now below threshold of hearing. 5, For a given setting of the AR fader there is a level of direct sound below which the reverberation has no audible effect. This also varies with the setting of the listener's loudspeaker.

**167**

*The assessment of relative sound volumes is done by ear, subject to some reference level which is determined by meter.*

# Volume control: meters

The maximum permitted volume may be sharply defined. In AM radio '100 per cent modulation' means quite literally the point above which the peaks of the signal are greater than those of the carrier wave and will momentarily extinguish it; on a vinyl record there is a physical limit to the wall thickness between grooves. In practice, however, in present-day terms 'full modulation' generally indicates an upper limit for some designated low level of irreversible distortion.

Similarly there is a lower limit to programme level below which noise of one sort or another becomes noticeable. We must therefore control and where necessary compress the signal to make the best use of the range between noise and distortion. Within the accepted range, judge the relative levels by ear, but use a meter to check the result.

Meters are also used to ensure that there is no uncalled for loss or gain between items of equipment; to control relative levels between different performances; and to check that levels remain within the bounds desirable for good listening.

In music recording studios, multitrack techniques ideally require separate metering for each channel that is being recorded. Using the conventional display, about eight meters can be read. For a larger number it is best to have them in line with the fader and rising on a vertical scale to form a graphical display.

The two main types of meter are the VU meter (favoured in America) and the PPM (widely used in Europe). A bargraph may simulate either.

### VU meter
The face of the VU meter has scales for both percentage modulation and decibels. It may be a direct-reading instrument − i.e. requiring no special amplifier. In a studio-quality meter the long time-constant (as much as 300 milliseconds is used to damp unreadable fluctuations) prevents transient sounds from being registered at all. It under-reads on sharply percussive sounds and speech (at '100 per cent modulation' these are distorted).

A particular disadvantage of the scale is that 'percentage modulation' has little to do with relative levels as perceived by the ear, and that about half of the range is occupied by the 3dB above and below the nominal 100 per cent modulation. Very little natural sound varies over so narrow a range. Nevertheless many users feel they do get sufficient information.

### Peak programme meter
The PPM is a programme aid as well as an engineering device. Using a special amplifier for conversion of the signal it reads logarithmically (i.e. in decibels) over its working range of about 30dB. A typical PPM has a time constant of 2.5 milliseconds for the rise and a slow fall (time constant 1 second, giving a fall of 8.7dB/second).

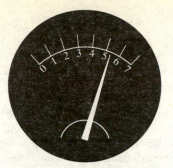

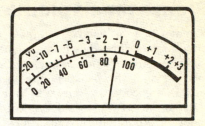

**PEAK PROGRAMME METER (PPM)**
The markings are white on black.
Each division is 4dB; '4' on the
meter is a standard 'zero level' and
'6' is full modulation, above which
distortion is to be expected.

**VU METER** The lower scale
indicates percentage modulation and
the upper scale decibels relative to
full modulation.

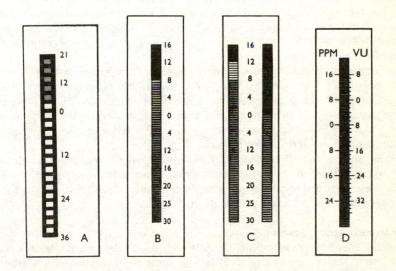

**BARGRAPHS** A, A simple LED bargraph gives a rough guide to level (or
overload) in an individual channel or group. B, Plasma bargraph: mono. C, Plasma
bargraph: stereo (or any pair of channels). Above a given level (here +8 on the
PPM), the plasma glow is brighter still, to indicate overload. A further type of
display simulates the bargraph on a VDU. D, Bargraphs can be programmed to
offer a variety of displays including both PPM and VU.

# Programme volume

A meter can be used to suggest or check levels. For example, if a discussion is allowed its normal dynamic range with occasional peaks up to the maximum, a newsreader who speaks clearly and evenly will sound loud enough with peaks averaging about 6dB less. A whole system of such reference levels can be built up: see first table opposite.

Radio and television stations with a distinctive style and a restricted range of programme material have only a limited number of types of junction and it is easy to link item to item. But for a service (still available in many countries) which incorporates news, comedy, drama, popular and classical music, religious services, magazines, discussion programmes and so on, problems of matching between successive items can become acute; a listener expects to adjust his volume only with increasing interest in a particular item. An increase in volume that coincides with a reduction of interest is irritating.

**Junctions between speech and music**

Two rules which generally smooth junctions between speech and music are given in the second table opposite. The apparent contradiction can be resolved by starting speech 2dB down from its normal level and then raising it by that small difference. These levels assume listening with at least moderate attention with the volume set accordingly. In these circumstances announcements should peak less than music. But if the listener's volume is always assumed to be low, a higher relative level of speech is tolerable: in the worst conditions an announcement may have to be 8dB *above* music.

Problems of matching are of less interest to stations whose main audience may be listening in noisy or unfavourable conditions (e.g. in a car or on poor equipment such as a small transistor radio), or whose principal concern is maximum coverage – as in developing countries where a small number of transmitters cover a wide area and communication takes precedence over quality.

Films and many other programmes on television require a volume setting that is lower on average than is usual for advertising or promotional links. This appears to be an intractable problem – which is left to the audience to solve with a 'mute' button.

**Preferred listening levels**

An experiment on preferred listening levels (third table, opposite) shows that sound balancers prefer to listen at marginally higher levels than musicians; and both very much higher than most members of the public. People professionally concerned with sound need to extract a great deal more information from what they hear, and the greater volume helps them to pick up the finer points of fades and mixes, etc., and check technical quality. But it must always be remembered that the state of affairs at the receiving end may be very different.

RECOMMENDED PEAK LEVELS for a radio service with a full range of output. A restricted range of output may permit a narrower range of levels. Here, the levels given are relative to 100 per cent modulation at the transmitter. They were obtained by using a peak programme meter (PPM).

| Programme material | Peak level, dB |
|---|---|
| Talk, discussion programmes | 0 |
| News and weather | −6 |
| Drama: narration | −8 |
| Drama: action | 0 to −16 |
| Light music | 0 to −16 |
| Classical music | 0 to −22* |
| Harpsichords and bagpipes | −8 |
| Clavichords and virginals | −16 |
| Announcements between music (depending on type of music) | −4 to −8 |

* or lower for periods of up to half a minute

LISTENERS' PREFERENCES FOR RELATIVE LEVELS OF SPEECH AND MUSIC
Based on the results of a BBC survey. This included classical and light music (but not pop music) and was designed to measure preferences for listening in reasonable conditions at home. These are the averaged results:

Speech following music to be 4dB down
Music following speech to be 2dB up

PREFERRED MAXIMUM SOUND LEVELS

| | Public | | Musicians | Sound-balancers | |
| | men | women | | men | women |
|---|---|---|---|---|---|
| Symphonic music | 78 | 78 | 88 | 90 | 87 |
| Light music | 75 | 74 | 79 | 89 | 84 |
| Dance music | 75 | 73 | 79 | 89 | 83 |
| Speech | 71 | 71 | 74 | 84 | 77 |

These figures were obtained by BBC experiments in 1948, before the advent of either FM radio or popular music in its modern forms. But the trends shown here remain valid. (The figures are given in dB relative to $2 \times 10^5$ Pa.)

# Manual control of music and speech

About 110dB separates the thresholds of hearing and of feeling. The significant sounds (including music) that we hear in our daily lives cover much of this range. But only 45dB may separate the noise level of a quiet room and its occupant's preferred maximum level of music. So the natural or possible range of sounds must be compressed to meet the preference of many listeners, as well as to hold levels between noise and distortion levels. In practice, different ranges apply to AM and FM radio, and to analogue and digital recordings.

**Controlling music**
In the concert hall, music may have a range of 60–70dB. In BBC practice it is compressed to about 22dB (peak values) with quieter passages not exceeding half a minute. Records (CD and DAT in particular) may be allowed more than this.

Automatic control without the anticipation of quiet or loud passages would destroy the music, but manual control can enhance the listener's enjoyment. In order to avoid overmodulation, fade down gradually over a period of half a minute or more; anticipate very quiet passages similarly. Try to preserve the nuances of light and shade. Steps of 1½–2dB at a time will not be noticed by the audience; most faders are marked in 'stops' of about this size.

**Controlling speech and sound effects**
Speech is controlled in a different way and over a narrower range. The maximum range is in radio plays, where BBC practice allows 16dB (again, on peak values), with the average at 8dB below the maximum to allow for the dramatic effect of louder passages. Even so, shouting has to be held back (making it sound distant) unless the performers restrict their own volume and project the effect of shouting. Manual control of levels may be exercised more abruptly than for music if the adjustment is made at the end of the gap between one voice and another. A sudden adjustment by as much as 6dB made during the first syllable following an unexpected change in voice level may be barely noticeable.

The *volume* of a percussive sound effect such as a pistol shot or car crash must be suggested by the *character* of continuing sound. Fortunately this necessary convention is accepted by listeners.

**Recording for film**
In recording for film, the minimum of control should be exercised at source. The purpose of this is not to match the voices in different shots: these can be put on separate tracks and matched at the dubbing (re-recording) stage. Rather, it will help the editor with the background atmosphere – for example, tiny gaps that are opened out can sometimes be filled by cutting in sound trimmed from other parts of the same take.

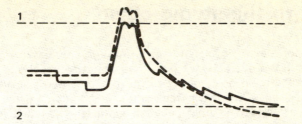

MANUAL CONTROL OF PROGRAMME VOLUME   Method of compressing a heavy peak to retain the original dramatic effect and at the same time ensure that the signal falls between maximum and minimum permissible levels 1 and 2. Steps of 1½−2dB are made at intervals of, say, 10 seconds.

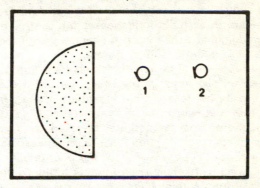

VOLUME CONTROL AND PERSPECTIVE   Fading up a quiet passage is like moving closer. But if this is done on a single microphone the perspective remains the same. A pleasanter effect may be achieved by mixing microphones at two distances: microphone 1 is used to bring forward the quiet passages and microphone 2 takes over in the loudest parts of the music.

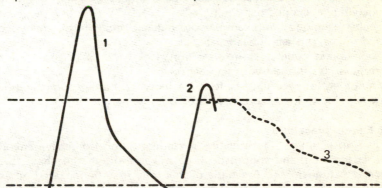

CHANGE IN DYNAMICS OF A SOUND EFFECT   An effect of which a dominant element is sheer volume of sound, such as a rifle shot, 1, must be held down close to the 100 per cent modulation level, 2 (though some distortion due to overmodulation is acceptable). The loudness of the sound must be suggested by the echoing reverberation that follows it, 3. Additional sounds may be used to confirm its nature: the classical example is the ricochet.

**173**

# Links to the studio chain

In this book the main signal traced through the desk is that which originates in the microphones (and other input sources) and leaves the desk after the main gain control to go to a recorder, a local or cabled audience, or to a broadcast transmitter. In addition to this, there are generally a number of other circuits: some (such as that for artificial reverberation) are plugged into the main studio chain; others provide supplementary inputs or feeds ('sends') out from the desk. (There are also lines such as production talkback to the studio, which are essentially independent of the programme signal.)

A foldback switch (which may be pre-set and left) feeds the output of selected faders to a studio loudspeaker for cue (or possibly mood) purposes; an additional switch in each channel taps it for feed to public address loudspeakers in the audience area.

The output from some of the channels may be split to provide a 'clean feed' that does not pass through the main (master) control. This allows studio output to be fed to a remote location without sending back the contribution from that source.

Remote telephones may sometimes be used as a source, e.g. for immediate news coverage or phone-in programmes. The band-width is typically 3000Hz, or may be less if there are poor-quality links. Feed the incoming call through an amplifier and limiter to the control desk. Isolate the outgoing call from studio chain.

To make effective use of aural judgement the balancer needs good listening conditions and high-quality loudspeakers. Sound is monitored for deficiencies of various types:

1. Production faults such as miscast voices, stilted speaking of the lines, uncolloquial scripts, bad timing.
2. Faulty techniques, for example poor balance and control, untidy fades and mixes, misuse of acoustics.
3. Poor sound quality, as in distortion, lack of bass or top, or other irregularities in the frequency response.
4. Equipment or recording faults such as wow, flutter, hum, tape hiss, noises due to loose connections or poor screening.

### The line-up procedure

To line up equipment to a common standard, an electrically-generated tone is fed from the control desk or mixer through the chain to the recorder or transmitter. A sample of this tone may be included on each recording used for professional purposes, so that replay equipment and subsequent recordings may also be lined up to the original standard. It is also common practice to take 'level', that is, to listen to a sample of the material to be recorded and check its volume on a meter. Fed through the chain (but not recorded) this serves as a test of the system in more practical conditions and confirms the identity of the source.

**174**

**FLEXIBLE AUXILIARY SEND
SWITCHING** This is used for public
address, studio feedback, 'echo' send
and feeds to remote locations which
require a mix that is different from
the main studio output. 1, Feed from
the channel (or group) input.
2, Remote cut. 3, Channel (or group)
fader. 4, Auxiliary send switching.
5, Mono send output fader. 6, Send
output switch. 7, Stereo ganged
output fader. 8, Stereo ganged output
switch. 9, Prefade-listen. 10, Channel
out to group bus or main control.
11, Output to mono send buses.
12, Output to stereo send buses.

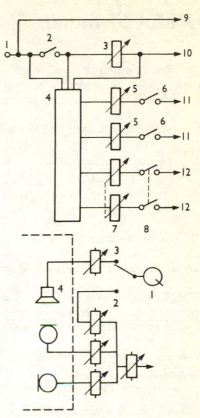

**ACOUSTIC FOLDBACK**
1, Reproducers, which are normally fed
direct to the mixer via switch contact,
2, may be switched, 3, to provide
an acoustic feed to the studio
loudspeaker, 4.

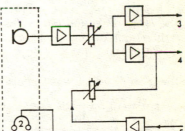

**CLEAN FEED CIRCUIT** For multi-
studio discussion a speaker in the
studio can hear a distant source on
headphones without own voice.
'Clean' cue is also provided.
1, Microphone and 2, Headphones or
'deaf aid' for speaker in studio.
3, Clean feed to distant studio.
4, Combined studio output.
5, Incoming line.

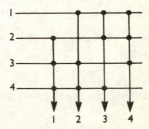

**MULTIWAY WORKING** In this
example four remote sources each
receive a broadcast-quality mix
without their own contribution. This
matrix can be achieved by the use of
'auxiliary sends' or 'independent
main output' facilities in the central
mixer console.

**175**

# Useful formulae

*An understanding of these relationships is not essential to those with a purely practical interest in microphone use.* But they will be useful to those with a mathematical or engineering background.

**Frequency, wavelength and the speed of sound**

$$f\lambda = c$$

where $\lambda$ is wavelength
      c is the speed of sound
      f is frequency in hertz (Hz)
      1Hz is one cycle per second; 1kHz is 1000Hz.

The speed of sound varies with temperature:
$$c = 1087 + 2T \text{ ft/sec}$$
where T is the temperature in degrees Celsius.

The speed of sound also varies with the nature of the medium. In fully saturated damp air it is some 3ft/sec (0.9m/sec) faster than in dry air. In liquids and solids it is much faster.

**Volume, intensity and power**

$$\text{Volume} = 10 \log \frac{I_2}{I_1} \text{ decibels}$$

where $I_1$ and $I_2$ are the intensities.

The range of sound intensities between the threshold of hearing and the threshold of feeling (if this is accepted to be 120dB) is $10^{12}$ or 1 000 000 000 000 : 1.

The gain of an amplifier is also measured in decibels:
$$\text{Gain} = 10 \log \frac{P_2}{P_1} \text{ decibels}$$
where $P_1$ is the power input and $P_2$ the power output. But power is proportional to the square of voltage, so
$$\text{Gain} = 10 \log \left(\frac{V_2}{V_1}\right)^2 = 20 \log \frac{V_2}{V_1} \text{ decibels}$$
A range of 1 000 000 000 000 : 1 in intensity is equivalent to only 1 000 000 : 1 in voltage.

Note that the voltage scale is used for microphones: dBs of voltage gain are not the same as dBs of increase in sound intensity.

**176**

# Further reading

*Alkyn, Glyn*. Sound Techniques for Video and TV. *Focal Press* (2nd Ed., 1989).
> Mainly mono, but far more detailed on sound than Millerson's book.

*Bartlett, Brian*. Stereo Microphone Techniques. *Focal Press* (1991).
> Guide to the theories behind the use of free-field, boundary layer and binaural stereo pairs.

*Borwick, John*. Microphones, Technology and Technique. *Focal Press* (1990).
> A good all-round account, though with less emphasis on performance.

*Gayford, Michael* (ed.) Microphone Engineering Handbook. *Focal Press* (1994).
> Offers detailed technical, and where appropriate, mathematical descriptions of design and resulting performance characteristics for a wide range of types – even including a section on the promise of optical microphones. Many chapters are contributed by specialist engineers of particular market leaders which inevitably somewhat limits the selection of examples.

*Huber, David Miles*. Microphones Manual, Design and Application. *Focal Press* (1988).
> Most directly useful when describing the characteristics of individual instruments and how to exploit them in 'microphone placement'; less so when discussing the complexities of microphone design. American terminology.

*Millerson, Gerald*. The Technique of Television Production. *Focal Press* (12th Ed., 1990).
> A highly analytical study of the medium, including a section on the contribution of sound.

*Nisbett, Alec.* The Sound Studio. *Focal Press* (6th Ed., 1994).
> Extends beyond the field of *The Use of Microphones* to include a full account of programme construction, sound effects, radiophonic techniques, editing, and the role of sound in television and film.

*Oringel, Robert*. Audio Control Handbook. *Focal Press* (6th Ed., 1989).
> An elementary introduction with a strong emphasis on American equipment, with photographs and claimed performance characteristics.

*Potter, Kopp and Green-Kopp*. Visible Speech. *Constable*, London (1966). *Dover Publications*, New York.
> A clear description of the characteristics of the human voice.

*Robertson, A.E.* Microphones. *Iliffe*, London (2nd Ed., 1963).
> Describes the engineering principles behind many types of microphones. Technically complex, but worth searching out.

*Rumsey, Francis*. Stereo Sound for Television. *Focal Press* (1989).
A short conversion course for those familiar with the mono basics.

*Talbot-Smith, M.* (ed.) Audio Engineers Reference Book, *Focal Press* (1994).
A useful source book on the design, manufacture and installation of many types of audio equipment.

*Wood, A.B.* The Physics of Music, *Methuen*, London (7th Ed., 1975).
A standard primer on the subject.

# Glossary and index

### Note on differences in British and American usage

This book is designed to be read in both America and Britain, as well as many other parts of the world. The reader is asked to forgive the mid-Atlantic terminology that often results. Differences of usage appear not only between countries but even from one organisation to another: both BBC and NBC have their own 'house' terminology. Further anomalies may appear in translation from other languages, or by the whim of the engineers or salespeople for manufacturing companies in the description of their products.

There are variations in ways of describing the job this book is about, the place where it is carried out, and the equipment used.

The American term audio operator broadly describes the job. But I betray the English origins of this book by avoiding the term in the text: 'audio' and 'video' are used much more in America than in Britain where the older 'sound' and 'picture' are preferred except in certain compound terms of American origin or for differentiating between signal feeds in television recording systems. In common usage in Britain a video is a cassette recorder (or recording). In BBC radio an audio operator is called a studio manager. Television 'sound supervisors' and film 'sound recordists' are not unreasonable names – although purists may object to 'recordist' as a way of avoiding confusion between the person and the machine, the recorder. Sometimes he or she doubles as 'sound engineer' or 'sound technician'; better perhaps to say 'sound man (or woman)' or 'sound balancer'.

### The place and the equipment

The place where much of the job is done might most reasonably be called the control room or, in television, sound or audio control. BBC radio is bound by its own history: there, 'control room' was the name given to the main switching centre, and the room that is part of a studio suite is called a control cubicle. The name was originally accurate: it started life as a structure like an overgrown telephone box in the corner of the studio.

The control desk is also called the panel (BBC radio) or the board (US usage). The master control (US) is also called a main gain control, and a sub-master control is a group fader. A British outside broadcast has Americans puzzling: it turns out to be a remote; while a nemo on the NBC board might confuse a British sound engineer, who would call it an outside source. Readers may add their own examples from these pages.

### Metric conversions

In this book, conversions from imperial to metric measures are often deliberately imprecise. It would be perverse to render 3ft as 0.91m where 'ball-park' distances are intended.

**A and B signals** (29, 31, **78–79**, 80–81, 109, 152–153) Left and right components of stereo. In *AB stereo* these are generated and/or processed and transmitted separately, not combined as MS (middle and side) signals.

**Absorption** (**34–35**, 88–91) Loss of sound energy due to friction as the air moves back and forth in the interstices of a porous material (a *soft absorber*) or by transfer to another vibrating system from which less sound is subsequently re-radiated. See also *membrane absorber, Helmholtz resonator.*

**Absorption coefficient** (**34**) The fraction of sound energy which is absorbed, usually on reflection at a surface and unless otherwise stated for a frequency of 512Hz at normal incidence.

**Acoustics** (**30, 32–34**, 42, 74–75, 82–84, **90–94, 104–107, 110–111**, 134, 162) The behaviour of sound, and its study. The acoustics of a studio depend on its size and shape and the amount and position of absorbing and reflecting materials.

**Acoustic control system** (32, **104–105**) A system of microphones, computer-controlled mix-and-delay circuits and loudspeakers which is used to extend the reverberation time of a hall by a variable amount. Acoustic feedback is not used.

**Acoustic holography** (**105**) The use of a computer and loudspeaker arrays to reconstruct a two- or three-dimensional sound field to simulate that in an auditorium with a different shape and acoustics. The term 'holography' is an analogy, not an accurate description of the method.

**Amplification** (9, 48–49, 130, **150–151, 176**) A gain in strength, usually of an electrical signal.

**Analogue signal** (8–9, 150, 154) A continuously-variable signal which corresponds directly to the original waveform, and which can be used to reproduce it. The waveform is not sampled and not converted to a series of numbers (as in a digital audio signal, q.v.).

**Antinode** (22–23) The part of a stationary wave where there is maximum displacement.

**Artificial reverberation (AR), 'echo'** (9, 74, 92, 150–151, **162–167**) Continuation of an audio signal simulating the natural decay of sound within an enclosed space. See also *digital reverberation, echo chamber, echo plate, springs.*

**Atmosphere** (86, 172) The normal background sound at any location.

**Attack** (20, 164) The way a sound starts. See also *transient.*

**Attenuation** (154–155, 160–161) Fixed or variable losses, usually of an electrical signal. See also *fader, compression, limiter.*

**Backing track** (120) A pre-recorded musical accompaniment to which the soloists can listen on headphones as they add their own performances.

**Baffle** (77, 118) A small acoustic screen which causes a local variation in the acoustic field near a microphone. It distorts the high-frequency sound, by setting up a system of standing waves.

**Balance** (8, **74–93, 102–149**) The choice of microphone positions to pick up an adequate signal, to discriminate against noise and provide an appropriate ratio of direct to indirect sound. It may also include the creative modification of the electrical signal.

**Balance test** (**75**, **102**, 116) A trial balance, or a series of trial balances, which should preferably be judged by direct comparison.

**Bargraph** (**168**−**169**) In audio, a meter showing volume as a linear (usually upright) display. It may act as either as *PPM* or *VU meter* (q.v.).

**Bass** (44, 54, 82, 157, 159) Lower end of the musical scale. In acoustics, the range (below about 200Hz) in which there are difficulties, principally in the reproduction of sound, due to the large wavelengths involved.

**Bass tip-up** (**44**−**47**, **50**, 53, **56**−**57**, 82, 113) A selective emphasis of bass which occurs when a microphone responding to pressure gradient is placed where there is a substantial reduction in sound intensity between the two points at which the sound wave is sampled. It is most noticeable when the microphone is close to the source and so is also called 'proximity effect'.

**Bi-directional microphone** (**38**−**39**, **42**−**51**, 81, 82, 84−85, 88−91, 103, 115, 121, 131, 167) One which responds to sound from its front and rear but not to sound from its sides and above and below.

**Boom** (46−47, 54, **68**, **94**−**101**) An arm, usually telescopic and mounted on a floor stand or dolly, from which a microphone is slung.

**Cable** (37, **68**−**69**, **98**) Electrical wiring, e.g., to carry audio signal, power supply or both.

**Cancellation** (**14**, 40−43, **52**−**54**, 76) Partial or complete opposition in phase, so that the sum of two signals approaches or reaches zero.

**Cardioid response** (**38**−**39**, **46**−**51**, 54, 63, 82, 84−85, 92, 128, 132) Literally, a heart-shaped directional response.

**Cavity resonance** (**16**, **34**−**35**, 40) See *Helmholtz resonator*.

**Coincident pair** (**76**−**79**, 92−93, 106−109, 121, 123−128, 138−141) Two matched directional microphones (often in a single housing) angled to pick up information from different but overlapping parts of a sound field. It is usually arranged that the sum of their outputs is an acceptable mono signal and their difference contains (stereo) information on position.

**Clean feed** (174) U.S.: mixed-minus. A cue feed to a remote programme source which includes all but the contribution from that source.

**Coloration** (**32**, 82, 102) Distortion of frequency response by resonances at particular frequencies.

**Compatibility** (**78**) Measures to ensure that a stereo signal produces acceptable monophonic sound when reproduced on standard mono equipment.

**Compression** (66, 102, 130, 150, **160**−**161**, **172**−**173**) Control of sound levels to ensure that all wanted signals are suitably placed between the noise and distortion levels of the medium, and that relative levels are acceptable to the intended audience. *Manual* and *automatic compression* are used for different purposes.

**Compression ratio** (160–161) A selected degree of automatic compression, e.g. 2 : 1, 3 : 1, or 5 : 1. It is set to operate at a given onset volume, e.g. 8 dB below full modulation.

**Condenser microphone** (36–38, **46–50**, 59–61) This depends on the electrical quality of capacitance, i.e. the ability of neighbouring and oppositely charged conductors to store energy between them. A condenser is a device for doing this, and in a condenser microphone the two components are a diaphragm and a base plate. Variations in their distance apart produce corresponding fluctuations in capacitance and so generate an electrical signal. See also *electret*.

**Connector** (70–71) See *DIN, Lemo, XLR*.

**Contact microphone** (**64–65**, 114, 118, 130, 163) One which directly picks up the sound transmitted within a solid material.

**Control** (**150–175**) The adjustment of programme level (in the form of an electrical signal) to make it suitable for feeding to a recorder or transmitter.

**Cottage-loaf response** (38–39, **50–51**) A bi-directional response in which pick up at the front is more sensitive and covers a wider angle than that at the rear. See *supercardioid response*.

**Dead room** (**88–91**, 103–104) A room with very thick sound absorbers (often 1 metre deep). A *dead acoustic* has little or no reflected sound.

**Decay** (32, 162, 164, 167) The way in which a note ends; or in which a sound or its reverberation dies away.

**Decibel, dB** (**26–27**, 39, 168–173, **176**) A measure of relative intensity, power or voltage.

**Delay** (104, 153, **163–166**) Storing a sound for a moment, usually in a digital store, then recombining it with the original signal.

**Diaphragm** (10–12, **37–41**, 46–48, 58, 60) That part of the microphone which responds to air pressure − or pressure gradient, if exposed on both sides.

**Diffusion** (32, **34**) Breaking up sound waves by means of irregularly distributed reflecting surfaces.

**Digital audio signal** (7, 9, 150, **154**, **164–165**) Audio information which has been converted from *analogue* form (in which the electrical waveform is directly related to the sound waveform) to a binary code. While in this form it is not subject to the gradual accretion of noise which continuously degrades analogue signals.

**Digital delay** (**164**) Temporary storage of a signal in memory, so that it can be reproduced after a designated interval.

**Digital reverberation** (**164–165**) Reverberation generated by using a digital signal and random access memories.

**DIN** (70–71) German industry standard, e.g. as applied to microphone connectors.

**Directivity** (**51**) The front-to-back ratio of sound picked up by a microphone.

**Distortion** (9, **36**, 74, 118, 168, 172) Unwanted changes of sound quality, generally by the introduction of electrically generated tones, or by changes in the relative levels of the different frequencies present.

**Dummy head technique** (71, 109) A pair of microphones arranged to mimic the relative position of the ears. A baffle between them reproduces the screening effect and path-difference due to the head. This produces a spatial effect, best heard on headphones.

**Dynamics** (160−161, **170−173**) The way in which sound volume varies.

**Echo** (9, 92, 150−151, **162−167**) Literally, the discrete repetition of sound at least a twentieth of a second later; colloquially, artificial reverberation or AR (q.v.).

**Echo chamber** (**162−163**) Reverberant room, through which a signal is fed via loudspeaker and microphone.

**Echo plate** (162−164) A sheet of metal which is used to provide artificial reverberation. It is vibrated by one transducer; another (or two for stereo) responds to the reflected wave motions.

**Eigentone** (32) A characteristic resonance due to the formation of standing waves between parallel walls.

**Electret** (36−37, 48, **60−61**, 84) Miniature, lightweight condenser microphone in which the diaphragm or baseplate carries a permanently embedded electric charge. Early development was limited by the mechanical properties of materials (such as teflon) which would hold a charge indefinitely without loss. A good performance is achieved by the use of a metal (e.g. tin) diaphragm over an electrostatically charged baseplate. This can now be made of silicon oxide (surface-treated to exclude water) which may act as part of the head-amplifier chip.

**Electromagnetic wave** (8) Radiant energy travelling at the speed of light. This includes gamma and X-rays, light, radiant heat, and radio.

**Electrostatic microphone**, (48) See *condenser microphone, electret*.

**End-fire** (46−47, 51, 80−81) Polar response with axis in line with body of microphone.

**Envelope** (20) The way in which the volume of a sound varies in time; its dynamics (q.v.).

**Equalisation, EQ** (9, 60, 94, 130, 150−151, **156−159**) Changes in the electrical signal, nominally to correct for frequency distortion introduced at any stage in an audio system. In practice it is also used for creatively distorting the frequency response still further, the result being judged by ear.

**Exponential** (18, 27) A rate of growth in which doubling occurs at equal intervals. See *logarithmic scale*.

**Fade** (**150−155**, 172−173) Gradual reduction or increase in an electrical audio signal by the use of a fader or 'pot' (potentiometer).

**Field pattern** (**38−39**) Polar response (q.v.).

**Fader** (**154−155**) Potentiometer ('pot') controlling the volume of an audio signal.

**Figure-eight response** (38−39, **42−45**, 48−51, 92, 106) Also called 'figure-of-eight'. A bi-directional microphone response in which the front and back are live but opposite in phase. See also *bi-directional*.

**Filter** (44, 150, **156**–**159**) A network of electronic elements (generally resistances and capacitances) which allows some frequencies to pass and attenuates others.

**Fishpole** (**99**) A hand-held microphone boom.

**Flutter echo** (32) A rapid fluctuation in volume which is heard when a staccato sound reverberates between parallel reflecting walls.

**Foldback** (144–147, **174**–**175**) A feed of selected sources to a studio loudspeaker for the benefit of the performers.

**Formant** (**20**, 22, **24**–**25**, 158) A broad frequency resonance associated with a sound source, e.g. a voice or a musical instrument. It is caused by the physical characteristics (notably the dimensions) of the resonant system.

**Frequency** (**12**–**13**, 18–19, 26–27, **40**–**41**, 156) In pure tones, the number of complete oscillations that an air particle makes about a median position in one second. Complex sounds are made up by adding many such simple patterns of motion (or frequencies).

**Frequency response** (**26**–**27**, 36, **40**–**41**, 43–66, 156–159) The way in which the relative levels of the different frequencies in a sound or audio signal are changed in passing through a stage or electrical component in its path (e.g. by a microphone). *Frequency correction* may be introduced to restore or otherwise deliberately change the frequency response. This is also called *equalisation*.

**Fundamental** (**18**–**25**) The primary and usually the lowest component of a musical note, and that which defines its pitch.

**Gain** (**176**) Amplification, generally calculated in decibels.

**Gate** (**161**) A switching circuit that passes or cuts a signal in response to an external stimulus.

**Gooseneck** (**59**, 60, **122**–**123**, 125, 126–127, 143) Section of a microphone mounting that is flexible enough to bend to and hold a desired shape and direction.

**Gun microphone** (**52**–**55**, 72, 96, 99, 147) Microphone fitted with interference tube to make it highly directional.

**Guy-wire** (**69**) Line pulling suspended microphone to desired position.

**Haas effect** (**30**–**31**) An effect which occurs when sound arrives at the ears from different directions with a time difference of a few milliseconds or more: all the sound seems to come from the direction of the first signal to arrive. This limits the field within which 2-loudspeaker stereo can be heard.

**Harmonics** (**18**–**23**, 25) A series of frequencies that are all multiples of the lowest frequency present (the fundamental).

**Head amplifier** (48–49, 59, 61) A small amplifier within the microphone casing or nearby which converts the fluctuating capacitance of a condenser microphone into the form of an alternating current which is suitable for transmission by cable to a mixer or recorder.

**Helmholtz resonator** (**16**, **34**–**35**) A cavity within which air can be made to expand and contract at a frequency which is characteristic of its size and shape. If a soft absorbing material is placed in the mouth of the cavity, it will selectively reduce sound at the resonant frequency.

**Hertz, Hz (12−13, 176)** Number of cycles or excursions per second in a pure tone.

**Howl-round** or **howl-back** (164) Closed circuit, e.g. microphone, amplifier, loudspeaker and sound path back to the microphone again, in which the overall gain exceeds the losses of the system.

**Humidity (104,** 110, 162, 176) Damp air transmits sound better than dry air, in which upper harmonics are attenuated in a distant balance. (Because of this, in dry conditions a close balance sounds more brilliant than any performance heard at normal distance in a concert hall.)

**Hydrophone (64−65)** Transducer which converts sound within a fluid, particularly water, to an electrical signal.

**Hypercardioid response** (50) Imprecise manufacturers' term; probably the same as supercardioid or cottage-loaf − but this should be confirmed by looking at a polar diagram.

**Impedance (36)** The combination of resistance, inductance and capacitance that serves to reduce the signal in an alternating current. An inductance selectively reduces high frequencies; a capacitance discriminates against the low; a resistance acts equally on all frequencies.

**Intensity of sound (16−17, 26−27, 44, 176)** The sound energy crossing one square metre.

**Interference tube (54−55)** An acoustic channel which, attached to a microphone capsule, confers highly directional properties. Sounds approaching from an angle to the axis are reduced or eliminated by phase cancellation.

**Lavalier** (60) Microphone suspended round the neck. Also called neck or lanyard microphone.

**Lemo (70−71)** Small connector with a sleeve and pins pointing in both directions.

**Level** (161, 167−174) Volume of the electrical signal. A *level test* is used to find suitable settings for (a) the source fader, to allow for expected variations in sound volume, and (b) the master control, to feed the signal onward at a level which is appropriately placed between the noise and distortion levels of the following equipment.

**Limiter** (151, **160−161)** An automatic control to reduce volume when the signal rises above a level that would introduce significant distortion.

**Line up (70,** 174) To arrange that the signal passes through all items of equipment at an appropriate *level* (q.v.). This is achieved by the use of *line-up tone*, often at 1000Hz, which is fed through the entire system and should produce a standard reading on meters at every stage.

**Lip-ribbon microphone (56−57)** One which is held at a close, standard distance from the mouth to discriminate against ambient noise. Equalised bass tip-up further reduces low frequency noise.

**Location** (86) Place outside a studio used to record sound and/or picture.

**Logarithmic scale** (**18**, 26−27, 168, **176**) One which converts a particular form of growth ('exponential', q.v.) back to a linear scale. Differences in sound intensity or frequency which increase in the ratios 1 : 2 : 4 : 8 : 16 : 32 : 64 appear to the ear to grow by equal intervals, so it is convenient to represent them by a scale which also has equal intervals − 0 : 1 : 2 : 3 : 4 : 5 : 6. This is a logarithmic scale.

**Loudness** (**26−27**, 170−172) The subjective aspect of sound intensity.

**Loudspeaker** (8−9, **28−31**) A transducer which converts an electrical signal into sound. Like the microphone at the beginning of the chain, it is essentially an analogue device.

**M and S signals** (78−79, 152−153) Literally, 'middle' and 'side' components of the stereo signal, obtained by adding and subtracting the left and right stereo signals. It is convenient if 'M' is also an acceptable mono signal, with 'S' containing the additional information required for stereo. The algebraic sum and difference of the M and S signals is, once again, the left and right components of stereo.

**MS microphone** (80−81, 94, 96) A pair of capsules designed to pick up the middle and side components of stereo directly. They are mounted in a single casing, usually in an end-fire configuration.

**Membrane absorber** (34−35) A damped resonating panel which will respond to and selectively absorb a range of sound frequencies.

**Meter** (9, 151, **168−169**) Device for measuring voltage, current etc. The *VU meter* and *peak programme meter* (q.v.) are adaptations for measuring audio-signal volume.

**Microphone** (7−11, 24, **36−67**, **76−81**) A device for converting sound to electrical energy.

**Midlift** (124, 126, 130, 136, **157−159**) Deliberately-introduced peak in the middle- and upper-frequency response. See also *Presence*.

**Mix, Mixer** (9, **150−155**) The electrical combination of audio signals. In a *mixer* each source is first controlled by its own fader.

**Modulation** (160, **168−171**) Superimposition of the audio signal on a carrier wave of higher frequency. *100 per cent modulation or full modulation* corresponds to the maximum acceptable audio signal level beyond which overload distortion occurs.

**Monitor** (8, 9, **30−31**, 74−75, 170−171, 174) Check sound quality by ear. A *monitoring loudspeaker* is used to check the aesthetic quality as well. (In addition, picture monitors are used in television, both in the control room and on the studio floor).

**Mono, monophonic sound** (**28**, 32, 74−75, **78**, 82, 102−103, 112, 142−143) Sound combined to be reproduced through a single loudspeaker. If several loudspeaker are used, the signal to each is the same.

**Mouse** (62−63, 84, **142−143**) Microphone in soft, acoustically transparent housing attached to solid, reflective surface, which acts as a pressure zone (a.v.).

**Moving-coil microphone** (**36−38**, 46−47, 128−129) One in which a coil attached to the diaphragm moves in the field of a magnet.

**Music balance** (102−149) See *balance*. *For individual instruments see contents list*.

**Newtons per square metre, N/m$^2$ (26) See** *Pascal*.

**Node** (19, 22−23) In a stationary wave, a point at which there is no displacement.

**Noise** (9, 36, 54−55, **56−57**, 62, **72−73, 86−87**, 88, 92, 160−161, 172, 174) Unwanted sound or audio signal.

**Noise reduction system (150)** Analogue systems divide the audiofrequency spectrum into several bands: each is then separately and automatically lifted to its optimum signal-to-noise level before recording, and is reduced accordingly on replay. This permits multiple re-recording without the introduction of appreciable noise from the tape itself. (It can also be used around any other potentially noisy element in a sound system.) The use of digital signals serves a similar purpose.

**Obstacle effect** (28, 40−41) A sound is not impeded by obstacles which are smaller than its own wavelength but is reflected or absorbed and also diffracted by those which are larger.

**Omnidirectional response** (**38−39**, 41, 60−63, 82−83, 108−109) Responding equally to sound from all directions.

**Outside source** (150) British term for remote source.

**Overtones** (18−23) Individual component frequencies in a sound which, when added to the fundamental, help to define its musical quality.

**PA, public address** (150) A feed of selected sound sources to audience loudspeakers.

**Pan, steer** (106, 131, 140, 142, **152−153**) Change the relative strength of left and right components of a stereo signal in order to change its apparent position within the reproduced sound field.

**Panpot** (**152−153**) A 'panoramic potentiometer' which is used to pan (q.v.) or steer a signal to left or right.

**Parabolic reflector** (**52−53**) A reflector which will concentrate sound from a distance and in a given direction to a single point. It is efficient only at wavelengths less than its diameter.

**Pascal (Pa)** (37) Unit of sound pressure. 1Pa = 1 newton per square metre (N/m$^2$). This has replaced an older measure, dynes per square centimetre: 1Pa = 10 dynes/cm$^2$. A common reference level, $2 \times 10^{-5}$ Pa, approximates to the threshold of hearing at 1kHz.

**Peak programme meter, PPM** (**168−169**) A meter used for measuring the peak values of programme volume.

**Phantom power** (**48**, 60−61, 68, 151) Power supply, one leg of which employs both wires of the audio circuit.

**Phase** (14−**15**, 28, 39, 42−46, 48, 52−53, 153) The stage which a particle responding to a pure tone has reached in vibrating about its median position. Particles which are at the same stage in this cycle of movement are said to be *in phase*.

**Phase cancellation** (42, **52—53**, 108, 164) The superimposition of two waves where one is positive and the other negative, so that their total is less than either on its own.

**Phasing** (**164—165**) An effect in which two similar or identical signals are very slightly separated in time, so that the waveforms are enhanced at some frequencies and cancel at others. If the time separation is changed, a hollow, sweeping effect is heard. Also called flanging.

**Phon** (**26—27**) A unit of subjective loudness. Phons equal decibels (measured objectively) at 1000Hz, and at other frequencies are related to them by contours of perceived equal loudness.

**Pitch** (**18**, 22) The subjective aspect of frequency. In harmonic series, the frequency of the fundamental.

**Polar characteristic, polar diagram, polar response** (**38—59**, **76—81**, 92, 104) These describe the way in which the response of a microphone varies with the angle of incidence of a sound. Since this will change with frequency, it is given for a representative series of pure tones. For each of these the response along the main axis of symmetry (generally a line normal to the diaphragm) is taken as unity, and the response at other angles is related to this.

**Popping, pop-shield** (**72—73**) Break-up of audio signal as diaphragm is blown out of its normal range by vocal plosives such as 'p' and 'b'; and a screen between mouth and microphone which prevents this.

**Post-balancing** (**154**) Treating (by equalisation, etc.) and mixing sound that has already been recorded on multitrack tape.

**Pre-hear** (**150—151**, 155) A means of sampling a programme source before fading it up and mixing it in to the studio sound. Also called 'prefade-listen', PFL.

**Presence** (50, 82, 124, 130, 136, 140, **158—159**) Bringing 'forward' an instrument (or voice) by selectively amplifying a range of frequencies which contains much of its character.

**Pressure gradient** (14, **38—39**, **44—45**, **48—49**, 62) The difference between two successive points in a sound wave. A microphone which measures pressure gradient (on opposite sides of the diaphragm) will have a directional response, whereas one which measures the pressure at a single point will be omnidirectional.

**Pressure zone or boundary effect** (**62—63**, 84, **142—143**) The effect of a hard, rigid surface on the pressure and pressure gradient of the sound field close to it. Cancellation at a right-angle to the surface can be used as part of the directional response of a microphone. See also *mouse*.

**Progressive wave** (**22**) A wave which travels through a medium (as distinct from a standing or stationary wave).

**Proximity effect** (**44—45**, **56—57**, **72—73**) See *bass tip-up*.

**Pure tone** (10, 174) A sound or signal containing one audio frequency only. See also *line-up, sine wave*.

**Quadraphony** (8, 106) Sound using four distinct signals which go to four loudspeakers − conventionally two in front which reproduce most of the directional information, and two at the rear which add reverberation. It is possible for all four to carry direct sound, but this severely limits the ideal listening area.

**Radio microphone (66−67**, 142) Microphone attached to a small radio transmitter, with a receiver to link it to sound control.

**Reference level (26, 166−167, 171, 174)** Since decibels are a measure based on ratios there is no absolute zero, and levels are given relative to some arbitrary reference level. For sound a useful reference level is $2 \times 10^{-5}$Pa, as this roughly corresponds to the lower limit of human hearing at 1000Hz. See also *line-up*.

**Resonance (16**, 34, 40, 112) Natural periodicity; reinforcement associated with this.

**Response (36−65**, 156−159) Sensitivity, frequency and polar characteristics of a microphone.

**Response selection (156−159)** The corrective or creative manipulation of the frequency content of a signal.

**Reverberation (9, 32, 42**, 50, 74−77, 82, 88, 92, 94, 102−112, 116, 138, 162−167) The sum of many reflections of a sound in an enclosed space.

**Reverberation time (32−33**, 90, 104, 158, **162**, 166) The time it takes for a sound to die through 60dB.

**Ribbon microphone (36−37**, 38−39, **42−46**, 50, **56−57**, 82, 90−91, 116, 120, 124) One in which a narrow strip of foil, corrugated for greater flexibility, is suspended in a magnetic field. A fluctuating current is produced by movement of the foil with air pressure − or, more commonly, pressure gradient.

**Scale (13, 18−19)** Division of the audio frequency range by musical intervals, i.e. frequency ratios. The more harmonious intervals have simple frequency ratios, e.g. 1 : 2 (octave), 2 : 3 (fifth), 3 : 4 (fourth), etc.

**Scale of width (74−77, 102−103**, 110, **115**, 140) The relative width of the stereo image within the audio field between left and right loudspeakers.

**Screen (34−35, 88−91**, 103, 126, 131−133, 148) A free-standing sound-reflecting or absorbing panel used for the local modification of studio acoustics.

**Sensitivity (10, 36−37**, 43) Microphone output measured in decibels relative to one volt per pascal.

**Separation** (103, 126, 131−133) The degree to which the signals from different sound sources are kept apart for the purpose of individual treatment and control.

**Shelf (157−159)** A dip in frequency response obtained by the use of a filter (or equaliser).

**Shotgun microphone (52−55)** See *gun microphone*.

**Sibilance** (24, 82, 136) The over-emphasis of 's' and 'ch' sounds in speech.

**Side-fire** (80−81) Polar response with axis at right-angle to body of microphone.

**Signal** (8−9, 160, 168, 174) The required information content of a sound field or of an electrical or electromagnetic transmission.

**Signal-to-noise ratio** (36) The ratio of information content to unwanted hiss, rumble, hum and other unwanted background noises, measured in decibels.

**Sine wave, sine tone** (10−11) A wave containing a single frequency; a pure tone (q.v.). In mathematics, 'sine function' describes the shape of this simplest type of wave. The term is avoided in this text.

**Sound (10−35)** A series of compressions and rarefactions travelling through air or another medium, caused by some body or bodies in vibration.

**Soundfield microphone** (80−81) Proprietary name for a microphone with tetrahedral array of capsules.

**Speech balance** (24, **82−93**, 142, 172) See *balance*.

**Spill** (132, 144−145, 156) Sound picked up by a microphone other than that intended.

**Spin** (164) An effect obtained by recirculating an original signal repeatedly through the same system. Any imbalance in the frequency characteristics of the system is rapidly enhanced. See also *howl-round*.

**Spotting** (**106**, 126, 138) Setting additional microphone to selectively enhance some part (usually an instrument or group) within an overall balance.

**Spreader** (152−153) A device which converts a mono signal into a form of stereo, in which it occupies all or a broad part of the audio stage.

**Springs** (162) Reverberation-producing device in which a signal is sent along metal arranged in a coil, to be reflected many times at discontinuities in the material of which it is made. The springiness of the coil is not actually used.

**Stand** (58−59, **68−69**) Microphone mounting.

**Standing wave, stationary wave** (**22−23**, 32, 40, 91) The sum of two equal waves travelling in opposite directions. This may be caused by reflection at a wall or at the end of a pipe.

**Stereo, stereophonic sound (28−31**, 50, 74−80, **92−93**, 102−103, **106−110**, 112, 116, **138−143**, **151−153**, 163, 169) Sound combined to be reproduced through two or more loudspeakers, each with a different signal, in order to give an impression of spatial spread.

**Studio (sound studio) (32−35**, 83, **88−91**, 92, 95, 103, 114) An enclosed space designed or primarily used for microphone work.

**Supercardioid response** (38−39, **50−51**, 83, 92−93, 124−125, 130, 132, 136) Unclear term for the much more descriptive 'cottage-loaf' response. In this book it is taken to be a polar response intermediate between cardioid and bi-directional. See *directivity*.

**Talk-back** (98, 174) Use of a microphone in the control room which is linked to a loudspeaker or headphones in the studio.

**Tetrahedral array (80−81)** A set of four microphone capsules the signal from which can be reduced to give good directional information in three dimensions and can be further reduced to two, with a choice of direction and polar response (including a capacity to pan and 'zoom' — i.e. change the polar response — using an existing 4-channel recording).

**Tone** (151, **174**) In audio practice, a single-frequency signal or sound. See *sine wave, zero level tone*.

**Tracking** (132, **154**) Building up a recording in successive stages. Later tracks are recorded to the replay of those already on tape.

**Transducer** (64) A device for converting audio information from one medium (sound, electrical current, electromagnetic transmission, disc, tape, etc.) to another.

**Transformer** (37, 43, 57, 131, 151) A device which isolates the direct current components of an electrical circuit while permitting the signal to pass with no significant loss of power, but changing voltage and impedance as required. Many microphones produce an electrical signal which is unsuitable for feeding along long cables or into subsequent equipment; the transformer provides the necessary matching.

**Transient** (**20**, 102, 116, 118, 124) In this context, often the irregular initial part of a sound before a regular waveform is established; an important part of the character of musical instruments.

**Velocity of sound** (10, 13, **176**) At room temperature this is approximately 1120ft/sec, and for most practical calculations may be regarded as constant. In liquids and solids it is faster.

**Volume** (26–27, **168**, **176**) See *level*.

**VU meter** (168–169) Volume unit meter, used in much American equipment for measuring audio signal levels. It shows percentage modulation and is not linear in decibels.

**Wave, sound wave** (9–**17**, 22, 29, 32, 52–54, 62) A succession of compressions and rarefactions transmitted through a medium at a constant velocity, the speed of sound.

**Wavelength** (10–**13**, 52–54, 176) Provided that the wave is perfectly regular (i.e. a sine wave or pure tone) this is the distance between successive peaks.

**Windshield, windscreen** (36, 46, 54–57, **72**–**73**) Shield which fits over a microphone to contour it for smoother airflow, thereby reducing or eliminating wind noise.

**Wireless microphone** (66–67) See *radio microphone*.

**XLR** (**70**–**71**, 81) A robust connector system used for microphones and cables.

**Zero level tone** (174) Electrically generated tone at a standard reference level used to line up electrical equipment. In BBC practice this is one milliwatt into 600 ohms using 1000Hz pure tone.